He Ran All The Way

He Ran All The Way

The Life of John Garfield

ROBERT NOTT

FOREWORD BY Julie Garfield

LIMELIGHT EDITIONS   NEW YORK

First Limelight Edition July 2003
Copyright © 2003 by Robert Nott

Published in the United States by Proscenium Publishers, Inc.,
New York

Manufactured in the United States of America

LIBRARY OF CONGRESS CATALOGING-IN-PUBLICATION DATA
Nott, Robert.
  He ran all the way : a biography of John Garfield / Robert
Nott.—1st
Limelight ed.
    p. cm.
Includes bibliographical references.
  ISBN 0-87910-985-8 (pbk.)
  1. Garfield, John. 2. Motion picture actors and actresses—
United
States--Biography. I. Title.
PN2287.G377N68 2003
791.43'028'092--dc21
                                    2003000423

Contents

Foreword

FRIENDS OF MINE WHO ARE INTO ASTROLOGY SAY THAT one characteristic of my birth sign, Capricorn, is a constant reappearance of people and events from the past. I don't know a great deal about astrology, but I remember mentioning my fascination with it to my mother, who had a lot of trouble believing in anything besides Marxism: "Mom, isn't it interesting that both Daddy and Sidney [Sidney Cohn was my stepfather] were both Pisces?"

"Well, what's so interesting?" she challenged.

"Well, they both married you." She shut up about astrology after that.

I guess I must be a classic Capricorn, because my past is always coming back to me, and I mean in every way: lovers, kids I went to school or camp with, who always show up expectedly in my life, but most of all the people who knew my father or remember him or were connected with him in some way and never forgot that.

In the fall of 1989, I got a call from a young man who wanted to write a play about my father. He'd gotten my number from a mutual friend. I agreed to meet with him, even though I secretly hated him for bringing the most painful part of my past back to me, for what felt like the millionth time in my life, and also because I still hadn't even begun to forge my own artistic work about my father.

"The past rears its ugly head," people often say. For me the past isn't so ugly so much as it's sad: sad to have been robbed of my father, the charismatic movie star, at the age

vii

of seven; sad that I'd never had the opportunity to work with him
or talk to him about our mutual passion, the craft of acting; sad that
my father, who'd given so much of his time and energy to his country's war effort, had been so badly brought down by the Blacklist
that he became virtually unemployable; sad that my father died of
a massive heart attack at the ripe old age of thirty-nine. Doctors
have explanations for what causes death, but in my family we
knew that it wasn't precisely a heart attack that killed my father—
it was more like an attack on his heart, by his own country and by
his close friends, including those he had most revered: the Kazans
and the Odets, the ones who betrayed their own kind to save their
careers.

My father's ghost comes back to me when I meet people who say,
"I knew Johnny," even though I know they didn't because nobody
who really knew him called him anything but Julie, and when I
meet the ones who did know him and who sadly launch into their
"I remember whens." And the ghost also appears when I unsus-
pectingly turn on the damn TV and there he is, looking so open, so
alive, and so unreachable.

I've spent much of my life hiding from all the hard facts about
my father, like a safe little rabbit in her hutch. If I'm suddenly hungry for carrots, I slowly peep my head out to see if it's safe, and if it
is I then hop along in blissful denial that at any moment some crea-
ture may appear from anywhere and whip out a mirror to my father's past, shattering whatever delusions I've clung to about his
infidelities and other weaknesses of character. I've kept him as a
God because I need to, but—in his integrity, in his refusal to name
names—was he not godlike? How many could have held out like he
did? Could I have?

So here was this young guy (or should I say this young fool?) who
thought he was going to actually get my father's real story out there
for the first time. Little did he know how difficult that was going to
be, for my father's work has been buried. Yes, it's true that during

his seven-year prison term with Warner Brothers he made a lot of rotten B pictures, but there were also amazing ones, like *Force of Evil, Body and Soul, The Postman Always Rings Twice, The Breaking Point.* Why were they buried along with the rest? I think it's a shame that they did it: some kind of universal shame that this country helped kill the very thing it had nurtured. Why is it that a country or a person can so easily destroy its own? Is it some kind of inherent fear of facing oneself? Like Judge Kaufman's statement, after he sentenced the Rosenbergs to death, that a Jew was capable of and completely justified in killing a Jew—if that Jew happened to deserve it.

Robert Nott—that was the name of the guy who came to talk about my father. I thought, what a funny name, but kind of catchy too, like—not, not ever, never, a name of nothing—or maybe not. This young Mr. Nott walks into my little apartment on West 44th Street and he's all open, all heart. There's something about the comb of his hair or the shape of his head, or maybe it's the way his clothing hangs on him that kind of brings back the forties. It was as if he'd returned from that time my father had lived in. It even occurred to me that it could be my father coming back, to tell the true story for all the world to know, or maybe just a close friend of his.

Robert Nott was consumed with John Garfield's life and career. He was determined and unflappable in his search for the truth, and best of all, he was full of soul, full of sensitivity and awareness of the kinds of questions he needed to ask, and the pain they might cause. I knew from the moment I met him that he deserved to succeed in this effort of his, because it was coming out of something so pure, so sincere and so full of love, it was as if he were on a mission to enlighten and to set the record straight about John Garfield, one of the most innovative figures in the history of American cinema.

Nott never did write a play; he wrote this biography instead. He talked to loads of people I knew, many of them dead now. I'd occasionally get a call from one of them: "Some guy who's writing a book wants to talk with me about your father. Is he OK?" "Yeah, he's OK. He's a great guy," I'd answer. "Tell him everything you know. He's going to write something very good, I just feel it."

And he did.

Julie Garfield

Julie Garfield

Introduction

I FIRST ENCOUNTERED JOHN GARFIELD ON THE LATE LATE
Show sometime back in 1974. There he was on the small
television screen in my living room, getting his brains
knocked out by Artie Dorrell in a great boxing movie called
Body and Soul. I fell in love with the guy right away.

Garfield was the first actor to play characters who somehow managed to lose even when they were winning. He is
generally considered to be the first "rebel" actor in film
history; the one who opened the door for all the other
cinematic anti-heroes to step through. Marlon Brando,
Montgomery Clift, Steve McQueen, Paul Newman, Robert
DeNiro and many others walked through that door; somehow Garfield became obscured by it.

Not that Garfield has been entirely forgotten. People
can recall the titles of a few of his films, like *The Postman
Always Rings Twice,* but he hasn't developed much of a
contemporary following. For instance, when I told one
friend that I was writing a biography on John Garfield, he
asked, "Wasn't he married to Greta Garbo?" He was thinking of actor John Gilbert, who never married Ms. Garbo.
Others can relate only to the feline comic strip character,
Garfield.

And while I have discovered a considerable number of
dedicated John Garfield fans, he does not attract the
cultists of a James Dean, a Marilyn Monroe, or an Elvis
Presley. Perhaps because Garfield died at age 39 in 1952,
and his fame was buried with him. Our current culture has

room for only a limited number of cult pop icons: Dean, Monroe, Presley, and maybe Humphrey Bogart. Garfield has fallen through the cracks.

I initially began this project in 1989 as a play; a one-person show spotlighting Garfield sometime during the last week of his life. Researching Garfield's life and career with an eye towards discovering more about both the man and the actor, and why his reputation had eroded over the years, eventually I got in touch with Garfield's daughter, Julie. After deciding that I was the real thing, she agreed to support my efforts. Upon meeting her brother David in Los Angeles a little time later, he suggested I drop the play idea and write a book. "No one's done it yet—not the right way, anyway," he said. By 1992 I had changed my approach and set about writing a biography. (Incidentally, since that time I've discovered that at least two plays have been written about Garfield with the same sort of set-up I envisioned.)

Over the next eight years, I conducted some 75 interviews in connection with the project. I reviewed all of Garfield's films, combed film libraries and archives for information on him, and, through the Freedom of Information Act, obtained his extensive FBI file—a thousand pages of mostly blacked-out government analysis and conjecture that doesn't add up to much. I wanted to tell Garfield's life story and wasn't particularly concerned with labeling him as a leftist or a Method actor or a womanizer or a victim of the McCarthy era. Garfield was one of those actors whose off-screen activities mirrored his on-screen persona: he was uneducated, didn't always think things out too clearly, loved women (too much, if such a thing is possible) and adhered to his own personal moral code that allowed him to cheat on his wife but not to rat on his friends.

From always admiring Garfield as an actor, I came to admire him as a human being for his simplicity and honesty. But I like his flaws—and he had a lot of them—most of all. He lived and worked by instinct. He didn't always know where he was going, but he was pretty sure that he was going to get there, and even if he didn't make it you sensed the journey was going to be exciting and unpredictable.

Throughout the book I call Garfield "Julie" because that's what everyone who knew him called him. They still do, fifty years after his death. And it is to "Julie" that I dedicate this book.

He Ran All The Way

Prologue
May 23, 1952

"He came like a meteor, and like a meteor he departed."

—RABBI LOUIS I. NEWMAN

AT 1 P.M. ON FRIDAY, MAY 23, 1952, THE FRONT DOOR-bell rang at the Central Park West apartment of John and Robbe Garfield. When Joseph Bernard, a friend of the Garfields, answered the door, he found two New York City policemen standing there. They wanted to speak to Mrs. Garfield, they said. Bernard told Robbe and she expressed surprise about the unexpected visitors. With her husband's funeral service to begin in an hour, she couldn't figure out what the NYPD might want. Had the visitors been from the F.B.I., she would have been less surprised, for they had her late husband under surveillance for suspicion of commu-nist activity for the past 18 months.

Going to the door, Robbe found the officers holding their hats in their hands and shuffling their feet to and fro obvi-ously uncomfortable with their task. "It's about your hus-band," one of the officers said. "We'd like to ask you to consider holding an open casket service for the public. We have a feeling that there's going to be a lot of mourners showing up. There's already about a thousand of 'em on Amsterdam Avenue and traffic's coming to a standstill. We're expecting at least three times that to show by two o'clock."

Robbe had deliberately planned a small, quiet service

3

with a closed casket; friends only. So much had been taken from her lately—her peace, her privacy, and her husband—that she resolved to have her way in, at least, this one matter. "I'm sorry," she replied and started to close the door, "I can't do that."

The two officers fidgeted more and the spokesman of the duo put in: "Mrs. Garfield, we're pretty sure that if you don't open the ceremony up to the public, there'll be a riot."

Robbe's mind momentarily returned to a warm autumn day some fourteen years earlier, when her husband had picked her up at the Pasadena train station upon her arrival in California. "Why couldn't I come into Union Station [Los Angeles]?" she asked him. "If I show up at Union Station I'll cause a riot," he told her. Everything had seemed so simple then. He was going to be a movie star. She was going to change the world.

Robbe sensed panic in the voices of the two policemen. Years later she would describe their approach as "begging." Affected by their plea, she briefly conferred with Bernard, as well as with writer Clifford Odets and director Lee Strasberg. All three men felt it might be in Robbe's best interests to agree to an open casket service. The three did not entirely convince her, but Robbe agreed, resigning herself to another lost cause. The officers thanked her and left.

An hour later, when Robbe arrived at Riverside Memorial Chapel on Manhattan's West 76th Street, the officers' predictions were absurdly unrealistic. There were not, as they had suggested, 3,000 mourners, but probably twice that many, if not quite the 10,000 that the New York newspapers would report the next day.

The mourners came from all boroughs of the city and from all walks of life. There were businessmen taking a long lunch break to pay their last respects to a fellow New Yorker. There were housewives, many carrying toddlers so tiny that they had to be lifted to view the body in the oaken bier. There were younger girls, "bobby-soxers" as they were called, teenagers too young to really know what love was all about, who were crying over their fallen idol. And then there were working-class stiffs, men clad in their dirty trousers and weathered jackets, lunch boxes in hand, who came by to bid farewell to one of their own.

Garfield's son David, then 8 years old, recalled vividly the large presence of African-American mourners, a "sea of black faces," as he later put it. This was not unexpected, for John Garfield was known for his defense of the "little guy," both on and off the screen. Some said he paid for his beliefs with his life; others that he was a traitor to his country. One of the onlookers called Garfield a communist, and another came to the actor's defense. A fistfight erupted before the police could pull the two men apart.

Everywhere that day, there were police. Fifty white-gloved officers were dispatched to the chapel at the last minute to manage the crowd, which was jamming the thoroughfare and stoops of 76th Street and Amsterdam Avenue. The windows of 76th Street's brownstones were filled with onlookers and curiosity seekers. Still, the crowd was quiet, respectful and reserved. All 600 seats in Riverside Memorial Chapel were filled, as were the aisles. The chapel doors remained open, and the crowd blocked the doorway and stairs outside. Joe Bernard could not bring himself to look at the casket. It was difficult for him to accept that the Golden Boy was dead.

In the chapel's back row, a short, stocky, gray-haired woman wept. Her name was Dinah Cohen Garfinkle, the deceased's stepmother. She had never been able to quite fill the shoes of Garfield's biological mother, and he had never quite been the son she wanted him to be. He had sent her a monthly check for $85 since his father's death 10 years before. Coincidentally, she received the last check on the day of the funeral, but only for the sum of $50. A note with the check explained that as he was no longer working steadily, Dinah's monthly stipend would be decreased for the time being. Garfield's fortunes had sunk to an irreversible low, and with his death, so did Dinah's.

"God loves a shining mark, a single blow," said Rabbi Louis I. Newman, who presided over the service. Newman went on to describe Garfield as "almost an American legend." Despite the Lord's

love of this shining mark, Newman continued, "as if to temper his
soul, the hammer blows of circumstance descended mercilessly
upon him."

The hammer blows came first from the House Committee on Un-
American Activities (HUAC), whose members included Garfield in
their fervent search for communists or anyone resembling a communist, during the height of the Red Scare. Next came the rebuff
from the movie studios, who were no longer willing to employ an
actor under suspicion. Then, when Garfield testified before HUAC
in March 1951, his refusal to name names was considered ambivalent and elusive, so the Federal Bureau of Investigation began investigating him. To top things off, many of Garfield's friends went
out of their way to avoid him for fear of being judged guilty by association.

Rabbi Newman read the Third Psalm and excerpts from philoso-
pher Bertrand Russell's *Free Man Worship.* "He came like a meteor,
and like a meteor he departed," Newman said. It's unlikely that
Garfield's spirit found peace in the departure. For weeks afterward,
the media capitalized on his fame and fall, publishing a series of articles that questioned the actor's loyalty to his country. Opening fire
with a right-wing diatribe, journalist Victor Riesel asserted that
Garfield was on the verge of informing on his friends in order to
salvage his own career.

Naming names. That was an unpardonable act that John Garfield
could not commit. His desire to hold out was just one of the attributes that endeared Garfield to the average guy and gal on the street.
In retrospect, the outpouring of support and sympathy from New
Yorkers should not have been unexpected. After all, John Garfield
really was one of them. He had come up from the streets of the city's
Lower East Side, fought his way in and out of the public school system, and had managed to attain his goal of becoming a working
actor. He was a regular fellow; Julius Garfinkle from Rivington
Street, and he remained a regular fellow after he went to Hollywood
as John Garfield to portray regular fellows in films for the Warner

Bros. studio. You could say that he actually attained the American Dream: he was a movie star. And he never changed, really.

"You felt that here was one who had not been corrupted by success," journalist Archer Winston wrote after Garfield's death. "He was still trying to reach out for the good job, the work or art that might say something to those that listened." But who was listening? Garfield, who five years earlier was nominated for an Oscar for Best Actor for the 1947 film *Body and Soul*, had been reduced to playing summer stock and brief Broadway revivals. "I'll act anywhere," he told columnist Darr Smith in 1951, when his career was on the ebb, "if people want to see me."

They wanted to see him now. Thousands passed by the casket to pay their final respects. Around 5 P.M., Robbe ordered a halt to the public viewing. A throng of another 500 pressed against the chapel doors, hoping to get a last look. Robbe relented, and the procession continued.

At 8 P.M., Robbe and a few close friends retired to an anteroom for a small reception, after which Bernard and Strasberg accompanied her back to her apartment. The crowds still came to pass by the body, keeping the chapel open until near midnight. All in all, a reported 6,000 mourners filed past the casket to say good-bye to a guy they felt they knew.

Even dead, John Garfield could attract a crowd.

CHAPTER ONE

Birth of an Antihero

*"The streets were our playground and our
jungle—and you behaved like an animal or
you got your block knocked off!"*
—JOHN GARFIELD

IN THE ANNALS OF NEW YORK CITY'S HISTORY, MARCH 4,
1913 was just another day. A look at the day's newspaper
headlines say it all: An unidentified man was shot and killed
on East 39th Street; on East 112th, three thugs broke into a
woman's apartment, tied her up, and threatened to poison
her baby if she didn't give them money; in the East Bronx,
Mrs. Bertha Sachs offered two men two dollars each to burn
down the tenement house she worked in. Unfortunately for
Mrs. Sachs, the two men turned her in to the police.

In Washington D.C., that same day, President Woodrow
Wilson, a Democrat, took office. Over 40,000 people
marched in the celebratory parade, and, for a country still
testing its strength in the Industrial Revolution, his inaugu-
ral address seemed fitting:

> But the evil has come with the good, and much fine
> gold has been corroded. With riches have come in-
> excusable waste. We have squandered a great deal
> of what we might have used, and have not stopped
> to conserve the exceeding bounty of nature, with-
> out which our genius for enterprise would have
> been worthless and impotent...

9

Some forty years later these same words could have been used as a eulogy for John Garfield. He was born Julius Jacob Garfinkle on March 4 in a two-room tenement on Rivington Street in New York's Lower East Side. Little is known of the background of his parents, David and Hannah Garfinkle. David was of Russian Crimean descent, and according to Garfield's cousin Sylvia Maishlash Nonkin, Hannah (whose maiden name was Margolis) may have hailed from the Ukrainian town of Zhitomer. Julie knew literally nothing about his grandparents, and chose to learn little about his own father and mother.

The Garfinkles had come to America in 1909 to escape the religious pogroms against the Jewish people in Russia, two among some two million Jews who immigrated to the United States between 1880 and 1920. Roughly 90 percent of them remained in New York City. Russian Jews made a home in what was then the city's Garment District, near the intersection of Canal and Essex Streets and East Broadway. David Garfinkle's first job was as a pants-presser in a garment factory. Eventually he would operate his own tailoring shop.

In those days, the Garfinkles moved frequently—from Allen Street to Orchard Street to Hester Street, before ending up on Rivington, which was known as Pushcart Alley. (Asked to describe Rivington Street years later, Garfield said, "Mostly pushcarts, I guess.") From Orchard Street to the Bowery, Grand Street was one huge shopping center, not unlike an outdoor mall. Consumers could buy just about anything they wanted here, so the area attracted upper-class society women looking for bargains, tourists, thieves and pickpockets, as well as the locals.

The Garfinkle's Rivington Street flat was a slum apartment; there was no heating in the winter. Each floor's residents had to share a single toilet. Kitchen sinks doubled as tubs, and baths were taken in cold water or not at all. This may explain why Garfield, in later years, eschewed baths in favor of showers. At the Garfinkle's, the kitchen served as a bedroom for young Julius, and much to his dismay he found himself sharing his bedroll with tenement rats during the winter months. In the summer, the family climbed out on the fire escape or up to the roof for a more comfortable night of sleep. Pneumonia and consumption (tuberculosis) were prevalent. This was not an auspicious environment to be born into.

Yet these squalid surroundings seemed to foster achievement. A boy with brains and talent might find some incentive to get out of the slums. John Garfield came from the same neighborhood that wrought and molded other entertainment greats like Paul Muni, Edward G. Robinson, George and Ira Gershwin, Eddie Cantor and Leonard Bernstein. There were two venues for improving one's lot in those days: school or crime. David Garfinkle accepted, as God's plan, his fate as a pants-presser, and he espoused the notion of hard work and schooling. Others chose the path of crime. Gangsters have always provided a model for impressionable youngsters, and the Lower East Side's share of hoodlums was no different. They may not have equaled Al Capone, Dutch Schultz or Bugsy Siegel, but local gangsters like Dopey Benny, Pretty Amberg and Little Augie were having enough success to suggest that crime did pay. (Even the ends these gangsters met did not necessarily dissuade youngsters from following the same path: Dopey Benny went to prison, Amberg was blown up in a car bomb, and Little Augie died in a hail of bullets on Norfolk Street, just off of Rivington.)

And it was here that Julius Jacob Garfinkle (Julius was shortened to "Julie" and Jacob was dropped) grew up. The youth of Julie's generation were so eager to assimilate into American culture—more than their parents—they soon began abandoning the "old" ways. To his distress, David found himself a devout Jew in a world of non-Jews. "The spirit was freer here," recalled immigrant Abraham Hyman of the Lower East Side. "You did things that you were not supposed to do in the old country." The men shaved their beards and discarded their skullcaps while the women gave up wearing wigs. It was easy for a child born into this proverbial melting pot to skip going to synagogue and pass up the Sabbath meal altogether, opting instead to spend time in one of the city's concrete playgrounds.

Even when he was a young boy, there was a hint of the devil in Julie's eyes. He was stocky without being plump, and by his early teens he would work off his baby fat through sheer energy. He was fortunate enough to sport a clear complexion—no acne problems for him—and his dark hair, combed neatly to one side with a part on the left, was generally well kept. Early on he developed a stutter, though perhaps a byproduct of his lack of self-confidence. On the outside, however, he was all charm. His personality matched that look of devilry in his eyes; he kept busy swimming in the East River, teasing organ-grinding monkeys, chasing ambulances and playing stickball in the street. Full of mischief, Julie soon perfected a variety of practical jokes, though few of them could be considered clever. His favorite was to climb on a rooftop, tie a piece of brick to a rope and drop it on unsuspecting passersby.

On any given day Julie could wander to the Bowery just north of his neighborhood and see drunken men lying in doorways. Chinatown could be explored too, but territory was to be respected. There being safety in numbers, Julie soon turned to the local street gang for protection. Vacant lots were turned into battlefields with fists, rocks, clubs and bottles serving as weapons. Julie would later attribute a scar on his leg to a sledding accident, but it may have actually been a result of a street fight.

Perhaps Julie would not have turned to the streets had it not been for the death of his mother, Hannah. She died in 1920, when Julie was seven years old. No death certificate is recorded for her, but Julie would always say Hannah died of "worry." Julie and his younger brother Max (born 1918) became unofficial orphans, for David Garfinkle had little time to be a father to his two boys. After his wife's death, David chose to distance himself, emotionally and physically, from his children. "They shipped me off to an uncle's house," Julie later recalled, "telling me only that my mother was ill. When I returned a few weeks later, I naturally expected to find her there. When I finally realized why she wasn't, the shock was harder to bear because I'd had no preparation for it."

Hannah's death facilitated the breakup of the family. David had neither the time nor the means to support two children on his own. "My father was an average guy who couldn't cope with two kids without a wife," Michael (Max) Garfield said. "He wanted to get rid of us both." The boys briefly stayed with relatives in Brownsville, an area Julie dubbed the bowels of Brooklyn. There he joined another street gang.

In later years, Julie tended to exaggerate his involvement in these gangs. "I suppose it was a fifty-fifty chance then which I would achieve—Sing Sing or Hollywood," he once boasted. He said he was the leader of two different gangs, and it may be true, for he possessed a charismatic personality. Still, Julie acknowledged that the worst crimes he ever committed were swiping vegetables from street vendors and baiting cops to chase him. He was probably more of a threat to himself than others, for he lacked an inherent toughness. "I never felt Julie was a fighter," journalist Sam Shaw said. "Even in a great picture like *Body and Soul*. There was no meanness in him. He didn't have that streak of killer in him." Michael J. Coppola, a classmate of Julie's in junior high school, agreed. "He wasn't that tough. He was a really nice kid. I don't know where they got that image that he was a tough guy."

They got that image from Julie himself. Cast in one gangster film after another at Warner Bros. in the 1930s and 1940s, he would revel in playing up his screen image to the fullest. "I was a bad boy," he said in a typical Hollywood interview. "And I lived in a bad neighborhood. I knew so many things a boy shouldn't know. I did so many things a boy shouldn't do." He continued to exaggerate his criminal achievements, saying later in an absurd boast: "I might have wound up the no. 1 gangster in this town."

Nevertheless, it is true that he was out on the streets running with the gangs a lot. They taught him loyalty—a strong lifelong personality trait for Julie—and they taught him how to steal. A deeply religious man, David took the teachings of the Talmud seriously and didn't look kindly upon Julie's street activity. The Garfinkle

apartment had become a mini-synagogue where David prayed continually. David had aspirations to become a rabbi; Julie would describe his father as a "cantor on weekends and holidays," which
was not an unusual description, for while in the old country, the
rabbi was considered a great man to be respected, in America rabbis and cantors found regular work hard to come by. Thus, many of
them became "rabbis for hire," rending services at births, weddings
and holy festivals for a fee. "Father wanted to be a cantor but he
never achieved it," Michael Garfield said. "But I really don't recall
religion being impressed upon us as children. I don't even know if
Julie went to Hebrew School." Michael's inability to recall such details is probably due to the fact that he remained with relatives in
Brooklyn while Julie was shunted from one relative to another before returning to David's care. The boys were raised separately and
did not bond as brothers.

Working ten to fifteen hours a day as a pants-presser and praying
all night left little time for David to be a father. David had little patience for Julie's disinterest in school or religion, but in Julie's view,
if it was religion that had succeeded in turning David into a no-
nonsense, self-righteous would-be cantor, then he wanted no part of
it. "Julie and my father did not get along," Michael recalled. "My father was an immigrant. He came to this country and went right to
work in a garment factory. He figured that Julie should keep his
nose to the grindstone in order to be successful. Julie didn't see it
that way." Discussions between Julie and David soon turned into
arguments; arguments into beatings.

When things got too unpleasant at home Julie would disappear
for days at a time. He stayed with friends, with family, or on the
street. At least once he hitched a ride to Bridgeport, Connecticut,
where a sympathetic uncle lived. "Not having a mother, I could stay
out late," Julie later said. "I didn't have to eat regularly or drink
milk at four o'clock. I wanted the attention that I missed at home, so
I became leader of a gang and that way I got attention and (was) recognized as important." The gang members would not judge him.

They were all cut from the same cloth and Julie had all the prerequisites necessary to join them: no interest in school, no job, and no
job prospects.

He learned early on never to back away from a fight. He didn't
always win—his short stature at the time (about 5´5˝) was a handi-
cap, but he fought with a ferocity that made up for his physical
shortcomings. "The classier kids crossed the streets when they saw
me coming," he later said. So did some of the not so classy kids.

The Garfinkles moved constantly, ending up in the Bronx by
1925. There David met, courted and married a quiet woman named
Dinah Cohen, who was easily dominated by her new mate. "She
was not a bad person but she was a stupid person," Robbe Garfield
Cohn said of Dinah. "She did whatever her husband told her to do."
Julie's cousin, Sylvia Maishlash Nonkin, said Julie didn't hit it off
with Dinah: "Julie didn't like his stepmother at all. She was a cold
fish." Julie's own view of stepmothers was like a page from a child's
fairy tale. "There was no convincing me that a stepmother could be
anything but a wicked ogre," he said, "and I acted accordingly."

Dinah was no wicked ogre. She took pains to win Julie over
though he was eager to challenge her authority. She understood that
he was simply seeking that which he had not yet found—love. It
was something he would seek for the rest of his life, and sometimes,
even after he had found it, he didn't realize what he had. He would
easily confuse a surface affection for the real thing, and yet, when
someone like Dinah showed a genuine concern, Julie disregarded
her attentions and sought reassurance elsewhere. Still, Dinah took
an avid interest in his schooling; and the principal of P.S. 32 once
calculated that she spent more time in school than Julie did, as she
was perpetually called down to explain her stepson's absence.

Julie looked for excitement everywhere. When he was about 12
years old, he agreed to a dangerous stunt on a dare. He climbed to
the roof of a five-floor tenement building and hung upside down
over the edge by cradling his knees over the tip of the roof. It was an
outrageous deed; one that won him the admiration of the entire

neighborhood, and was typical of the length to which he would go to attract notice. Hanging from the roof—that's how John Garfield wanted to live.

He discovered another way to garner attention: acting. Whenever he found an audience of three or more he would climb on a box or a piece of furniture and act out impromptu scenes from nonexistent plays. "Even when he was a small boy he would get a soapbox, put the kids together, and make a speech," Dinah Garfinkle recalled in 1952. "Sometimes he even arranged street shows and charged the kids a penny to see them. And he was always the principal actor in the shows he arranged." So he was producer, director, writer and performer; quite an ambitious undertaking for a preteen boy.

It wasn't unusual for a boy like Julie to "play actor" in those days. Silent movies were capturing his generation's imagination, and growing up in the heart of the Yiddish theater district, Julie was bound to develop an appreciation for the genre. Second Avenue was a prime thoroughfare for both the Yiddish theaters and the movie houses, and even the devout David Garfinkle could be persuaded to attend a Yiddish production at The Thalia or The Windsor. The Yiddish plays have since been described as one part soap opera, one part morality play. Typical of the fare was the Yiddish version of *Hamlet,* which, opening with a the wedding feast, portrayed both Claudius and Hamlet as rabbis, replaced the bloody battling with family bickering, and ended with Claudius being exiled to Siberia! Julie was stage-struck at once.

Despite his interest in acting, Julie actually hated school. He bounced an ink bottle off a teacher's head at P.S. 32 and for one term (in 1925) left school altogether in favor of a job selling newspapers on the street. While many immigrant parents encouraged their children to leave school in order to work (the better to sustain the family), both David and Dinah realized that an education might be Julie's only hope of escaping the tenements. On the advice of a friend Dinah looked into a new junior high school in the Bronx that had, thanks to the offbeat and dedicated work of its young principal, established a reputation for dealing with "problem children." The school was P.S. 45; the principal was a man named Angelo Patri.

P.S. 45 is located on Lorillard Place, off 189th Street in the Belmont section of the East Bronx. In 1926 the neighborhood was primarily Italian, though there was a smattering of Jewish and black families. The nondescript H-shaped building suggested little other than a typical New York City public school, but inside the walls Patri was working miracles.

Patri had been born in November 1877, the son of uneducated Italian farmers. He came to America with his family in the 1880s and later attended City College of New York before finding work as a teacher in one of the city's public schools. But college had not prepared Patri for the rigors of teaching in a mismanaged school system, and he soon discovered the eternal challenge of disciplining unruly students. Patri was a student of pedagogical principles and methods, and while reading John Dewey's *Ethical Principles,* which states that conduct is the real test of learning, he discovered a fundamental element of teaching: "The teacher must watch and guide; he could not force." This became Patri's mantra. He dove back into the school system and worked his way up to the principalship of P.S. 45 in 1913. As a bold first step, he established a relationship between the school and the parents of the students, thus laying the groundwork for the future PTA

Patri learned to take a keen personal interest in every one of his students, particularly those who ranked above—or below—the average level of accomplishment. For these students he decided to emphasize their natural talents instead of the basic three R's of education. Instead of concentrating on multiplication tables, students who displayed a penchant for art could spend time in workshops painting or drawing. To his staff Patri stressed that it was their duty to ask their students what they wanted to do with their lives. In short, he became a fierce advocate of arts education in the public school system. This method was widely questioned in the first years of Patri's rules, but by 1926 P.S. 45 was considered the model of efficiency and success in New York City. Patri's influence outside the school system grew as well; he wrote a regular column for *The New York Post* and penned five books on education.

Dinah Garfinkle shared with her husband what she had heard of Patri's success with problem children and they decided he was the man for Julie. Patri's creed, as exemplified by the school song, paralleled David's own beliefs:

> *As we gather day by day,*
> *Pledge we loyal friends to stay,*
> *All honor and respect display to P.S. 45.*
> *For her sake let's sing the sweeter,*
> *Work the harder, work the fleeter,*
> *Work so nothing else can beat her, P.S. 45.*

It's unlikely Julie thought much of these lyrics, but all the same his parents sent him off to live with yet another uncle, on Prospect Avenue, off 189th, and enrolled him in P.S. 45 in January 1926. He didn't win new friends easily. "He was a sad kid," recalled classmate Michael J. Coppola. "A loner. Maybe because he was Jewish and felt out of place with all the Italians here." The Italian and Irish-Catholic gangs made it clear that their territory was off-limits to Jews, and it didn't take Julie long to learn the meaning of the word *kike*.

He hated the neighborhood and he hated this school. As often as he could, he skipped class. One day he didn't skip high enough. While trying to catapult himself over the chain-link fence that surrounded the school, Julie tumbled down the other side and landed in Patri's prized flower garden. It didn't take him long to make a shambles of the flower bed, and soon a teacher collared him and escorted him to Patri's office.

Julie had not yet met Patri. He probably expected a beating from the principal—a common punishment in the 1920s—but he was up against a different sort of man. Standing at five and a half feet (approximately the same height as Julie) and possessing a craggy face and an unruly mane of white hair that looked like a wild fire, Patri suggested an absent-minded professor forever searching for a lost pencil. The principal indulged his passion for bright colors by sporting an orange or a green tie with his white suits. He could have been an out-of-place explorer. "He was only a little bit of a man," Coppola recalled. "But he was very snappy and very classy, and everybody loved him."

Patri pretended to putter around the office while feigning indifference to Julie's plight. Rather than chide the boy for trying to escape, he turned to him and said simply, "You know, even flowers have a right to live." The words had an effect on Julie. "He made me see that flowers are tender, beautiful living things to be cared for and protected," the future actor said. "He gave me the idea that people are like that too, and the heart, and ideals. And some of the things inside our own hearts and minds that we better not trample either." (Keep in mind that Julie retold this story often, changing the specific details but always crediting Patri with some equally heartfelt, and sometimes quite corny, statements.)

Julie was suspicious of adults, but Patri appeared to go out of his way to help him. A few days after the flower-bed incident, Patri showed up at Julie's uncle's apartment. When the principal noticed that Julie had to sleep in the hallway on a pile of coats (his uncle displayed no more interest in the boy than David had), Patri bought Julie a mattress and a suit of clothes. Patri also used his influence to get Julie a job in the vegetable market across from P.S. 45. This personal interest Patri took had a positive effect on Julie. "He didn't have a father figure in his life," Coppola explained. "Mr. Patri came into the picture and showed him respect and love, and I suppose he found his father figure in him." Patri himself confirmed this, telling reporters that he and Julie were like "father and son." In dialogue more appropriate for a Warner Bros. crime drama, Julie claimed that Patri saved him from the electric chair. Unlikely as that sounds, one of his gang mates, an Italian kid named Capuato, reportedly did end up in the electric chair in Sing-Sing.

Julie had a penchant for talking back ("He liked to shoot off his mouth," actor/director Joseph Pevney said.), so Patri put that talent to use by enrolling him in an oral English class taught by Margaret O'Ryan. If Patri was now playing father to Julie, then O'Ryan became his surrogate mother—the first of many. Through O'Ryan's patient work, Julie began to lose his stutter, though he would sometimes draw upon it to imbue his screen portrayals in later years. With O'Ryan pushing him, he joined the school's debating team. She sensed that Julie had talent and cast him in several school assembly plays.

Outside of drama and speech class, he was a lousy student. Academically speaking his first semester at P.S. 45 was not a good one, though he managed to pass English, history, speech, geography and shop with D or C averages. He failed algebra twice. He did get a B in conduct from O'Ryan, which made him happy. That summer he attended school, barely scraping by in every subject except algebra. This lack of achievement in math would lead him to place his business and financial affairs in the hands of others in later years.

During the fall semester his grades improved slightly, but his favorite class remained drama. His confidence was bolstered when O'Ryan cast him in the school production of *The Division of Sir Launfal*, a morality tale about the search for the Holy Grail. You could say this was his official stage debut, and Julie loved the applause. O'Ryan thought he was good enough to play the part of Marley's ghost in the holiday theater production of *A Christmas Carol*. The acting bug bit him hard. "He found himself in that acting class," Patri would later say. "The moment he started to play a part he forgot himself. He was the king or the beggar—or whatever the part."

Acting offered Julie a chance to immerse himself in a world of make-believe. "Julie became obsessed with the stage," childhood friend Arnold Forster said. "His only concern and thought was for acting. Everything he did was tied to that central focus. If I were a psychiatrist, I might say that he was trying to escape the real world from whence he came." And the easiest way to escape, of course, was to assume another identity. Unlike his father or street urchin peers, the audience didn't judge Julie for anything other than his acting. Their applause meant that they liked him—a powerful incentive for a kid who didn't know what the word *love* meant.

O'Ryan and Patri were surprised and impressed with Julie's ability to grasp direction and develop character. Once, during an acting exercise, O'Ryan ordered him to stand in the corner until he understood what it was like to be blind. He amazed her by returning fully immersed in character, as if he had been born blind. "I've seen Julie do it many times," Patri said. "He would go off and stand alone for a few minutes. Then you could actually see him shed his own self. He would come out completely in the part." Shedding his own self probably wasn't hard, because Julie didn't like who he was at this point in his life; his instinctive ability to adopt another character played a vital role in his future success as an actor. The school stage would become his second home; there, at least, he was good at something.

His success at acting inspired him to work harder in other classes, and he managed decent grades in a few courses for a while. Mainly intrigued by the challenges of acting and speech, he agreed to represent the school in an oratorical contest sponsored by *The New York Times*. The topic was "the Constitution," for which Julie wrote an essay on "Franklin, The Peace Maker of the Constitution." Patri was a great admirer of Benjamin Franklin and had once written a short essay about him. Julie borrowed the essay and noticed how Patri had made a point of comparing Franklin's struggles with those of the daily immigrant in New York City. It was a stretch, but Julie stretched it even further by tossing the personalities of George Washington, Thomas Jefferson and John Adams into the mix and making Franklin the brainstormer behind the American Revolution. He liked to interchange fact with fantasy; it made for good storytelling. Patri was dumbfounded. "I don't know where Julie got the idea that Franklin was the great mind behind the Revolution," he later told reporters. "But I remember how beautifully he handled it."

The judges may not have cared about the factual inaccuracies in Julie's speech. They liked his presentation, which was confidently hammy and very theatrical. He won the borough championship against eight contenders and moved on to the final debate in a Manhattan municipal auditorium. There he took second place, losing to a competing teen from Keukok. Years later, he mixed fact and fiction again and told everyone he actually won the debate. Was anybody really going to check into the facts?

After the final debate the contestants were invited to a sit-down dinner sponsored by *The New York Times*. At the table Julie noticed a small bowl of water in front of him. He had no idea it was a finger bowl, so he picked it up with both hands and sipped from it—an act more in line with something one of The Three Stooges would do. He had a lot to learn.

CHAPTER TWO

Robbe

"Robbe was a center that Julie could hold onto."

—GERRY SCHLEIN

ALTHOUGH TECHNICALLY A YEAR BEHIND IN HIS STUDIES, Julie graduated from junior high school in 1928, a half-semester after his peers. (For the record, he scored an A in both speech and drama class.) In January 1929, he entered the tenth grade at Roosevelt High School, which was located just one block west of P.S. 45., but Julie had no intention of staying in school. He had already decided to drop out and pursue an acting career full time. Patri had managed to obtain a dramatic scholarship with the Heckscher Foundation for Julie to study theater and due to Patri's prodding, he survived his first semester of high school. Cast in a production of *A Midsummer Night's Dream,* he somehow ended up playing both Bottom and Quince (an amazing feat, when you think about it). But by the fall semester Julie proved that old habits die hard. Without a Patri to guide him, Julie resorted to the usual antics. "At Roosevelt High he achieved a mark for ineptitude that is likely never to be broken," journalist Kyle Crichton wrote of Julie in a 1939 *Collier's* article. "He cracked nary a book, did nary a sum, answered nary a question." What he did do, apparently, was shoot spitballs at the teacher, which got him expelled. He managed to transfer to Textile High, where he lasted for about a month. Despite his lack of political knowledge, he considered himself fervently anti-Hoover. When one of his teachers began a long-winded discourse on the merits of Hooverism, Julie responded with a string of obscene noises and words. He was told to get out and stay out.

He lasted a little longer at his third high school, DeWitt-Clinton, as a result of Patri's pleas and because the school boasted a drama club called The Fordham Players. "That was a very prestigious name for a bunch of high school kids doing plays," Julie's friend and co-actor Arnold Forster said of the group. What surprised Forster was how Julie made up for his short stature when he was acting: "On the stage he seemed bigger than he was."

At the age of 14 Julie still seemed more interested in acting than in sex. And as much as he came to love sex in later years, most friends agreed that it always ran a distant second to performing. His neighborhood pals such as Eddie Kogan, Ernest Pendrell and Joe LaSpina would sit around and talk about sexual conquests, and while Julie would join in the discussions, he later admitted that none of them knew what they were talking about. As a young teen Julie was darkly attractive, sensual even, and while he may have seemed like a prime catch to the neighborhood girls, he did not fit the image of the perfect suitor that most fathers entertained. After a date with young Frances Chaney, Julie was invited in to meet her parents. They were cordially cool towards him. After he left, Chaney's father turned to his daughter and said, "If you ever bring that bum home again I'll throw him out!"

Father shouldn't have worried. Around this time Julie met another woman who would win his heart. Her name was Rose Seidman. She was a year younger than Julie but she was his kind of woman: short, dark, Jewish, with a trim figure to boot. She also had a fierce independent streak. She hated the name Rose and changed it to Robbe (pronounced Robbie) by the time she was 16. Julie first met her at a block party in the Bronx. He tried to make small talk. She wouldn't bite. He asked if he could walk her home. She said no. They would not meet again for over a year.

Rose Seidman was the second of two children born to Max and Lena Seidman, who, like the Garfinkles, were Jewish immigrants from Russia. Max claimed to have been a member of the czar's military band, where he played his cornet sitting on a big white horse (or so he liked to tell it). Lena had a more humble job working in a cigarette factory. Like David Garfinkle, Max worked as a pants-presser in New York City, though he moonlighted as a cornet player at nightclubs, wedding receptions and brothels. In America Lena became a housewife, and concentrated on raising her two daughters, Rose and Anne. The Seidmans' living circumstances were slightly better than the average immigrant's, but they were still working-class people. They lived in an apartment on East 4th Street for years. Robbe's maternal grandmother lived with them. Her paternal grandmother, she was told, had died after slipping on a banana peel.

Like Julie, Robbe spent a lot of time at the Yiddish theater. It was an easy life for a while. Then one day Robbe went picking berries in rural New Jersey. While out in the field she fell and cut her arm on a rock, a seemingly minor incident. By the time she returned to the city her arm had swelled to twice its normal size and she was in intense pain. Her mother called a local doctor, who performed an impromptu operation on the kitchen table. He used a steak knife to cut into Robbe's arm. This action aggravated the wound and infection set in. The Seidmans rushed their daughter to Mt. Sinai Hospital by streetcar.

There, doctors diagnosed her condition as osteomyelitis, an infection of the bone marrow caused by bacteria. There would be no easy cure, but when the doctors suggested amputating both arms, Lena told them in Yiddish to go to hell. Robbe spent the next few years more or less living at the hospital. "I spent a lot of time at Mt. Sinai," she could later say with a smile. "In fact, I got to know it better than I knew my own home." According to Robbe, her parents were banned from visiting their daughter at the hospital. It seems that every time they bade Robbe good-bye after a visit, she would burst into tears, and the swelling in her arm would reignite. Lena couldn't be kept away from her daughter. When night fell, she climbed up the fire escape to her daughter's room to visit with her, often bringing the young girl chocolates. These nocturnal visits ended after Lena slipped on the fire escape and bounced down the wrought-iron stairs on her derrière.

Eventually, the doctors did cut away some of Robbe's left arm, leaving it shorter than the right. For the rest of her life she wore long-sleeves to keep her disability a secret. The experience left a positive mark on Robbe, for through it she developed a sense of fortitude and a tolerance for pain. By the time she was 10 years old she figured she had taken all the hard knocks life had to offer. She was wrong, but the accident and it's aftermath prepared her for just about anything the world would throw at her.

The world would throw a lot at Robbe, as it turned out. The Lower East Side of the 1920s was a hotbed of politics. American unions such as the Amalgamated Clothing Workers Union and International Ladies Garment Workers Union formed there during this time period. People talked about politics and bomb-making, even though nobody really knew how to make a bomb. The Seidmans were, to some degree, part of that sociopolitical movement. "My father was very liberal about everything," Robbe recalled. "I used to go to demonstrations with him when I was very young because he wanted to teach me."

It wasn't hard for her to understand why unionism—considered a daring form of socialism in those days—was important to the workers. Lena had told Robbe a horror story that made the young girl's hair stand on end. And it wasn't make-believe. It was the story of the Triangle Shirtwaist Company factory, on the Lower East Side, that had burst into flames in March 1911. For the workers (mostly women) inside, there had been no escape, for the company had shut and barred all the fire escape doors. To escape the flames, many of the women threw themselves out of the windows, to their death. By the time the fire was extinguished, over 140 people had perished. Lena Seidman knew some of the women who died in that conflagration, and her retelling of the incident kindled within Robbe a different sort of fire. As a young woman she chose to join the struggle against inequality and prejudice, participating in demonstrations and street marches that called for unionization and equality for minorities.

Unfortunately, Boss Tammany and the Republicans controlled the Lower East Side and did not sympathize with these causes. Tammany toughs appeared at marches and threw anything they could get their hands on at the marchers. Robbe attended one such demonstration wearing a new hat and dress that her mother had made for her. Protesters threw cabbages and rocks at her colleagues on the line. Robbe was not so lucky. She was bombarded with feces. "A whole pile of shit hit my head," she recalled years later. "And it spoiled my whole day, needless to say." Once again, Robbe learned a hard lesson: When it came to politics, anything goes.

Soon after that incident, the Seidmans relocated to the West Bronx in the mid-1920s, and it was there that Robbe first encountered Julie at the block party. After their brief meeting and her subsequent rejection of him, neither figured on seeing the other ever again.

Back at the Garfinkle residence, Julie let his father know that he was quitting high school in favor of the stage. Julie figured two more years of school would hinder rather than help him, and as he wasn't learning anything anyway, what was the point? David might have accepted his son's leaving school if it was to earn a decent wage, but this acting business was another thing altogether. "I remember him telling me how his family felt about his wanting to be an actor," friend Robert Brown said. "It seemed egocentric to them for him to want to be an actor. For what was an actor but a bum?"

"My parents thought that the quicker I went out and earned money, the better," Julie explained. "They needed money but that didn't bother me. I wanted to be an actor!" He found little sympathy among his relatives. "Julie should be something practical, making more money," they would complain to David. To make matters worse, Julie had quit his job at the vegetable market and was no longer selling newspapers. Yet he needed money more than ever in order to attend drama school.

The story goes that the prominent stage actor Jacob Ben-Ami caught Julie's performance in *A Midsummer Night's Dream*. Word reached the young thespian that Ben-Ami was impressed, though whether this was on the up-and-up is debatable, since Julie was naïve. Nonetheless, he took the news to heart and wrote Ben-Ami a letter soliciting advice on his future. To his surprise, Ben-Ami responded, suggesting that he apply to The American Laboratory Theater (known as the Lab), an organization run by Richard Boleslavski and Mme. Maria Ouspenskaya, two graduates of the Moscow Art Theatre. Julie promptly made an appointment for an interview.

He spent hours going over his two lines of dialogue: "Jacob Ben-Ami, who happens to be a very dear friend of mine, sent me here. I would like to audition." When he met the rather formidable Mme. Ouspenskaya, he managed to spit the lines out, while adding that Ben-Ami had recommended him for a scholarship. (He was becoming quite skilled at lying.) Then he sweated bullets worrying that she might just phone Ben-Ami to check the facts. "I died a thousand deaths before I was able to leave that room," he later told a journalist. Luckily Ouspenskaya didn't call his bluff. Instead, impressed by his audition piece (a poem by Edgar Allan Poe) she agreed to enroll him in the morning class on a one-month trial basis. If he showed promise, she told him they would award him with a seven-month scholarship.

Julie was ecstatic, but his father considered the whole acting business a childish occupation and wondered how Julie was planning to get by financially. Angelo Patri answered that question by staking Julie five dollars a week for the next eight months. In Julie, Patri saw potential; a kid who could do right given the proper chance. He figured if the boy had the guts to con his way into the Lab, then he should be able to go after his dreams. And Julie had plenty of dreams.

CHAPTER THREE
An Actor's Life

"The stage has an indefinable excitement."
—JOHN GARFIELD

THE AMERICAN LABORATORY THEATER WAS FOUNDED IN 1923 by Richard Boleslavski, a Polish-born actor who had worked with the Moscow Art Theatre before the Russian Revolution. The Moscow Art Theatre's driving force was Constantin Stanislavsky, generally regarded as the man who developed what has become known as the Method system of acting. Stanislavsky established the Moscow Art Theatre in 1898, building an ensemble of actors who approached their roles methodically, working towards a more realistic portrayal through personal identification with their stage characters. Boleslavski and Ouspenskaya had been two of the premier actors of the company. When they arrived in America they opened the American Laboratory Theater on MacDougal Street with financial backing from Herbert and Miriam Stockton. Boleslavski saw the theater as a laboratory; a place for experimentation and discovery.

Julie tried to fit in at the Lab. He didn't immediately grasp what Ouspenskaya meant when she talked about sense memory work (in which an actor reaches back into his past for a personal experience to summon forth a feeling or emotion necessary for a stage scene) though it was an approach he would learn to rely on more and more in the future. He was primarily concerned that the intimidating little lady would discover he was a phony. Every time that

Jacob Ben-Ami visited the Lab, Julie hid in the boiler room for fear
of being found out.

Julie entered his first semester at the Lab in October 1929, on the
eve of Black Thursday and the Great Depression. New students
were called "sheep," which sounded little better than "bum" to
Julie. Ouspenskaya frightened him. Tiny, wizened and constantly
sporting a black cigar in her mouth, Madame used her piercing eyes
to bore into a student's psyche. She no doubt evoked the screen
image of the Gypsy Woman she later played in the 1941 horror film
The Wolf Man. Ouspenskaya enjoyed reducing her students to tears,
for she felt that in order to begin training an actor she had to break
down all of their defenses. Julie's introduction to ballet class was
less emotionally stressful but more physically painful because the
instructor, a Miss La Sylphe, ominously wielded a sharp switch to
keep the students hopping.

1929 was the final full year of existence for the Lab. Despite limited success (one Lab production, Clemence Dane's *Granite*, actually made it to Broadway in 1927), the company suffered continued
financial setbacks, which the advent of the Depression aggravated.
During Julie's first semester with the Lab, half of the students had to
drop out for lack of tuition monies. In addition, Boleslavski left the
Lab for Hollywood to direct the film *The Awful Truth*. He stayed
there until his death in 1937. The lack of incoming tuition combined with diminishing box office returns and Boleslavski's departure led the Lab to close its doors in the summer of 1930.

The Lab's effect on Julie was important, for not only did it offer
the young actor an introduction to a well-rounded curriculum, but
it gave him the chance to rub shoulders with the likes of Lee Strasberg, Harold Clurman, Ruth Nelson, Stella Adler and Eunice Stoddard (all future members of the Group Theatre). And eventually, he
would figure out just how to use sense memory to color a portrayal.

In the summer of 1930 Julie applied for an apprenticeship at Eva
LeGallienne's famed Civic Repertory Theater on 14th Street. Julie
was looking for experience, and at the Civic Rep, he got it: experi-

ence sweeping the floors, cleaning the toilets, building the sets, taking tickets and playing stagehand. Now and then he got a bit part onstage. LeGallienne, a strict disciplinarian, was respected for her attempt to bring theater to the masses (top ticket price was $1.50).

Julie had, by now, reached his full height—five foot seven—and at seventeen he possessed a boyish charm and ebullient personality. The local girls thought he was cute, and Julie picked up on this aspect, using it whenever necessary to get his way in both business and pleasure. The girls liked him, and he liked them back, but before he could do much about it Robbe came back into the picture. She visited the Rep in order to meet a girlfriend who happened to be in the apprentice program with Julie. He asked her out on a date. While there was an element of "wolf" in his attitude, he also seemed naïve, a trait that Robbe found disarming. She agreed to go out with him.

The couple were soon spending hours talking on park benches, taking in the early talking pictures at the local movie house, and making out wherever and whenever they could. He fell for her harder than she fell for him, partially because he was so desperate to have a stable relationship with someone who showed him affection. She developed a nurturing attitude towards him from the beginning, an attitude that ensured that she would have to play mother as well as lover and wife. Robbe's parents weren't happy about her new beau. "No Jewish parents want their daughter to marry an actor," she said years later. "Because an actor was a bum."

Julie didn't think so. He wanted to act, and he couldn't describe why he wanted to act. He never would clearly articulate why he loved the theater, but Robbe noticed that he was never so happy as when he was in rehearsal or onstage in a play. She thought it had to do with his desire to prove that he was good at something. "Acting is a vanity-thing," she explained. "For what are actors but big children looking for approval?" Julie didn't find approval with LeGallienne. He still had an aura of the street tough about him, and one day she accused him of stealing another performer's shoes. Julie

was more hurt than scared, particularly after the real culprit was
flushed out and LeGallienne refused to apologize to him. He left the
Civic Rep with the hope of getting some work on Broadway—he
was optimistic if nothing else. Before he could start making the
rounds his old pal Joe LaSpina, who was then working in a gas station in Indiana, sent him a letter asking Julie to join him on a cross-
country jaunt. Julie was not yet 18 and raring to go.

David Garfinkle was furious when he heard Julie's plan. Robbe
was more hurt than she wanted to admit, but she decided to maintain a cool facade. "I'm going away," he told her one night, sounding like a fugitive from a chain gang who was about to go into
eternal hiding. "I feel this is my need." Robbe simply shrugged.
"Everybody knows their need," she replied. He was baffled and disappointed. The two had not yet become lovers and he was hoping
to get a lusty farewell from her. "I was shoving off, really, and she
didn't give me a tumble," he said. Robbe wisely realized he needed
to get the wanderlust out of his system. He said good-bye and promised to write, but she didn't believe him. She didn't really think
he'd go, she later said, but a few weeks later his postcards began arriving from all over the country.

With less than five dollars on him, Julie packed a knapsack and
headed to the front door. David intercepted him, so Julie turned and
bolted out of the back door. Within an hour he had managed to get
a lift to Cincinnati with a passing motorist. It was early autumn,
1930, and though the country's road system was not comprised of
the highways of today, somehow he managed to hitch a ride as far
as Indiana, where he met up with LaSpina. The duo headed to Nebraska on a ticket of youth, hope and luck, working their way across
by washing dishes, picking wheat and doing any and all odd jobs.
Julie would sometimes recite Kipling's "Gunga Din" for handouts at
kitchen doors while LaSpina offered pen-and-ink sketches to potential dinner hosts. Nebraska provided a few weeks of work in the
wheat fields, and when the harvest season ended the boys headed
further west.

Crossing the Rockies was no easy chore. Few cars passed the two travelers, and those that did weren't stopping to pick up a couple of hobos. An early winter frost made the going more miserable. Julie liked to tell a story about an experience the two had in Wyoming, where they spent the night in an abandoned cabin in the middle of nowhere. The cabin was filled with tin cans; Julie and Joe tore into them, hoping to find something to eat. Instead they found ore samples left by a local prospector. There was an old stove, which LaSpina lit, and the pair bedded down near it, hungry but warm. When they awoke, they discovered that a box situated next to the stove was filled with dynamite and blasting powder—an explosion waiting to happen.

Now they took to riding the rails, learning quickly how to tell how far away a train was by its whistle, and detecting its speed by the chuffing of the steam in the cylinders. They became pros at boarding a train between the tender (the car carrying water and coal) and the first mail car. Often they would travel "blind," as the railroaders called it, lying underneath the cars wearing rags tied around their heads to keep the cinders from cutting into their eyes. The rails took them to Nevada, where they lived in a hobo camp for a month. Julie earned his keep by reciting Poe's *The Raven* over and over again. He considered it "the best training for the stage a man could get."

They kept company with vagrants, criminals and the first casualties of the Great Depression—the unemployed. Julie would later romanticize the entire experience, but it was not all fun and games. In Nebraska the boys watched helplessly as a fellow hobo fell to his death under the cars of an oncoming freight train. In Utah Julie stumbled across a railroad "bull" (cop) who opened fire on the errant youth, narrowly missing him as he zigzagged across the rail yard.

By October Julie and Joe made it to Los Angeles. Julie joked about breaking into the movies, but it was just that, a joke, and the reality of their situation soon set in. The only work they found was in the fruit fields, where they picked peaches and ate peaches until they were sick to death of peaches. Julie would later tell journalist Ida Zeitlin that he tried to join both the Navy and the Marines at this time, which was probably another lie. "I'm picking fruit," were the only three words he wrote on a postcard to Robbe from the San Joaquin Valley.

Before long both of them were yearning for home. Joe wanted to go straight back to Indiana while Julie wanted to take a roundabout route back to New York. Julie had not yet learned how to drive, but somehow he managed to bluff his way into a truck driving job. Within minutes of taking the wheel he managed to run the truck, loaded with cantaloupes, off the road. He was promptly fired; his only severance pay being squashed cantaloupe.

But Julie had perseverance. He managed to make his way through the Southwest, hitchhiking and working from southern California to Arizona, New Mexico and Texas. "I'm doing six days for vagrancy," he wrote Robbe from a jail in Austin, Texas, and it was true. He got out and headed north to Nebraska, where he again managed to find work in the wheat fields. He returned to New York sometime in November, and by the time he arrived in his step-mother's kitchen he was deathly ill. He had contracted typhoid fever from taking a drink of water from a contaminated well in Nebraska. He welcomed 1931 in a hospital bed.

Robbe visited Julie in the hospital. She was sporting a dark tan, even in late autumn, and when David Garfinkle stopped by and saw her chatting with Julie, he began yelling at her in Yiddish and pursuing her with a cane. He thought she was black and he didn't want his son consorting with a black woman. "He was a very stupid, non-caring person," Robbe said of David Garfinkle. Though the typhoid fever caused irreparable damage to his heart, Julie recovered. Joe LaSpina was less lucky. He died shortly thereafter, in the Midwest, of tuberculosis.

Rested, reanimated and armed with a heavy dose of self-confidence that came with the feeling of having nothing to lose,

Julie started the new year by making the acting rounds. He played bit parts with Fritz Lieber's Shakespearean Players for a while, before ingratiating himself with director Herbert Biberman. Biberman was one of the guiding forces of The Theatre Guild, a production company formed in 1919 that vowed to present "the best drama of one's time." And while most of New York fell for it—The Theatre Guild was one of the most respected theatrical organizations of the era—not everyone was won over. "The only fundamental difference between the new theater and the old is that the former sells better stuff," one critic wrote. "These theatres always will begin with a play, and never with a group of actors that may be appropriately considered part of it." The critic was Harold Clurman.

Clurman was a passionate, fast-talking (though soft-spoken) 29-year-old play reader for the Guild. An avid theatergoer since early childhood, Clurman had studied the work of the Moscow Art Theatre and had written a thesis on French theater based on his experiences in Paris. Clurman wanted theater that made "men more truly alive," where director, actor and playwright all worked together to realistically depict life as it unfolded in 1930's America. Clurman's dream would slowly come to life. So would Julie's.

Julie was financially surviving thanks to a job selling Margaret Sanger-endorsed diaphragms to medical offices (the women secretaries blushed when he came in). He knew he needed to gain more experience in the theater, and he understood the value of theatrical training. He enrolled in acting classes held in the basement of the Civic Rep. One of the guest lecturers was 24-year-old Clifford Odets, an aspiring playwright and actor who had played small roles in several Guild productions. Julie and Odets were immediately drawn to each other; the younger man saw in Odets another father figure in the mold of Angelo Patri. Julie was fascinated with Odets' rambling dissertations on life, theater and women, while Odets was constantly amused by Julie's candor and innocence.

Odets told Julie of the newly formed Group Theatre, which was spearheaded by Clurman, Lee Strasberg and Cheryl Crawford.

Strasberg, 12 years Julie's senior, had been born in Poland but grew up in the same neighborhood as Julie. A high school dropout, the serious and sometimes downright icy Strasberg became a working director and actor at the Students of Art and Drama Club at the Chrystie Street Settlement House on the Lower East Side. After seeing the presentation of the Moscow Theatre's 1923 season in New York City, Strasberg realized that Stanislavsky had created a process in which the actors literally became the characters onstage. He liked that approach, and soon after tried to adapt it to his work at the Theatre Guild, though with little success. There he met Clurman, and the two men became friends, talking endlessly about what theater should be, and bemoaning what it was not.

Crawford had been the casting director for the Guild. Like Clurman and Strasberg, she was excited by the prospect of forming a unified company that would work as an ensemble to present plays that "said something." Unlike the two men, Crawford was generally calm, quiet and open. She struck some as having a missionary's sensibility, and perhaps it's no surprise that she once dreamt of becoming a missionary. Crawford was as unhappy with the Guild's lackluster offerings as Clurman was, and soon she joined him in organizing experimental play readings on Sunday nights. These staged readings provided the basis for the creation of the Group Theatre.

The Group was in its infancy when Julie met up with Odets, the fascinating and ultimately impossible-to-know playwright/actor. Robbe would sum Odets up as "a strange man" while another colleague described him as "a suit of clothes with some utter stranger inside them, who is known as Odets." That Julie got along well with Odets, as well as Clurman, Crawford and Strasberg, is a testament to his easygoing nature. Everyone tried to help Julie because no one felt threatened by him. He came off as a talented nonprofessional with no educational background, no knowledge of theater history, and no ambition to do anything except act. Instinct, everyone agreed, was his strength. He had a natural talent for making friends offstage, and for making the right choices when it came to acting onstage.

Julie told Odets about a Broadway play he was going to audition for, T.C. Upham's *Lost Boy*. It was about a very Julie Garfinkle-like youth, a victim of society who ends up in a reform school. While Julie rather optimistically hoped to land the lead role, he was lucky to land the relatively small part of another delinquent named Bill. What's most amazing about it all is that director James Light cast the inexperienced actor in such a prestigious production. Though Julie bragged to family and friends that he was appearing on Broadway, it turned out he wouldn't be appearing there for long. *Lost Boy* closed within two weeks at the end of January 1932. So much for stardom.

The experience garnered Julie his Equity card as well as a new name. In the program for *Lost Boy*, his last name is listed as Garfield, a further Americanization to his name. How or why he chose that name is a mystery; he never explained it. That's the name he used when he bounded into the casting office of Elmer Rice, the playwright-director who was looking for actors for the Chicago company of his latest play, *Counsellor-At-Law*. The play, which had opened on Broadway in December 1931 with Paul Muni in the lead, was an unqualified success. Muni played George Simon, a Jewish lawyer who had worked his way out of the ghetto and into a successful law practice, only to find everything falling apart when he knowingly helps a guilty client commit perjury. Julie read for the part of a shoeshine boy, but Rice was so taken with the actor's off-the-cuff delivery that he cast him as office boy Henry Suskind, a larger role. (Julie's childhood friend Eddie Kogan got the part of the shoeshine boy.)

Otto Kruger would play the lead role in the Chicago production, while Vincent Sherman was cast as a radical opponent of Kruger's. Sherman was a good-looking 28 year old from Georgia (though there was little trace of a Southern accent) who aspired to be a lawyer.

Sherman shared a dressing room with Julie. Like Patri and Odets before him, Sherman ended up playing surrogate father to Julie. Acting fired Julie's interest in cultural and national events. "He was so eager to find out everything there is to know about life," Sherman recalled. "He wanted to know about art, painting and music. I've never seen such eagerness to learn in all my life. I'd buy a *New Republic* and *The Nation* and let him read them, and he'd just devour them; he ate them up." Julie may have chewed and chewed, but one wonders whether he digested anything, for while his interest in cultural affairs was sincere, his understanding of politics and world events remained surface-deep.

Sherman and Julie would stay up through the wee hours of the night talking about theater and life. "We lived in New York at that time," Sherman recalled. "And there were nice-looking men on street corners selling apples for a nickel, and people jumping out of windows, knowing there were no jobs to be had. You wondered, 'What the hell is going on in this country?' because here was one of the richest countries in the world, with all the resources in the world, and there were bread lines everywhere. It was pathetic."

Sex was a welcome distraction from the country's ills. While in Chicago, Julie found out that the local chorus girls and bit players were competing to see who could get him into bed first. One of them finally succeeded, pulling him into a spare bedroom during a cast party. It may have been his first time, but he was smart enough to use a contraceptive. (Robbe recalled that Julie was the one who provided her with one of the Margaret Sanger diaphragms when they made love for the first time.) He was just past 19 years old, and as with acting, Julie was a quick study when it came to the opposite sex. And also as with acting, he got hooked. He may not have seen his one-night stand as being unfaithful to Robbe, for the two hadn't officially consummated their affair. But unfaithfulness, when it came to sex, never gave Julie cause for remorse. Sex was something he was good at, and it reassured him that he had talent. That was something no one could take away from him.

Counsellor-At-Law opened in May 1932 at Chicago's Erlanger Theatre and played to full houses until Kruger returned to the New York production to replace Muni, who had left to go to Hollywood to film *Scarface,* a violent crime drama. Julie wasn't put out to pasture, for when Muni rejoined the New York production in the autumn of 1932, Julie reprised his role. He stayed with the play until the spring of 1933, telling everyone that he was a working actor. This time he wasn't lying.

CHAPTER FOUR

The Group

*"I didn't learn a thing about acting until I
joined the Group Theatre."*
—JOHN GARFIELD

ASKED TO DESCRIBE WHAT HE MEANT BY THE TERM
"group," Harold Clurman would hem and haw until finally
he had to say something: "A theatre is created when people
with common interests and tastes unite to deliver ways and
means whereby they may give their group feeling an adequate theatrical expression." That may not have been a
clear enough definition for some people, but Clurman knew
what he wanted even if he couldn't properly express it.

Clurman felt that the main problem with American theater was that the focus was on the play, and not the players.
Fellow Guild members Morris Carnovsky, Phoebe Brand,
Ruth Nelson and Franchot Tone listened sympathetically,
for like Clurman, they were all interested in presenting contemporary plays that had a connection to the then-current
social scenario. While most of those affiliated with the
Group Theatre were definitely sympathetic to liberal cause
and thought, this did not necessarily make them communists. "The Group Theatre was definitely not a political
group," former member Martin Ritt asserted. In Phoebe
Brand's view, however, everyone was "touched" by the
communist cause.

It was coincidental that the first official Group production (or co-production, as it was financed by the Theatre

Guild) was a Russian play entitled *Red Rust,* which opened at the Martin Beck Theatre on December 17, 1929. The play was not a success, though it did garner some kind reviews, with the *Nation* noting that this style of theater was what made the Soviet theater so successful in that it was "closer and more literally faithful to the contemporary life of its age than any other theatre in the world." This is what the Group, as the new theater company was now called, was striving for.

Following the path of the Moscow Art Theatre the Group's directors—Clurman, Strasberg and Crawford—planned to assemble an ensemble of actors, go away for the summer to train and rehearse and then return to New York City to mount two productions. The three directors interviewed and auditioned dozens of hopeful performers, including Odets. Despite the commercial failure of *Red Rust,* the Guild agreed to back the Group's next production, Paul Green's *The House of Connelly.* Crawford rented a house, barn and dining hall in Brookfield Center, Connecticut, for the summer of 1931. The Group Theatre was on its way.

It was during these summer rehearsals that the actors first studied Stanislavsky's "system," under the tutelage of Strasberg, and which Strasberg labeled a "method." The actors were asked to try to recall the events of a particular experience—the time of day, the place, the people involved, how it made them feel, etc.—that would allow them as actors to recreate the moment and apply it to the play. Playwright Green tried to describe how this method worked: "The directors would take a particular actor or actress and say 'Here's a part in the play. Now you go over there by that tree and lean your head up against the tree and do all you can to bring back a feeling, an experience in your life that is similar to what the scene is about. An emotion—or an emotional experience.' Emotion was a great word with them." Green's analysis of the method sounds remarkably similar to the instructions Margaret O'Ryan had given Julie when he was asked to portray a blind man. How successful each actor was depended on their willingness to open themselves up to memory and emotion. Julie turned out to be particularly adept at it, always managing to inject a huge dose of instinct into the proceedings.

As for *The House of Connelly,* it heralded great things for the Group and theater in America. It opened at the Martin Beck Theatre on September 29, 1931. Twenty-two curtain calls were required of the actors and the reviews seemed to warrant the public acclaim. "It is not too much to hope that something fine and true has been started in the American theatre," critic Brooks Atkinson wrote. But hope was all that kept the Group going for the next two years. Their next four productions, *1931, Night Over Taos, Success Story* and *The Party,* were financial and critical failures. The Group was beginning to look like a one-hit wonder. And then Crawford unearthed Sidney Kingsley's play *Crisis,* a hospital drama. When it opened at the Broadhurst Theatre in September 1933 under its new title, *Men In White,* the play was an immediate hit. American audiences responded to the play's major theme—sacrifice and devotion for the sake of humanity—and the play won a Pulitzer Prize, before MGM bought the film rights and turned it into a successful film starring Clark Gable.

The Group had arrived, and they made it clear that they were planning to stick around. *Men in White* had everyone in New York talking about the Group, and Julie wanted to be part of that talk. He was then studying acting at The Neighborhood Playhouse with Sanford Meisner, another member of the Group. Julie's fellow students included future film director/actor Joseph Pevney and actress Helen Golden Levine. Levine likened Julie to a jungle cat forever ready to pounce on its prey. "He was always wound up tight like a spring," she recalled. "He put on this virtuoso performance in drama class, but I don't think he was too interested in the other types of classes that they taught."

Levine was right. Julie paid little attention to movement and voice classes. He wanted to act, and he felt the other classes simply diluted his energy. His raw talent indicated that he would go on to bigger and better things. "He was so much better than the rest of us," Levine recalled. "It was virtually apparent from the first day." One day Meisner asked the students to improvise a scene in which they faced conflict. Julie made up an agonizing sequence wherein he portrayed a patient having his tooth pulled in the dentist's chair. The scene made his fellow students wince. "It was excruciating," Levine said. "You could barely watch him; it was so painful." Julie was probably just utilizing his own brand of the Method, for in real life he dreaded dentists. (A 1943 newspaper piece entitled "Dialogue From A Dentist's Chair" made fun of his fear, discussing in detail his writhing and moaning during an interview in a dental office.)

Julie left the Neighborhood Playhouse to join the cast of the Theatre Guild production of *Peace on Earth,* an anti-war drama penned by George Sklar and Albert Maltz (Maltz would later write two John Garfield screenplays for Warner Bros.) He had a small role, as a messenger boy, but it was work, and he earned twenty-five dollars a week. To supplement this income, he took a job at Macy's alongside Robbe, who was working there as a salesgirl. Julie didn't last long, for he would take time out from selling ties to do impromptu impersonations of Edward G. Robinson and Paul Muni in the store aisles. The sales manager fired him.

What he wanted was to join the Group. In a sense it was like joining a gang: he would be among friends who would not judge him (or so he thought) and who would act as a surrogate family. Odets tried his best to get Julie into the company. But as neither Clurman nor Strasberg thought Odets was talented, his endorsement of Julie was hardly taken seriously. Bobby Lewis, another Group member, probably deserves the credit for getting Julie into the Group. Lewis was teaching acting in the basement of the Broadhurst Theatre, and Julie, egged on by Odets, enrolled in the class. One day Lewis suggested to Julie that he use a Picasso painting of a young boy as a base to work with for an improvisational scene. Lewis wanted him to recreate the physical pose within the art piece and imbue it with an inner life of his own. One can only imagine what the final product looked like, but Lewis was impressed enough to ask Strasberg and Clurman to come watch Julie in action. Lewis asked Julie to recreate the scene

again, and he did, to Clurman's satisfaction. After some consideration, Clurman and Strasberg agreed to add Julie to their apprentice
roster, which included Elia Kazan, for the 1934 season.

By the time the news reached him, Julie was in Vermont. In 1933,
through Patri's influence, he had landed a job as assistant social director at the Twin-A-Wani Lodge, an upscale retreat for those who
still had money. (His immediate supervisor was the not-yet-famous
playwright Sidney Kingsley.) Julie mounted some theatrical productions while at the lodge, and the following year—1934—he was
invited back as the social director. Robbe accompanied him.

Julie and Robbe were still enjoying a passionate, lively relationship. But you wouldn't exactly call it love—at least Robbe didn't.
While in Vermont she began a romantic relationship with the son of
a local hotel owner. The young man had class, as well as a certain
panache that Julie lacked. When Julie got the news that the Group
wanted him to join them for summer training in Ellenville, New
York, Robbe wasn't sure she wanted to go with him. Julie begged
her, believing that if he could get her away from his rival's home
turf, he could win her back. The rival, however, was tenacious. He
offered to drive Julie and Robbe to Ellenville himself. Robbe accepted the offer and Julie ended up in the back seat—odd man out.

The driver did himself in. Trying to impress Robbe with his driving skills, he failed to negotiate a sharp turn and ended up running
the car through a wood fence and off the road. Julie was thrown from
the car and into a nearby clump of bushes. The rival was dazed, but
Julie was bleeding from the nose, and when Robbe saw this, she
claimed she fell in love with him on the spot. The Vermont suitor
drove back home alone; Robbe and Julie hitched a ride to Ellenville.

They hooked up with the other Group members at Mount
Meengha Lodge, a hotel located two thousand feet above sea level
in the Catskill Mountains. The hotel was luxurious by 1934 standards, boasting both a swimming pool and tennis courts. Robbe was
amazed at the spectacle that greeted them: "Stella Adler was
dressed in a mink stole like some rich woman—this was in the mid-

dle of the summer during the height of the Depression—and Bobby Lewis was playing a record, Afternoon of a Fawn, and acting it out as it played on the gramophone. And I immediately thought to myself, 'What am I getting into?' What they were getting into was an artistic hotbed of theater, politics and sex.

The Group spent the summer rehearsing Melvin Levy's *Gold Eagle Guy*, which they planned to mount in the autumn. They also found time to have affairs with each other (except for the love-and-lust-struck Odets, who kept striking out with women), and drink and talk about how theater and communism could change the world. Robbe felt at home in this last topic. "We were idealistic," she would later say. "But it was so wonderful to sit up all night and talk with people who were so sincere about everything they were doing, and how it could change the world."

Change, many of the Group's members felt, could only come about through and by the people. The Communist Party offered the most hope, for it alone embraced unemployment relief, equality for all people (regardless of race) and government support for welfare. No other political party offered a cure for the country's ills. "If you weren't a member of the party," Helen Golden Levine said, "or at least a fellow traveler, then you just weren't in the swing of things." Robbe joined the Communist Party around this time. So did Odets, Kazan and several other Group members. Julie didn't, though he later told friends that he tried. He just wasn't taken seriously. "The Group considered him something of a lightweight, both as an actor and a politician," said Helen Levitt, Julie's secretary in later years. Robbe later acknowledged that Julie's interest in world affairs and politics ran no deeper than the surface. He could sit and listen to Odets scream about using art to change the country over a bottle of scotch, but come morning he was more interested in learning his lines.

The Group members argued amongst themselves about which acting approach was more successful: Stanislavsky's theory that the appropriate feelings of each character should stem from the action of the play, or Strasberg's diluted formula wherein the actor was to find the appropriate emotion before considering the action of the play. Stella Adler had studied with Stanislavsky and was a fervent follower of *his* system; Strasberg was adamant that his own method was more appropriate. Members began to choose sides in an ever-increasing battle of wills and ideals between the two acting coaches. Julie, forever able to remain on good terms with just about everyone, pledged allegiance to both.

All the Group felt the same way Robbe did about Julie—that he was young, naïve, childlike and very much in need of protection. "Our first impression of him was that he was adorable," Phoebe Brand recalled, as if talking about a pet monkey. Her husband, Morris Carnovsky, agreed: "The one word that instinctively and immediately derives from his action is charm." Equally amusing was Julie's penchant for malapropisms, a result of his attempt to impress even though he didn't know what the hell he was talking about.

"I'll observe his looks; I'll cut him to the quick, if he but belch, I'll know my course!" Julie exclaimed one day, reciting dialogue from Shakespeare's *Hamlet* to impress Brand and Carnovsky. Instead the pair broke up laughing. The correct verb was 'bletch', not 'belch.' Julie ended up sounding like Jimmy Durante. Shakespeare would never be his forte. The Group newsletter, "The Flying Grouse," which was initiated by Luther Adler and Roman Bohnen in February 1936, included a column titled "Counterfeit Presentiments" that poked fun at the Group. Morris Carnovsky wrote one such column that played up Julie's malapropisms:

> SCENE: Lee's apartment. The radio plays the Missa Solemnis. The victrola plays a Balinese dance. Lee is reading simultaneously "Die Entwicklung des Basso-Buff im Weltpolitick des 20 Jahrhunderts" and "The Cadaver of Gwendolyn Gwynne." Julie bursts in.

> JULIE: Give me some advice, Lee. I have developed a new atrophicy in my diction. With me this is tantamount. I

would gladly listen to you all day, for you know my ambition. It is to play a cultural man and speak monosyl-
labic. To say to the dame, "Madam softly downs the
couchy moon! Pray dismiss Parker House, your butler,
and lay with me ere I smack you down!"

Julie would do anything to attract attention. He once climbed a
barn roof and performed a live-wire type act on the ridge while
everyone gathered below to watch. Julie lost his balance, fell, and
slid down the roof, à la Oliver Hardy, landing in a mound of dirt on
the side. Miraculously he sustained only minor injuries. Robbe was
furious, but Strasberg was impressed and asked the young apprentice if he would take a fifteen-foot leap onstage for a scene in *Gold
Eagle Guy*.

Rehearsals for the play were not going well. It rained all summer
long; the eight dogs roaming the grounds all contacted ringworm
and died off one by one. The actors fell ill as well. Tension between
the Strasberg and Adler camps rose, and Group member Art Smith
and his wife seemed to spend more time organizing the kitchen
help into a union than working on the play. Labor activists were invited in to lecture during the rehearsal process, distracting everyone. Kazan later testified that some of the lecturers were prominent
leaders of the Communist Party.

The play's plot didn't win anyone over either. *Gold Eagle Guy*
dealt with the rise of a shipping magnate (Julie kept referring to him
as a magnet) during San Francisco's Barbary Coast era. The accent
in the script was on capitalism, a fact that amused and angered
many in the Group. During one rehearsal Luther Adler uttered a
much-repeated (and apt) criticism of the play: "Boys, I think we're
working on a stiff." Most everyone agreed.

Odets, given little to do in the play and growing increasingly disillusioned with the Group, spent more and more time writing two
plays. One he called *Paradise Lost*, while the other, tentatively titled *I Got the Blues,* was about one thing he truly knew: the lower

class losers of New York City. The play was a biting social drama with comic undertones about a Jewish family in the Bronx struggling to keep alive (both physically and emotionally) in an uncertain world. One of the play's main characters, Ralph Berger, was clearly modeled on Odets' close friend Julie Garfield.

Julie was still a kid at heart, and like a kid he enjoyed practical jokes. During the 1936 run of *Johnny Johnson*, he shared a dressing room with Joseph Pevney and Morris Carnovsky. Carnovsky had been trying to impress upon Julie the importance of truth in theater. Julie had his own sense about truth in theater and asked Pevney to help play a gag on Carnovsky. One evening while Carnovsky was onstage, Julie dabbed red make-up across his throat and on the small sink in the dressing room. Then he set out a razor blade—also adorned with red makeup—and tilted his head back as if he had just slit his own throat. "When Morris comes up you scream like crazy like I done myself in, okay?" Julie ordered Pevney.

When they heard Carnovsky's footsteps approaching the dressing room, Pevney put on his best act, moaning and crying and screaming, "Julie, Julie, what have you done?" Carnovsky ran in and said, "What's the matter?" Pevney pointed to Julie's stiff body and then pretended to faint. Carnovsky, aghast, screamed out "Oh, dear God!" and then started to faint himself. This in turn frightened Julie, who suddenly jumped up. Seeing the reanimated corpse of his friend only terrified Carnovsky more, and he collapsed on the floor.

There would be no further "truth in theater" demonstrations from young Garfield. And yet that gag surpassed, in ingenuity, most of the other jokes Julie perpetrated, from stuffing rubber frogs and snakes into the underwear of his female costars to making prank phone calls that had no punch line. The strangest aspect of it all is that Julie himself was a prime target for practical jokers and con men. He probably would have made a bid on the Brooklyn Bridge.

CHAPTER FIVE

Awake And Sing!

> *"A man making a thousand dollars a week has*
> *no reason to be a Communist. Everything that*
> *I've got I'll share...if that is Communism,*
> *then I'm a Communist!"*
>
> —CLIFFORD ODETS

ENSEMBLE WORK WAS THE RULE OF THE GROUP. A FA-
mous story illustrates this. A young actress named Katharine
Hepburn attended an early lecture by Clurman, and when
she was asked what she thought of the Group's plans,
replied, "This may be all right for you people, if you want
it, but you see, I'm going to be a star."

In 1935, Julie didn't have "star" written all over him.
Members of the Group appreciated the raw talent that Julie
possessed, a talent that made him a unique asset to the company. "He was the Group's most valuable actor," Martin Ritt
explained. "There was no one else in the Group like him."
Unlike a J. Edward Bromberg (known as Joe) or a Morris
Carnovsky, Julie was basically unstudied, but he managed
to inject truthfulness into every scene he played because he
followed his instincts. This ability to draw from his own experiences ingratiated him with the Group members (for
wasn't that the very approach that Stanislavsky advocated?)
and ensured him of success in Hollywood. No other member of the Group could—or would—make the transition to
motion pictures as easily as Julie. Carnovsky, Bromberg, the
Adlers, and even Kazan proved to be a bit too technical in

their film performances. They filled the screen with larger-than-life characterizations that come off as mannered. Julie segued naturally into film because of his natural ability to find truth in almost every action he took. Though in later years no Group member other than Ritt would admit it, Julie's success in Hollywood caused envy.

The Group suffered their first defection to Hollywood in January 1933 when Franchot Tone left to sign a five-year contract with MGM. Tone, a graduate of Cornell University whose monied background placed him in a position of sharp contrast with other members of the Group, had been with the company since its inception in 1929. He fared well in Hollywood at first, appearing in two classic films, *Mutiny on the Bounty* and *The Lives of a Bengal Lancer* (both 1935). To complete this rosy picture of success, he even married a bona fide movie star, Joan Crawford. Though the Group had a difficult time forgiving Tone for his defection (Group member Michael Gordon likened it to leaving the Church), forgive him they did, especially as Tone sent them money to keep them afloat during the tough times. Even so, overall the Group was not prone to forgive star-struck members. "We were hostile to anyone going to Hollywood at the time," Phoebe Brand would note.

Alan Baxter and Joe Bromberg both decided that Hollywood had more to offer them than the Group did, and followed Tone west. Bromberg, missed more due to his versatility, found steady employment at 20th Century Fox. Baxter never quite made the grade in Hollywood, and ended up playing the same hood role over and over, a fate that Julie himself would barely escape while under contract to Warner Bros.

Had Hollywood called, Odets would probably have taken the next train west. Odets was frustrated with the Group's reluctance to give him substantial roles as an actor. It seemed as if they kept him on simply as a reward for his dedication. He believed firmly in the Group idea, especially when it came to using theater to change society. Recalling the bitter New York taxi strike of 1934, Odets fashioned an outline for a play, *Waiting for Lefty*. Five short, somewhat unrelated scenes showed how taxi drivers came to the conclusion that a strike was necessary to protect their jobs and wages. Isolating himself in New York's Hotel Bellevue, Odets knocked the play off within a matter of days. He then read the play to the Group actors, though he did not invite the Group's trio of leaders as, in the past, he had never found their comments the least bit encouraging. The actors loved the piece and began to work on it in their free time under the supervision of Odets and Sanford Meisner. What appealed most to the actors were the short, fast-paced scenes that seemed to speak for working class America in the 1930s. "My God, Joe, the world is supposed to be for all of us!" Edna tells her husband, a cabbie. Another cabbie, Benjamin, is a former hospital worker who was fired because he's Jewish. He's ready to take on the world: "Maybe get killed, but goddamn! We'll go ahead!" And the final cry, started by the cabbie, Agate, but picked up by all his fellow workers: "Working class, unite and fight! Tear down the slaughter houses of our old lives! Let Freedom really ring!" Odets couldn't have predicted that when the play was finally produced, audience members would so identify with the play's theme they would take to their feet during the opening night production and scream in unison with the actors. The playwright was about to hit the American Theater with a one-two punch that would make everyone sit up and take notice of the Group.

When the Group's directors finally saw a rough production of the show put on by the actors, both Clurman and Crawford were politely supportive. Strasberg's only comment was to Clurman: "Let 'em fall and break their necks," because he believed that the Group needed him to survive. In recent weeks, however, his authority had been challenged, not only by Stella Adler but by actress Ruth Nelson, who chased him out of a rehearsal of *Gold Eagle Guy* when the director went to great lengths to belittle another actress in front of the entire company.

"Strasberg was weird," said Martin Ritt, who joined the Group in 1937. "He wanted full control. He had no hopes in Odets—Odets couldn't act, Odets couldn't write—but once Odets proved himself with *Waiting for Lefty,* then Strasberg wanted to anchor him to the Group." Julie was one who always looked up to Strasberg for direction and never turned against him as some others would.

Gold Eagle Guy bombed, as Luther Adler had predicted, opening and closing in November 1934. Strasberg decided that it was time to call it a season. Clurman disagreed even though he did not have a sufficient script ready for production. Crawford, for her part, had been searching for a play that would appeal to the Group's sense of social justice and equality for all. The three leaders didn't realize that they had such a play at hand—Clifford Odets' *Awake and Sing!* When the three directors told the actors that there were no immediate production prospects, the actors replied that they would find a script and produce it themselves. Odets reminded Strasberg about his play, *Awake and Sing!.* "You don't seem to understand, Cliff," Strasberg remarked coolly, "we don't like your play." The actors told Strasberg that *they* liked the play, and while that may not have won over the arrogant director, the commercial and critical response to the initial production of *Waiting for Lefty* changed everything.

Waiting For Lefty was scheduled to make its debut as a one-night benefit for *New Theatre* magazine on January 6, 1935, at the Civic Repertory Theater on 14th Street. It was a bare-bones type of production. There was no set; lighting cues were minimal. The play would succeed or fail based on the weight of the story and the performances of the actors: Morris Carnovsky, Art Smith, Ruth Nelson, Russell Collins, Paula Miller, Luther Adler, J. Edward Bromberg, with Phoebe Brand and Julie as two young poverty-stricken lovers named Florrie and Sid.

Robbe sat next to Clifford Odets in the audience, along with actors Herbie Ratner and Lewis Leverett. As planned, when the actors onstage began yelling, "Strike!" on cue before the final curtain, Odets, Ratner and Leverett were to stand up and join them. They did. So did 1,400 other people. The entire audience, mesmerized by the play's realistic depiction of Depression-era life, stood and began crying out "Strike, strike!" The cast, including Julie, froze momentarily, stunned by the response. "It was an absolute bombshell," Robbe recalled. "Clifford couldn't believe it. We thought the whole theater was going to come down around our ears." The audience continued roaring its approval for forty-five minutes. Clurman called Odets up on stage to take a bow, and audience members spontaneously rushed the stage to hug him. After the actors removed their makeup and exited the theater, they discovered throngs of people waiting to speak with them about the play. American theater suddenly had a point of view. It was intimate, communal and political.

Only one theater critic was present. Henry Senber of the now-defunct *Morning-Telegram* witnessed the spectacle, and in his review he spoke for the future of the Group. "One left the theatre Sunday evening with two convictions," he wrote. "The first was that one had witnessed an event of historical importance in what is academically referred to as the drama of the contemporary American scene. The other was that a dramatist to be reckoned with has been discovered."

Within six months *Waiting for Lefty* was being produced nationwide. Odets was being approached by impresarios, Broadway producers and Hollywood talent scouts. Julie benefited from Odets' growing fame. In Julie, Odets saw the Ralph Bergers of the world, young men who were trying in vain to understand and challenge the harsh realities of everyday life. Berger was the first part to garner Julie some critical notice and attention. Some of Berger's dialogue seemed to have come from Julie's mouth. "I never in my life had a birthday party," the young idealist cries, echoing Julie's own feelings. "Every time I went and cried in the toilet when my birthday came." *Awake and Sing!*, directed by Clurman, provided the Group with its second successive hit within months.

Today it's easy to dismiss *Awake and Sing!*, as dated, but the dialogue continues to resonate with a plea for a better life for those who have been forgotten by society. The Bergers—Myron, Bessie, Hennie and Ralph—will do anything (well, almost anything) to improve their lot in life. The play rang with the sort of realistic dialogue that Odets was so good at committing to paper, and the script was punctuated with a socialistic cry for revolt. "If this life leads to a revolution it's a good life," grandfather Jacob Berger declares. "Otherwise it's for nothing."

When it opened at the Belasco Theatre in February 1935 it was a critical and a commercial hit. Julie won favorable reviews. "Julie Garfield plays the part of the boy with a splendid sense of character development," Brooks Atkinson of *The New York Times* wrote. Julie paid close attention to the notices (he always would) for he needed them to bolster his confidence. He still wasn't sure of himself, even onstage. "He never really thought much of himself at times," Robbe said. "He always needed reassurance."

On January 27, 1935, Julie and Robbe married. The Seidmans catered the affair at a Bronx meeting hall and all the members of the Group were invited. The ceremony was scheduled for a Sunday evening when all the theaters would be dark. Unbeknownst to Julie and Robbe, the Group had already scheduled a benefit performance of *Gold Eagle Guy* for that night. Robbe waited at the meeting hall alone, sipping wine during the long wait and eventually got quite drunk. When Julie arrived, he was loaded too, for on the taxi ride to the meeting hall he and Kazan downed a quart of scotch between them. To make matters worse, Robbe's father, who was leading the wedding band, was inebriated. David and Dinah Garfinkle were not amused. So it was a boisterous ceremony, but Robbe looked beautiful in a wedding gown of her own making.

Afterward Joe Bromberg drove the newlyweds to their new home. It wasn't the Ritz. They had to take what they could get, a studio apartment on Riverside and 72nd Street. As Julie carried Robbe over the threshold she noticed, through the open door of the room across the hall, a woman sitting on the bed casually rearranging her clothing. "I could see right away she was a whore," Robbe said. "Because you don't hang around actors without learning a lot of things that you wouldn't have learned if you stayed in Washington Irving High School." The prostitute turned out to be one of many unsavory characters who frequented the place.

The Garfields didn't stay there long. Rent was difficult to make, so one night Julie threw some suitcases and bags filled with personal belongings out the window to the street below, and the couple climbed down the fire escape and disappeared into the darkness. This became a familiar routine with the Garfields during the mid-1930s.

They moved to a small apartment in Greenwich Village. Robbe called it a mud hole, but they did their best to entertain friends. Robbe cooked spaghetti—the only dish she claimed she could make—for the couple's starving artist friends. Julie surprised everyone by playing Beethoven's Seventh Symphony on victrola for dinner music. (Many of his friends thought he would much rather listen to Jack Benny on the radio.) Carnovsky was teaching a course in music appreciation and Julie was an apt student. When actor Joe Pevney visited the Garfields one night for spaghetti and Beethoven, Julie stood leaning against a bookcase listening to the classical recording with pride. "He was so excited, standing there, leaning against the furniture and listening to this beautiful music," Pevney recalled. "And then he turns to me, smiling, and says, 'How 'bout that Beethoven, Joe? Ain't he fuckin' great?'"

The Garfields eventually landed in a five-floor walkup on 23rd Street; an apartment building that also housed Roman and Hilda Bohnen, Morris Carnovsky and Phoebe Brand, and Ruth Nelson and Bill Challee. Romantic relationships continued to thrive within the Group, with Paula Miller marrying Strasberg, Clurman and Stella Adler becoming lovers, and Cheryl Crawford taking up with actress Dorothy Patten. Odets continued to strike out in his efforts to seduce the Group's resident actresses.

Carnovsky would recall the spirited battles that Robbe and Julie fought in that apartment house: "The walls were quite thin, and you

couldn't miss a sound there. They had such an intimate relationship at the time that the fights they had were quite bitter. And I always felt that she was the one in control, because every time it
ended with him crying, in real tears, 'Robbe, Robbe!' as if pleading
for forgiveness."

Robbe liked to be in control, and much as David Garfinkle dominated his second wife, Robbe liked to dominate Julie. "I think she
was a ball-buster," one of Julie's friends would later say. It was
Robbe's feeling that Julie was much more immature and undevel-
oped, and she assumed that he needed her much more than she
needed him. This is not to say that she took Julie for granted, for it
was obvious to everyone that the Garfields were very much in love
during this period.

"Nobody misses the good old days like they say, especially during the Depression," Robbe once said. Yet she would always fondly
recall the life she shared with Julie in 1930s New York. She cooked
spaghetti on a small gas plate that sat on the toilet in the bathroom.
They could walk anywhere and feel safe, and make out in Tomp-
kins Square Park if they wanted. They went to the movies all the
time, although she later said that she never dreamed that one day
Julie would be acting in one. Robbe handled the bankbook and lead
the way in political matters. "Robbe was a total political animal,"
Arnold Foster said. "And extremely intelligent. When she initially
took Julie under her wing it was partially because he was a guy
without a family. And how she related to him was how she related
to the problems of the world." In that sense, Robbe wanted to take
care of—and improve the lot of—Julie.

Julie followed her without always knowing where he was going.
Robbe and Odets campaigned to get 100,000 signatures on a petition to encourage the government to pressure Nazi Germany to release imprisoned Communist leader Ernst Thaelmann. Robbe
understood the ramifications of the petition; Julie may not have. It
was just a signature to him. He had a better sense of what it was he
was fighting for when he took part in a battle to get rehearsal pay for

members of Actors' Equity. The governing Equity council, which included Group members Morris Carnovsky, Margaret (Beany) Barker and Joe Bromberg, established a Cuts Board and fought for rehearsal pay, their cause aided in part by a small but vocal cadre of Communist Party members.

"Communist" was not a dirty word in 1935. Nor could one have foreseen any danger in the 1930s being associated with communism. But thousands of miles away from New York, Hollywood was making a film called *Red Salute,* starring Barbara Stanwyck and Robert Young, in which the good guy, border patrolman, takes on the bad guy—communists. And though the film would come and go without making much impact, it was the precursor to countless red-scare films of a later era in which that word "communist" sounded very frightening.

CHAPTER SIX

Golden Boy

*"He (Julie) was a very ambitious man, and I
guess he needed to be considered special."*
—MARTIN RITT

FOR EVERY TIME THE GROUP GOT A HOLD OF A GOOD SCRIPT
and turned it into a hit, they would inevitably turn around
and choose another script that had "stinker" written all
over it. They were counting on Odets to finish *Paradise
Lost,* but as he was taking too much time, the Group's leaders chose Nellise Child's play *Weep for the Virgins.* The
play revolved around the lives and loves of three sisters
working in a San Diego fish cannery. Julie got the part of
Hap Nichols, a sailor smitten with Violet Jobes, played by
Phoebe Brand. *Weep for the Virgins* opened on November
30, 1935, and closed eight days later. It was a mess. Theater
critic John Witney suggested that the whole thing was akin
to taking a sleigh ride down a hill without the snow. Another critic, Percy Hammond, at least had praise for Julie:
"Mr. Garfield as the sailor-man is vigorously magnetic."
Years later Brand would cite her scenes with Julie in this
play as her all-time favorite.

The Group still hoped that *Paradise Lost* would salvage
their season. It didn't. It opened early in 1936 and closed
eight weeks later. The play was Odets' favorite but never
caught on with the public; some critics even suggested that
the final speech, in which protagonist Leo Gordon tells his
wife that "the whole world is for men to possess," was com-

munist propaganda. The public and press were beginning to associate the Group with communism, so Clurman, Crawford and Strasberg drafted a letter to the New York newspapers in which they stated that the Group did not produce plays based on particular issues, such as social responsibility, but on what they had to say. It angered many of the actors to see the Group's leaders attempt to disavow their beliefs.

Interorganizational problems continued to chip away at the Group. Early in 1936 Bromberg left for Hollywood. Though he would return to the Group, Odets followed suit by writing a screenplay, *The General Died at Dawn* (1936), for Paramount. Hollywood didn't bring him happiness. "I felt a strange sort of sadness about him, as if there was something gnawing at him," actor/writer Ted Allan said. "I think he was disappointed that his early success as a playwright, and the fame and fortune that came with it, did not bring him real happiness." Once in Hollywood Odets married Academy Award-winning MGM star Luise Rainer, but even she did not make him happy. After trying his luck within the studio system of the 1930s, where political haranguing was frowned upon, Odets vowed never to return to Hollywood—unless he was broke.

More of the Group's members entertained the notion of going Hollywood about this time. Stella Adler headed out in 1937, made a few B films and returned a failure. Kazan tried it in 1940 and made two films for Warner Bros. (who insisted that he change his last name to Cézanne!) Roman Bohnen believed that the movie companies were really only interested in two Group actors: himself and Julie. The talent scouts, like the critics, were drawn to Julie's magnetism. But he wasn't considering going to Hollywood. The Group still had a lot to teach him, and it's unlikely that he felt bold enough to leave their protective enclave. Plus he was about to participate in the new Group production, *Johnny Johnson,* a musical written by Paul Green and Kurt Weill that dealt with the horrors of war.

In the interim the Group managed to slip another failure under their belts: *The Case of Clyde Griffiths.* After that they retreated rather than advanced to Nicholas, Connecticut, for another summer of training and preparation. There was widespread hope that a touring company of *Awake and Sing!*, orchestrated by Luther Adler, would help turn things around. The touring company (which included Julie) played in Baltimore, Chicago, Cleveland and Newark from April through June 1936.

While on tour in Chicago, the Group had a friendly reunion with Alan Baxter, who was in town on a publicity tour for his latest film (in which he played a gangster). Baxter never pretended to enjoy Hollywood, and he truthfully told the other actors that film work required little more than a lot of patience and one or two facial expressions. ("I credit my Group gleanings with whatever personality comes across from my pan," Baxter wrote in a letter to Luther Adler that appeared in the second issue of "The Flying Grouse.") Baxter was forgiven for going to Hollywood; Bromberg was not so lucky. The Group was rather discriminating in their anger towards defectors: they had forgiven Tone and Baxter but forever disparaged Bromberg and Garfield. One could argue that Baxter and Tone were rather listless as film actors, while both Bromberg and Garfield gave colorful performances that brought attention and acclaim, and maybe it was just plain jealousy. Garfield's daughter Julie would later suggest that all the other male members of the Group envied her father because of his success with seducing starlets.

Still, the tour's opening night did not bode well for the future. Julie and the cast were shocked when Luther Adler's line, "What the hell kind of house is this; it ain't got an orange!" was met with a barrage of oranges thrown by a group of college students in the balcony. Julie was dodging fruit when Stella Adler stopped the show, calmly walked downstage and addressed the audience with the line, "It's up to you ladies and gentlemen out there to protect the actors." And the ladies and gentlemen did just that, ejecting the fruit-throwing hooligans. The show recovered (after an opening night like that it could only get better), doing well in Chicago and in Baltimore. Cleveland was another story, for audiences were sparse and critical response was mild. Newark was worse. Box office receipts were negligible and morale plummeted, leaving low spirits when the tour wrapped in June.

Fortunately, there was summer camp in Connecticut. Julie began to show interest in other facets of theater, taking courses in fencing, ballet and music appreciation (from Kurt Weill himself). Strasberg gave a class on the fundamentals of acting while Stella Adler ran a scene study class. There was time for play, as when the Group got together and entertained the locals with selections from their works. The new apprentices (which included Lee J. Cobb) amused everyone with their original spoof *Waiting for Odets*. Odets was there, trying to work on a new play, and he brought his new bride, Luise Rainer. They rented a small cottage off the hotel grounds, isolating themselves from the rest of the Group. Everyone was put off by Rainer's Hollywood attitude, and she in turn found the Group to be pretentious. "Just because they leave one button open on their shirt doesn't make them artists," she told her husband.

Clurman unwisely chose this chaotic time to propose a reorganization of the company. To open up this discussion, he gave a detailed critique of the Group actors—including Julie—and their craft. He proposed that he become managing director and Crawford and Strasberg play supporting roles. This proposal would more or less give him creative control over the Group's future. The response from the actors was mixed, with strong criticism coming from the communist wing of the Group. But, when the issue was put to a vote in July, the members ended up unanimously supporting the proposal. The Actors Committee, which had been formed in order to represent the actors' point of view, elected new leaders as well: Roman Bohnen, Carnovsky, Kazan and Stella Adler. It was as if everyone thought that by switching roles around, everything would turn out all right.

Unfortunately, the Group's problems were more severe than personnel changes could solve. They were producing offbeat, revolutionary fare in a conventional and commercial theater world and the novelty was wearing off. Broadway audiences wanted theater to be different, but different in a sort of predictable way. What the Group needed was a commercial success that also said something and they thought they had it in the anti-war musical *Johnny Johnson*.

Rehearsals began in late summer under Strasberg's direction. Russell Collins played Johnny while Phoebe Brand was the woman he loved. Most everyone else, including Julie, had relatively minor roles; the set was really the main character. Playwright Paul Green, who wrote the book, described *Johnny Johnson* as a play with three separate parts. "The first act is a comedy, the second a tragedy and the third a satire," he said. There and then, the Group should have known they were in trouble.

Despite their reputation for presenting the best drama of their time, few of the Group's productions were commercial successes. *Johnny Johnson* would be another flop. The preview was worse than the barrage of oranges in Chicago. By the end of the nearly three-hour play, only twenty people remained in the 1,400-seat 44th Street Theatre. By opening night (November 19, 1936) the show was in better shape thanks to some all-night rehearsals and judicious editing. Many Group members felt the show had been salvaged; their feelings were borne out by the standing ovation they received on opening night.

Several reviewers enthused about the play, but most theatergoers reacted the same way critic Richard Watts of the *Herald-Tribune* did. He wrote,"It attempts to cover too much ground and rushes off in too many directions at the same time, with the result that the final effect is one of confusion and opportunities missed." Many critics remarked unkindly about the lack of singing ability among the Group's actors. The play hung on through the holiday season before closing in January 1937.

They had tried something daring and failed. Morale sank ever lower. Matters weren't helped by the "Report of the Actors Committee to the Directors of the Group Theatre," completed later that year, that criticized the poor choice of plays, the management of *Johnny Johnson,* the poor wages paid to the actors (Julie was then making $40 a week) and the three directors themselves. Crawford was accused of being a martyr because she always accepted the least-fulfilling jobs and complained about it, Strasberg was criticized for his tendency to strike fear rather than inspiration in the actors, and Clurman was criticized for not following through on his initial promise to organize the Group. Strasberg and Crawford reacted by resigning in March. Clurman stayed on and told the actors that they were free to look for work elsewhere. For Julie, the future looked unclear. And then a voice from his past called to him.

Helen Golden Levine, Julie's classmate at the Neighborhood Playhouse some years before, was working for producer Millard Blaugh in the William Morris Agency. Blaugh was about to produce Arthur Kober's comedy *Having Wonderful Time*. It was slight fare about a Catskills resort, but it had all the earmarks of a Broadway hit. Levine had been reading with all the young hopefuls who came to try out for the role of Chick Kessler, the lead male. No one seemed to be right for the role. Blaugh, Kober and director Marc Connelly wanted someone who was fresh, fun and Jewish. Levine thought of Julie: "I came to understand what they didn't like about the people that they had heard, and one day it dawned on me that Julie Garfield was the boy for this part. So I bundled the script under my raincoat and went to the theatre where Julie was doing one of the last shows of *Johnny Johnson,* and I said, 'Julie, would you be interested in leaving the Group for a real Broadway hit?'"

He wasn't interested at first, but when Clurman told him he was free to seek work elsewhere, he changed his mind. Levine asked Julie to come to her apartment, where the two worked all night on the script and the role of Chick. Levine told Julie exactly what the producers were looking for, and she helped him procure an audition that week. When Julie showed up, he read the role just as Connelly, Kober and Blaugh wanted it. "They thought it was a miracle," Levine recalled. "How did he hit on everything just the way they wanted it? He was perfect, and they hired him on the spot."

Katherine Locke, who played the female lead, Teddy Stern, was not privy to the audition. "I read with most of the actors who auditioned for the part," she said, "But funny enough, not Julie. He just showed up one day at rehearsal and I realized he was cast. I found him to be naïve and innocent, but he wanted to improve himself. Though he wasn't versatile, whatever he did was powerful. What he had gained during his tenure with the Group was brought to the show, and later to Hollywood."

What Julie brought with him from the Group was confidence. He also brought elements that weren't helpful when it came to doing sitcom-type comedy. Marc Connelly, a rather large man ("like Humpty Dumpty," Levine said), liked to direct by the show-and-tell method. He would get up and run through each part, acting out each role and giving the actors line readings. For Julie, accustomed to delving deep within his past to find the proper emotion for each action, this was foreign. Connelly, in turn, would lose his temper with Julie's constant quest for motivation. "Connelly didn't want any of this Group Theatre soul-searching that Julie was trying to do," Levine explained. "Julie wanted to justify each step. And Connelly would yell at him, 'Never mind! Do as I do!' " It was not a harmonious relationship, and Connelly decided to fire Julie. Locke interceded. She was already taking a protective stance towards Julie (as all women would) and she asked Connelly to give her some time with him. "Julie, don't go into the cellar for this one," she urged him. "Just relax, let it come out naturally, and let's have some fun."

To aid Julie in his quest Locke persuaded him to accompany her to Benno Schneider's acting class. Schneider was a respected acting teacher whose style was to allow each actor to bring his own personality into the role. In a sense it was not unlike Stanislavsky's original method, for Schneider wanted the actors to use their own character traits to color their performances. He didn't promote sense memory work or endless analyzing, however, choosing instead to encourage his actors to work on instinct. This brought Julie back to his initial training with Miss O'Ryan, and his confidence soared. Schneider basically encouraged Julie to be himself.

It's probably not too far-fetched to suggest that Julie had lost sight of himself in the mid-1930s. As a boy, he had shown initiative, even if it was criminal initiative, and he wasn't afraid to pull goofy stunts or go with the flow of a moment, whether it came to work or school or women or acting. Within the Group, he became just another member; a less noticeable member at that. When one talks of the Group Theatre today, one thinks of Kazan, of Odets, of the Adlers, of Clurman, of Bobby Lewis and Lee Strasberg, and not of John Garfield. Like a worker in a factory, Julie had submerged individuality in the greater good of the organization. He didn't really come into his own until he went to Hollywood. His participation in *Having Wonderful Time* was a step in establishing his independence and individuality.

Julie always took his craft seriously. One day Schneider gave the entire class a scenario for improvisation: a group of people lost in an impenetrable jungle had to find their way out. After allowing the exercise to continue for some time, Schneider called the actors over to discuss the improvisation. He noticed that Julie was missing and sent out his own search party to find him in the confines of the rehearsal hall. One of the others spotted Julie high up in the rafters of the building, scanning the horizon for a way out of that jungle. Garfield learned a great lesson from Schneider, a lesson that James Cagney and other film actors of that era already knew: Believe in what you're doing, and the audience will believe it too. Schneider's motto was simple: "You're either an actor, or you're not." Julie was an actor.

But Julie couldn't do everything. One day Schneider assigned Locke and Julie the balcony scene from *Romeo and Juliet.* It was a disaster. Julie had plenty of practice murdering Shakespeare while training with the Group; now he played Romeo as a dead end kid from Rivington Street. The scene ended and Schneider turned to Julie and said, "I think you better try something else."

Julie reintegrated himself with Connelly and returned to rehearsals for *Having Wonderful Time.* It was a lucrative gig. One day he said to Locke, "Boy, what a job! They're paying me more money than the Group ever did." Locke asked him how much. "$300 a week," he replied. Locke was furious; she was getting $250!

Having Wonderful Time opened at the Lyceum Theatre on February 20, 1937. It was an immediate hit with audiences who just wanted to sit back and laugh (at a top ticket price of $3.30). Reviews were polite and positive. *Variety* noted that "there is practically no story, but that is not important. It is genuine and stirring writing by someone who, very obviously, knows whereof he speaks." The whole cast was praised, with Julie pretty much being lumped in with the rest of them. *The New York Times'* critic Brooks Atkinson, forever a Garfield fan, wrote that the actor had "the sort of perceptions that make an admirable character of Chick Kessler, and he also knows how to convey them in the theater."

Socially Julie avoided the cast and crew. He was on good terms with Levine and Locke but otherwise he struck the ensemble as distant. Levine has a photo of the cast and crew taken at the one-hundreth performance; Julie is noticeably absent. When he did hang around with the cast, he regaled them with stories of his childhood. Where he once may have lowered his head in shame at his dubious beginnings, he now viewed his background as a badge of honor. One of his proudest achievements to date, he told the cast one day, was stealing tires off cars in the Bronx.

Locke left the show, being briefly replaced by Sydney Fox before Levine took over the role of Teddy Stern. One scene called for Julie to kiss Levine onstage. He let her have it, but she didn't think it was anything special. He did. "Howdya' like that kiss?" he asked her afterwards, winking. "Wasn't that something?" Levine was baffled. She didn't know if Julie was playing wolf or putting her on. But when he did kiss someone passionately, he told them that he learned how to kiss that way from Robbe. It may have been Julie who provided the contraceptive, but maybe Robbe wasn't as inexperienced as he believed.

Robbe was his lover, friend, teacher, and political advisor. He needed someone like her because, although he liked having friends and lovers, he couldn't give a damn about much else and would just as soon let someone else handle the details. More important, she was like the mother he never had. When Frances Chaney, who had dated Julie years before, came backstage to congratulate Julie on his performance in *Having Wonderful Time*, he pulled Robbe forth as if she were a trophy. "He was so proud to be married to this wonderful girl," Chaney recalled. "It was very sweet and very touching."

What was neither sweet nor touching was the Group's reaction to Julie's performance in *Having Wonderful Time*. They tore him apart, taking pains to tell him just how shallow his part was. What had happened to the method? Carnovsky asked. Julie didn't have an answer. He was hurt, but he wouldn't show it (he made a lifelong habit of hiding his true feelings). The Group felt that *Having Wonderful Time* represented traditional Broadway; everything that they were against. "The Group hated him for being in that play," Robbe recalled. Levine believes that while the Group were more or less ambivalent about the play itself, they didn't like the idea that Julie was in an unqualified Broadway success. "Everyone of them wanted to see their names up in lights on Broadway," she said. "But another part of them really did want to make this Group thing work."

Having Wonderful Time ran for 132 performances in Manhattan before it moved to Werba's Brooklyn Theatre, where Joe Pevney took over Julie's role as Chick Kessler. One night before the Broadway show closed Odets came backstage to see Locke and Julie. He told them he was writing a play about a prizefighter and a gangster's moll specifically for them. They were elated, which is unfortunate, because neither of them ended up playing the leads. The play was *Golden Boy*.

As a piece of theater, *Golden Boy* is almost pure commercialism, just sprinkled with social philosophy. The basic story concerns an artist who turns in his violin for a pair of boxing gloves, not only to make money but to be somebody: "Artists and people like that are freaks today," the golden boy says. "The world moves fast and they

sit around like forgotten dopes...I'm out for fame and fortune, not
to be different or artistic!" Joe Bonaparte, the artist cum boxer
golden boy, was really two parts Clifford Odets and two parts Julie
Garfield.

Julie believed the lead role was going to be his. Robbe recalls
Odets giving the script to Julie, who then began memorizing his
lines. Julie left *Having Wonderful Time* in late August, telling Connelly that he was going to play the lead in the next Group production. But by the time *Golden Boy* began rehearsing on September
13, Luther Adler was Joe Bonaparte and Julie was playing Siggie, a
cab driver. Siggie, a self-proclaimed outcast, has several Garfield
traits. "You can't insult me," he proudly tells Papa Bonaparte, "I'm
too ignorant!" It was a part that seemed tailor-made for a younger
Julie Garfield, not the recent Broadway success. Julie believed in
the power of a promise and could not figure out why Odets had
gone back on his word. Casting Adler was Clurman's doing. Odets
had come to the conclusion that Julie did not have the emotional
maturity that the role called for, but it was not his decision to cast
Adler. The Group wanted—indeed, needed—a commercial success,
and Julie's name on the marquee would not ensure that. So Clurman chose Adler (who at 34 years of age was perhaps too old for the
part) to play Bonaparte and then turned to Hollywood to solve the
rest of the problem.

The beautiful blonde screen actress Frances Farmer had scored a
big hit in Hollywood virtually overnight with her performance in
the Paramount film *Come and Get It* (1936). She was signed to the
usual seven-year contract with the studio, but it was a contract she
would never fulfill. Fed up with Hollywood, she rebelled against
Paramount and headed east with her husband, actor Leif Erickson.
Erickson and Farmer had heard about the Group and wanted to
join; Clurman sensed box-office success and took them both in.
"The Group wanted her," Martin Ritt recalled. "They wanted her
prestige, her money and everything she meant." Casting Farmer in
the role of Lorna, the gangster's moll, caused a considerable rift

within the rank of the Group. Several members felt Clurman had
sold out. The only other female role, as Siggie's wife, went to
Phoebe Brand.

Clurman held fast and assembled a terrific ensemble of support-
ing players for the production, including Kazan as the gangster
Fuseli, Roman "Bud" Bohnen as Tom Moody, the gangster, and
Bobby Lewis as Bobby Gottlieb, an unscrupulous fight promoter.
Two young newcomers, Karl Malden and Martin Ritt, joined the
Group to play smaller roles.

When the play opened at the Belasco Theatre on November 4,
1937, Kazan, Ritt and Pevney, among others, came to believe that
Clurman had made the right choice with Adler. Julie could not see
it that way. The critics were wowed over by both the writing and
Adler's powerful performance and went out of their way to praise
the actor. Burns Mantle of *The Daily News* went so far as to write,
"None of the younger actors could have done better," as if he had
heard of Julie's disenchantment. Some reviewers, such as *The Observer's* Ivor Brown, were kind enough to praise Julie's work in the
play. And film actor, Spencer Tracy, who was taking a vacation in
New York City, stepped backstage to introduce himself to Julie and
compliment him on his fine comic performance. That was almost—
though not quite—enough to blunt the blow of losing the lead.

Julie remained convinced that he had been robbed. Joe Bonaparte
was his baby; he had identified with the character immediately and
had learned most of the lines before rehearsal began (Julie was always a quick study with lines). While Robbe sympathized with his
plight, she felt he should grin and bear it and act like a grown-up.
But he had always made major decisions—to leave school, to hitch-
hike across country, to join the Group—on a lark. So, when both
MGM and Warner Bros. approached him about taking a screen test,
he jumped at the offer. He didn't tell Robbe. Instead he approached
Helen Golden Levine and asked her to test with him at the Warner
Bros. in New York City office. They chose a scene from *Having
Wonderful Time*. "He was better than I was, but even he was not

good," Levine recalled of the test. "We didn't know what to do in front of a camera in those days. But there was still something very special about his talent."

That something special was enough to lead both studios to make offers of long-term contracts. The Warner contract was more attractive because it called for a two-picture commitment (within six months) with the usual clause that gave the studio the right to bind Julie to seven years of movie-making. Julie liked the offer because he figured there was no way he would survive more than two pictures in Hollywood. His pay would be astronomical by 1938's standards: $750 per week.

Without consulting Robbe, he signed the contract. This was a unique move; one that suggested a desire for making his own way in the world. He even waited a few days to tell her the news. As Robbe put it, she "hit the roof." She had news for him: she was pregnant. Julie saw that as a sign that he had made the right decision, as the $750 weekly salary would help support the baby. "I was very unhappy that he wanted to leave," Robbe explained. "Not just New York, but the Group too." Julie told Robbe she could stay in New York. He would make his two films and be home by summer's end, for there was no way that Warner Bros. or anybody else out there would want to keep him around.

He knew the Group would kill him once he told them the news, so he waited until the last moment when he was forced to give two weeks' notice. As he expected, the Group reacted with self-righteous indignation. They held a meeting to discuss Julie's decision (as if they had any say in the matter), informed him of his limitations as an actor and told him they wouldn't speak to him for the remainder of the run. Morris Carnovsky, who saw himself as Julie's mentor, was particularly upset by the news. In his view Julie had fallen into the very trap that Carnovsky had warned about in a November 1937 article for the *New York Herald-Tribune;* "Many of our most genuinely talented young people prefer to make their marks as successes in the conventional and material sense of the word to retaining their integrity," he told the interviewing journalist. (Carnovsky himself would venture to Hollywood repeatedly over the next decade to play character roles in an array of films.)

Julie offered to send the Group money to help keep them afloat, but that was like offering to buy friends, and the promise did not assuage the Group's anger. They gave Julie the cold shoulder. Neither Kazan nor Ritt (both of whom would go on to have successful directing careers in Hollywood) blamed Julie. Kazan felt the Group was being "a bit snobbish" about Julie's decision. In his autobiography Harold Clurman erroneously blames Robbe for Julie's choice, suggesting that she advised him to leave the Group. Robbe denied this claim, reiterating that she was as upset with Julie as the Group's members were. Norman Lloyd, who was then working with Orson Welles in the Mercury Theatre, understood both sides to the question. "This was the great lie we lived," he said. "The lie was 'Oh, we're great artists, you see, we want pure theater.' But secretly, the truth was, we all wanted to go to Hollywood."

Those last two weeks of Julie's tenure with the Group were horrible. One night he told them that he had made a mistake and pretended that he was miserable (maybe he was). Some of the Group, like Carnovsky and Brand, forgave him. Others never did. The truth is, they probably all realized that Julie could be bigger and better than any of them.

Robbe couldn't have known it at the time, but Julie's decision to sign a movie contract signaled the first of many changes to come in their relationship. She couldn't have predicted that she would no longer be the only one Julie looked to for support, advice, love or sex. As a member of the Group, she was just that. In Hollywood, he would be his own man. It was as if he was abandoning shorts in favor of long pants.

Warner Bros. gave Julie a train ticket to California on the Super Chief. (For some reason, as soon as he arrived in Hollywood Julie began to embellish his life story, telling journalists that he drove

across the country in a beat-up 1933 Chevy coupe. Not true obviously.) Robbe walked Julie to Grand Central Station to kiss him
good-bye. She would soon quit her sales job and move in with her
parents to await the birth of the baby.

As Julie was about to board the Super Chief, Bud Bohnen, still in
makeup from his matinee performance of *Golden Boy*, raced
through the gate at Grand Central, threw his arms around Julie and
begged him to get off the train. Julie was shaken by the experience,
but he stuck to his guns. He was on his way to the city of dreams;
one big candy store where a kid like him could have his pick of the
goods for the taking. And Julie learned very quickly how to take.

CHAPTER SEVEN

Hollywood

"This place (Hollywood) is an anesthetic. Nothing has reality."

—JOHN GARFIELD

HE WAS HALFWAY ACROSS THE COUNTRY WHEN HE BEGAN to doubt himself. What the hell was he thinking? Everything that was dear to him—his wife, his friends, his career, his city, his fans (yes, he had fans now, and some of them even asked for his autograph)—was back on the East Coast. And here he was, throwing it all away for a long shot at Hollywood and $750 a week. All of a sudden his decision didn't seem so smart; he was filled with self-doubt, and one wonders whether he didn't consider grabbing his bag and jumping ship, just as he'd done so many times before when he rode the rails across the country in 1930. Hollywood wouldn't miss him. Warner Bros. wouldn't really give a damn (just who were the Warner brothers, anyway?). He could get back to Robbe within a couple of days if luck was with him. But he needed the money. That's what he kept telling himself. His New York earnings of $40 a week wouldn't be enough to support a wife and a baby back in the city. He did some breathing exercises; something he had learned from Mme. Ouspenskaya in his days at the Lab. They were supposed to calm you down.

He looked away from the window. His eyes met a stranger's gaze. Maybe it wasn't a stranger. The guy sure looked like someone Julie knew—a movie star. Robert Taylor, to be exact. He was just sitting there, reading the paper. He looked up and nodded at Julie, and Julie nodded back. How they started their conversation is unclear, but by the time they finished, Julie had made a friend and Taylor had assured him that making movies wasn't a bad way to earn a living. Taylor, MGM's pretty boy, promised he would have Julie over for dinner one night. (Taylor and his wife Barbara Stanwyck were the first to invite the Garfields to a Hollywood party later that year.)

Things got better—and funnier—when he arrived at Union Station, Los Angeles. Joe Bromberg met Julie dressed up for his role as an Indian potentate in the Peter Lorre film *Mr. Moto Takes a Chance.* Bromberg helped Julie find a place to stay—a room in a boardinghouse on Sycamore Street—and a car, a 1932 Ford that Julie hoped to resell after he made his two films. He just wanted to make some money and get out. "I went to Hollywood to be a failure," he said in 1939. "I wanted to be a failure. My purpose was to earn some money quickly, so that we would be prepared when our child was born." Julie wouldn't fail—at least, not at Warner Bros.

The Warner brothers—Abe, Harry, Sam and Jack—were Polish-Jewish immigrants who had come up the hard way. They entered the motion picture business almost by accident (didn't everybody in those days?) by renting a projector to show the 1904 Western *The Great Train Robbery* in between vaudeville acts. One of the vaudeville acts the brothers were promoting was brother Jack and sister Rose. The duo lacked one vital ingredient for success, namely talent. The film rentals, however, were making money, and the four boys decided to look into the movie-making business.

The routine of the next ten years was one step forward, two steps back for the Warners. But they had guts. They began producing their own films, a lot of which were bad, but then they hired an orphaned German shepherd named Rin Tin Tin and turned out a slew of dog films that cleaned up at the box office. Rin Tin Tin kept the wolf away from the door throughout the 1920s, until Al Jolson pretty much succeeded him as Warner Bros. biggest box office attraction.

Sam Warner convinced his brothers that talking pictures were the future of Hollywood, and the company put all of its money into a movie about a cantor's son who chooses the theater over the synagogue. Though the film had no spoken dialogue, per se, the Warner Bros. sound machines would offer audiences the spectacle of Jolson singing on the screen. "Wait a minute," Jolson ad-libbed as the sound machines began, "You ain't heard nothin' yet." And that was that. Released in the autumn of 1927, the film called *The Jazz Singer,* made millions for the Warner Bros. It also ushered in the sound era.

Ironically, the night before *The Jazz Singer* premiered, Sam Warner died of a stroke. Jack and "Major" Abe continued on. The most gregarious of the trio, Jack, remained in Hollywood as Vice-President in Charge of Production, while Harry, as President, and Abe, as Treasurer, manned the studio's New York office. The studio, located at the corner of Sunset and Bronson, expanded; it brought First National Pictures, which gave the Warners access to more studio space as well as some 4,000 cinemas to screen their films.

Warners built up their stable of stars throughout the 1930s; a stable that included James Cagney, Edward G. Robinson, George Raft, Paul Muni, Humphrey Bogart, Errol Flynn, George Brent, Wayne Morris, Jeffrey Lynn, Eddie Albert (later to gain fame on television's *Green Acres*), Bette Davis, Kay Francis, Geraldine Fitzgerald, Ann Sheridan, Miriam Hopkins, Joan Blondell, Barbara Stanwyck (sometimes) and a trio of singing actresses known as the Lane Sisters. An incredible array of talented character actors included Claude Rains, Ralph Bellamy, Allen Jenkins, Jack Carson, Alan Hale Jr., Frank McHugh, Gale Page, May Robson and The Dead End Kids. Another newcomer to the studio was former radio newscaster and future president, Ronald Reagan.

A permanent acting company had been formed that had an identity all its own. "They had all these wonderful stock people," contract player Jeffrey Lynn recalled. "You didn't see that kind of company at any other studio." And no other studio—not even

MGM—worked so hard to tailor scripts to its stars, though quite often the stars didn't like the tailoring job. Despite the abundance of "star" names, ensemble acting was the rule at Warner Bros. As another rule, contract players generally worked on three substandard films for every good one. If a star did not want to work in one of these substandard films, he or she could refuse and take some time off without pay—this was called suspension, suggesting a public school punishment—but the time off was added to the seven years of the original contract.

The so-called studio system has had its share of critics, but contract player Jeffrey Lynn, who came to Warner Bros. in 1938, felt that it worked under Jack Warner's rule. "The studio system *did* work, and part of the credit for that has to go to Jack Warner," Lynn said. "He was a smart man. And Warner Bros. made the right decisions and picked the right people. They chose a lot of intellectual writers, and you'd never expect that from a studio that made gangster films."

Warner Bros. was *the* gangster film studio. It seems right that the studio, once on the edge of financial failure, would produce films that revolved around the underdog trying to make it to the top against all odds. And the underdog in a typical 1930s Warner Bros. film was just your common guy or gal, someone trying to improve their lot in life, even if it meant turning to crime. "Warner is the only major studio that seems to know or care what is going on in America besides pearl-handled gunplay, sexual dalliance, and the giving of topcoats to comedy butlers," a 1937 *Fortune* magazine article stated. Jack L. Warner told the press that movies should play a role in the cultural and educational development of the world, and brother Harry told *Fortune,* "The motion picture presents right and wrong, as the Bible does. By showing both right and wrong, we teach the right."

Well, maybe, but the Warner Bros. heroes often turned to crime, and they sure looked like role models to impressionable Depression-era youths. While many of the Warner films of that period can be seen as morality plays, the irony is that no other studio did so much to glamorize the gangster. And the studio's players seemed to represent America during the Depression. Cagney, Robinson, Muni, Raft and Bogart characterized the steelworkers, the meatpackers, the truck drivers, the lineman, the oil drillers, and the innocent (or not so innocent) fugitives from justice. Their female counterparts like Bette Davis, Barbara Stanwyck and Joan Blondell were born to play tenement girls, poverty-stricken mothers, molls and B girls (or worse). Movie audiences of the 1930s, who were fighting a daily battle to survive the Depression, could identify with these cinematic depictions of crime, poverty and injustice. "Warner pictures are hence as close to real life as Hollywood gets," the *Fortune* article noted.

It's fair to say that the closest thing to the social consciousness prevalent in the New York theater was found in the Warner Bros. films. Julie typified the Warner type—dark, brooding, street-smart and a native New Yorker to boot (is it coincidence that Muni, Cagney, Raft and Bogart, as well as Garfield, were all New York City-born?). Other movie studios were emphasizing the heroic attributes of their leading men. MGM, for instance, had Clark Gable, Robert Taylor and Jimmy Stewart demonstrate that with a lot of hard work and a little faith, just about anything was possible. Everyone emerged a winner at MGM. At Warner Bros., there were no winners. The characters Cagney, Bogart, Robinson and Raft played worked just as hard as Gable, Taylor and Stewart, but the odds were against them. Crime didn't always pay, but it was often the only option for a Warner Bros. character. Unable to find his rightful place in society, the Warner Bros. hero ended up in prison or in the electric chair or dead on the snow-covered steps of a city church. Julie couldn't have known it in 1938, but he was going to fit right in to the Warner mold.

His expectations were low. "I came to Hollywood fully expecting to hate it and with myself all set for the kick in the pants that I felt sure I would get," he said in 1939. He got kicked, all right, first by Jack Warner, when he was sent to Warner's huge art deco office to meet the studio head. (In later years Warner discontinued this practice, but in the 1930s it was a rule.) With a Cuban cigar hanging out of his mouth, Warner did a silly soft shoe for Julie before vigorously clasping his hand. Then he called his new contract player Jimmy, or Johnny, or Joey, or something similar. Julie was baffled. It's easy to conceive of Jack Warner as a stereotype; the cigar-chomping, back-slapping, hard-driving studio head with a penchant for bad jokes. And, according to those who knew him, that was just what he was. "He was the kind of guy who, if he liked you, he'd take a step towards you, and then stop and say 'Gee, I better not, he's liable to ask me for a favor.'" explained contract director Vincent Sherman. Robbe, who would meet Warner later that year, deemed him "a total cliché."

"We're going to call you Jimmy, right?" Warner asked, casting Julie a sideways glance. Jimmy Cagney was the biggest star at Warners in 1938, and while there may not have been room on the lot for two Cagneys, they could certainly accommodate two Jimmys. Julie said he was known as Julie. Warner frowned; to him Julie was an effeminate name, and it sounded Jewish. James Garfield was better. Julie pointed out that James Garfield was the name of a dead president. At least that's the way Julie liked to tell it in later years, though it's quite possible that he had never heard of President James Garfield. Warner agreed that could be a problem, and the two quickly worked out a compromise. The actor would be John Garfield. Julie didn't kick. What did it matter, anyway? He'd make his two films and be back home in time for Labor Day. "My friends still call me Julie," he told Bosley Crowther of *The New York Times* later that year. "And Julie I'll always be."

His argument with Warner over his screen name was just the first salvo in a seven-year war, a war Julie really couldn't win. If the studio system didn't beat him down, the movie scripts would. Maybe Julie should have expected that his first film would be a potboiler. But for an actor accustomed to working with Elmer Rice, Irwin Shaw and Clifford Odets, perhaps it wasn't too unrealistic for him to anticipate something comparable at Warner Bros. But *Girls on Probation,* the first film offered to Julie, wasn't comparable to Shaw or Odets. It was a stinker. The title said it all; Julie was to play a young lawyer who stops a good girl from going bad. It was a B film that the studio threw to Julie in order to see if he could carry the ball. Fortunately, before he was officially signed for the film, another all-American ball carrier, one Ronald Reagan, took over. Julie was sent to test for a supporting role in the Errol Flynn/Bette Davis costume soaper *The Sisters,* which was set in San Francisco in 1906, just in time for the big earthquake. The promise of working with Davis and Flynn enthused Julie, and he showed up for the screen test with all his lines memorized. Dialogue director Irving Rapper offered Julie a script to work with; the actor declined. He did his screen test opposite a now-forgotten contract starlet; she read from her script, Julie tossed off his lines like a pro. The New York accent was prominent.

"What the hell is this?" Rapper asked when the scene was complete. "Where do you come from?"

"The Group Theatre," Julie answered, and then, almost as an afterthought, he added, "In New York."

Rapper was harsh. "I suggest you go back there." Julie didn't get the part in the film; B western star Dick Foran did.

He said he had come to Hollywood to be a failure, and so far he was right on track. But then some unexpected casting problems on the set of a medium budget film led the studio to give Julie another chance. The film was about a musically inclined family and the twists and turns their lives take when some outsiders enter their domain. Based on a *Cosmopolitan* short story called "Sister Act", by Fannie Hurst, the film, *Because of a Man,* was scheduled to start shooting within two weeks on the Warner lot. The film's musical family, the Lemps, were comprised of four sisters and their widowed father. The three Lane Sisters—Lola, Rosemary and Priscilla—and actress Gale Page were cast as the quartet of sisters and character actor Claude Rains as their father, Adam.

The casting problem revolved around the two male leads, Felix Deitz and Mickey Borden. Deitz was a charming but shallow composer who wins the affections of daughter Ann (Priscilla Lane).

Borden was a cynical pianist who believed that the fates were work-ing overtime against him. Warner Bros. wanted Errol Flynn to play Deitz, but Flynn demurred, suspecting (rightfully) that the Borden character was going to steal the film. Actor Burgess Meredith, pen-ciled in for the role of Mickey, also turned down the film, opting to tour Europe with a theater production of Maxwell Anderson's *The Star Wagon*.

Julius J. Epstein and Lenore Coffee were adapting the story for film, with uncredited help from Epstein's brother Philip. Julius Epstein said he wrote the role of Mickey Borden with actor Van Heflin in mind, so both Epsteins had a vested interest in who played the part. But when they met Julie on his arrival at the studio, they took a liking to him. Soon he was enjoying lunch with them at the writers' table in the Warner Bros. commissary. There was an ul-terior motive to the Epsteins' hospitality, according to writer Ring Lardner Jr.

"The Epstein Brothers brought him to the writers' table mainly because he was the butt of their jokes," Lardner recalled. "Julie was very naïve. The Epsteins used to make things up to tell him. They'd treat him like the new player on the ball team who is told to put some mustard in the pitcher's glove to soften it up, or something like that. And he fell for it every time. It was a question of how much they could get him to believe."

They could get him to believe a lot, as it turns out. One night shortly after he arrived in Hollywood a phone call wakened him from a deep sleep. The caller identified himself as Julie's old pal, Jimmy Hart.

"Jimmy who?" Julie asked.

"Jimmy Hart," the voice on the other end of the line said. "Don't you remember me? I worked with you at the Civic Rep, with LeGal-lienne."

"Oh, yeah," Julie said, still unsure. "How are ya'?"

"I'm in a bad way," Hart replied. "I just came in on the Super Chief to see if I could break into films. I was hopin' you could help me. I'm down here at Union Station and I'm out of dough. I got no place to stay. I figured I could call you, being you're still a regular fellow, right?"

Julie mumbled that he'd drive down to Union Station to pick Hart up. He dressed and drove the ten miles to the station in the predawn morning. Julie searched Union Station but never found Hart. Instead of going back to bed, he grabbed a quick breakfast (grapefruit and coffee) and headed to the studio early.

"You look awful," Julius Epstein said to Julie when he saw him. "Didn't you get any sleep last night?"

Julie told the Epsteins the saga of the mysterious Jimmy Hart. The Epsteins broke up laughing and told him they had placed the phone call to him as a gag. Julie laughed with them, though he wasn't so sure it was funny. The Epsteins would repeat, with some variation, this phone gag over the next few years; Julie fell for it almost every time. Still, the Epsteins liked him. A certain brooding air that Julie assumed the Epsteins recognized as a trait of Mickey Borden. They recommended Julie for the role, and on April 8 he tested with a brief scene from the film. Michael Curtiz, who was to direct the film, had seen Julie's original Warner Bros. screen test and now recommended him to the studio head, so Julie had an ally there. In the interim, Jeffrey Lynn tested for the role of Deitz.

"When I went to see my test," Lynn recalled, "I also got to see Garfield's test. Now I'd never heard of this guy John Garfield, but after I saw the test I said, 'Who ever does get in this picture with him better step aside, because he's got the film.' And I was right." Julie was confirmed for the role of Borden, and shooting began in early May. No one involved with the film thought it would be anything more than a mild success.

Because of a Man, retitled *Four Daughters* by Jack Warner before it was released, might best be described as a comedy with tragic undertones. As the Lemp Sisters, the Lane Sisters play classical music, dream of getting married (or not getting married), and crack wise with their gruff but lovable father. Their Aunt Etta (the wonderful May Robson) cooks dinner and waxes philosophical about love, music and men. Felix Deitz shows up to write a composition for Mr. Lemp and ends up flirting with all four sisters (none of them seems to mind). Deitz hires an old pal, Mickey Borden, to help him orchestrate the composition.

Borden's a character, no doubt about it. His hair is heading straight towards the ceiling, his tie is at half-mast and his cigarette perpetually hangs out of his mouth, curled over his lower lip like a permanent extension. Accustomed to living on the wrong side of the tracks, Borden is amused by the Lemps' middle-class lifestyle. "A rug on the floor, the smell of cooking in the kitchen, a piano, and flowers," he cynically notes. "It's homes like these that are the backbone of the nation." Not only a dark cynic, but a rebel, Borden also gets a lot of funny lines. "Talking about my tough luck is the only fun I get," he tells Ann; there's something inherently sad about him, and there's something comical about him too. Borden is unconventional; maybe even a little crazy, and Julie played him with just the right balance of humor and despair. Even when he's on the inside, he somehow ends up being an outsider.

"Don't you ever get tired of being a swell guy?" Borden asks the ever-sweet Deitz at one point. "It would bore me stiff." Borden has all the prerequisites necessary to make him a screen rebel: he wants to live fast and die young. "That's the way I'm leaving this world," he tells Ann at one point. "Lightning." Julie swings wonderfully from breezy comedy to sardonic self-deprecation in the span of his first scene, a roughly ten-minute piece of byplay between himself, Robson and Priscilla Lane. At one point Etta grandly offers Mickey a cup of tea. He accepts with a bite: "You needn't look so noble. Tea is only a little hot water."

Julie gives a superb acerbically comic performance. He bats a pair of Robert Mitchum eyes years before there was a Robert Mitchum. Playing a character who continues to tempt the fates, Julie exudes an economy of energy, doing a lot with a little, and the camera fell in love with him. So did most of the women in the

movie audience. Mickey is begging for love, much like Julie Garfinkle was, and women instinctively wanted to mother or bed him.
Watching him is like witnessing a meteor shooting across the skies:
it's exhilarating to see, but you better enjoy the moment because
you just know it can't last.

As for the rest of the plot, well, Borden convinces Ann to forsake
Deitz (Mickey is not an entirely sympathetic character in this scene)
and coerces her into marriage. The two try to make a go of it but
after only four months it's obvious that the fates are working on
Mickey again. Realizing that Ann and Felix are still in love, and that
Felix can offer her stability, Mickey goes out in typical Warner Bros.
style: he tempts the fates by driving wildly through a snowstorm.
The fates chew him up and spit him out, leaving him near death in
a hospital bed. (In a neat touch, the scenarists of the film *don't*
allow Mickey to smoke one final cigarette on his deathbed.) In the
last shot, set up to make the audience leave the cinema happy, Felix
and Ann swing merrily on the family gate—the sort of scene Hollywood could never get away with in a film of today.

Julie's signature scene was set at the piano, where Borden goes
on and on about his losing battle against the fates. He has talent, he
tells Priscilla Lane, but just enough to get by on. He bets five dollars
on a horse that he could have bought for seven dollars. He claims he
wouldn't win first prize in a musical competition even if he were
the only contestant. It's the fault of the fates: "First they said, 'Let
'im do without any parents; he'll get along.' Then they decided, 'He
doesn't need any education. That's for sissies.' Then right at the beginning they tossed a coin. 'Heads he's poor; tails he's rich.' So they
tossed a coin with two heads." Movie audiences ate that dialogue
up, and the antihero was born.

Maybe *Four Daughters* shouldn't hold up today, but it does. All
the actors give winning performances that suggest they were having a lot of fun during the shoot, and the dialogue is still sharp
and funny over 60 years later. Rains is good, the Lanes are better
than average, Lynn isn't bad at all, and Julie is terrific. Lynn *was*

right—the film belonged to Julie, though no one knew that when the film wrapped in late June.

Julie rarely discussed his approach to film acting, but in a lecture he gave at the Actor s' Laboratory in Hollywood years later, he recalled this first film job. "I was very frightened, and very upset because I didn't like the script," he said. "I worked very hard the way I worked on a play, and I was baffled by the set. That (Mickey) was a colorful part and I'm not being modest in saying that any actor could have played the same hit. It was that kind of thing."

Julie was right and wrong. Mickey Borden is a wonderfully written character, but it's difficult to imagine any other actor of the era making the same impact (certainly not Burgess Meredith, nor Fred MacMurray, another candidate for the role). Julie brought an intensity, an anger, a sense of having lived a lot longer than 24 years, to the role; elements that were part of his own life. Stanislavsky probably would have been proud—Julie was able to inject truth into every scene. He later said that he based Mickey on pianist Oscar Levant, an acquaintance from New York. But the role of Mickey Borden seems almost autobiographical, and some of the dialogue sounds like it came not from the screenwriters' imagination but from Julie's mouth. Mickey was an orphan. So was Julie, to some degree. Mickey hitchhiked across the country. So did Julie. Mickey never had a birthday party, never finished school and had never known a happy home. Ditto Julie. And like Julie, Mickey found some happiness in the form of a loving, supportive and stronger partner.

The studio dropped the little film on the market in the late summer. Everybody involved had to go to work on another film. To fulfill his initial two-picture contract, Julie had a second picture to make, and that film was an action-packed B called *Blackwell's Island*. Julie was given top billing (he was billed sixth in *Four Daughters*). The story was loosely based on the Welfare Island Raid of 1932, in which law enforcement officials stormed an island prison where corrupt jailers shared power with the inmates. Julie played a crusading reporter who infiltrates the prison to write an exposé.

(Such things happened with alarming regularity in the Warner Bros. films of the late 1930s.) Bill McCann was the director, and Rosemary Lane followed Julie out of *Because of a Man/Four Daughters* to play his love interest. They shot the film in less than 30 days during the summer of 1938. Julie couldn't have been too enthusiastic about the script. Had he come to Hollywood just to play cops and robbers in a speedboat? (The bullet-ridden finale took place on the East River.)

And yet Julie adapted to film making immediately. No matter what the circumstances, he always approached his work as a professional. If the script required him to stand in a prop speedboat before a rear projection screen and fire a prop machine gun while a prop man threw prop water in his face, he'd give it his all. He'd grasp onto whatever threads there were in the plot and do his best to make his character as realistic as possible. If *Blackwell's Island* did nothing else for his career, it certainly proved that he could carry a film.

He probably carried it without benefit of the Method. Morris Carnovsky visited Julie on the Warner lot one day and asked him whether he was using his Group training at the studio. Julie sidestepped the question but ended up in a heated argument with Carnovsky about the role of the Method in film acting. Carnovsky felt that Julie was rebellious about utilizing what he had been taught with the Group in film. "He made some remark derogatory to the Method," Carnovsky recalled. "He dismissed the possibilities of using the Method in Hollywood."

"He was a natural," Robbe would later say of Julie's ability to adapt his acting style to film. While some of the Group's members argued that Julie never successfully grasped their method of work during his tenure with them, Julie was, to some degree, adhering to Stanislavsky's notion that an actor become the character. (Supposedly two of the film actors whom Stanislavsky admired greatly were Spencer Tracy and Gary Cooper, both men who offered little more than their own personae on film.)

Unlike character Mickey Borden, Julie was full of optimism. "Do you remember that scene at the piano?" Joseph Pevney asked of one of Julie's more famous scenes from *Four Daughters.* "That was Julie." Benno Schneider's teaching may have had more influence over Julie's acting style than the combined Group membership.

Julie would never go through the rigorous self-torture that so many so-called Method actors go through today. He learned quickly to go with the flow of things, playing a scene with his natural instincts and engaging in a give-and-take with his fellow performers. When the other actors (such as Claude Rains) were good Julie was even better. He would soon lean more and more towards the James Cagney method, which, according to its founder, was based on three simple words: Just do it.

Having completed his two films for Warner Bros., Julie returned to New York early in September. He wasn't yet a household name, but journalist Frederick James Smith was interested in interviewing him. "I'm scared of the way they build you up in Hollywood, force you, hothouse you," Julie told Smith. "It's too easy to go soft and lose your identity. I want my happiness inside." He said he did not find film acting to be challenging. And he felt that the lure of the easy money made screen actors lazy. "There [in Hollywood] everyone seems to be a success with plenty of money to spend. Here [New York] actors are constantly struggling. I think that is necessary, for when an actor doesn't face a conflict he loses confidence in himself. I always want to struggle, because I believe it will help me accomplish more."

Robbe was eight months pregnant and glad to have her husband home. They both figured that the Hollywood "thing" was over. Julie had made his two pictures for the studio, and it didn't seem likely that Warner Bros. would pick up his option. He just didn't think he was that good. And then *Four Daughters* was released.

The success of the film may be difficult to understand today. It's an old-fashioned homage to middle America, but in its time it was a blockbuster, for audiences hoping to escape the sight of men

standing in soup lines and the sound of war in Europe were easily
seduced by the story line, which reaffirmed faith in the family unit.
Even so, it's unlikely that the film would have been anything other
than a mild success had it not been for Julie's participation. The
sneak previews in both Los Angeles and New York indicated that
most of the audience members were going wild over Julie. Ring
Lardner Jr., then a fledgling screenwriter with Warner Bros., recalled the impact of Julie's screen debut: "I already knew him from
the making of the picture, but I remember when I first saw the film,
that I was absolutely startled by the effect of that character coming
on the screen and taking over. I didn't realize he had that power,
that magnetism."

Many of Julie's friends felt the same way. It was somewhat surprising to see Julie—considered a lightweight by those who knew
him—project such power on the screen. His initial appearance
about a third of the way into the movie gave *Four Daughters* a bolt
of energy. *The New Yorker's* review of the film described Julie as
Mickey Borden best: "Just as we adjusted our senses to the generally
amiable, good-natured comedy of the gentle sentiments...the door
opens and this young man of lowering aspect, a mean and embit-
tered wastrel, ambles in and distracts us entirely from the nice
things of life. Of course our spirits are immediately refreshed by his
arrival..."

"This newcomer to Hollywood introduces a species of personality which may possibly become a fashion," critic John Moshter ac-
curately noted. *The New York Times'* Bosley Crowther, who wrote
of the film, "it may be sentimental, but it's grand cinema," felt
Julie's interpretation of Mickey Borden was "the most startling in-
novation in the way of a screen character in years." Another reviewer wrote that it was impossible to discern who was coming up
with Mickey's dialogue—the screenwriters or John Garfield.

Naturally, the Epstein Brothers and Lenore Coffee had written
the dialogue; Julie had just made it his own. He was down to earth,
honest and real. Film historians have cited Mickey Borden as being

the first screen rebel character in cinematic history, which in turn makes John Garfield the first antihero of film. He was prototypical of all the young men of the Depression era: the guy trying hard to fight the fates and finding himself defeated at every turn. Unlike the characters played later by James Dean and Marlon Brando, John Garfield's rebels invariably did have a cause. They wanted a piece of the American pie, a place to live, a shot at life. Audiences of the late 1930s understood that aspect of his character all too well.

And he was sexy. There was something sensually languid about John Garfield, an inner force that suggested he could be a demon in bed. Which other male stars of that period project such sexual charisma? Certainly not Jimmy Stewart, nor James Cagney nor Humphrey Bogart (whose screen characters probably wore a shoulder holster to bed). Maybe Clark Gable, but Gable was tough. John Garfield was sensitive, and his vulnerability, as an actor, set him apart from the rest of the pack. Men may have wanted to emulate him, but women wanted something else altogether, as Julie would soon discover.

Women flocked to him. First and foremost, this was the main pitfall of Julie's overnight success. Life imitated art, with every woman imagining she was Priscilla Lane and that Julie was Mickey Borden. At first the actor thought it was all a joke, but pretty soon it became apparent that it was the real thing. "After he did *Four Daughters* every extra girl on the lot was dying to seduce him," contract director Vincent Sherman recalled. "And he did not yet know how to handle success. He was hot and heavy and they just came along, one after the other." At first it was just the extras and the bit players and the coatcheck girls and the waitresses. Later his array of would-be suitors and conquests would include costars and cinematic sex symbols. Hollywood had the sweetest candy store in the world, and pretty soon Julie didn't have to ask. The women asked him.

Film director/writer Abraham Polonsky believed that the sexual affairs were just part of the business of Hollywood. "When you're a real star in this town there's no way you can avoid some sort of sexual confrontation," he said. "It's pushed all over you. It's part of the way people show their admiration for you, get pleasure out of their association with you." Julie often responded to these sexual advances because they reaffirmed that he was good at something (besides acting). Many of his friends believed that his promiscuity was just another symptom of his quest for approval. To Julie, a successful seduction provided the reassurance he needed that he was special. Actor Joseph Bernard, a friend of Julie's, once got up the nerve to ask him just why he felt the need to continually stray. "Sometimes they tell you that you're the best at this, or the best at that," Julie responded. "And sometimes you just want to prove it to yourself."

His prowess in bed became as legendary as Errol Flynn's. In Julie's case it is likely there could have been more talk than action, but it is impossible to whitewash him. He liked women. And they liked him. And while his womanizing did not become so obsessive that he considered leaving his wife (nor she him), it would place his marriage and his health in considerable jeopardy time and again. Robbe would eventually discover her husband's infidelity. Why she chose to continually forgive him is unclear, though everyone who knew the couple agreed that they were very much in love, infidelity and all. A pattern developed wherein Julie would stray when he felt insecure. Sometimes he could keep the affairs a secret; sometimes he couldn't. Robbe found a way to put up with it for nearly 15 years.

By the end of 1938 more pressing professional matters were facing Julie, namely his immediate future with Warner Bros. *Four Daughters* was a commercial and a critical hit. Jack Warner and company realized that much of the film's success was due to Julie's performance. The studio placed a full-page ad in *Variety* touting John Garfield as the star of the year. They also took up the option on his seven-year clause, designating him a star player rather than a featured player. He got a raise, from $750 a week to $1,500 a week. Jack Warner began campaigning to get Julie a nomination for an Academy

Award for Best Supporting Actor. All of that was good news. Julie
was tied to the studio until 1945. That wasn't necessarily good news.

Not knowing how to describe Julie's screen appeal, both Warner
Bros. and film critics suggested that he was the "new Cagney." (As if
the old one wasn't good enough.) Comparisons were to be expected,
particularly in light of Julie's work in *Blackwell's Island,* in which the
actor plays a fast-talking, happy-go-lucky, wise-cracking tough guy,
the total antithesis of Mickey Borden. One wonders whether the studio wasn't deliberately trying to turn Julie into another Cagney, for
the spirit of Cagney certainly inhabits Julie's performance in the film.

But Cagney played winners. Even when he is gunned down in
the last reel of *The Roaring Twenties* (1939), Cagney dies a hero.
John Garfield's characters would not be so lucky, nor so noble. More
often than not, they were the losers of the world. Both actors had an
inner force that detonated onscreen. Abraham Polonsky, who knew
both men and worked with Garfield on two later films, felt Julie projected more humanity. "Garfield projected so much energy and
power," Polonsky explained. "Like Cagney did, only in a different
light. Because Cagney's never generated a feeling for his character,
a feeling of getting on with the people he loved. Cagney had the
force, but Garfield had the force *and* the humanity."

Jeffrey Lynn was not surprised with the response to *Four Daughters.* He felt director Michael Curtiz deserved most of the acclaim.
"Remember that scene at the piano with Garfield and May Robson
where she offers him tea?" Lynn said. "Well one day Curtiz called
the whole cast together, and he told us the story as he saw it. And
what that scene meant to all of us. He must have talked for almost
an hour, and as he finished tears were streaming down his face. And
no one said anything. We couldn't speak! We were so entranced by
this tough Hungarian weightlifter telling us about this slice of
American life, and if I had any doubts about the film, I forgot them
there and then. I figured if he was going to be that serious about the
film, then I knew I had to be." Curtiz liked Julie's no-nonsense instinctive approach, and as a director he managed to get more out of

the actor—particularly when it came to economizing—than any other film director Julie worked with. (Curtiz and Garfield would make a total of four films together.)

Julie was in New York when the word came that the film was a hit. Success did not go to his head overnight, but he was a bit presumptuous in an interview with Bosley Crowther when he said "The public wants quality and entertainment in pictures, and if the star doesn't have a story with those in it, the public doesn't want any part of it. I go up to the Bronx now and see how people live. It makes your hair stand on end! But that's life, and an actor must participate in it if he wants to be a true artist. So if I can't do pictures that say something about it, I don't want to be in pictures." (Julie would make 31 films in all. How many of them said something about life is open to debate.)

He had visited the Bronx to see Angelo Patri and address a class of German refugee children. Julie told them that, if they wanted something bad enough, they could overcome all obstacles and make it. Julie's sudden popularity as a screen idol gave him a newfound, somewhat unrealistic, belief in the American Dream. After all, if Julius Jacob Garfinkle from Rivington Street could make it, couldn't anybody? Patri was delighted with Julie's success. David Garfinkle, on the other hand, was indifferent. The enormity of his son's success was lost on him; reportedly he never saw one of his son's films. Julie later said his father had only attended some of the Group Theatre productions because he had given David free passes. Though he never openly displayed his feelings about his father's indifference to his success, that aspect of their troubled relationship must have caused Julie considerable pain. Later, Julie could retaliate by omitting any reference to his father or stepmother in interviews. Reading some of the interviews he gave from the mid-1940s on, one gets the impression that he was an orphan from day one.

Warner Bros. summoned Julie back to Hollywood. It was agreed that Robbe would stay with her parents until after the baby was born, and then she would take the train west to join him. In the interim, Julie would find them an appropriate place to live in Hollywood. When he returned, Jack Warner assured him that from now on, John Garfield would receive nothing less than star billing in A productions.

But there was still a B film, *Blackwell's Island,* waiting to be released. Warner Bros. quickly turned it into an A, or at least a B+, invested another $10,000 and hired Michael Curtiz to reshoot some scenes. What effect Curtiz had on the finished product is impossible to judge, but the film is a reasonably exciting crime drama, and Julie appears to be having a ball. The critics were kind and the public was satisfied. The commercial success of this minor film affirmed Warner's hunch that John Garfield was star material.

Julie wanted more *Four Daughters*-type films rather than another *Blackwell's Island,* and to that end he made it a habit to hang out with the studio's screenwriters at their lunch table in the commissary. He continued to socialize with the Epstein Brothers and Ring Lardner Jr., as well as Howard Koch, John Huston and others, figuring he'd have a chance to get in on the ground floor of the next good picture. He accepted the fact that these writers would make him the brunt of their jokes. "What do you hear from the fates, John?" they would yell to him across the commissary, which led everyone to laugh. Julie accepted the jesting in good humor. In return, he hoped to garner an education from the writers, for from them he picked up the latest news on politics, writing and world affairs.

He didn't always know what they were talking about, or how he should contribute to the conversation. "He would try to join in on the conversation and sometimes he would use a word or phrase that was wrong," Vincent Sherman recalled. "His desire was to be with the writers, and I understood that and appreciated that. I didn't think it was anything to laugh about, but sometimes the writers would make fun of him and laugh about it."

Julie's malapropisms continued. He used "congenital" in place of "congenial," "idiosyncrasy" when referring to the plural of "idiot," and "poignant" instead of "pungent" (or visa versa). Friends accepted the malapropisms as an amusing part of Julie's persona, and looked forward to his next faux pas. Sometimes he did make them up on purpose to get a laugh, but just as often he used a word to try and impress someone, only to see his ill choice garner laughter.

He tried to learn everything at once and quickly, as if to make up for his lack of opportunity and education. He solicited advice on what books to read from Dalton Trumbo, Lee Strasberg and John Huston, which resulted in shelves and shelves of unread books in his home. He took an obsessive interest in sports, playing handball, tennis and bowling with a fury that surprised and scared his colleagues. Friends recall Julie perpetually clad in tennis shorts, practicing his serve for hours until he couldn't move his arm anymore. He pulled his right arm out of its socket when he went bowling for hours on end one afternoon. He did nothing in moderation.

Poker became another pastime. He liked to gamble but wasn't good at it. Martin Ritt called him a pigeon. He lost nearly all the time. On the screen, he may have been a good actor, but offscreen he telegraphed his poker hand with all the subtlety of a ham actor in a melodrama. He believed that he could always draw to an inside straight. His poker mates included some of the great wits of the time, including members of the famed Algonquin Round Table set: George S. Kaufman, Russell Crouse, Ira Gershwin, and sometimes Harpo Marx. These wags counted on Julie's malapropisms to keep them laughing and his poor gaming skills to keep them winning. "Whenever he goes to New York we feel like sending a bodyguard to make sure he returns," Kaufman joked from Hollywood.

On the rare occasions when Julie did win, he felt guilty about keeping the money. During the war years he once played craps with some visiting soldiers. After he took some of the soldiers' money he began to feel embarrassed about it. He obliged the soldiers to take the money back. He didn't play for the money, but to belong, to be part of a group, to find a place among his peers and betters.

Julie needed to be liked; he still had that insecurity that stemmed from his lack of family. "Everybody he spoke to, he used charm with," secretary Helen Levitt recalled. "He needed everyone to like him. He really worked at it." Elia Kazan agreed: "He wanted to be liked, to be valued, to be esteemed."

To really be esteemed, of course, he had to prove he was a great actor. He later said he wanted to be as good and acclaimed as his idol, Laurence Olivier. At age 24, Julie was a success. He was a movie star, the embodiment of the American Dream. He truly believed that he would be given the type of roles that made the careers of great actors like Olivier. But Julie was in for a shock. There would be few films of the quality of *Four Daughters* at Warner Bros.

As John Garfield, he was now expected to report to work on the studio's assembly line. And working on the assembly line at Warner Bros. was not much different than serving time in a factory. You punched in, did your job, and went home. And there wasn't much thought given to retakes.

CHAPTER EIGHT

The Assembly Line

"I worked constantly [at Warner Bros.]. Every-
body did. It was from one picture right into
another. You never had a breather."
— ACTRESS ANN SHERIDAN

THE FIRST THING THAT STRUCK ROBBE GARFIELD ABOUT
California upon her arrival in October 1938 were the oranges. Oranges had once been a luxury to her. Now she
could drink all the orange juice she wanted. She should
have paid heed to comic Fred Allen's description of Hollywood: "It's a great place to live—if you're an orange."

Julie picked the very pregnant Robbe up at the train station in Pasadena and drove her to their West Coast home.
She wasn't happy with the digs, because there were just
that: digs. Julie had picked a studio apartment with a Murphy bed. Robbe wasn't prepared for a long stay in Hollywood; she arrived in town with just three dresses and one
pair of shoes. "I was just coming to case the joint," she later
recalled. "I wasn't going to stay."

She didn't have a choice. Julie was tied to Warner Bros.
for seven years. As yet he had only a faint inkling of what it
was like to work under the studio system. He had made one
minor film classic and one pretty good action film, which
wasn't a bad ratio for a two-picture deal, but from now on
he would be expected to make between two and five films a
year. Warner Bros. expected employees to punch in, go to
makeup and wardrobe for costuming, show up on the set

ready for work, do what they were told to do as quickly and efficiently as possible and then punch out, often later than 5 P.M. Julie
was making $1,500 a week, but the money wasn't easy.

While Jack Warner and the powers that be in the front office realized that Julie had scored a success as the "eternal outsider" (as
one critic put it), they also realized that crime did indeed pay and
the Warner back lot often resembled gangland Chicago during the
days of Prohibition. From 1930, when Edward G. Robinson played
Little Caesar for the studio, through the early war years, the studio
propagated a string of gangster films featuring Robinson, Cagney,
Bogart and Raft. Julie was expected to pick up a machine gun and
get in line with the rest. The studio tried to mold Julie in the tough
guy vein while alternating this approach with films that called for
him to reprise, with variations, his Mickey Borden character. With
few exceptions, from 1938—1941, Julie's string of films at Warner
Bros. would cast him as either the young, misunderstood rebel or
gangster with a chip on his shoulder. The Epstein Brothers and
Lenore Coffee had helped make Julie into Mickey Borden, and now
the mold was set. Unfortunately, other screenwriters trying to ape
the Epstein style drew only broad strokes to paint the screen characters that Julie would play in ensuing films. The actor would have
to rely on his training, his talent and his natural charm to survive
the next four years on the Warner assembly line.

Jack Warner told the press Julie would next appear in a gangster
film called *Bad Boy*. Julie read the script. It was about two brothers;
one good, one bad. Julie asked for rewrites. The studio pretended to
accommodate him while dusting off an old 1933 Douglas Fairbanks
Jr. property, *The Life of Jimmy Dolan;* a story about a brash young
boxer who takes it on the lam after being framed for murder. The
title for the remake was prophetic: *They Made Me a Criminal.*

Julie plays champion boxer Johnny Bradfield. His manager kills
an inquiring reporter while Johnny is in a drunken stupor, frames
Johnny for the murder and he has to take refuge on a date farm in
Southern California. There he meets the pretty young owner of the

farm, Peggy (played by Gloria Dickson, who reportedly had an affair with Julie during production), her grandmother (the reliable May Robson) and the Dead End Kids. Johnny, a cynical outcast of society, soon teaches the kids how to cheat, steal and lie. But the love that Peggy, Grandma and the boys show him is enough to make him mend his ways. Money is needed to save the farm (no kidding), so Johnny agrees to battle a brainstorming boxer. By publicly fighting, Johnny draws the attention of a determined detective (Claude Rains). He saves the farm, loses the fight and is promptly arrested. For the final scene, he's headed back to the hoosegow, but when the detective sees how Peggy and the kids revere Johnny, he has a change of heart and lets the former champ off the hook. *Time* magazine noted that the film was "a straightforward story of regeneration by fresh air and pure love."

A simple film with a story as old as the hills and stereotypical characters, *They Made Me a Criminal* is a decent film; one of the better early films Julie made. The film really suffers in that the screenplay never delves into Johnny's feelings about his sudden misfortunes. He seems to take to the life of a date farmer without a second thought. Some of the dialogue rings familiar too, as when Peggy says to Johnny, "You don't believe anyone's on the level, do you?"

Busby Berkeley, veteran of famous 1930s musicals, directed the movie. Berkeley was used to taking his time in setting up shots, and for a picture that Jack Warner viewed as another assembly line quickie, Berkeley envisioned it as the film that would prove his range extended beyond musicals. He was working at a snail's pace and so the front office flooded him with memos begging him to move quicker. Apparently he ignored them all. One fascinating memo from the Warner files has Unit Manager Frank Mattison writing to the front office that "the picture has made John Garfield a Bolshevik, and I can see now that he is going to be tougher and tougher to handle on each succeeding picture... unless he works with a director other than Berkeley." Whether Mattison was referring to Julie's politics or to his unhappiness over moving so slowly on what he must have regarded as subpar material is another thing.

The Dead End Kids were hellraisers both on and off screen. They had pushed Leslie Howard into a tank of dirty water representing the East River on the set of *Dead End* (the film that made them famous), had pulled Bogart's pants off on the set of *Crime School*, and tried to give grief to Cagney on *Angels With Dirty Faces*. They were kinder to Julie, perhaps because they saw him as being one of them, but still they played their share of practical jokes on him. Julie couldn't figure out why visitors to the set asked him to take them on a tour of nearby Indio, California (where the film was being shot). Later he discovered that the Kids were sending the tourists over to him. Another day one of the Kids told Julie that Berkeley wanted to speak with him privately in the desert about a mile away. Julie walked the mile. Berkeley wasn't there. No one was. For some time, the Dead Enders sent him on similar wild-goose chases, until he got fed up with it, and then he nearly drowned a few of them in the hotel pool one evening. Cagney had stood up to them and Julie finally did the same, and that ended the practical jokes.

Julie got along well with Ann Sheridan, who was cast as the secondary female lead. An early scene called for Sheridan to passionately kiss Julie on a couch. Berkeley told Sheridan, "Hold it until I say 'cut!'" Sheridan did as told. Berkeley never yelled cut. Julie tried to squirm away but Sheridan held fast, knocking him off the couch and onto the floor. The cast and crew loved it. Moviemaking is a tedious business and any distraction is welcome. Julie was the perfect fall guy for such occasions; and, as it turned out, Berkeley and Sheridan had prearranged the entire bit to make him uncomfortable. Oddly enough, whatever his offscreen reputation as a lover, Julie disliked onscreen lovemaking.

Although *They Made Me a Criminal* made money, Julie didn't have time to count the profits, for Robbe insisted on moving in order to prepare for the baby. She chose a two-bedroom house in the San Fernando hills that was owned by RKO starlet Helen Mack.

Mack was leaving Hollywood and wanted to rent the house; neither Julie nor Robbe wanted to buy property at the time. The Garfields thought the house was unique. So did the chamber of commerce. Tour buses pulled up in front of the house on a daily basis, not because John Garfield lived there, but because the house was considered a prime example of Spanish Colonial architecture.

Daughter Katherine Hannah was born on October 28, 1938. Julie and his stand-in paced the halls of the hospital, nervously pitching pennies all night. When he saw the beautiful Katherine, Julie fell in love with her right away. "How can anything look like me and be so pretty?" he said of his new daughter.

While Robbe learned the ABCs of motherhood, Julie went back to work. Warner Bros. was casting Paul Muni's latest biographical epic, *Juarez*, and they offered Julie the supporting role of Porfiro Diaz, one of Juarez's generals. He was excited at the prospect, since the cast included Bette Davis, Brian Aherne, Claude Rains, Gale Sondergaard and Gilbert Roland. "It's the story that counts, not the player," he told the press, explaining his reasoning for accepting a supporting role.

Juarez chronicles the quest for control of Mexico between dethroned President Benito Juarez (Muni) and Napoleon's puppet Emperor Maximilian (Aherne) in the years following the American Civil War. Claude Rains was Napoleon and Davis played Aherne's love interest, who wanted him to retire and let Mexico solve its own political problems. Even with that powerhouse cast and the combined writing talents of John Huston, Wolfgang Reinhardt and Aeneas MacKenzie, the film did not succeed. It creaks along, hampered by poor scripting and a lack of action. In his autobiography, *An Open Book*, Huston placed the blame for the film's failure square at Muni's feet. Muni, Huston asserted, felt he did not have as much dialogue as Aherne and insisted that his brother-in-law be brought in to write additional scenes. All this tinkering has the film just going on and on without making much of a point. As for Julie, he's clearly out of his element portraying a Mexican officer; he looks silly sporting a goatee and carrying a pistol on his hip. A Jewish street kid playing a Mexican soldier? Even the employees of Warner Bros. didn't buy it. Every time Julie wandered into the commissary in costume, the writers would yell out in unison, "He's the best god-damned lookin' schlemiel in Ol' Mexico!"

Julie laughed with them, but he realized he had made a mistake. He was glad to have taken the chance at something different, but Diaz was too different. Some of the overly simplistic dialogue how-ever, which helped define America's philosophy in the pre-war years, he must have loved. "Democracy?" Diaz proclaims at one point. "Why, it means liberty; liberty for a man to say what he thinks. To worship as he believes. It means equal opportunity." The critics weren't impressed. "John Garfield, who used to be Jules, is more John than Jules, though his tongue is the tongue of Jules," wrote *The Brooklyn Daily Eagle*. "He is earnest, but only a forthright, earnest young man making believe he is Porfiro Diaz." Diaz's son was not impressed either. He threatened to sue Warner Bros. over Julie's portrayal of his father, suggesting that the actor played Diaz like Tarzan. Jack Warner never let Julie stray so far from type again.

Some of the film was actually shot on location in Mexico City—a rare extravagance in those days—and Robbe got to accompany Julie there for a short period of time, but dysentery and diarrhea marred the so-called vacation. While in Mexico City, Julie received word that his father was seriously ill, so he chartered a plane and flew to New York City, leaving Robbe behind. David, diagnosed with cancer, was confined to a bed—a bed he would remain in until his death three years later. Father and son had little to say to each other. David was not interested in his son's Hollywood life, and Julie was not in-terested in hearing about the tailoring business or God's will.

Staying behind in Mexico City, Robbe grew lonely. She was con-cerned about her father-in-law (even though she didn't like him), about the state of her marriage and whether she was still attractive after having a baby. A young, handsome teenage boy made her feel

better about herself, however absurd it seemed; at 25 she found herself engaged in a flirtation with an 18-year-old actor named Montgomery Clift. The bisexual Clift was in Mexico City with conductor
Lehman Engel, but Engel was left out of the picture when Robbe
and Clift began wandering off to swim or picnic together. Robbe acknowledged that she was attracted to him. "He was a beautiful
young boy," she recalled. "And I kind of fell for him." She said she
did not allow her hands to follow her eyes, but she felt that sense of
maternal nurturing that had initially attracted her to Julie.

When the filming in Mexico City wrapped, with Julie returned
from New York, Engel and Clift hitched a ride with Julie and Robbe
from Cuernavaca to Acapulco, where they would all board a states-
bound ship. The car trip was awful. Everyone had cramps and the
quartet made endless pit stops. Julie, no great shakes as a driver,
lost control of the car at one point and veered off the road and
through a guardrail. No one was seriously hurt, but Robbe turned to
see Julie sitting on the ground with blood pouring from his nose
and tears forming in his eyes, and she recalled the first time she fell
in love with him in the aftermath of the earlier accident. As odd as
it sounds, she later acknowledged that her love was rekindled by
this car crash. Yet this, too, marred their relationship somewhat:
Robbe wanted Julie to need her, but he wanted more and more to
test his independence and be his own man.

Before leaving Mexico City Julie agreed to appear on writer Ted
Allan's radio show "Good Neighbor." Allan often recruited American talent for the English-language program, broadcast from Mexico
City, and Julie proved a willing candidate. Moments before they
were to go on the air, Allan was told that the sound effects props
and equipment was missing—the records, the props, the instruments, everything. It made no sense, but there was no time to or-
ganize a search party. Julie didn't care. "Julie and I had to do all the
sound effects with our voices," Allan recalled. "Make the gun
shoot, make the horse gallop, hit the pots and pans together; all that
stuff with our voices." Julie had a ball. Later, after they finished the

program, Allan and Julie stepped into a small anteroom to chat. There, on the shelves, they discovered the sound effects props and equipment. Julie thought it was very funny.

Years later Allan called Julie's ability to laugh at himself as an important character trait. "He had a delicious sense of humor," Allan said. "But you never really got to see that side of him in his films." Julie was very funny and had an easy way with a comic line (as did Cagney and Bogart). He wanted to do a film comedy and asked Jack Warner to find him one. Warner didn't acknowledge Julie's request, and when he announced Julie's next picture, it didn't sound very funny. It was a crime film, appropriately titled *Dust Be My Destiny*.

This movie, directed by Lewis Seiler, has Julie playing Joe Bell, an ex-con and a "nobody with a capital N" who is unjustly sent to prison. Released from prison, Joe rides the rails to Florida, where he encounters more trouble while trying to do the right thing. Joe is sentenced to 90 days in a prison farm, where the foreman happens to be a temperamental drunk with a penchant for violence. Fortunately for Joe, the foreman's daughter, Mabel, falls for him, and even more fortunate, Mabel is played by Priscilla Lane. Joe tells Mabel that all he wants out of life is a place to hang his hat, and since that is just what Mabel wants as well, they get married.

As early as 1939, a John Garfield film formula existed, and this film followed the formula to the end: Joe inadvertently causes the death of Mabel's father, and the young lovers flee from the law while Joe develops a considerable chip on his shoulder. Joe is another cynic who feels the fates are against him ("What's the use?" is an oft-heard line in these early Garfield films), but through Mabel's patient love and a series of encounters with simple, everyday folk (a lovable old codger, an amiable milkman, an understanding newspaper editor and so on), Joe's icy exterior slowly melts. Still, spending a honeymoon on the run is no party, and Joe considers turning to armed robbery. "It takes courage to steal," he tries to explain to Mabel. "It don't to beg!" Before he can hurt himself, or anyone else,

Mabel turns Joe in. When he is brought to trial, he is surprised to find that the witnesses for the defense are all the stock characters he met on the road. Joe's lawyer sums up the film's point of view in his final argument: There are a lot of Joe Bells looking for a place to hang their hat, and this country had better help them find it.

Joe is cleared and he and Mabel get that place to hang their hats. *Dust Be My Destiny,* written by Robert Rossen (another product of Rivington Street) was one of Warner Bros.' last attempts to portray the difficulties faced by young people traveling the country's by-ways during the Depression. Julie wasn't happy with the film, but like *They Made Me A Criminal,* fine ensemble acting helps it immeasurably. Julie and Priscilla Lane worked at developing their screen relationship, and the middle portion of the film, which deals with the couple's problems while on the run, is particularly well played by both stars. A brief, nearly silent sequence where the two decide to split up is worth the price of admission, especially when Julie has to rely on just his facial expressions to convey his true feelings. It's a beauty to watch but a difficult scene to explain on page, and it indicates what the film could have been had more thought been put into the direction and script. Julie injected Joe Bell with a sense of angry desperation that was rarely seen in his early screen work. He really captures the uncertainty of a young man waiting for a tomorrow that will never come.

Completed early in 1939 and released that September, *Dust Be My Destiny* opened to good box office. It may not rate an entry in a listing of Top Ten John Garfield Films, but it's fairly good, flaws and all. It's interesting to see how the film captures the time period and the way people struggled to make the best of things. Julie worked well with Lane, an actress he personally liked but professionally disparaged*, and the duo enjoy a nice give-and-take onscreen rapport. In fact, the film probably represents Lane's best work as an actress.

---

* Garfield had a tendency to make fun of the acting talent, or lack of, of Lane, Ronald Reagan and Maureen O'Hara, among others.

Less happy was a near tragedy that occurred on the set one day. Julie, Bobby Jordan and Billy Halop were filming a scene that called for them to run alongside a moving train in a real rail yard. Halop slipped in a puddle and stumbled onto an adjoining track in front of a train coming from the opposite direction. Fortunately, Jordan instinctively reached out his arm and pulled him to safety. During his days riding the rails, Julie had witnessed similar events with more tragic endings and he was visibly shaken.

After *Dust Be* My Destiny and between April 1938 and January 1939, Julie made five films for Warner Bros. There was literally no time to breathe between pictures. Even on Saturday, the assembly line was forever waiting. "You finished one film on Friday and went in on Monday to start the next one," Vincent Sherman recalled. "Sometimes Saturdays too—unless you wanted to take a suspension. From 1938, when I started there [Warner Bros.] until 1952, when I left, I didn't stop. I don't think I had one day off in those fourteen years."

By 1939 and 1940 Julie was spending more time at the studio than at home. Not that he really had a home to call his own. The Garfields always rented, moving from place to place like fugitives from justice themselves. Julie didn't want a home to own him. "It gets you," he told journalist Frederick James Smith around this time. "Pretty soon you're at its mercy. You're working to support a lot of chairs and stuff." Robbe didn't mind, because she never considered Hollywood her home. "I wasn't planning on living out there," she said. "I wasn't making a nest."

Still, they had their own way of nesting, even in a rented house. Upon returning from their first trip to a grocery store, Julie would pull a large salami out of a bag and hang it on a hook in the kitchen. "Now we live here!" he proclaimed to Robbe.

The Garfields' neighbors were the battling Bogarts. Bogart was then married to actress Mayo Methot (who Julie called "method"), and it was a union of discord. The Garfields were unprepared for the nightly war that waged across the street from them, when vases would crash against the wall, chairs would fly out of windows (presumably past Bogart's head) and screaming fits would last into the early hours of the morning. Robbe and Julie would sit up and listen to the commotion and wonder whether they should call the police. In the morning Bogart would casually dismiss it all. Later on the Garfields joined the Bogarts on a studio publicity junket for Errol Flynn's Western *Dodge City,* and the fighting started all over again. The Bogarts' hotel room adjoined the Garfield's room, and they didn't disappoint. "They kept us up all night," Robbe said. "We'd almost fall asleep and then we'd hear another piece of furniture smash." Compared to the Bogarts', the Garfields' marriage looked downright solid.

During the day Julie worked, even when he wasn't filming. There were photo shoots to coordinate and press interviews to give. When it came to publicity, Julie was among the more cooperative stars, according to PR man Bob William. But the actor would use the press interviews to indirectly communicate with his boss, Jack Warner. He spoke loudly about his efforts to get good scripts, comparing his efforts to the fights he had on the streets of New York in his youth. "As a kid, I sold *The Bronx Home News* on a street corner," he said in one 1940 interview. "I kept that corner until I surrendered it of my own accord. I'll keep my ground I think is right, too, until I surrender it of my own accord. But when that day comes, they'll be planting me." It sounded like dialogue from one of his films.

The films kept coming down the assembly line. The Garfield character in *Dust Be My Destiny* wasn't killed off because he had to return, under an alias, for films like *East of the River, Castle on the Hudson* and *Flowing Gold,* all future Garfield potboilers. But Mickey Borden had died and this now posed a problem. Jack Warner wanted a sequel to *Four Daughters* with a starring role for John Garfield and ordered the Epstein Brothers to fashion such a sequel. How, the Epsteins asked, were they to do this when Mickey had died in the original? Warner didn't care how they did it; they were just to do it.

So the Epsteins took Thomas Wolfe's *Fly Away Home*, adapted it, and managed to cram all the actors from *Four Daughters* into it. Jeffrey Lynn knew why the studio was doing it: to make money. He said of the film, "I never felt like I fit in. I always felt like I was outside the door listening in. And I don't think the other characters fit in either."

Lynn was correct. The film, titled *Daughters Courageous*, was tailor-made for Julie, with some emphasis on the supporting characters played by Priscilla Lane and Claude Rains. The other actors simply trod water, if that. The entire cast and the director of *Four Daughters* were brought back for this story of a wandering husband (Rains) who returns home after a 20-year absence to discover that his wife is about to remarry. His four grown daughters—Priscilla, Lola, Rosemary Lane and Gale Page—experience mixed emotions over his return. Julie is a drifting rebel, one Gabriel Lopez (a Hispanic, perhaps drafted by the Epsteins as an in-joke relating to Julie's role in *Juarez*). Unlike Borden, Lopez isn't a cynic and he is given a nice sense of humor and a casual indifference to life that make him come off as a distant cousin to Cary Grant's character in the 1938 screwball comedy *Holiday*.

Daughters Courageous has its admirers, but it cannot be called a good film. In it, the four daughters do ridiculous things: they tear their clothes on thorn bushes, display their bare backsides to each other, giggle incessantly, act like 12-year-olds and things like that. Rains' performance is good, and so is Julie's, who has some funny lines and seems to be enjoying his love scenes with Priscilla Lane. The film also boasts one great gag at the expense of the Group Theatre delivered by Claude Rains. The critics were wise to Warner's ruse and were quick to note that the film was a poor variation of the previous year's *Four Daughters*. But the public didn't care. Warner had another commercial hit, and Julie's stock on the lot rose considerably.

Still, the executives on the lot weren't always happy with Julie's on-set preparation. Hal B. Wallis, the *Daughters Courageous* producer, had plagued Curtiz with memos criticizing Julie's work as an actor. "Watch him," Wallis wrote Curtiz in one such memo, "be-cause I have a feeling that he will have his own ideas about how he should play the part, and we want to make sure he plays it the way we want him to." It was the first memo of many that Wallis would dictate concerning Julie's acting, and indicates how much control film producers wanted over any project, including the acting. Wal-lis was right about one thing, Julie did like to bring his own ideas about character to rehearsals (when there were rehearsals). Curtiz was one director who would listen to Julie's suggestions and work to incorporate the actor's ideas. In this sequel, both men wanted to make Gabriel Lopez a fresh character and not just another version of Mickey Borden and, for the most part, they succeeded. As an actor, Julie resented executives and producers butting in to tell him how he should play a scene. This aspect of movie-making would always annoy him, and fueled his desire to escape the studio system.

Nevertheless, he was fairly content at Warner Bros. in his first few years there. Elia Kazan, who showed up on the lot in 1939 to act in two films (*Blues in the Night* and *City for Conquest*), felt that Julie was "a hell of a lot happier than he let on" at Warner Bros. Jef-frey Lynn also felt Julie was happy during his honeymoon days at the studio. Yet Julie took pains to bite the hand that was feeding him. In a magazine article entitled "I'd Like to Write as I Please," the actor sounded off about Hollywood, his image as a trouble-maker and the kind of films he wanted to make. "I think that Hol-lywood, as it is now constituted, does its utmost to over-develop the actor's ego and so spoil him for the simple business of living, either with others or himself."

He went on about the type of roles he was expecting to play, hint-ing that he would return to New York and Broadway if his wishes weren't fulfilled. "I want good parts in good pictures," he wrote. "When those are no longer forthcoming I expect to exercise my op-tion to return to the stage." (He had insisted upon such an option in his studio contract.) Of his own image Julie wrote, "I'm just a young fellow trying to get along in this funny Hollywood world." He

would always try to portray himself as a simple everyday guy, a
"mug" who did not plan to be seduced by Hollywood. Success
would not go to his head, he asserted. But many of Julie's friends
and colleagues thought he was using his newfound stardom to
mouth off. "I have always talked plainly and too much," he wrote in
the article. "Now I am expected to talk in parables and to keep
silent too much." It's unlikely he knew what a parable was.

Time magazine, in its review of *They Made Me a Criminal,* described Garfield as "outspoken…and an amateur left wing politician." It was an apt description. He could pretend to be more
informed about world affairs than he was, making comments that
baffled his co-stars about the next revolution and such, but when he
went down to the corner newsstand to get a copy of *The New York
Times* to read about world events, he would inevitably turn first to
the newspaper's entertainment section. Still, with Robbe leading
the way, Julie began to gravitate towards ultraliberal political
groups in Hollywood.

"Hollywood was a liberal community then," screenwriter Paul
Jarrico explained. "The writers, the directors, and to a lesser degree
the actors were largely left of center." Hollywood wanted to present
itself as a community that cared, and for Julie, who had worked his
way up quickly from uneducated street waif to equally uneducated
movie star, it was important to maintain a connection to his roots. He
appeared sincere in his efforts to help those less fortunate than himself. Actress Betsy Blair (then the wife of Gene Kelly) recalled Julie as
always being one to financially support liberal causes. But intellec-
tually he remained lost in the Hollywood cadre of communists and
communist sympathizers, a group that included screenwriters Ring
Lardner Jr., Albert Maltz and John Howard Lawson, director Herbert
Biberman, and his fellow actor from Group Theatre days, Joe
Bromberg. Politics was often the main topic of discussion when this
group got together, but that wasn't the only tie that bound them.

"People got together socially," Jarrico recalled. "It wasn't always
for political reasons. They got together to play poker, to drink, and to

dance. It was a normal social life going on which often included non-communists as well as communists, and people who were fairly left of center even if they were not in the Party. And John Garfield was someone who was fun to be with even if you didn't think he was a brain surgeon or a first-class scientist. And his best friends were red—more than just liberal—they were red. And he knew they weren't bomb throwers or dangerous people to associate with."

It was Robbe who felt more at home among this political group. She was the one who took part in the passionate discussions about war, race, equality and the Depression. Julie never quite penetrated the Hollywood liberal community's depths. Often he would fall asleep at parties when political discussions came up. Julie was never considered an artist of any real intellect. The "intelligentsia," as Robbe described the leftwing writers in this group, did not take Julie seriously either as an artist or a political citizen. "A lot of the Party guys in that group, such as the writers, looked upon him as a very soft, weak, ambivalent type of guy," journalist Sam Shaw said. "I don't think they respected his artistry. From their point of view, he was a nice schmuck." He would always give money for some worthwhile cause, rarely questioning its worth. Mostly he wanted to talk acting. "He was involved in a kind of generous way," director/writer Abraham Polonsky explained. "Sure, he supported the liberal causes, but he wanted to be a famous actor. He didn't want to change the world!"

Liberalism was taken for granted by Julie. But remarks such as the one he made to the cast of *Daughters Courageous* gave the more conservative members of the Hollywood community the idea that Julie was a communist. For no reason in particular, he announced one day, "Come the Revolution we'll all be eating strawberries and cream." No one around him knew what he was talking about. To Julie, it must have sounded like the right thing to say, but it was no doubt no more than a line he had overheard at a recent party.

He was a liberal, but never a communist. He signed political petitions as easily as he would sign an autograph for a fan. He put his

John Hancock on a petition endorsing the Medical Bureau of the North American Committee to Aid Spanish Democracy, which meant that he supported efforts to send humanitarian and medical aid to the Loyalists in Spain. He allowed his name to be used as chairman for The American Friends of the Chinese Army when Japan invaded China. He also sponsored a call for a boycott of all Japanese goods under the auspices of the American League for Peace and Democracy. At the time, these were all innocent-sounding organizations; a decade later they would sound more ominous. He may have signed or sponsored or taken part in dozens of such petitions, benefits and boycotts without thinking any of it through.

Garfield was right when he wrote that Hollywood wanted to keep him quiet. While Warner Bros. was one of the most liberal movie studios in town, they were not above influencing their employees when it came to questionable outside activities. When Julie told the studio he was planning to accompany actor Melvyn Douglas to San Francisco to appear at a dinner dance benefit for longshoreman Harry Bridges (who was then deemed an undesirable alien due to his Communist ties), Warner Bros. strongly urged him not to take the trip. He heeded their advice. The studio did, however, allow him to participate in the more innocuous 1940 "Salute to Roosevelt" radio broadcast, along with Edward G. Robinson and Humphrey Bogart.

In the late 1930s there was not yet a "Red Scare" in America but the seeds were being planted to create one. Back in the early 1930s New York Congressman Sam Dickestein (whose district included Rivington Street) had attempted to create an investigative arm that would keep track of subversive activity in America. In January 1934 his resolution was passed, and later that year the first hearings, which focused on Nazi organizations in America, were held. Those early hearings pretty much set the ground rules for the future House Committee on Un-American Activities events, giving the chairman of the committee as much leeway as he wanted when it came to questioning witnesses, yet allowing witnesses little to no right to defense counsel; making the prosecutors also the juries and judges.

During 1937 Dickestein presented a resolution that would authorizie a standing committee with the power to investigate just about anyone. In May 1938, Texas Congressman Martin Dies lead the House in passing an amended version of Dickestein's resolution by a vote of 191—41. Committees such as these quickly gained ground so much so that in August 1938 Congressman J. Parnell Thomas (one of Dies' underlings) could demand an investigation into the WPA's Federal Theatre and Writer's Projects. The WPA Projects, which subsidized free theater, had produced over 100 shows of varying quality, shows that featured lower-class heroes of the type John Garfield played in Warner Bros. melodramas. Thomas denounced the entire project as "a hot bed of communism" (a popular phrase at the time) because he had heard that a New York chambermaid with no stage experience had been given the lead role in one WPA play because she was a communist. It seems an unlikely scenario to base an investigation upon, but it made headlines, and Dies and Thomas loved headlines.

Hollywood made headlines too. And it did on August 13, 1938, when Dies and Thomas announced that they were sending investigator Edward F. Sullivan to Hollywood/Los Angeles to look into Communist infiltration of the movie and shipping business. After a brief visit Sullivan returned and said, "All phases of radical and communistic activities are rampant among the studios of Hollywood," although he offered no proof of his charge. Lack of proof would become another regular aspect of the witch hunts. Dies told the press that 90 percent of the mail he received was in support of the Committee's investigations, yet his initial foray into Hollywood was really a failure. He was pretty much ridiculed when he suggested that nine-year-old Shirley Temple was a communist because she sent greetings to the French Communist newssheet *Ce Soir.*

California Assemblyman Sam Yorty did manage to set up an investigating committee to determine whether the State Relief

Administration was rife with communists. This committee (known as the Little Dies Committee) was chaired by Congressman Jack R. Tenney, who later became one of the driving forces of the 1940s witch hunts. In 1941 this committee reorganized in a fact-finding committee known as the State Committee on Un-American Activities, and became the predecessor of the more powerful House Committee on Un-American Activities (HUAC).

Dies cited John Garfield by name as a "commie" as early as 1938 because the actor had joined the Hollywood Anti-Fascist League and the American League for Peace and Democracy. Julie joined these organizations for two reasons. First, he believed in what they stood for; like equal rights for minorities and women and government support for the homeless, and second, he wanted to belong. He could join a political organization as easily as he could join a poker game. He just wanted to be in on everything. But as Abraham Polonsky noted, Julie did not want to change the world.

What he probably did want to change was his scripts at Warner Bros. When Julie read the script for his next film off the assembly line, something called *Mama Ravioli,* he felt the storyline—about two brothers on opposite sides of the law—sounded familiar. That's because *Mama Ravioli* was *Bad Boy* under a new title. Again he said no. The studio sent him a few more potboilers like *Festival in Manhattan, Flight Angels, Hell's Kitchen* and *Invisible Stripes* (in this he was to play the younger brother of George Raft). Julie turned them all down and then told the press that he wanted to play Davy Crockett, hero of the Alamo. That was certainly wishful thinking, or a private joke on the part of the actor. Nobody at Warner Bros. was laughing.

In the meantime, Jack Warner's lobbying had paid off and the actor was rewarded for his work in *Four Daughters* with a nomination for Best Supporting Actor. (Other Warner Bros. employees nominated that year were Bette Davis for *Jezebel,* James Cagney for *Angels With Dirty Faces,* and director Michael Curtiz for both *Angels With Dirty Faces* and *Four Daughters.*) Julie wouldn't attend the Academy Awards ceremony. "He didn't expect to win," Robbe said. "But some people at the studio thought he was going to get it." *Newsweek* had already labeled John Garfield as "the outstanding film find of the year" while the New York Film Critics had Julie running third in their choice for Best Actor (behind Cagney, and Spencer Tracy for *Boys Town*). The other nominees for Best Supporting Actor didn't look too hot, but when the awards ceremony was held on February 28, 1939, at the Biltmore Hotel, actor Walter Brennan picked up the Oscar for Best Supporting Actor for his work in *Kentucky*. Brennan's performance is good, but it didn't generate the electricity of Julie's work in *Four Daughters*. It's not implausible to assume that Hollywood wasn't ready to reward a newcomer with the coveted Oscar. "They didn't like the idea of this guttersnipe from New York coming in and taking the kudos away," Robbe tartly remarked.

Shortly after the awards ceremony the Garfields visited New York City. Julie returned to P.S. 45 at Angelo Patri's request to speak to the graduating class of 1939. While Julie never did come around to explaining just why he chose acting as a career, he did tell the class, "I must be in the theater; otherwise I'd die." Julie lauded both P.S. 45 and Patri, crediting them with his success. When he finished his speech Patri surprised him by presenting him with a leather briefcase as a token of appreciation. It was almost like receiving a diploma.

While Julie was in New York Clifford Odets tried to talk him into returning to the Group to appear in one of two Irwin Shaw plays. *The Gentle People,* an allegory about fascism, concerned a New York thug's threatening hold over two old fishermen, while *Quiet City* dealt with a successful capitalist who looks back with troubled conscience at the unethical paths he chose in life. Julie would not commit to either project, which frustrated Odets (Franchot Tone returned to New York to play the lead in *The Gentle People*.) Maybe Julie sensed that the Group's brief glory days were over. For one thing, Clurman was still trying to rely on movie stars to bolster box office sales. The Group had not enjoyed a commercial success since *Golden Boy*. Odets himself was having trouble writing; neither of his two most recent works, *Rocket to the Moon* and *Night Music,* displayed the depth and strength of his earlier writing. "When we talked about it later on, we realized that the Group was breaking up anyway," Robbe said. "Julie was not the catalyst. A few years later it [the Group] was gone."

The actors who had remained faithful to the Group began to feel as Julie had in 1937. In 1939, the Group Theatre was floundering; a year later it was all but disbanded. The Group's last official production was 1940's *Retreat to Paradise*. Most of the Group members moved to Hollywood the following year, where a contingent of them would create the Actors' Laboratory (Lab), a sort of West-Coast version of the Group.

The Garfields returned to Hollywood to find Julie even more heralded on the Warner lot. He seemed to have a gift for predicting the future when he told the press, "Never will I get such a reception again. My future performances will always be compared with my role of Mickey Borden." The actor had the misfortune of coming out of the starting gate hellbent for stardom, and it was questionable whether he could fulfill his early promise. The critics already felt that the studio was wasting a fine commodity. "If you repeat the title of *They Made Me a Criminal*, you can almost fancy you hear the voice of John Garfield accusing the Warner Brothers," *The New York Times* film critic Bosley Crowther wrote. "But they all have to go through the same mill at Warners."

Julie did not want to go through that particular mill. His friends and co-workers reminded him that all of the studio's big stars had served their apprenticeships in the same fashion. Cagney, Robinson, Muni, Bogart and Raft all had to cut their teeth on crime dramas; some of them would never shed their prison clothes. But, encouraged by his Academy Award nomination, Julie decided that he wanted to challenge himself and take a chance. And when an opportunity for such a chance arose, he grabbed it.

The Epstein Brothers were busy adapting Maxwell Anderson's stage comedy *Saturday's Children* for Warner Bros. Producer Hal B. Wallis had penciled in James Stewart and Olivia de Havilland as the leads. Both actors opted out at the last minute. Vincent Sherman, who had scored a hit with his directorial debut, a B horror flick called *The Return of Dr. X* (starring Humphrey Bogart as a zombie), displayed some interest in the story. Warner was impressed with Sherman's work ethic and assigned him *Saturday's Children*. Julie let Warner know he wanted the lead in the film, and with Sherman and the Epsteins behind him, he got it. Shooting began right before Christmas 1939.

The film is a wonderful departure for Julie. He plays office accountant Rims Rosen, an eternal dreamer who plans to travel the world and invent everything that needs inventing. He's a shy optimist, quite the opposite of the antagonistic rebels the actor had played. Rims thumbs his nose at despair and disillusionment until his desire for independence is challenged by his love for Bobby, an office secretary (played by Anne Shirley, an underappreciated actress of the era). Bobby is a sensible girl who wants a career of her own, but she lets her sister Florrie (Lee Patrick) talk her into tricking Rims into marriage. "Women only have one weapon," Florrie claims. "Marriage!" Rims and Bobby marry but it doesn't take long for the disenchantment to set in. Bobby loses her job and gets pregnant. Rims is forced to take a pay cut. He begins to sense that Bobby duped him into marriage. The marriage begins to falter and crumble; when Bobby's father Henry (Claude Rains) sees what is happening, he decides to commit suicide so the couple can collect on his life insurance. Henry fails at his task, but the near-tragedy forces Rims to face up to the responsibilities before him. Flush with renewed optimism, he announces that he will work harder and longer for the good of the family. "We're Saturday's children," he notes. "We're young. And that's the best guarantee for the future."

Despite this somewhat unbelievable finale, *Saturday's Children* is a little gem of a film, a romantic comedy still awaiting rediscovery. Julie made real efforts to insure that Rims was unlike any of his previous screen characters. He altered his speech pattern, speaking with a slow deliberation. To look like an urban version of Harold

Lloyd, he added a pair of spectacles and he played the comic moments with subtlety—a grace he had forsaken in most of his post-
Four Daughters films. A quality of childlike innocence and
vulnerability remains to Rims, a side of Julie's persona that never
again would be so fully exploited on film.

Julie's ability to grasp simple direction on film in order to flesh
out a scene was apparent. In one scene he is called to play drunk.
Julie overplayed it and Sherman wasn't happy. He took the actor
aside and said, "The marvelous thing about a drunk is that he's trying to pretend he's sober. Now you've had too much to drink, but try
to appear sober and don't slur your words and do all the usual stuff.
Keep it simple." Julie nodded, took in Sherman's direction, and got
it right on the next take.

James Wong Howe was the cameraman on the film. Wong Howe
and Sherman collaborated on a prolonged gag at Julie's expense.
One scene called for Anne Shirley to bathe her husband in the tub.
Julie hated baths. Clad in swimming trunks, he climbed into the tub
for a take. Wong Howe told him that something was wrong with the
camera. Julie stepped out of the tub. They set up the shot again.
Julie got back in. Another take was ruined by something or other,
Wong Howe said. Over a four hour period, while the press stood by
to take publicity shots (at Sherman's request), Julie climbed in and
out of the tub repeatedly. By four o'clock he was shivering on the
drafty sound stage. Two hours later Wong Howe announced that the
day's work was all for naught. "The shots are ruined," he told the
cast and crew. "The film has emulsion scratches on it." Sherman
matter-of-factly announced that they would shoot the entire sequence again the next day. Julie wasn't happy, but pretty soon he
caught on to the joke. Sherman told him they had actually managed
to get the shot on the third take. Still, the final joke was on Sherman
and Wong Howe, for the bathtub scene never made it to the screen.
Perhaps it was too intimate for movie audiences in 1940.

Saturday's Children was released in May 1940 and won over the
critics. "Particular praise is in store for John Garfield, the sallow

Romeo with the sad face and troubled soul, who falls into the part of the harassed young lover as though it had been written for him alone," *The New York Times* noted. Julie loved the film, and Sherman felt they all had something special in the can. But despite everyone's hard work and high hopes, the film did not find an audience. In retrospect, one wonders if this was due to the film's odd structuring, beginning as a comedy, touching upon social drama and then veering into tragedy (or melodrama) before swinging back to comedy again. It's a mixed-bag sort of film, and mixed-bag films generally don't go over well. Sherman explained that "it wasn't the kind of film that people went out of their way for. It was a sweet picture, and it got very good reviews, and Johnny was very good in it. But it didn't make any money."

It didn't lose money either, but that was little compensation to Jack Warner. His studio wasn't about to make films that broke even just to make John Garfield happy. The studio immediately announced a string of films that would reinforce John Garfield's image as the tough guy with the heart of gold. *Saturday's Children* should have been the beginning of a second film career for Julie, the chance to broaden his range as Cagney had done. Instead, John Garfield was sent back to the rogue s' gallery. And if he thought that the films he made before *Saturday's Children* were mediocre, he really needed to brace himself for what was coming next.

CHAPTER NINE

Heavenly Express

"To me heaven is just a place where you sit
down with a couple of other guys and an
idea and not too much dough and you work
it over and say,' Let's do it!' "

—JOHN GARFIELD

THINGS GOT WORSE. JULIE'S NEXT FILM WAS *CASTLE ON the Hudson,* a remake of the 1933 Warner Bros. film *20,000 Years in Sing Sing,* which had starred Spencer Tracy. Julie described the film to reporter Frederick Woltman as a story about "a wise guy who goes to the electric chair for a woman." That was about it. The wise guy's name was Tommy Gordon, but he was indistinguishable from Joe Bell, Johnny Bradfield, and Mickey Borden. Anatole Litvak was picked to direct; the leading lady was Ann Sheridan, and Pat O'Brien played a kindly warden. Julie didn't like the script and only agreed to do the film under two conditions: 1) that the studio retain the original ending, wherein Tommy goes to the electric chair for a murder he did not commit, and 2) a bonus of $10,000.

At least screenwriters Seton I. Miller, Brown Holmes and Courtney Terrett gave Julie some opportunity for buffoonery in the film, such as an amusing bit where Tommy, on death row, receives a letter from the IRS threatening to arrest him for evasion of income tax payment. Another gag was an inside joke referring to *Saturday's Children.* "I was pinched on a Saturday, sentenced on a Saturday and sent

118

here (Sing Sing) on a Saturday," Tommy says, appraising the fates' grudge against him. "And I was born on a Saturday."

"It's funny how the theater helps you," Julie told a visiting reporter on the set. "All I did was imagine I was playing to a studio audience. I disregarded the camera and concentrated on the people watching me." His theater training could only do so much; *Castle on the Hudson* was standard prison fare. "This is merely a routine notice that Mr. John Garfield, formerly of the Group Theatre, who was recently sentenced to a term in Warner Brothers, is still in prison," one critic noted.

He must have felt like he was in prison, because in the spring of 1940 he decided to go over the wall. Kermit Bloomgarden, who had produced a few of the Group's productions, approached Julie in Hollywood with Albert Bein's play *Heavenly Express*. Julie read the play, liked it, and decided to exercise his contractual option to return to the stage. Almost immediately, the actor began to brag about his triumphant return to Broadway—prematurely, it turns out.

Julie still didn't understand Hollywood. He wanted to do *Waiting For Lefty*, or Dalton Trumbo's *Johnny Got His Gun*, or the story of Angelo Patri. The studio wanted him to play *Bad Boy*, a.k.a. *Mama Ravioli,* now known as *East of the River* but still the same lousy script. Julie knew that the strong base he had built with *Four Daughters* was steadily eroding under the Warner system. He no longer embodied the dynamic loser/lover who men wanted to emulate and who women wanted to bed. He was a Cagney wannabe, a lesser Bogart, the recipient of George Raft's hand-me-downs. He was being offered opportunities, but they were opportunities at other studios. RKO wanted him for Sidney Kingsley's *They Knew What They Wanted* opposite Charles Laughton and Carole Lombard. Warner refused to loan him out. Columbia, having bought the film rights to *Golden Boy,* wanted Julie as Joe Bonaparte. Warner wouldn't deal with studio head Harry Cohn (they were feuding at the time) and the role went to newcomer William Holden. For the second time, Julie missed out on playing the role that Clifford Odets had created for him. Years later Julie told actor Robert Blake that not being able to play Joe Bonaparte on film was "one of the biggest heartbreaks of my career."

So when Bloomgarden asked him about *Heavenly Express*, Julie said yes—perhaps too quickly. Playwright Bein had tried to convince Harold Clurman to produce the play back in 1932, but Clurman found the play impossible to stage. Bloomgarden should have heeded Clurman's concerns. The play, Bein explained, was about a bum's version of the universal scheme of things. Bein had spent years riding the rails as a hobo and had once fallen from a speeding locomotive and in the days following that fall, Bein suffered recurrent hallucinations in which speeding trains and ghostly passengers raced through his head. That experience, he said, was the impetus for writing the play.

In *Heavenly Express* Julie was to play The Overland Kid, a mystical hobo spirit who rides the rails searching for lost and lonely tramps. Once he finds them, he spirits them back to heaven through his guitar playing. This was obviously not the sort of role Jack Warner would have given the actor. Julie knew the script needed work, so he invited Bein, Bloomgarden and director Bobby Lewis to his Hollywood home so the four of them could brainstorm and do rewrites. There the quartet worked on lightening the tone of the play by stressing comedy over drama, but there were still a lot of dead people in it. Julie agreed to help financially back the production, as did Clifford Odets. Julie's constant put-downs of Hollywood, coupled with his griping about his untapped acting ability, fueled his desire to return to Broadway. "He hated Hollywood," director Irving Rapper recalled of this period in Julie's life. "He hated (Errol) Flynn, he hated all the things that were not New York. He'd say 'Irving, you come from the theater, you're real. These guys, Jesus Christ! I want to go home—they're phonies!'" He didn't really hate Hollywood, but there's no doubt that 1940 was turning out to be a miserable year for him. And he did miss the stage, unlike other stage actors who turned to film and never returned.

"The theater is the place to learn things," Julie said. "The place where an actor is sometimes allowed to take chances." He wanted to take chances, and he envisioned *Heavenly Express* as his springboard to risk-taking and renewed success. He was aware of the pitfalls that the play presented. "I'm going to take a good hard shot at this play in which I've sunk a lot of time and thought," he told one reporter at the time. "If it flops after all my loving care I'll be half convinced that the theater is not for me. Then I'll go back to Hollywood, start accumulating possessions, work forty hours a week and settle down."

He had planned to be in New York with the play for six months. He was there less than a month. *Heavenly Express* closed after three weeks. Its failure is not difficult to understand. Bein's track record was not exactly confidence winning; both his previous plays, *Little Old Boy* and *Let Freedom Ring,* had flopped. Bein and Bloomgarden were counting on John Garfield's name to be the selling factor, but that in itself could not overcome the script's deficiencies. The reviews were not kind. "Only Grade B allegory, likewise Grade B Bein," *Variety* wrote. Richard Watts Jr. of *The New York Herald-Tribune* stated that the play was "a vague, hollow and curiously aimless work," adding that it was the first ineffective performance that he had seen Julie give. Brooks Atkinson of *The New York Times,* perhaps overjoyed to see Julie return to the stage, was kinder, but most of his praise went to the actor, not the production: "As the Overland Kid, Mr. Garfield plays with a glow of youth and a touch of Ariel— altogether the most winning angel of death in the theater."

"He loved being in it, but they came to expect something else from it," Robbe explained. That was the irony. Julie had left Hollywood and the gangster roles that the studio had forced upon him only to find that New York audiences were disappointed that he wasn't playing one of life's losers. Audiences weren't ready for John Garfield as a ghostly balladeer who collects the dead. It baffled the critics *and* disappointed audiences. "It's questionable whether it will interest the average playgoer," *Variety* said. It didn't. Julie told everyone that it was worth the effort just to try something different, but the play's failure depressed him so much that he did not even attempt to return to Broadway for another eight years. "He thought it was no use," Robbe said. "Nobody wanted to see him in anything different."

Hollywood wasn't unhappy that he failed. Columnist Louella Parsons wrote, "Now that John has learned his lesson he will come back to the Hollywood he professed to dislike a much chastened young man." Jack Warner was equally content, feeling that Julie's failure would give former stage stars Bogart, Cagney and Robinson food for thought about trying the same thing. Warner quickly planned to put Julie back in prison, if only on film.

Julie saw it coming—but let it be said that he didn't quit easily—and he lobbied for the role of composer George Gershwin in a biographical film that the studio was planning. He really didn't stand a chance. Director Irving Rapper tried to explain why. "He'd be poignant in the part and he'd be great in Allen Street, but do you see him with a high hat and two beautiful girls?" Rapper said. "He (Julie) never wore a tie in his life!" The part of Gershwin went to newcomer Robert Alda (Alan's father). Julie didn't hold it against Alda, but the incident only intensified his displeasure towards Jack Warner.

The relationship between Warner and Garfield was much like that between Warner and just about everyone else on the lot: indifferent at best, horrible at its worst. "Give an actor a break," Warner once said, "and he'll fuck you." When he wanted something from a star Warner could be charming and somewhat generous; when he felt a star was being ungrateful the studio head could turn nasty and tyrannical. Actress Viveca Lindfors, who came to Warner Bros. in the late 1940s, felt that Warner and his underlings had little use for personal relationships: "There was really no need on their part to have a human relationship with anyone on the lot. It was as if they were really afraid to have a relationship with the people they worked with. That was very cold. There was no warmth."

Bob William, one of Warner's key publicity agents, recalled a dinner he had with Warner during which they discussed Julie's situation at the studio. The two sat alone at opposite ends of a very long table—another sign of the distance Warner liked to keep. "Warner had a problem acquiring properties for Garfield, because he (Garfield) wanted to play a dramatic role in a more civilized atmosphere," William said. "He really wanted to play the district attorney or the romantic." Warner wasn't about to line up district attorney roles or romantic leads for Julie. And the actor, who liked to take risks and inject life into three-dimensional characters, was really tiring of playing the same old rebel/loser/convict type. His weariness begins to show by 1940 in films like *Castle on the Hudson* and *East of the River.*

Still, complain as he might about his work, he enjoyed being a movie star. He could tell everyone that he was still Julie Garfinkle from Rivington Street, but as John Garfield he was an internationally known film star, one who was sought out for interviews, parties, opinions and sex. Some of his friends thought Hollywood wrought permanent changes in Julie. Morris Carnovsky would say that Julie simply adapted to the situation as called for: "I think he learned how to dominate every situation. And he learned how to wrangle life in Hollywood."

That wrangling continued to involve extramarital affairs. He could invite a woman into his dressing room for a quickie just as easily as he might try to seduce one in his own home (if Robbe was away). When the pictures he was making were bad and he felt his acting talent was in question, he could always reassure himself by a good performance in bed. There's some truth to director Martin Ritt's comment on Julie's infidelities: "He didn't know how to handle stardom." It wasn't difficult for Julie to simply accept that the women—many of whom hit on him long before he developed a notion to seduce them—came with the territory.

He did comprehend that the affairs were morally wrong. "I've made mistakes," he would later tell publicist Sid Garfield (no relation). "Success came to me when I was too young to evaluate it." That success brought a number of vices. Yet this basically unsophisticated, uneducated, good-hearted waif, cast adrift in a town notorious for its lack of integrity, had become an overnight movie star before he was 25 years old. Aside from amorous women, he was continually encountering the fast-talking agents and producers, the prospective business managers and the intellectual (and sometimes pretentious) screenwriters. "He would have had to be made of iron to withstand it," friend Gerry Schlein said.

Success did bring a certain amount of confidence too. Director Vincent Sherman felt stardom made Julie feel suddenly quite important. This led the actor to voice his opinion more and more, which was fine, except he quite often didn't know what he was talking about. "Suddenly you're a star, and suddenly they start asking you questions about everything," Sherman said. "About politics, about world affairs, economics, philosophy—everything. And they quote you. Well, that gives a young person who is immature the feeling that he is something far greater than he ever thought himself being."

One example: In the spring of 1939 an article in *The New York Daily News* under the headline "Keep U.S. Out of War, Urges John Garfield," quoted Julie as saying, "I wanted to fight to give out the true facts of what's going on, and maybe if every actor did that, we'd have no war to worry about." He urged Hollywood to produce films that promoted pacifism. "Hollywood can play a big part in mobilizing for peace," he went on. "It can make pictures that keep people's minds clear and sane, or it can make pictures that warp the entire nation with distortions and lies." Most likely Julie gave little afterthought to his statements.

Perhaps he wasn't always the brightest guy in the world, but he meant well, and quite often he displayed integrity when he made a political or social stand. When *Heavenly Express* previewed in Washington D.C., Julie took time out to appear as a guest of the National Negro Congress at the Phillis Wheatley YMCA, a segregated organization (for blacks only). He denounced the Jim Crow attitude of the South and urged his audience to band together as one nation. He also urged them to read *Johnny Got His Gun.* Appearing before an all-black audience and calling for equality for all races was not the most popular thing for a movie star to do in 1940 (name another film star of the era who would take that risk). But if Julie felt the urge to spout off about things he was uninformed about in press interviews, then let it be said that he also used his newfound fame to speak out on behalf of those less fortunate than himself.

If he was anti-war in 1938 and 1939, it was because he was following Robbe's lead. But in August 1939, when the famous nonaggression peace pact was signed between Russian leader Joseph Stalin and Adolph Hitler, Julie—and a lot of his peers—began leaning towards American intervention in the war. By the summer of 1940 Hitler had conquered Poland, Norway, Denmark, Luxembourg, Holland, Belgium and half of France. By the beginning of 1941, Britain was pretty much standing alone against the Nazi juggernaut. To a lot of the left-leaning communist sympathizers, Stalin's signature on the nonaggression pact meant appeasement. Robbe wanted to validate Stalin's decision, though she didn't know how. Julie neither condemned nor condoned Stalin's decision at the time. It's probably fair to state that he gave no thought to his own political actions. Sometimes he liked to talk for the sake of talking, and he could always find reasons to qualify his comments. "I pay taxes," he once said. "Exercising the rights of citizenship is an American principle. If I don't exercise them, why have them?"

Julie discovered he had fewer rights to exercise at Warner Bros., however. His next film, *Flowing Gold,* directed by Alfred E. Green, relegated him to second feature status, which clearly signified how far and fast his screen career was falling. *Flowing Gold* is a B action film loosely based on a Rex Beach story about two guys, a girl and an oil well, with Julie and Pat O'Brien as the two guys and Frances Farmer as the girl. Despite its status, *Flowing Gold*, shot quickly in the summer of 1940, is enjoyable in a campy sort of way. The structure is weak but the film moves like lightning, thanks to the actors' performances and some spirited direction from Green. It may not seem like a better film than *Castle on the Hudson* or *They Made Me a Criminal,* but it is a lot more fun to watch. Slick dialogue spits out like tacks on an upholstery assembly line and there's a raucous bar brawl, an amusing scene with Julie watching Farmer flail around in the mud (later immortalized in the 1983 bio-pic *Frances*), a bizarre romantic subplot involving a ukulele player and an overweight woman, and a wonderfully corny finale wherein Julie saves the day with a crane. In terms of characterization, John Garfield was still on the run, not from the law, but from Warner Bros. "You got some chip on your shoulder," a burly character says to Julie early on in the film. "Wanna try to knock it off?" our star responds, ready for a fight.

"*Mr. Garfield is still Mr. Garfield,*" *The New York Times* noted, "which is good enough to make one wish that his producers would cease casting him in the same role film after film." While the reviewers were finding it more difficult to be kind to Julie's career, there is no indication that the public was tiring of the "John Garfield film" at this time. All of the actor's films—except for *Saturday's Children*—turned a tidy profit for Warner Bros.

Working with Frances Farmer must have been some consolation for Julie. The shine on her star was dulling, and *Flowing Gold* was a comedown for her. And following her work on *Flowing Gold,* Farmer began a slow slide into despair; within two years she was arrested for public intoxication, and her mother had committed her to a mental institution. There the actress suffered degradation at the hands of other inmates and the guards. In her autobiography, *Will There Really Be A Morning?,* Farmer made little mention of John Garfield or *Flowing Gold,* but their scenes together truly sparkle.

The film gave the studio writers another chance to have some fun at Julie's expense. After the first week of rushes, Julie received an official memo, typed on Jack Warner's letterhead, which read:

> Dear Julie—have just seen your first week of rushes and never, in all my years in the business, have I seen such in-

credible hammy acting. Who do you think you are, another goddamned Muni?

The letter, signed by Jack Warner, went on to suggest that Julie could be replaced by "a good actor, perhaps Ronald Reagan."

Furious, Julie stormed to Warner's office to tell him where to stick the letter. Warner wasn't around, but two of the studio's writers were. They simply laughed as Julie described the letter to them. He caught on fast and laughed with them, telling them that he knew it was a gag all along. They knew better.

After finishing *Flowing Gold* he reported immediately to another set on the back lot to play in *East of the River,* which had started out some time back as *Bad Boy.* The script had haunted Julie, like the fates haunted Mickey Borden, yet the actor felt there was no sense in fighting. Simply put, the story has a gangster and a lawyer as brothers, a girl in between them, and a loving mother who tries to make things right. The lawyer gets the girl; the gangster gets a prison term. The film, arguably Julie's worst, is mediocre and barely worth mentioning.

During filming, the actor lived up to his reputation as one of the bad boys of the Warner lot. He blew take after take, conveniently forgetting his lines, giving about 50 percent of himself in every scene. He called in sick a lot, once telling the studio that he had a cold sore on his lip. Jack Warner called Julie up to his office for a private chat, which probably wasn't pleasant. Julie said he didn't mind performing in a crime drama now and then, but couldn't the studio alternate that sort of thing with some really meaty, offbeat roles? Warner reminded him that Rims Rosen in *Saturday's Children* and Porfiro Diaz in *Juarez* had been meaty, offbeat roles, and neither film set the box office on fire. Unfortunately, Warner had a point. With Julie's Mickey Borden roles, the studio had, perhaps, created something of a Frankenstein's monster, but audiences were demanding more of the same. Julie returned to the set and finished the shoot without further complaint.

"Julie always tried to make the best of it," Robbe recalled. "He had to accept it, in a way. It was his livelihood, and a damn good livelihood at that. We lived very nicely and our families lived very nicely. And that was part of it—the money."

The money was a big part of it. So was the fact that Julie couldn't relax. He loved to work. He told reporter Charles Darnton, "To work successfully the actor must keep everlastingly at it. I still have to do things in pictures I don't want to do in order to be able to do the things I want to do." But he must have wondered whether it was all balancing out. In 1940 he made *Castle on the Hudson*, *Flowing Gold* and *East of the River* in order to have the freedom to do *Saturday's Children* and *Heavenly Express*. The first three mediocrities were all financial successes; the latter two, whatever their merits, disappointed at the box office. To date, 1940 was the lowest point of John Garfield's professional career. And he turned down two other poor scripts, *Flight Angels* and *A Child Is Born,* that same year.

It was also the year that Humphrey Bogart began moving up the ranks at Warner Bros. Cagney and Robinson were still at the peak of their film careers there, and George Raft, despite minimal acting talent, was developing into a top box-office draw for the studio. In terms of rank, John Garfield was behind Cagney, Robinson and Raft and probably on equal footing with Bogart. He no longer seemed like the studio's exciting new find. He was becoming more and more like just another face on their contract player list, and one could wonder whether he really wasn't just a character actor who had somehow been thrust into a position of stardom.

And yet by playing to this very strength, he began turning things around. He was a character actor, and a good one, capable of breaking out of the stereotyping that Hollywood forced upon him. Looking at the Garfield body of work from 1941 through 1944, one realizes that he made a decision somewhere to segue (quite easily and successfully) into the category of supporting player, without really stepping back. Taking second billing to bigger stars in big pictures—which is sort of the case with *Four Daughters*—would offer him serious acting challenges and allow him to revitalize his box-office power.

"The only way to protect a career is to appear in good material," he said around this time. Though happenstance, he got some good material. Warner Bros. had bought the rights to Jack London's novel *The Sea Wolf* in 1938, hoping that Paul Muni would play Captain Wolf Larson. The material was still sitting on the shelf until producer Hal B. Wallis revitalized it as a vehicle for Edward G. Robinson two years later. Robert Rossen, who had penned *Dust Be My Destiny*, was given the chore of adapting the novel to the screen. Michael Curtiz would direct. The script contained two strong supporting male roles: Van Weyden, the writer who slowly earns Larson's respect, and George Leach, a rebellious sailor who fights against Larson's tyranny. Stage actor Alexander Knox was cast as Van Weyden (both Jeffrey Lynn and Arthur Kennedy tested for the role) and he proved to complement Robinson well. Warner hoped that George Raft would play Leach, but the actor wasn't impressed with the script. Turning the role down, Raft wrote Wallis, "This is little better than a bit part." Jerry Wald, a young screenwriter who was hired to assist Rossen, suggested Julie for the role of Leach. ("They were both 'deese, dem' and dos' type of guys," publicist Bob William said of Wald and Garfield.) Julie wanted the role; he had actually read some Jack London novels and said he felt a kinship to the author. Jack Warner consented; he wanted to get his young rebel before the cameras again.

The making of *The Sea Wolf* was a happy experience for everyone involved. Julie became close friends with Robinson, who would end up serving as another father figure. The older actor tried to impart a sense of culture to Julie, giving him a crash course in the history of art (Robinson amassed one of the most impressive art collections in Hollywood), while passing on some tips on how to deal with Warner executives.

In the field of malapropisms, Julie found a peer in Curtiz. Describing the story of *The Sea Wolf* to the attentive cast one day,

Curtiz broke into tears and claimed that the scenes would be so exciting that they "would make your blood curl." He wasn't much
help to Julie when it came to the film's love scenes with Ida Lupino
(playing a female convict who somehow happens on board). "You
love her, see?" Curtiz said, in a manner befitting Chico Marx. "You
are crazy for her. It happened all of a sudden. You don't understand
it. So you love her. There. Now you do it." Julie was befuddled. Another day, a prop man told Curtiz that the water in the storm scenes
was too noisy for the sound equipment. "Can't help it," Curtiz
replied. "We only got hard water in California."

The Sea Wolf stands as a well-constructed testament to the studio
system of yesteryear. The screenplay manages to remain faithful to
London in retelling the story of a demented superhuman, a brute
cursed with the ability to think, who believes that it is "better to
reign in Hell than serve in Heaven." Robinson and Knox were terrific, both overshadowing Julie's supporting role as Leach. Despite
an opening sequence that suggested Julie was about to play another
fugitive rebel (he is seen dashing about street corners in the fog), his
George Leach is a determined optimist, much like Julie himself.
"You gotta fight, you can't quit," he tells Lupino at one point. "It's
something in me that tells me I gotta keep on fighting, that tells me
there is something for people like us." Leach keeps on fighting and,
in a memorably chilling climax, finds an escape for himself and
Lupino while both Knox and Robinson go down with the ship .

Released in May 1941, *The Sea Wolf* was a tremendous success.
Crowther of *The New York Times* wrote, "When *The Sea Wolf* is
topside, it rolls along ruthlessly and draws a forbidding picture of
oppressive life at sea, of a captain who rules his men without mercy
and without heart." Julie, Crowther noted, played his part with
"concentrated spite." His spite was probably aimed at Warner Bros.

Jack Warner always said he was searching for good material for
his youngest rogue, but the truth is he generally ended up sending
Julie scripts that were hand-me-downs. George Raft, for instance,
had turned down *East of the River* and *The Sea Wolf*. His first

Warner film was 1939's *Each Dawn I Die,* a prison saga which teamed him with James Cagney. Raft imbued his roles with a sense of cool detachment that only carried him so far. As an actor he was limited and he made no discernible effort to get better. But in Warner films like *Invisible Stripes* (1939), *They Drive By Night* (1940) and *Manpower* (1941) he proved to be a potent box-office draw. Still, he was no judge of material. While he was wise enough to turn down stinkers like *It All Came True* (a Bogart vehicle) and *East of the River,* Raft also passed on classics like *The Sea Wolf* and *The Maltese Falcon* (the latter cemented Bogart's stardom). Raft would leave Warner Bros. in 1942, and his star faded away by the end of the decade. And yet, at the end of 1940, Julie and Bogart were running neck and neck behind Raft at the studio. Bogart had not yet achieved stardom, but the studio saw him as having potential; oddly enough, Julie was for some reason considered low man on the totem pole. An illuminating story circulating about this time had producer Hal B. Wallis telling Bogart, "Look, you want Raft's roles. Raft wants Eddie Robinson's roles, Robinson wants Muni's roles."

"That's simple," Bogart is reported to have shot back, "All I do is bump off Muni and we all move up a step." A funny line, but note that John Garfield's name is not included in the story.

Julie had his defenders. Sticking by the writers' table had garnered him roles in *Four Daughters, Juarez, Saturday's Children* and *The Sea Wolf.* When he heard that Warner Bros. had bought the film rights to Irwin Shaw's *The Gentle People* (which he had turned down on Broadway), he began lobbying for the role of Goff. He had to wait his place in line, however, behind Cagney, Raft and Bogart. Cagney and Raft turned it down. Bogart wanted it. He had just completed a minor gangster film, *High Sierra,* that turned out to be his first unqualified hit, and he was beginning to flex his muscles on the lot. "It seems to me that I am the logical person on the lot to play Gentle People," Bogart wired Jack Warner. "I would be greatly disappointed if I didn't get it." Bogart could have—and probably should have—played the role, but a number of factors played a hand in Julie getting the lead. For one thing producer Hal B. Wallis and screenwriter Jerry Wald both liked Julie. Further, Ida Lupino was playing the female lead, Stella Goodwin. Lupino had acted opposite Bogart in *High Sierra* and reportedly didn't enjoy the experience. On the lot, the rumor was that Lupino didn't want to work with Bogart again, and that she vetoed his casting. Whether she had that sort of power at Warner Bros. in 1941 is questionable; 50 years later she would deny that she had. But Bogart had played a ribald joke on Lupino that earned him her rancor. Ann Sheridan later told the funny story of how Bogart had talked Lupino into lobbying Jack Warner for the rights to the novel *The Memoirs of Fanny Hill*. Bogart told the actress that the story was a classic; one that every female star in Hollywood was yearning for. Lupino had never read the book; still she begged Warner to attain the rights for her. Only later did she realize that Fanny Hill was one of the most renowned madams in history, and that her memoirs were extremely erotic. The story made Lupino something of a joke on the Warner lot, and she wasn't amused. For whatever reason, Bogart missed out on the film and Julie found himself with his first strong leading role in some time. He began shooting *Out of the Fog* (the film title for *The Gentle People*) in February 1941.

The Gentle People of Shaw's play are two kindly fishermen, Jonah and Olaf (played on film by Thomas Mitchell and John Qualen), who just want to live out their lives peacefully, dreaming of the day when they'll run a larger fishing operation. Along comes Goff (Garfield), a gangster with no past, who offers them "protection" in exchange for extortion money. The two fishermen refuse to cooperate, so Goff sets about destroying their property, seducing Jonah's pretty daughter Stella (Lupino) along the way. Unable to get help from the law, Jonah and Olaf decide to kill Goff. The gangster has one weakness: he can not swim. So the duo take him for a boat ride across the bay under the pretense of negotiating with him. But the two are pacifists and can't bring themselves to commit murder. Goff catches on to their scheme and decides to kill them, but in attempting to turn the tables on them in the rocking boat, Goff falls overboard and drowns. The pair return to shore expecting to be arrested but discover that no one really misses Goff.

Is it a fable about fascism and the rise of the Nazis and how pacifists must be roused from their sleep? Shaw himself said of the play, "It's a fairy tale with a moral. In it justice triumphs and the meek prove victorious over arrogant and violent men." The political parallels were not lost on the film's star. In an interview with the *Boston Daily Record* Julie said, "The film has something important to say. It shows how men such as I portray are kicked around until eventually they turn against society, adopting the Fascist idea of seizing what they want."

One of the screenplay's flaws is that it doesn't offer much of a substantive backstory to explain how Goff was kicked around by society. Julie has to portray an almost entirely unsympathetic character, one who is difficult to like. After playing a good supporting role in *The Sea Wolf*, it's likely that Julie saw *Out of the Fog* as a comeback film, a way to reclaim his leading man position in A pictures at the studio. But the film didn't generate the excitement that the studio hoped for. Perhaps audiences were not ready to accept Julie as a totally unlikable villain, although preview cards had indicated that the film would be a hit. Many critics were nonetheless pleased to see him tackle something different. Howard Barnes felt that the film was "a work of genuine distinction" and said Julie gave "what is unquestionably his greatest screen portrayal as the petty hoodlum who turns gentle people into killers."

Warner Bros. didn't agree with Barnes. One day Wallis sent director Anatole Litvak an angry memo in which he complained about Julie's acting. "He lapses into the Group Theater type of performance," Wallis wrote, urging Litvak to get "more life" into the actor. Litvak paid no more attention to this memo than he did to studio pleas that he speed up filming. Like Michael Curtiz, Litvak knew what he wanted, and he was going to take his time getting it. After watching another week's worth of rushes, Wallis shot off another diatribe to Litvak regarding Julie: "Garfield is chewing up all the scenery in the place. He is becoming a thoroughly unreal character." During the filming of *Saturday's Children,* similar memos from Wallis had complained about Julie's tendency to underplay scenes; now he was griping about overplaying.

Looking at the film today, it's easier to side with Wallis than with Litvak or Barnes. Julie gives what is basically a one-dimensional performance full of hammy moments. Litvak did not keep Julie in check, and the actor goes over the top—way over the top—throughout the film. Some actors can get away with going over the top— Cagney and Burt Lancaster, for example, but Garfield rarely could. One has to wonder what Bogart could have brought to the role, or what Garfield might have done under the direction of Michael Curtiz. As it is, the film as a whole remains stage-bound, lacking movement or excitement. Call *Out of the Fog* an interesting failure if you will, but it was (and is) a failure all the same.

Accidents plagued the shoot. Julie told a visiting reporter that as a young street kid he never hesitated to pick on innocent bystanders. Perhaps he was waxing romantic, seeing shades of himself in the character of Goff, but he ended up playing the role a bit too convincingly. In a scene calling for Goff to knock down Stella's boyfriend, played by actor Eddie Albert, Julie didn't pull his punch, and Albert was knocked hard and fast against a box on the set. Albert began bleeding and had to be rushed to the hospital. Fortunately the injuries were not too serious. Later still, in the studio's water tank, Julie fired the prop gun too close to his head and fell prematurely from the rowboat into the deep. He surfaced with powder burns on his face and hair, and another day of shooting was lost.

The financial failure of *Out of the Fog* reinforced the studio's notion that there was a certain formula to follow when it came to a John Garfield film. To Jack Warner and company, the film's disappointing box office returns validated their belief that the public only wanted to see Julie as a rebel or a loser or a low-life gangster on the run. *Out of the Fog* was a step back. Now the studio offered Julie another B, a drama about jazz players called *Blues in the Night*. Julie turned it down, and the studio, in turn, put him on suspension. This meant he would spend time at home, without drawing pay, until he came around and did what the studio wanted. (*Blues in the Night* is memorable in only one sense: it provided Elia Kazan with the second and last acting role of his film career.)

So Julie took the summer of 1941 off without pay and spent the time with Robbe and Katherine. The Garfields also moved again, first to Van Nuys, then back to Beverly Hills, where they rented a house on Doheny Drive. Julie filled the bookshelves with volumes he said he was going to read, including a collection of Hebrew Scripture. Whether he was sincere or not is another matter altogether; he liked to act as if he was more educated than he really was. He said his favorite books were Stanislavsky's *An Actor Prepares,* anything by Jack London, and Romain Rolland's *Jean Christophe.* "It's my favorite theme," he said of the last book, "the struggle of the artist with his archenemy, the World." He probably had read the Stanislavsky book, as well as the Jack London novels, but it's doubtful he tackled Rolland. Robbe confirmed that Julie mostly read plays and film scripts.

In these early Hollywood days, the Garfields enjoyed hosting some "deliciously wild parties," as Robbe put it. There was always ample food and drink on hand, and if a guest became too intoxicated to drive home (or wake up) he could always find a room to sleep in the Garfield home. And no one seemed to mind when someone swimming in the pool "lost" their bathing suit. It was Hollywood in the years before the war, and everyone was happy. At these parties, a couple of guys were always sitting in the corner playing cards, and more often than not, Julie was one of those guys. He continued to gamble and he continued to lose.

That summer of 1941 gave Julie and Robbe time to get politically involved again. They entertained some soldiers from nearby Fort MacArthur, and worked with the Chinese Industrial Cooperatives, another innocuous sounding organization that later had the label

"Red Front" pinned on it, to support Chinese leader Chiang Kai-Shek in his fight against the invading Japanese. (When Madame Chiang Kai-Shek visited Warner Bros. on a fund-raising tour, Jack Warner committed one of his most famous gaffes. After Kai-Shek made a speech at the Executive Dining Room thanking Jack Warner for his generosity, Warner stood up, looked her in the eye and said, "Gee, that reminds me, I forgot to take in the laundry.")

The Garfields were living so well that they hired a cook and a maid and a nurse for Katherine. Robbe still wanted to do most of the cooking, and Julie still enjoyed eating that cooking. When Julie was on suspension and had more free time between films, he would often eat so much food that he would have to go on a forced diet to drop the added weight before the next film started production. He was never picky about food; eating almost anything. He was not, however, a heavy drinker in these early Hollywood years. He drank to be sociable, preferring whiskey and scotch, the hard stuff, and usually passed out after imbibing about three drinks.

During this time Julie was forging a stronger bond with his in-laws than he'd had with his own parents. The Seidmans no longer considered him a "bum," so Robbe invited Max and Lena to come to Hollywood for a visit and the Garfields threw a huge party for them. Julie invited several Warner Bros. stars and contract players to the party. Julie was so taken with Robbe's parents that he introduced them to everyone as his own father and mother. Max Seidman, in turn, hit up all the Warner celebrities for autographs.

It was a good summer for the Garfields. When their marriage was tested by Julie's infidelities, his neighbor, artist Charlie Schlein, would take him to the mountains for some rest and relaxation. Julie confided to Schlein about his infidelities and talked about how much he loved Robbe and Katherine. "What was really important to Julie," said Charlie's wife Gerry, "was his marriage and his family. He was a good father. He loved his daughter. His marriage may have been rocky at times, but he loved Robbe. I think she was solid. He depended on her a great deal. She was a center that he could hold on to."

The one word most widely used to describe Robbe is *strong*, and perhaps she was too strong for Julie's good. Actress Viveca Lindfors, for one, believed this. "She was so strong that he probably didn't want her around," Lindfors said. "I mean, he was a weak sort of character in some ways." One can accept Lindfors' analysis in light of Julie's tendency to give in to temptation. He also took people at their word, placing a lot of faith in near-strangers. This undying faith led him to put his business affairs in the hands of another father figure, the man who would eventually lead Julie towards creating an independent production company, one Bob Roberts.

Roberts was an insurance salesman whose gift of gab made it easy to break into the Hollywood social circle. He didn't know a thing about the movie business, but he wanted to learn, and he talked a good talk. It's difficult to dig out any background information on Roberts. He was about five years older than Julie, and may have hailed from New York. The two had met at a poker game there in 1941, and Roberts offered to become Julie's manager, promising to help the actor secure the type of roles that he desired. Roberts had a knack for instilling confidence in other people, and he began encouraging Julie to break away from Warner Bros. (an impossible dream in 1941). Taken by Roberts' smooth-talking manner, Julie hired him as his manager, though he maintained an agent as well. Robbe, among others, had her suspicions about Roberts: "I didn't distrust him, really. It was a money thing. He latched onto Julie. He thought he could use Julie in some way, and Julie felt he was a good business manager. Roberts became his...everything."

He took over Julie's financial affairs. According to Gerry Schlein, Roberts urged the Garfields *never* to buy property in California as real estate prices would surely drop in the long run. He was left-wing, to put it mildly, and like Robbe he urged Julie to sign his name to various political petitions during this time. Whatever his failings, Roberts did have Julie's best professional interests at heart. Working in tandem with Julie's new agent, Lew Wasserman of MCA, Roberts managed to help secure a new contract with Warner

Bros. That contract gave Julie the right to work at other studios in lieu of a pay raise. This turned out to be a smart move, as did Julie's decision to play supporting roles, as he had in *The Sea Wolf.* Julie knew that he wouldn't have much of a film career left if he didn't fight for it.

Robbe could be hard on Julie's film acting. She taunted him about the mediocrity of his movies, and his willingness to appear in assembly-line potboilers. "You sit here, dashing off one part after another," she would chide, "It's beginning to look easy!" In truth, Julie's approach to film acting became casual and loose. Preparation for a scene—a given during his years with the Group Theatre—was shunned off in favor of a quick read and a few takes. (Though, to be fair, that was the studio system manner.) And while Robbe often supported Julie in his battle for better scripts at Warner Bros., she wondered at the same time if he wasn't hurting his career more by accepting suspension time. This unusual contradiction in personality was typical of Robbe's nature. "She didn't like Hollywood much," Phoebe Brand explained, "but she liked to live well, and they lived well."

It was Robbe who held the marriage together. When she believed in Julie, he somehow found the strength to strive for greater things. And if others in the Hollywood community did not take him seriously, Robbe did. That she tolerated his repeated extramarital affairs is amazing, but she was attracted to him and loved him very much. Their own sex life, according to at least one male friend, was quite good. The marriage survived Julie's infidelities mainly because Robbe possessed an amazing amount of patience and strength. And she came to understand early on that sex was part of the Hollywood picture. She certainly wasn't the only wife in Hollywood whose husband was cheating. (Whether Robbe indulged in any affairs herself is another question altogether.)

When Julie was happy at work, he was happy at home. But being a movie star wasn't enough to satisfy him. He wanted to be an acclaimed actor. "I signed a long picture deal," he told columnist

William Hawkins. "I found I was tied up in something I hadn't bargained for. It was the same sort of role, over and over, with no power of selection. But with it, of course, good money and safety. You find yourself satisfied with a job no worse than the last one. But the time comes when you stop and say, 'Is this what I want or is this something I can grow on?'" His growth as an actor had stopped. Within a year this would change, but in 1941 Julie was still another worker on the Warner Bros. assembly line.

That assembly line lured him back from his suspension with a story about Nazi saboteurs who try to force a female British agent to reveal national secrets while confining her to a Long Island estate under the pretense that she is ill. Far-fetched, maybe, but *Dangerously They Live* ("and that's the way they love," the ads proclaimed) was written to catch the wave of anti-Japanese and anti-German sentiment that was sweeping America. It remains a routine film, but Julie accepted it because he got to play a different type of role—as a medical intern with an eye for the ladies and fists geared for action. Raymond Massey and Moroni Olsen were the cultured bad guys. Newcomer Nancy Coleman was the British agent. Coleman had just completed *King's Row,* a real gem, and she recalled that neither she nor Julie really wanted to make *Dangerously They Live.* But there was little they could do. "I doubt complaining would have done any good," she said.

Coleman, like several of Julie's costars, said she never really got to know who John Garfield was. She rarely saw him on the lot unless they were shooting a scene from the film, and outside of their scenes together he had little to say to her. And then, near the end of filming, he called her up and asked her for a date, the sort of date that lasts all weekend and doesn't lead to anything more when it's over. "Of course I turned him down," Coleman said. "He had such a reputation."

Dangerously They Live, directed by Robert Florey, proved timely in one respect: The film included the plot device of an enemy sub lying off of the coast of Long Island, and not long after the film was released late in 1941, a German U-boat was sighted off of Long Island. (One critic joked that the Nazis must have taken their cue from the film.) Nancy Coleman saw the film as "another assignment." Julie must have shared her view. The film moves so fast that you don't have time to consider all the plot holes (there are secret panels, gunfights in hallways, the works), which make the film passably enjoyable.

Julie cooperated fully with publicity for this film. He made public appearances at film theaters in which he would recite the piano monologue from *Four Daughters* (a sad reminder of better days) or play in a comedy skit written by a studio contract writer. In those uncertain days preceding the country's involvement in World War II, *Dangerously They Lived* found a willing audience in Americans who wanted to see the Nazis get theirs (on screen, at least). "Strictly B-hive honey," *The Richmond New Leader*'s critic wrote of the film. Other critics begged Warner Bros. to give Julie another chance to show what he had to offer.

Completing *Dangerously They Live* capped an intense three and a half years of steady work for Julie. Never again would he have to work so steadily on material that was beneath his talents. He had survived the worst films of his career. There were changes ahead for him, for Hollywood and for the world.

CHAPTER TEN

The War Years

*"The only Japs I've ever seen are those slant-
eyes at Atlantic City. Those Japs always did
look slimy. Yep, shootin' Japs oughta be fun."*
—AL SCHMID (JOHN GARFIELD) IN
PRIDE OF THE MARINES (1945)

ASIDE FROM HIS DUTIES AS PUBLICITY MAN AT WARNER
Bros., Bob William was also responsible for exercising Errol
Flynn's two stallions. On the morning of December 7, 1941,
William was riding one of the horses in the Hollywood
Hills, not far from Flynn's La Jolla Drive ranch house. As he
rode past a small house, he heard the voice of radio an-
nouncer H.B. Carleton Bohem booming out of the window,
"This unprovoked attack on Pearl Harbor means war with
Japan." William swung the horse around and galloped back
to Flynn's corral, arriving to find Flynn, clad in a silk robe
and smoking a cigarette, standing outside. William reined
in the horse a bit too quickly and fell off at Flynn's feet. As
William rose, Flynn looked at him and said, quite simply,
"Bob ol' boy, this could be serious."

It was about 10 A.M. when Hollywood heard the news
about Pearl Harbor. America declared war on Japan the following day, and three days later Germany declared war on
America. Warner Bros. had a makeshift bomb shelter built
on the studio grounds overnight that several former employees insist was intended strictly for Warner Bros. executives. Air raid drills and blackouts became commonplace,

and soon the city of dreams was roused out of its slumber by the sound of coastal and anti-aircraft artillery firing at would-be Japanese bombers. Most of these bombers turned out to be errant barrage balloons.

Hollywood went to war, literally and cinematically. James Stewart, Clark Gable, Robert Taylor, David Niven, Victor Mature, Henry Fonda and Tyrone Power, among others, all enlisted. Four of Warner Bros. "stars of tomorrow"—Ronald Reagan, Jeffrey Lynn, Wayne Morris and Eddie Albert—departed for military service shortly thereafter. Julie hoped to join them.

Following his work on *Dangerously They Live* (but before the attack on Pearl Harbor), Julie was approached by theatrical producer Eddie Dowling about joining an entertainment troupe called The Flying Showboat. The troupe would tour American military bases on the East Coast and in the Caribbean. Dowling had already assembled Laurel and Hardy, dancer Ray Bolger, dancer Mitzi Mayfair, singer/actress Jane Pickens and Chico Marx (sans brothers Groucho and Harpo) for the troupe. Dowling wanted Julie to act as emcee. The tour, which would play Maryland, Florida, Puerto Rico, Antigua, Santa Lucia, Trinidad and British Guiana, was the first of its kind during World War II. Julie, eager to do what he could for servicemen, and prompted equally by the disillusionment with his film career, agreed to emcee. Jack Warner didn't protest.

The troupe left New York in November 1941. To put the entertainers at ease about the potential hazards involved in flying in a B-18, the pilots would ask one of the comedians to try on a parachute and have them clown around with it. Julie realized that this was a casual way of teaching the troupers how to don a parachute should the need arise. The production format was loose, props and musical instruments sparse. Julie would say a few words about how proud the country was of the boys in uniform and recite a dramatic piece, "The Jervis Boy Goes Down," written by Gene Fowler. Then he would tell some jokes—if one could call them jokes. "How many of you are from the South?" Julie would ask the crowds of GIs. The

Southerners in the audience would let out a raucous response. "I meant south of Brooklyn!" Julie cracked back.

The troupers performed in hangars, open fields, under and on the wings of airplanes, anywhere. The lack of technical support didn't matter to any of them. They were connecting to an appreciative audience desperate for entertainment. Temperatures in the Caribbean often broke 100, and it felt more like 150. Gnats and mosquitoes swarmed around the performers during lunch; Julie often found bugs in his food and sometimes in his mouth as he went to swallow. The tour gave all the entertainers a sense of what the servicemen were experiencing, isolated perhaps as they were on a remote island waiting for a war that might never come their way.

Julie enjoyed the tour. "I intend to go to the Screen Actors Guild and all studio heads I can reach and urge that some system be set up whereby actors and actresses can have the opportunity to give their between-picture time to entertaining servicemen," he said when he returned with the troupe to New York in early December. Julie felt that he could never do enough for the guys on the front line. Years later HUAC would overlook such patriotic actions when grilling Julie about his wartime activities.

President Roosevelt was impressed. Elected to an unprecedented third term in November 1940 (Bob Hope would quip, "It's not every day that Roosevelt is elected President. It just seems like it."), FDR wanted to recognize John Garfield's contribution. He invited the actor to the White House for a small reception in December. Julie was awestruck by the president and all the White House trimmings. FDR was surrounded by a contingent of Secret Service men and a line of servants and major-domos. Julie shook the president's hand, and then kept working his way down the line, greeting everyone in uniform, totally unaware that he was chatting with domestic help and not naval officers. He was still the kid from Rivington Street.

He returned to Hollywood to discover that MGM wanted to borrow him. Author John Steinbeck, an acquaintance of Julie's, had suggested him for the role of Danny in MGM's film version of

Steinbeck's novel *Tortilla Flat,* to be directed by Victor Fleming. The novel told of a neighborhood of lazy Californian fishermen in a sleepy seaside town. Spencer Tracy was set to play Pilan and Hedy Lamarr was slated to play Dolores. Jack Warner didn't want to let him go. Julie read the script and wanted to do it; he even threatened to leave for Europe as a war correspondent if Warner didn't let him go. The threat may have been an idle one, but Warner gave in, lending Julie to MGM in return for the services of Hedy Lamarr. Besides, Warner would benefit from the $5,000 per week salary MGM would pay them to use him because Julie was then earning $2,000 per week for Warners. The studio would pocket the other $3,000 and make a profit of $30,000 over the ten weeks Julie was at MGM.

For Julie to play Danny in *Tortilla Flat* was a gamble of sorts, a stretch that Warner Bros. would no longer let him take on the home lot. And stretch is a good word to use when describing *Tortilla Flat.* It proves to be a very easy-to-take movie but leaves little lasting impression. Danny is a simple Mexican paisano who inherits two houses and a watch from his late grandfather. With logic that would make Abbott and Costello proud, Pilan convinces Danny to trade the watch for three gallons of wine. Pilan and his friends accidentally burn down the first of Danny's houses. Then they move into the second house. Danny, meanwhile, falls for the fiery Dolores. She wants Danny to get a job. "I got no time for work," Danny says, while laying about strumming his guitar. But to impress Dolores he trades in his guitar for a vacuum cleaner, even though her house does not have electricity. Pilan steals the vacuum cleaner and trades it for more wine. There is much drinking and sleeping and singing. Actor Frank Morgan shows up as an old hermit named Pirate who loves dogs more than humans. Pilan starts trouble between Danny and Dolores. The two men have a falling out. Danny gets drunk and suffers a life-threatening accident in a fishing cannery. Pilan, feeling guilty, promises to repent if Danny's life is spared. Danny recovers and marries Dolores. He gives his second house to Pilan. Within a matter of minutes, Pilan and his friends manage to burn down that house too. Fade out.

While neither Julie nor Spencer Tracy are totally convincing as Mexican-Americans, they both give the film their all and the end result is undeniably charming. It's just the sort of film where nothing much happens. The supporting cast, which includes Allen Jenkins, Akim Tamiroff, John Qualen and Sheldon Leonard (all playing Hispanics!), is terrific. Julie knew the cast was full of hams. "I tried to steal scenes from Hedy, Hedy tried to steal them from Spencer Tracy, Tracy tried to steal them from Frank Morgan, Morgan tried to steal from me, and the dogs stole the show," Julie said after he saw the film. He was right about dogs, but Morgan took a fair share of the accolades at the time. The venerable actor, who played the title role in the 1939 classic *The Wizard of Oz*, garnered an Academy Award Nomination for Best Supporting Actor for his work in *Tortilla Flat*.

Danny would remain one of Julie's favorite roles. "Getting something like this, something so real you can reach out and put your hand on it, is like going back to the stage," he told journalist Charles Darnton. He developed a respectful professional relationship with Tracy, who was, along with Cary Grant, the biggest male star Julie ever worked with in film. For Julie, Tracy proved to be a good acting partner, for he liked to ad-lib or throw a curve into the scripted dialogue to see what sort of color he could bring to a scene. But the two men would not become friends. "You get to know people very well during the making of a film," director Abraham Polonsky said. "But two weeks after a film is over, your passions go elsewhere." As for Julie's relationship with the beautiful Hedy Lamarr, perhaps his nickname for her—Wildcat—hints at an intimate relationship. Lamarr's rather explicit 1965 autobiography makes no mention of an affair with Garfield, but the on-screen chemistry between the two stars led the Hollywood gossip mill to believe the two were involved.

Tortilla Flat proved to be a very mild commercial success, opening to passable reviews and equally passable box office in the spring of 1942. "One of his better performances," *Variety's* critic said of Julie's work in the film. But in a year where just about everyone was going to the movies, the star-packed *Tortilla Flat* was a commercial disappointment. It would remind everyone that John Garfield was capable of solid character work, but it still didn't make Warner Bros. want to offer him anything remotely similar. Julie would forever consider the film one of his best. "He would always talk about that film," actor Robert Brown, a friend of Garfield's, said. "I knew the song he sang from that film, 'Mrs. Morales,' and he and I would go from bar to bar in New York, singing it together."

Julie completed *Tortilla Flat* early in 1942 and then tried to enlist. He was rated 4-F due to a heart murmur. At 29 he was a health risk. As if to prove that he was fit, he took to the tennis courts the day after his physical results came in, playing set after set of tennis. Actress Geraldine Fitzgerald retained a distinct memory of a man trying desperately to push his physical strength to the limit. "He had a bad heart," she recalled, "But he still wouldn't slow down. He was always playing tennis, always doing something strenuous, as if he was trying to overcome this limitation. I thought it was very odd." Robbe found it sad. "He just couldn't relax," she would say years later.

If he couldn't serve in the armed forces, he'd do the next best thing: entertain. He joined a USO tour that played up and down the East Coast. At Fort Monmouth in New Jersey, he came across Army Corporal Jeffrey Lynn, and they paired up to appear in a comic sketch spoofing their screen images. Lynn would soon head overseas. Julie wanted to go with him. "I'll catch up to you pretty soon," he told Lynn. He probably meant it, but Lynn sensed that it would never happen.

Then Julie made a bond-selling tour drive through New England, selling nearly five million dollars in war bonds. He purchased $50,000 worth of bonds himself. He also made generous contributions to such patriotic organizations as the Marine Canteen, the Red Cross, the Royal Air Force Fund, and the Boy Scouts. He visited

New York's Stage Door Canteen, where soldiers could get a bite to eat and see visiting celebrities. Julie reasoned that a similar organization, located in Hollywood, could be an even bigger draw. Upon returning there he approached Bette Davis, who was good at getting what she wanted, and asked her to help him form the Hollywood Canteen. With the considerable talents of Jules Stein (then President of the Music Corporation of America) behind them, Julie and Davis managed to procure the support of various Hollywood guilds and unions. They found a small, abandoned theater on Sunset and Cahuenga which they leased for $100 a month. In no time at all studio craftsmen were spending their spare time restoring the theater. A supper dance at Ciro's (in connection with the premiere of the 1942 Cary Grant comedy *The Talk of the Town*) raised about $6,500. Labor costs were minimal, and props and set pieces were borrowed from Hollywood sound stages, sometimes legally, sometimes illegally, to give the Hollywood Canteen the aura of a studio set.

The Canteen officially opened on October 5, 1942. Admission was charged for opening night only, and over $10,000 was raised. All of it was given to veterans' hospitals in the Los Angeles area. Though officers were welcome on opening night, after that the canteen was for enlisted men only (this condition was imposed by Julie, who connected to the guys in the trenches). The Canteen ended up hosting about 2,500 servicemen a night. Often the hall would be packed from wall to wall with a waiting line stretching for blocks outside.

Davis was successful at garnering industry support for the creation of the canteen. Julie's forte was recruiting talent. He hit up all the Warner Bros. stars for help, and pretty soon people like Humphrey Bogart and Ida Lupino were either singing on the bandstand or washing dishes in the kitchen. Kay Kyser's band played there every Saturday night. Celebrity busboys like Charles Laughton and Spencer Tracy were called upon to emcee. Julie went there almost every night during the war years. "Johnny, Johnny, we want Johnny!" the servicemen would scream, and

Julie would oblige, climbing on the stage to tell bad jokes and extol the virtues of life in America. The GIs loved him.

Julie couldn't do enough for the war effort. Neither could studio head Jack Warner. "We felt that our studio was sort of a war industry," Warner wrote in his autobiography, *My First Hundred Years in Hollywood.* Warner Bros. probably made more war pictures than any other studio, and they made them as efficiently as their gangster sagas. And since gangsters were no longer the best screen villains (after all, wouldn't American audiences rather see the Germans or Japanese cut down by machinegun fire?), the studio realized that they had to recast their rogues' gallery of stars. Cagney became a fighter pilot for the RAF in *Captains of the Clouds.* Bogart was a merchant marine captain in *Action in the North Atlantic.* Raft was a trench coat-clad spy in *Background to Danger.* All three actors had a sense of authority that led audiences to accept them as officers or intelligence operatives.

But John Garfield was more of a mug, the average Joe, and as such he played enlisted men, and he played them well. In *Air Force,* the first official John Garfield war film, the actor played a cynical immigrant, one Joe Winoki. Winoki delivers his lines like a machine gun— rat-a-tat-tat. Imagine an optimistic Mickey Borden in uniform, and you get the picture. The film's plot revolves around the crew of a B-17, "The Mary-Ann," as the plane makes a fateful recon trip on the eve of the attack on Pearl Harbor. Despite dialogue that now seems contrived and hard to take ("Fried Jap goin' down," gunner George Tobias cracks after scoring a hit), *Air Force* is full of action and humor and tight ensemble acting. Director Howard Hawks didn't intend to use a star in a film that offered no star roles. Julie didn't care. He heard about the film in the Warner commissary, approached Hawks and asked for a role, declaring that he was indifferent to the size of the part or his billing. Hawks was impressed. "That's the only way to make a picture, I think," Julie wrote in a column for *Photoplay* at the time. "Subordinating the star roles to the action, to the facts." In the closing credits, Julie as the aerial gunner gets ninth billing.

Even with his limited footage in *Air Force,* Julie manages to be active in scenes where he has no dialogue, conveying emotion with subtle physical choices and listening to his fellow players without attempting to steal from them. He takes a back seat, but he makes you want to watch the back seat, even if you can't figure out just what he's doing back there. "He always had something going on in the back of his head," actress Viveca Lindfors said of Julie. "A vision or something, as if he knew something that no one else knew." Good actors like to keep their method of working a secret. *Air Force* let Julie be a character actor again. Shot in Tampa, Florida, in the spring of 1942 and released a year later, *Air Force* was one of Warner Bros.' biggest commercial and critical hits of 1943. It's success surely helped John Garfield reclaim his position as a powerful box-office draw nearly five years after he had made a similar impact with *Four Daughters.* (His run of mediocre pictures is almost entirely from the 1939 to 1942 era.)

Photoplay was one of the more legitimate fan magazines of the day, and Julie's article allowed him to express his thoughts about Hollywood and family. He enjoyed romping with Katherine in the backyard. "She was the apple of his eye," Robbe recalled. "He just loved her so much." Julie played the guitar, singing 'Mrs. Morales' over and over again, to his daughter's delight. He mastered fatherhood better than husbandry, apparently. "Women like Robbe are the salt of the earth," he wrote in the *Photoplay* article. "They can wait for things to germinate and then to grow." Julie was the one who had to germinate and grow. At age 30 he was still the New York street kid and he still wanted to play like one. Perhaps as a direct result of one of his affairs, the Garfields had separated, briefly and quietly, in the spring of 1942. Robbe was not a jealous woman, but she quite naturally couldn't figure out why he treated her with so little respect. She understood that sometimes he didn't go looking for "it," and that sometimes "it" found him. But it didn't mean he had to take it.

"He was approached by women a great deal," Phoebe Brand said. "They didn't give him a moment's peace. He couldn't walk on the

street or they'd accost him. He was subjected to all sorts of flattery
and adulation. He couldn't resist it." Writer Richard Collins recalled a typical lunch meeting with Julie at the Brown Derby in Hollywood. The waiter brought Julie a note from a woman sitting at an
adjoining table. "The waiters were always bringing over notes from
women who were interested," Collins said, "And sometimes he was
interested." He liked being the pursuer more than the pursued,
however, and took greater pains with women who initially rebuffed
his advances. Once, while Robbe was away, he brought a starlet to
his house and tripled his efforts to get her into bed, with no luck.
Near desperate, he exposed himself to her, and while she was impressed with the view, she still turned him down. He apologized
and drove her home, begging forgiveness. A few nights later he
called her to ask her for a date. She admired his nerve but felt sorry
for his wife. A year later, he tried to make a date with her again. He
was persistent, if nothing else.

Sometimes the women weren't pursuing just him. One of Katherine's nurses developed a rather unhealthy crush on Julie. When he
didn't return her affection, she got it into her head that Robbe was
responsible for his lack of interest. So the nurse grabbed a steak
knife and went after Robbe, initiating a chase that ended only when
Julie disarmed the woman. Robbe then took great joy in firing her.

Why did Robbe tolerate it all? Because she still loved her husband, because she got to accept the Hollywood lifestyle, and because she was realistic enough to understand that she couldn't turn
time back. "She knew what was going on," Phoebe Brand explained, "But she loved him." Friends, colleagues and co-workers
could dismiss Julie for his lack of intelligence or interest in world
affairs, but they genuinely liked him, warts and all. It was rare for
anyone other than Robbe to criticize him. The most common word
used to describe Julie, even years later, is sweet. So sweet, in fact,
that his friends could not or would not see past the sugarcoating.
He was undeniably charming. He imposed guilt on himself. And if
pressed, he really had a hard time maintaining a lie. "He was truth-

ful, naïve and dead-on honest," theatrical producer Robert Whitehead said. "He was lovable, and I think that's what made him
laughable too."

Robbe could only laugh so much. The affairs were just a big part
of a bigger problem. She missed New York City, her family and the
simpler days. "I wasn't crazy about Hollywood," she said. "I don't
think I even visited Warner Bros. more than three times in seven
years." She would, while living in Hollywood, summon up happier
images of their days in New York City, when she would fold their
sheets and clothes after washing them and have Julie sit on them in
lieu of not owning an ironing board. In Hollywood, because the
Garfields had a nurse, a maid and a cook, there was less for Robbe
to do, both in the community and in the house, so she felt less and
less necessary.

In New York she worked with people like Odets to lead the
charge in politics and socioeconomic issues. In Hollywood she was
reduced to driving a school bus and following rather unchallenging
Communist Party orders. Typical of the assignments, she recalled,
was a request to pick up and host a visiting female commandant of
a Russian merchant marine vessel. Robbe would accompany the
woman to a Soviet-American Friendship Rally at the Shrine Auditorium in Los Angeles, but no one noticed her—they all wanted to
see John Garfield, the movie star.

And yet the movie star could not separate himself from the
woman he loved. He relied on Robbe for support and advice. "He
needed her," Robert Brown said. "She was like the Rock of Gibraltar
to him. And when he found something he liked, like her, he stayed
with it." Robbe stayed with him, and the couple's reconciliation
begot their second child, son David, who was born in July 1943.
David had unruly dark hair and a constant look of questioning upon
his face; he was the close-but-not-quite splitting image of his father.

In studio relationships and negotiations, Lew Wasserman turned
out to be more sympathetic to Julie's cause than the actor's agent,
Arthur Lyons, had been. Lyons had represented Julie in Hollywood

since 1938; little is known about the agent other than he seemed
content to broker film deals with Warner Bros. without complaint,
no matter how weak the screen material was. With Julie displaying
a desire to break from Lyons and exert more control over his own
film career, Wasserman negotiated new contract terms with Jack L.
Warner, because in 1943 Warner wanted to keep Julie happy. Quite
suddenly the studio was without the services of many of its best-
known stars; James Cagney, Edward G. Robinson and George Raft
had all left the studio in 1942, and Reagan, Albert, Morris and Lynn
were serving in the armed forces. Of the prewar set, Humphrey Bogart, Errol Flynn and Julie were the last remaining heavyweights, and
Warner knew he was going to have to make concessions, although he
didn't enjoyed making them. "Won't it be wonderful when this war
is over and all the actors are starving again?" he mused.

Through Wasserman's efforts, Julie landed a second loan-out,
this time to RKO, to film the espionage thriller *The Fallen Sparrow*.
He wasn't the first choice for the part—James Cagney, Cary Grant
and Randolph Scott had all been offered it first—but Julie didn't
care. The film's political standpoint, while ambiguous, appealed to
him: Julie plays John McKittrick, an Irish-American Loyalist who
returns to New York City after fighting in the Spanish Civil War
only to discover that his best friend, Louie, has been murdered.
Louie, like McKittrick (or "Kit") was an American fighting the good
fight against the fascists in Spain. Kit is haunted by memories of tor-
tures in a fascist prison, and he believes that the main torturer, a
limping man, is still after him. Kit hooks up with Toni Donne (Maureen O'Hara), a dubious member of royalty who may or may not be
reeling Kit right into a lair of film noir proportions: our hero is
chased, beaten up, drugged and shot at, all the while dealing with
three dames (Patricia Morison and Martha O'Driscoll are the other
two) who may be pulling a double-cross or two. Meanwhile, the
limping man pursues Kit, both in real life and in his dreams. Finally, Kit discovers that he is looking not only for Louie's murderer,
but for the cure to his own nightmare.

The Fallen Sparrow, directed by Richard Wallace, an RKO journeyman, is top-notch entertainment, although it is no more politically and historically effective than a tourist brochure guide to Spain. No mention is made of the fascists being Spanish; it turns out they are Nazis working in Spain. Still, at least one movie studio was willing to acknowledge that there had been a civil war in Spain, and despite its vague political message, the film moves along well and remains an early example of noir with Julie in a Philip Marlowe-type role. The edge on the Garfield character was softened somewhat for this film—this was RKO, not Warner Bros.—with Julie being given some interesting character traits, such as a nervous tic, to play with. But the screenplay (written by Warren Duff, based on novelist Dorothy B. Hughes' book of the same title) did not allow Julie, as Kit, too much psychological conflict. Nor did the film actually state what Kit's, or the fascists', goals or beliefs really were. Kit describes his fight as a "personal battle between me and the little man in Berlin," the sort of dialogue that wartime audiences had to cheer.

The New York Times noted the film's flaws, but cited the film as "one of the uncommon and provocatively handled melodramas of recent months." Julie worked well with Maureen O'Hara, an actress he liked but apparently didn't admire (Robbe recalls Julie coming home from the shoot and making fun of the Irish actress' thespian talents). Of John Garfield films, *The Fallen Sparrow* occupies a slot right below the top tier. It remains one of his best remembered movies and it was a huge moneymaker when released in the summer of 1943.

Warner Bros. took note of Julie's work in the film in rather absurd fashion. Executive Steve Trilling saw the film and wrote to Jack Warner suggesting that the studio head contact Julie for a film. "John Garfield was excellent in *The Fallen Sparrow,*" Trilling wrote, "and if at any time he is available, would also like to make a deal for him at whatever terms we set up." Trilling must have overlooked or been unaware of the fact that Julie was tied lock, stock and barrel to Warner Bros. for three more years. Even his own studio didn't know him.

Between shooting *The Fallen Sparrow* (in mid-1942) and his next film, Julie appeared in court to sever all ties with agent Arthur Lyons, who had sued Julie, claiming the actor still owed him close to $5,000 in commission. Rather than fight the lawsuit, Julie paid Lyons off, happy to be rid of him. That July Julie petitioned to have his name legally changed. Supreme Court Justice Emmett H. Wilson granted the petition; officially and legally, Julie was now John Garfield.

And he played John Garfield in his next two films, *Hollywood Canteen* and *Thank Your Lucky Stars.* The plot of *Hollywood Canteen* (shot first but released second) revolved around two soldiers (Dane Clark and Robert Hutton) and their efforts to meet actress Joan Leslie at the Canteen. The Canteen served as a backdrop for an array of specialty numbers and guest star appearances, with Julie and Bette Davis playing themselves in brief scenes in which they sang the praises of the Hollywood Canteen. Warner Bros. contributed a good share of the film's profits to the real-life canteen, which pleased Julie and Davis, because the film was the studio's top-grosser in 1944. Even so, as far as John Garfield fans are concerned, there's not much to watch for in this one.

Thank Your Lucky Stars, another of those almost plotless all-star variety films with each guest star performing a brief song or dance or comic skit is slightly better. What little plot it has involves Eddie Cantor's attempts to line up an array of stars for a show to benefit Uncle Sam. Jack Warner announced that he would donate $50,000 of this film's profits to the Canteen, as well as secretly expecting every one of his contract stars to appear in the film for free. (Most of them did.) Julie's self-spoofing stint in the film is short, and there's something surreal and grotesquely amusing about his musical rendition of "Blues in the Night" (this after he roughs up Cantor backstage). Singing the song, he wasn't half bad, but he wasn't totally effective either, probably because he received word during the shoot that his father was dying. He finished his sequence in haste, and he and Robbe flew to New York City to see David, whose body, at age fifty-two, was withered away by cancer. On his deathbed he kept asking Julie why he wasn't in rehearsal for *Counsellor-at-Law*. David died on October 27, 1942, and was buried at Montefiore Cemetery in Queens. If Julie felt any sorrow over his father's death, it was probably for the relationship that he *didn't* have with him. "There was no relationship between them, so Julie wasn't exactly distraught when his father died," Robbe noted.

He didn't seem to have a brother either. Michael was serving in the Army at the time of David's death and was unable to attend the funeral. If he had, it would have been one of the rare times that the two brothers actually saw each other. Their separation at an early age had created a gap that could never be closed. Michael did move to Hollywood after the war but he and Julie were not close. Julie treated Michael with the same disregard he showed his parents, never mentioning him to friends or journalists unless specifically asked. Even then he was vague and insulting, once publicly referring to Michael as "one of the unemployed." For all practical purposes, as of October 1942, the Garfield family no longer existed. Robbe's parents Max and Lena, Robbe and his children were Julie's family now.

While he was in New York, Julie caught up with Clifford Odets, who was in a fairly permanent state of gloom. He had not written a hit play since *Golden Boy* in 1937 and despair was overtaking him. He told Julie that he felt he had lost his talent. Julie tried to encourage Odets to write another play, but the playwright responded by opening up his desk and bureau drawers and pulling out sheets of paper with dialogue written on them. "I've started all these plays but I can't finish them," Odets told Julie. Not only this but Odets' personal life was in disarray, for his marriage to Louise Rainer was coming to an end and his financial future wasn't looking bright. Despite David Garfinkle's recent death, Julie worked to cheer Odets, spending evenings with him at the playwright's Manhattan apartment and suggesting that he return to Hollywood to write screenplays. Odets couldn't really argue that it was against Group policy anymore, for almost every member of the Group was residing in Hollywood by 1942.

Phoebe Brand, Morris Carnovsky, Roman Bohnen, Art Smith, Joe Bromberg, Virginia Farmer and Lee J. Cobb were all on the West Coast, where they banded with Hollywood actors like Lloyd Bridges and Larry Parks to form an L.A. version of the Group Theatre, which was a one part performing arts group, one part school called The Actors Lab. The principles of the Group—and some of its politics—were retained in the Lab, which attracted up and coming Hollywood types and future Broadway performers (one of the Lab's youngest members was Joseph Papirofsky, later known as Joe Papp).

Julie wanted in to the Lab, just as he had wanted in to the Group a decade earlier. He rarely got past the front door. "The old Group Theatre people didn't take him seriously," said Helen Levitt, who was then serving as secretary for the Lab. "They still resented him for coming out to Hollywood earlier. Plus they considered him a lightweight. It was kind of an artistic snobbiness."

Yet when the Lab needed Julie, they would conveniently include him in their activities. In 1944 the Lab decided to produce John Hersey's play *A Bell for Adano,* a moving story of American soldiers in an occupied Italian city. They planned to hire actors who had served in the military during the war and to give proceeds to veterans' organizations. Kent Smith, a film actor with some name value, played the lead role in the production. Though there was no role in the play for Julie, the Lab believed some Hollywood names could help garner publicity. Levitt was asked to ask Julie if he would like to act as producer, and when he agreed, she then suggested that he ask Vincent Sherman to direct the production. Sherman was equally receptive but realized he'd have to get permission from Jack Warner. Warner was surprisingly amenable, provided Sherman cast Warner's stepdaughter, actress Joy Page, as the young Italian girl. (Sherman was considering Eva Gabor for the role.) Page, a minor starlet of the 1940s (she had a small role in *Casablanca* as the young bride who asks Bogart's Rick Blaine for help), was hardly the right type for the play, but the Lab compromised and soon the entire production was beginning to look like a Hollywood movie.

As producer, Julie had little to do. Sherman continued to direct at the studio by day and work on the play at night. Rehearsals went fairly well, though everyone had their doubts about Page's performance, and Warner was having second thoughts about letting his stepdaughter socialize and work with a group of radicals. All the same, the production ended up as a success, and a few years later the Lab asked Julie to act in their 1946 production of *Awake and Sing!*, which was performed at The Hollywood Bowl. In it Julie played the part of Moe Axelrod, the role Luther Adler originated on Broadway in 1935. Publicity photos for the play emphasized the sexual aspect of the relationship between Moe and Bessie Berger (played by Phoebe Brand), and ended up looking like commercial ads for a Hollywood sleazefest. But with Joe Bromberg directing and a lot of the old Group Theatre members in the cast, the play earned respectable reviews and did good business. Critic Virginia Wright found the play to be "vivid and honest" and praised Julie's work as Moe, stating that "Garfield plays him effortlessly, but with a smoldering, underlying force—a fury very different from the neurotic hysteria of the Bergers." It was Julie's first stage appearance since 1940.

The Lab was as politically motivated as the Group, and many members belonged to the Hollywood chapter of the Communist Party. Robbe continued to attend Communist Party meetings, and even hosted a few in her own home. Julie paid scant attention to the meetings, offering only surface support. "He was very sympathetic to all of us who were active," writer Ring Lardner Jr. explained, "but it was usually a question of him just giving his name and not taking an active part."

During the war years the communists found themselves being tolerated because they were joining the Allies in the fight against Hitler. Arnold Forster, Julie's childhood friend and later a lawyer for B'nai B'rith, felt that the communists were accepted during the war years because of President Roosevelt's embrace of Stalin as an ally. "The communists were part of the world in which Julie moved," Forster said. "That was really the liberal movement, the slightly left-of-center Rooseveltian democratic concept, which itself did not chase acknowledged Communists from their midst. As long as a Communist was willing to participate in a truly Rooseveltian mode, then he was accepted."

Thus, Julie's support of the American Committee for Yugoslavian Relief seemed harmless, as it would for other innocent-sounding organizations and events that he lent his name to: The American Rescue Ship, which contracted ships to carry Spanish refugees out of Casablanca; the Hollywood Democratic Committee, which supported labor-endorsed political candidates; the Joint Anti-Fascist Refugee Committee, for which Julie helped to secure close to $20,000 in donations to fight Hitler, and the "Replant the Scorched Earth of Russia" fund drive. Upon returning to work at Warner Bros., Julie probably forgot about his ties to these organizations, but his efforts would come back to haunt him by decade's end.

Unable to don a uniform in real life, Julie donned one for the camera in his next war film, *Destination Tokyo* (1943), a naval drama about the exploits of the submarine USS *Copper Fin,* ordered on a reconnaissance mission to Tokyo Bay. Cary Grant plays the sub's commander, an officer with a sense of humor and a paternal attitude, and he received top billing over Julie in the credits. (Grant was a bigger box-office draw at the time.) Julie plays a gabby sailor named Wolf who has girls—and nothing but girls—on his mind at all times. It's a marvelous comic performance, far removed from Mickey Borden. Wolf's descriptions of his encounters with women (who always seem to be stepping out of the bathtub clad only in a towel when he calls on them) are hilarious. "The minute I saw her I says, 'Up periscope!' " Julie quips in one off-color remark. A more serious and quite moving sequence has Julie listening to a dead comrade's phonograph record in the hope of hearing some racy dialogue. Wolf discovers that the dead man had recorded a love letter for his wife. It needed no dialogue for Julie to convey heartbreak; his face said it all.

Producer Jerry Wald wanted lots of war rhetoric in *Destination Tokyo,* and screenwriter Albert Maltz obliged. In one scene a

Japanese plane drops a bomb that fails to implode upon hitting the submarine. Naturally someone has to disarm the bomb, so commander Grant convinces a young sailor (Robert Hutton) to volunteer for the job. After the sailor succeeds in his mission, Grant holds the bomb's detonator in his hands and, turning to the crew, says, "It's got MADE IN THE U.S.A. stamped on it—the appeasers' contribution to the war effort!" The implications were clear, for the communists had been at the forefront of protesting the U.S. government's decision to export scrap metal to Japan in the late 1930s. Maltz also worked in some patriotic anti-Nazi talk, giving sailor Tin Can (played by Dane Clark, forever known as the poor man's John Garfield) a chance to explain why he hates the Nazis so much. The dialogue was harmless enough (they killed his uncle, a schoolteacher) but a decade later HUAC would not see the film's point of view in such clearcut terms.

Politics took a back seat to personal and professional affairs during the shooting of the film. Robbe was pregnant with son David, and Julie was in fine form on the set, clowning around with both Cary Grant and Dane Clark. Clark was one of the few actors to remain friendly with Julie through the years, as both men had much in common. Clark had grown up in Brooklyn, had boxed some, had tried unsuccessfully to get into the Group Theatre in the 1930s, and had come to Hollywood on a whim. There were stories that Warner Bros. hired Clark by in 1942 just in case Julie gave the studio trouble. ("I know he was hired by Warners to take Julie's place," director John Berry claimed.) For the most part, Clark was the studio's secondstring Garfield and he inherited a lot of films—mostly routine ones—that Julie probably would have made had he stayed on at Warner Bros. in the late 1940s.

Clark liked working with Julie and was relieved to discover that they were both about the same height. "I was so sick of playing opposite actors who I had to look up to, like Raymond Massey and Cary Grant," Clark recalled. Preparing for his first take with Julie, Clark was surprised when, after director Delmer Daves asked if everything was in place, Julie turned to the prop man and said, "Bring me my man-maker."

Clark was bewildered. "Man-maker?" he asked. "What the hell is a man-maker?"

His question was answered when one of the prop men set down a small box for Julie to step on. Suddenly John Garfield was several inches taller than Dane Clark. Clark was incredulous about the whole thing. Julie just smiled and said, "One day, when you're a star, you can have a man-maker too." The cast and crew broke up laughing.

CHAPTER ELEVEN

Between Two Worlds

*"All he (Julie) cared about was acting and
dames."*

—DANE CLARK

PRESIDENT ROOSEVELT INVITED JOHN GARFIELD BACK TO
the White House early in 1944 to thank him for his efforts in
support of the country's war drive, from his bond-raising
tours to the formation of the Hollywood Canteen. Though
the meeting lasted for less than a half-hour, Julie was hon-
ored. "There I was, a kid from the Bronx, meeting with the
President," he later recalled. "That's democracy—that's
wonderful."

The State Department had cleared the way for a USO
Tour of North Africa and Italy, places where bloody fighting
continued. Julie signed on to emcee the tour, which included comedian Eddie Foy Jr., dancer Sheila Rogers, ac-
cordionist Olga Klein, and actress Jean Darling (who had
been one of the early *Our Gang* members). The group called
themselves the USO Camp Show Troupers. Julie's willingness to join the tour was due to more than just patriotism.
He still had that need to prove himself; the same need that
stoked his desire for women.

The tour was scheduled to depart New York in February
1944. Julie's secretary, Helen Levitt, suggested that he meet
with writer Arnold Manoff to prepare some material.
Manoff wrote a piece for Julie that was considered by some
to be one of the best bits ever created for the USO tours. In

it, Julie portrayed a cab driver turned soldier who writes an affec-
tionate letter to his sergeant. The piece was from the point of view
of a character not unlike Julie's, a poor, uneducated New Yorker
who didn't quite understand what he was getting into when he enlisted in the Army. After the war, Julie would use the piece in stage
appearances promoting his films.

Julie had hired Levitt in 1942 to handle his fan mail. She recalls
her initial interview session with him as being bizarre: "I walked in
and he was performing, as if the important thing was that he entertain me. You'd think I was interviewing him for the job." To show
off how important he was, Julie often invited excuses to have Levitt
visit him on the Warner lot. "He'd come up with some reason to get
me on the set at least once during every picture because he liked the
idea of letting people know he had a secretary," Levitt said. "There
was never any particular reason for me to be there, but I went along
with it." Robbe treated Levitt more as a friend than an employee,
and the two women would often enjoy afternoon swims together in
the Garfield pool.

According to Levitt, between 1942 and 1945 Julie did not turn
down one script that was offered to him. He realized he needed
good material, and by returning to his ensemble roots he managed to
ensure that he could appear in quality productions. His new manager, Bob Roberts, had a hand in this, for Roberts saw the rationale
behind cooperating with Jack Warner. Warner, in return, renewed
his interest in John Garfield as a star player. But the next film Julie
made was to be among his worst. Called *Between Two Worlds,* it's
about a motley group of losers and lovers who are brought together
on a ship that may be heading to Heaven, to Hell, or somewhere in
between. A remake of an old Leslie Howard film entitled *Outward
Bound,* which had been a play, it was shot quickly in January 1944.
It was updated and reset in wartime London. Julie played Tom
Prior, a down-on-his-luck reporter who is not particularly surprised
or upset to learn that he is dead. Others on board for this dark joy
ride include Eleanor Parker and Paul Henreid as suicidal lovers,

Faye Emerson as another of the studio's B girls, and Sydney Greenstreet, who plays a slight variation on his famous "Fat Man" role from *The Maltese Falcon*. The part of a ne'er-do-well was nothing new to Julie, but it is difficult to accept him as an over-the-hill hack whose best days were behind him when the actor was barely 30 years old at the time of filming. Tom Prior is basically from the same family tree as Mickey Borden, only Prior's dead to begin with.

Despite its impressive cast, the direction of *Between Two Worlds* by Edward H. Blatt is poor, which makes it difficult to assess Garfield's performance, as he basically calls upon traits and mannerisms from previous movies. He is quite good in a brief, touching sequence in which he recounts his past indiscretions before reuniting with his dead mother, played by British actress Sara Allgood. Four years later, Julie was asked to name the worst film he had ever made, and he didn't hesitate: *"Between Two Worlds.* It was strange and it was mystic and it was bad." Curiously enough it remains one of the more fondly recalled films of the actor's career by many of his fans, perhaps due to its odd plotting, the strong ensemble cast, and Eric Wolfgang Korngold's memorable score. But Archer Winston of *The New York Post* summed it up best when he wrote that the film "will not contribute to your list of great moments in the movie houses... if you ask me, the ship symbolism is empty. I would rather go to Heaven in that new Lockheed Constellation or hell in a submarine."

Julie was probably happy to get the film out of the way just so that he could get off to Europe on his USO tour. He spent a few days with Robbe and his children before flying to New York early in February 1944. From there he and the Troupers departed on Valentine's Day for Newfoundland in an Air Transport Carrier. The beginning was not auspicious. The plane began to lose engine power over the mountains of the Azores Islands, East of Portugal, according to Darling, which forced the pilot to make an emergency landing once they made it to Italy. (That's an incredibly long distance to journey, over the countries of Portugal and Spain, making one wonder if Darling meant to say the Balearic Islands, which are located in between Spain and Italy.)

Once in Italy, the Troupers stumbled out of the downed plane and crammed themselves into an Army jeep that was to transport them the rest of the way to their headquarters in Naples. Half way to their destination, the jeep got caught in a mudslide. The jeep's driver managed to avoid going over a cliff, but the vehicle spun around and around in the mud, and jolted the entertainers against each other in the back seat. Unable to break the jeep free of the mud, the driver suggested that the group bed down in the ruins of a nearby building. February nights in the Italian hills were bitter cold, and the Troupers huddled together under blankets to stay warm, though neither Jean Darling nor Sheila Rogers wanted to sleep next to Julie—they just didn't trust him.

The beleaguered group made it to Naples the following day. From there they would make daily road excursions to field hospitals and front-line encampments, playing to entertainment-starved GIs. Jean Darling and Eddie Foy, both veterans of the vaudeville circuit, developed a musical-comedy act. Sheila Rogers could sing and dance, and she was good-looking, so she didn't have anything to worry about when it came to entertaining. Even the accordion player had something to hide behind. All Julie had was a monologue, so for added box-office insurance, he decided to spoof his tough-guy image, and he tailored the song "Blues in the Night" for the USO act by adding impromptu asides and exchanges with the audience. One of his favorite bits was to stop singing midway through the song and tell the troops a little secret. "You know, I don't really talk like this," he'd say, still sounding like a Dead End Kid. "Warner Brothers wants I should talk this way. I'm just puttin' on this accent." The GIs thought he was hilarious.

Jean Darling wasn't sure whether that part of the act was an act. "He was very serious about it," she recalled. "He wanted them to think he didn't talk like a New York street kid. I think he was trying to act better educated than he was." She came to realize, though, that the servicemen bonded with Julie because they saw in him their own backgrounds. "He talked to them like a regular guy," she said. Darling, Foy and Garfield often visited the field hospitals in an attempt to cheer the patients, many of whom were disfigured beyond recognition. It was a sobering experience.

So were their brushes with death. An enemy artillery shell narrowly missed the jeep on one occasion. And when the entertainers began to perform at the base of Mt. Vesuvius, the still active volcano belched enough smoke and ash out to convince the troupe that the show does not always go on.

One day Julie and Foy borrowed an Army jeep to go fishing in the country. They got lost on the way back and took refuge in a storage complex off the road. An enemy air raid on the area kept the duo up most of the night, but they felt they were probably safer hiding in this one isolated building than the rest of their troupe was back in Naples. They weren't. The next day they discovered that they had been hiding in an ammo dump that was a target of the Axis planes.

And yet, when the end result merited the danger involved, Julie was prepared to risk his life. An Axis air raid on Naples sent Jean Darling to a bomb shelter. Once there, she began thinking of her roommate, Sheila Rogers. Frantic, Darling raced back to their hotel through the streets of the city as bombs fell all around her. When she got to the room she shared with Rogers, she discovered the door was locked. Darling banged and banged on the door, screaming at the top of her lungs for Rogers to come out. The bombs continued to fall. Rogers finally appeared in the doorway of Julie's room with a bed sheet partially wrapped around her naked body. She cast Darling a furious glance and snarled, "For Christ's sake, go away, will ya'?" Then, as if performing a scene from a French farce, an equally nude Garfield stepped out, pulled Rogers back into the room, and closed the door behind him. Darling, somewhat disillusioned, returned to the shelter. Obviously her roommate had changed her mind about sleeping next to Julie.

In April, not long before the tour was to end, an officer of the Special Services of the United States asked Julie if he and the Troupers would be willing to travel behind enemy lines to entertain members of the Yugoslavian guerrilla movement. A band of guerrilla commandoes, lead by Tito (the communist leader), continued to resist the occupation troops of the puppet regime installed by Germany in Yugoslavia. The Special Services officer (whose name Julie would not recall) said that the gesture would be an important morale-builder for these partisans. The Camp Show Troupers agreed and traveled in the dead of night to the partisan camp where an interpreter translated the performance as best he could. In return the partisans staged a folk song and dance show for the Troupers. Julie thought the women guerrilla fighters were quite attractive, but as they all wore sidearms he steered clear of them. Colonel Vladimir Dedijer, commander of the partisans, presented Julie with a set of sidearms, a gift the actor would treasure. After the war, when Dedijer visited the United States, he stayed with the Garfields in Hollywood.

The USO Camp Show Troupers returned to New York City in late April 1944. Julie took the Santa Fe Chief to Los Angeles, where he was met by a reporter from the *The Los Angeles Daily News*. Asked how it felt to be performing under fire and living in foxholes, Julie replied, "It scared the hell out of me."

"There is no way of describing what those men go through," Julie said of the soldiers. "I don't think anybody at home can understand how a front-line soldier feels, lives and thinks." He said the soldiers were the most appreciative audience he had ever played to: "Those kids would sit in the rain and mud for hours just to wait and see us. They make you feel better than you really are."

The tour reignited Julie's desire to join the service. He took another Army physical, hoping his heart murmur wouldn't be detected, and somehow he passed, receiving a 1-A classification. He expected to be called up soon, but he didn't tell Robbe. She was mad enough about the cache of guns (including an automatic machine gun) that he had brought back with him from Europe as mementos. He also brought Robbe another surprise: a dose of clap, no doubt given to him by an Italian prostitute.

With Julie's return to the States, the Garfields moved again, to 1712 North Stanley Drive in Hollywood. This was a two-story house built by silent screen actor William Haines that had spacious rooms, a walled-in patio on the front lawn and a walled-in backyard. The room sported large bedrooms and an upstairs den where Julie could sit by the fire and read. A small gazebo was built into the backyard's rear wall. There was no room in the backyard for a swimming pool, so the Garfields took to visiting the Beverly Hills Country Club for water recreation.

Julie's seven-year contract with Warner Bros. was due to expire at the end of 1945, so the studio was doubly anxious to keep him happy in the hopes of re-signing him. What the studio came up with was a beauty of a film that was one part war saga and one part romantic drama. *Pride of the Marines* is the true story of Marine private Al Schmid, a normal guy from Philadelphia who found himself caught up in a war that he didn't understand. Schmid had been assigned to Guadalcanal in the summer of 1942; a place where bloody battling continued as the Japanese fought viciously to hold on to the island stronghold. In the early hours of August 21, 1942, Schmid and two of his fellow GIs, Corporal Lee Diamond and Private Johnny Travers, were manning a machine gun on the bank of the Tenaru River. Hundreds of Japanese troops stormed the lone machine gun nest, only to be repelled by the three men; Travers was killed and Diamond wounded. Schmid found himself alone for the rest of the predawn hours, fending off the swarms of Japanese soldiers and praying that he and his machine gun, affectionately nick-named Chloe, would hold out.

Schmid survived despite being blinded by a Japanese grenade during the assault. The brave Marine's story was one of the first to publicize the heroic efforts of the country's armed forces, and was turned into a book by journalist Roger Butterfield, *Al Schmid—Marine*. Jerry Wald bought the film rights for Warner Bros and assigned Albert Maltz to write the film version. Wald and Maltz agreed that they should emphasize both the heroics of the battle and the difficulties facing returning war veterans. They also agreed that there was just one actor at the studio who could play Schmid: John Garfield.

Warner Bros. saw the film as a great vehicle for flag-waving. *Sergeant York*, the studio's 1941 World War I saga starring Gary Cooper, had been a tremendous hit then, and Wald hoped to repeat the success of that film with *Pride of the Marines*. Schmid cooperated with Warner Bros. and invited Julie to spend a month with him at his Philadelphia home. Julie jumped at the chance to portray a living person and to study him on a daily basis.

"I met this kid and lived with him for a whole month, and I kept notes," Julie said in a lecture at the Actors' Lab in 1945. "I discovered certain things that I did were based on a conventional idea of blind people. They were all wrong. People who are blind have certain instincts. I found that they look up, sort of like a sparrow, as they never know exactly where the sound is coming from. On the basis of that alone, you can proceed to make a whole characterization." Julie's instincts were right on.

Shooting began in October 1944 and continued through the spring of 1945. Wald assigned Delmer Daves to direct and cast Eleanor Parker, a vivacious and talented new find, in the role of Schmid's girlfriend Ruth (Jessica Tandy was initially considered for the role). Screenwriter Maltz beefed up the role of Schmid's friend, Lee Diamond, to give actor Dane Clark a stronger supporting role.

Like other war films from that era, *Pride of the Marines* doesn't entirely date well, but long sections of it are just terrific. It packs a considerable punch in relating the story of Schmid, a factory worker who thinks the war is a lark (when he first hears of the bombing of Pearl Harbor on the radio, he confidently boasts that it's just another "Men from Mars" theatrical broadcast). What Schmid didn't figure on was falling in love with the free-spirited Ruth before he departs for the service on New Year's Day 1942.

The film cuts almost immediately to that fateful morning on the Tenaru River, where Schmid, Diamond and Travers make their stand in the machine-gun nest. In a tightly-filmed scene full of tension and action, the trio frantically fight off the invading Japanese forces, with Travers taking a bullet in the head and Diamond taking three in the arm. Schmid then mans the machinegun alone, gunning down some 200 enemy troops before a dying Japanese soldier ignites a grenade in the GI's face. Schmid, blinded, moans and screams and draws his pistol. Diamond believes Schmid is about to take his own life and begs his friend not to do it. "Shoot myself?" Schmid asks in amazement, blindly waving his pistol towards the enemy across the river. "Just tell me where they are, Lee. Tell me where they're coming from, and I'll shoot 'em!" The rest of the film deals with Schmid's attempts at recovery and rehabilitation, and Ruth's loyalty to him.

Maltz and Daves worked with the cast to create a moving story about returning veterans and their problems while remaining faithful to the basic tale of a normal guy who cannot comprehend how forces outside his control could alter his life so drastically. Julie was perfectly cast as Schmid, projecting charm, humor, sex appeal, fear, bitterness, self-pity and anger in the span of two hours of film time. It is perhaps his finest and fullest screen portrayal of the Warner Bros. period, and for once he plays a character whose anger is easy to understand. Suddenly he was, as an actor, displaying a strong sense of maturity. He definitely got better—and looked better—as he got older. His inner energy, always threatening to burst out and lead him over the top, was considerably harnessed. He got to play comedy in some of the early scenes, engaging in a nice, healthy, sexy relationship with the equally superb Parker (one of those actresses continually underserved by Hollywood), and there are moments of mild buffoonery in them where you swear he is doing another working-class imitation of Cary Grant.

Best of all is the tense attack on the machine gun nest, which rates as one of the most effective battle sequences committed to film. For about 15 minutes Daves, Maltz and the actors captured the sweat, fear, and blood of combat. Both Clark and Anthony Caruso (as Travers) are quite good in support, but once his comrades are put out of commission, the scene is all Julie's. Terror-stricken, he begs the machine gun, his last remaining friend, not to give out on him. "Don't jam on me, sweetheart," he pleads desperately, as if talking to a lover. The desperate fear in Julie's actions, played with just the right amount of economy, is indicative of what the actor could do when given the right script and the right director. "Why can't I shut you up?" he screams at the taunting (and unseen) Japanese soldiers across the river. Who knows what the actor in him was thinking at this moment, but whatever it was, it was beautiful. He had committed some fine portrayals to celluloid before, and it's not meant as harsh criticism of the actor to suggest that now, in 1945, he was really beginning to get interesting. Warners released the film in August 1945. The critics thought it a success and so did the public; it was Julie's biggest to date.

Dane Clark recalled that the atmosphere on the set was charged with the sense that the ensemble was developing something special. Clark said both he and Julie fell in love with Parker during filming, but the love did not translate into anything more physical than flirting. In one sentimental scene where their characters, Diamond and Schmid, must say good-bye to each other, Clark and Garfield schmaltzed it up, ad-libbing and hugging each other a bit *too* affectionately for Daves. After completing the overemotional scene, the two actors looked around to see everyone on the set crying. Julie, expecting an accolade, said, "Well, what do you think, Del?" Tears were rolling down Daves' cheeks as he said through his sobs, "It stinks! Do it again!" They did it again.

Before the filming for *Pride of the Marines* was even complete, Julie was assigned to another project, a crime drama written by genre specialist W.R. Burnett (author of *Little Caesar* and *High Sierra*). The project had been lying around the Warner vaults since before the war and George Raft had turned it down back in 1942. It's the story of a high-class con man, Nick Blake (Garfield), who gets in on a scam to fleece a beautiful young widow of her inheritance. Unexpectedly, he falls for her and finds himself turning against his own gang in an effort to save her. The film boasts a typical John Garfield title: *Nobody Lives Forever.*

A late entry in the gangster film cycle or an early sample of noir? *Nobody Lives Forever* is a little of both, with some soap opera thrown in for good measure. Julie's character is not so much drawn into the world of noir; rather he draws that world towards him. The film has enough noir elements: an isolated beach house, a gun-blasting finale on a fog-shrouded wharf, a tough guy working in an unfamiliar environment (sunny Los Angeles as opposed to dark New York City), and so on. But there's no femme fatale, per se, and the villains aren't particularly threatening. A lot of screen time is spend on the budding romance between Garfield's Nick Blake and Geraldine Fitzgerald's widow and allowing for some moments of comic relief from George Tobias. Julie glides through the film with a newfound confidence, giving the film an added zest that was lacking in his prewar crime melodramas. Former screenwriter Jean Negulesco directed the film, and a strong ensemble cast including George Coulouris as the villain, Walter Brenann as an aging con man called "Pop" and Faye Emerson as yet another gal from the wrong side of the tracks, backed Julie. Better than most of Julie's assembly line crime dramas, *Nobody Lives Forever* is a good, not great, film. Julie came to like Brennan, the actor who had beat him out for the Academy Award in 1938. And for a brief period Julie was playing Al Schmid in the morning and Nick Blake in the afternoon—a not unusual practice at Warner Bros. The long working hours turned out to be a welcome distraction from a personal tragedy.

When Helen Levitt decided to leave the Garfields' employ in order to manage the Actors Lab, she suggested that her friend, Hilda Wane, take over the job. Wane had been Danny Kaye's secretary, and the Garfields hired her on as a combination secretary/nurse. On Saint Patrick's Day weekend 1945, the Garfields agreed to let Wane take Katherine (age 6) to a friend's ranch near Vista, California, for an overnight trip. On the evening of March 16, Katherine complained to

Wane of a sore throat, but as the ailment seemed to be no more serious than that, Wane simply sent Katherine to bed early. The next
morning, the child's throat was causing her more discomfort, but as
her condition seemed manageable Wane saw no reason to call a doctor. Instead, she herded Katherine into her car and drove back to
Hollywood, figuring to let the Garfields take care of the situation. By
the time Wane reached the Garfield house on North Stanley, Katherine could barely breathe.

Julie was still sleeping when Wane brought Katherine into the
house. Robbe ordered Wane to call an ambulance and then wake
Julie. Robbe cradled the choking child in her arms. Katherine
looked up at her mother and asked, "Where's daddy?" Robbe
replied, "Daddy's coming, darling." A moment later, Katherine died
in her mother's arms. Julie rushed in to discover Robbe silently
cradling Katherine's lifeless body.

Julie reacted by loading the automatic machine gun, running into
the back yard and spraying the back wall with bullets. He then
dropped the gun and ran into the Hollywood Hills, crying and wail-
ing in aguish. A neighbor, Tyba Wilner, who heard his cries, later
said she thought that a wounded animal was lost in the hills. He
staggered down to the streets of Hollywood and wandered about in
a daze. Vincent Sherman was driving down Hollywood Boulevard
and saw the clearly distressed Julie staggering along the street, as if
drunk or overcome with rage. Sherman stopped his car and approached Julie, but before the director could say anything, Julie
blurted out, "God did this to me, Vince. He did this to me for all the
bad things I've done." Then he collapsed. The police, alerted to the
tragedy and the gunfire, confiscated the machine gun but did not
press charges against Julie.

The press reported that John Garfield's daughter had died of a
throat ailment—a nebulous diagnosis. Katherine had suffered from
asthma, and many felt that Wane should have taken the girl's condition seriously, though it's not clear whether Wane, a relatively
new hire, knew about the ailment. After the funeral at Reynolds-

Eberle Mortuary, Julie left Robbe alone and rather selfishly showed up uninvited at the home of actor Herbert Rudley. Rudley was playing poker with some friends and Julie joined the game. Rudley and his guests did not know how to bow out of the game without offending Julie, and so, despite their discomfort, the game continued. Julie gambled wildly, betting on hands that were hardly worth maintaining. Rudley's wife, Ann Loring, recalled the dark, discomforting game. "It was a terribly self-conscious game," she said. "The word dead is an oft-used poker term, and I remember everyone at the table was trying to avoid using it, especially when someone had a dead man's hand [two eights and two aces]. There was all this psychological self-guilt that all the men imposed on themselves in the game. It was just horrible."

Robbe had to handle her daughter's death with a stoicism born of necessity, because it was Julie everybody ended up worring about. He didn't let on that he was hurting inside while he was at the studio. Geraldine Fitzgerald and Robert Shayne, who appeared with Julie in *Nobody Lives Forever,* said they had no idea that he had suffered such a personal loss. "I truly didn't know that his daughter had died until some months later," Fitzgerald recalled. "He acted as if nothing was wrong." He couldn't always maintain that pose. One day he collapsed into the arms of publicity man Bob William, faint from grief or overwork.

Julie would wake up in the middle of the night crying out Katherine's name. He fell into periods of blue moods and dark depression, distancing himself from Robbe. Each of them chose different methods of dealing with the tragedy. She tried to get on with her life, taking time out to be extra patient and attentive with David (who was not quite three years old). Katherine's death also led Robbe to sever ties with the Communist Party and to cut back on participating in most political causes. For Julie, always willing to tell the press how he felt about his acting career, but rarely willing to unload his inner worries or thoughts on others, work was the only remedy. Working on both *Pride of the Marines* and *Nobody Lives Forever* obliged him to stay at Warner Bros. into the early evening. He sometimes stayed away from the house, sleeping in his studio dressing room. It is unlikely that he was with other women during this period. "I think after that tragedy he became a much more serious person," Vincent Sherman said. "He behaved much differently in terms of his relationships with other people, and other women."

And yet the death of Katherine would not make Julie a better parent to his son David, or his next daughter, Julie; he seemed to be less aware of his children's needs, and was incapable of giving them as much love and attention as he had given to Katherine. Perhaps he was afraid of getting too close and then losing them. Hilda Wane remained as Julie's secretary for a brief period. Julie did not blame her, but eventually she virtually drifted out of the Garfield's lives, though she would show up now and then at their front door, crying her eyes out over the memory of Katherine's death. Julie, who found it difficult to remain angry with anyone, was sympathetic. Robbe was less tolerant of the woman's behavior. Shortly thereafter, the Garfields dismissed all of their household servants, preferring to remain alone in their house.

On the professional front, there was some good news. By 1943 actress Olivia de Havilland had been on suspension at Warner Bros. so many times that the studio had added seven months to her contract for the time she spent not working for them. The actress felt this was an unfair practice and was eager to leave Warner Bros., so she petitioned the Superior Court of California for support. The court sided with De Havilland, and the actress left the studio early in 1945. The De Havilland decision, as it was known, affected the contracts of the entire Warner Bros. roster. Though Julie's original contract ended at the end of 1945, the time he had spent on suspension had added nearly two years to his contract. With the court decision made, he calculated the time he had been on suspension against the time left on his original contract and reasoned that by the time *Nobody Lives Forever* was complete he'd only have about eight months left to serve at Warner Bros.

The studio took stock of Julie's renewed popularity and offered him a lucrative seven-year contract, over which time he would earn one million dollars (compare that to the studio's offer to Humphrey Bogart for seven years at two million dollars!). Julie would also be given the right to make one outside film per year for another studio. He liked the million-dollar idea and seriously considered it although Robbe, Helen Levitt and Bob Roberts all urged him to branch out on his own. Ultimately, he only had to talk himself out of the deal. He walked up to Levitt one day at the Actors' Lab and said, "It's a million dollars they're offering me." Levitt told him that a million dollars wouldn't necessarily buy him happiness. Julie mulled some more and walked away. The next day he approached her again and said, "You know, a million dollars isn't enough money for seven years of unhappiness," as if she had been the one trying to talk him into renewing his contract.

Warner Bros. wanted to keep him. They almost needed to keep him. By 1945 the studio only boasted two major male stars: Bogart and Garfield. Errol Flynn's career was beginning to slump and most of the up-and-coming Warner Bros. stars of the postwar era, like Dane Clark and Zachary Scott, were hardly powerhouse performers. Studio head Jack Warner was getting nowhere with Julie and made his frustration clear in a September 1945 confidential memo to Mort Blumenstock (head of publicity and advertising), in which he wrote, "Impossible sign up Garfield after he makes one more picture for us. He has forgotten days when I picked him up when making six bits weekly. Nevertheless we will get along without him... don't want any trouble with him when we making last one, as he no pushover."

Bob Roberts felt Julie could do better if he formed his own company and had some creative control over his own output. Julie liked what Roberts was telling him. Roberts began to make contacts among some of the independents then cropping up around Hollywood. At the time a group of screenwriters, including Ring Lardner Jr., Dalton Trumbo and Lester Cole (all members of the Communist

Party, as was Roberts), was trying to form their own production company, Xanadu. Roberts convinced Julie to invest a thousand dollars in the company, money the actor would never see again. It was a small investment for building ties to the people who were writing the films, and Julie was always aware of the importance of a good script. Xanadu never got off the ground; Roberts was undaunted and began to make queries to other independent companies like Liberty Pictures and Enterprise.

It was one thing for an actor to free-lance in the heyday of the studio system. It was quite another for an actor to form his own company. Cagney had done it in 1943; Bogart would try it in 1949. Julie was one of the first actors (though not the first) to see independent filmmaking as the wave of the future. "The movies can't continue to give them [the audience] junk," he said in 1945. "I have a feeling that these independents that are starting up will be spearheads."

He would be one of the spearheads. But not before he took a phone call from the U.S. government ordering him to report to a Naval indoctrination station in Los Angeles. John Garfield was finally going to war. For him, it would last less than one day.

CHAPTER TWELVE

Breaking Out

"I served my time!"
> —JOHN GARFIELD, ON LEAVING
> WARNER BROS.

BILLY GRADY, MGM'S CASTING DIRECTOR, PAID A VISIT TO
Warner Bros. one day to ask Julie to play opposite Judy Garland in the western-musical *The Harvey Girls.* Julie turned
Grady down, which is too bad because it would have been
great to see John Garfield in color (John Hodiak took the
part). But he *was* interested in returning to MGM. And
when Joel McCrea turned down the role of drifter Frank
Chambers, a man driven to murder by a sexy siren in the
film version of James Cain's *The Postman Always Rings
Twice,* Grady offered the part to Julie. He took it, and
Warner Bros. let him take it, perhaps to make him happy,
perhaps just to get him off the lot and let someone else pay
him. Filming was to begin in May 1945 with Lana Turner
cast as Cora Smith, the adulterous wife who lures Chambers
into a noir nightmare of deceit and murder.

Julie received that induction notice from the U.S. Navy
before filming commenced. Robbe still knew nothing about
his efforts to get into the service. Now he tried to make her
understand that his inability to serve his country in uniform made him feel inadequate. He hated playing war heroes on the screen when all he was doing off the screen was
playing USO camps. During the filming of *Pride of the
Marines,* for example, Warner Bros. ordered him to San

Diego's naval hospital to play a scene (as Schmid) in uniform. Julie didn't want to do it. "Can't you get somebody else and stuff 'em in the uniform?" he asked director Delmer Daves. "I don't want to go down there with the real thing. There are those guys who have been shot up and what am I doing? An actor walkin' through there in a uniform." Daves and producer Jerry Wald were adamant that Julie do the scene as written. He did it and did it well, but that night he took out his angst in a bottle. According to costar Rosemary De-Camp, Julie joined pal Gene Kelly in an all-night drinking binge that ended in the destruction of a San Diego hotel room. "He [Julie] really tied one on because he was bitter about not being a real veteran," she recalled. "If he and Gene Kelly were in a hotel together, they tore it up."*

The induction notice pleased him; he hoped he would see action in the South Pacific as a Navy gob. There were farewell parties galore for Julie; Jack Warner even sprang for one. It was all for naught. Julie was out of the house by dawn and home by lunch. The Navy didn't want him. He had taken the Red Car (the trolley that bisected Los Angeles from east to west) to the induction center along with screenwriter Richard Collins and crooner Kenny Baker that morning. For passengers boarding the Red Car the ride downtown was memorable; they kept glancing towards Julie and Baker (who was then quite popular) and doing double-takes, as if trying to convince themselves that a major movie star and an Irish balladeer couldn't possibly be taking the trolley at six in the morning. Collins watched with amusement as passenger after passenger

---

* It may be odd to picture Garfield and Kelly as friends, but the two got along well. They played poker together—with Kelly usually winning—and worked out practical jokes to perpetrate on the public, including one where Kelly would pretend to be a purse-snatcher and Julie would pursue him through crowded streets. Kelly thought the world of Julie: "He was a lovely guy and a fine actor," he said. To see just how much Kelly revered Garfield, take a look at the 1955 MGM musical *It's Always Fair Weather.* Kelly's performance as a small-time hustler is clearly modeled upon John Garfield.

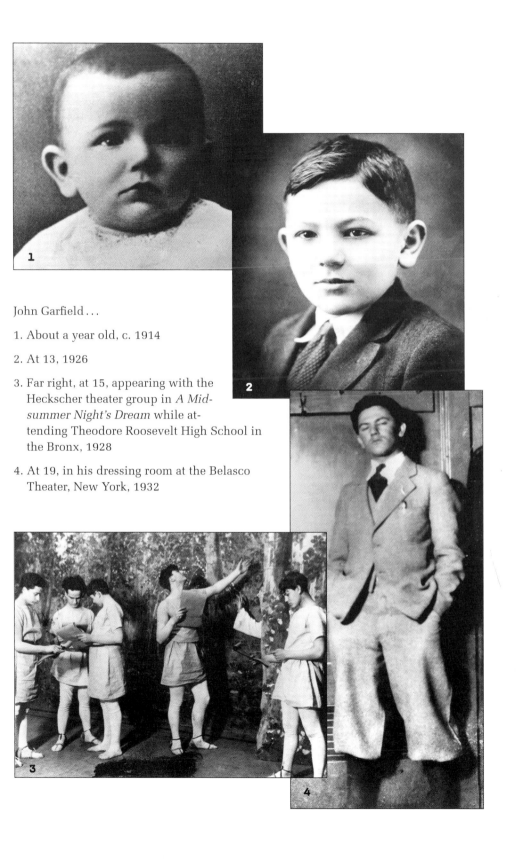

John Garfield...

1. About a year old, c. 1914

2. At 13, 1926

3. Far right, at 15, appearing with the Heckscher theater group in *A Midsummer Night's Dream* while attending Theodore Roosevelt High School in the Bronx, 1928

4. At 19, in his dressing room at the Belasco Theater, New York, 1932

Wedding picture of Julie Garfield and Robbe Seidman, January 27, 1935

LEFT: With Morris Carnovsky, Group Theatre, *Golden Boy*, 1937. (Garfield did not play the title role.)

BELOW: With Priscilla Lane, *Four Daughters*, 1938

ABOVE: Sitting in with the Swingsters, who supplied the rhythm for *Daughters Courageous*, 1939

RIGHT: With Priscilla Lane, *Dust Be My Destiny*, 1939

ABOVE: With New York traffic cop, getting a speeding ticket, 1940

OPPOSITE, TOP: With Spencer Tracy and Hedy Lamarr, *Tortilla Flat,* 1942

OPPOSITE, CENTER: With Harry Carey and George Tobias, *Air Force,* 1943

OPPOSITE, BOTTOM: With Cary Grant, far left, and Robert Hutton, far right, *Destination Tokyo,* 1943

John and Robbe at home with daughter Katherine and son David, 1943.

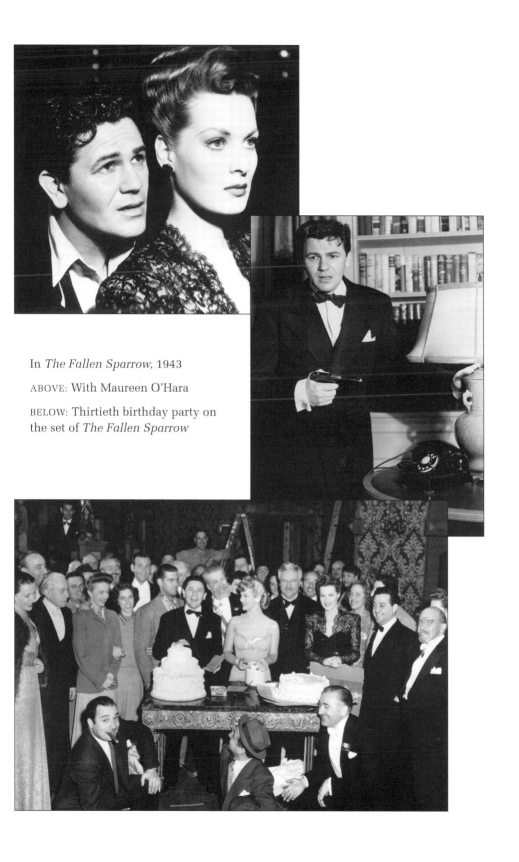

In *The Fallen Sparrow,* 1943

ABOVE: With Maureen O'Hara

BELOW: Thirtieth birthday party on the set of *The Fallen Sparrow*

OPPOSITE, TOP: In a foxhole in Italy, 1944.

OPPOSITE, BOTTOM: A studio publicity shot of John Garfield showing his wife, Robbe, weapons he brought back from his 1944 tour of North Africa and Italy entertaining Allied troops

ABOVE: With Bette Davis and Robert Hutton, *Hollywood Canteen,* 1944

Pride of the Marines, 1945

ABOVE: With Anthony Caruso and Dane Clark

RIGHT: With Eleanor Parker

OPPOSITE, TOP: With Warner Bros stars, *Thank Your Lucky Stars,* 1943

OPPOSITE, BOTTOM: Garfield, shortly before his Warner contract was to run out, with Jack Warner (center) and Robert Hutton

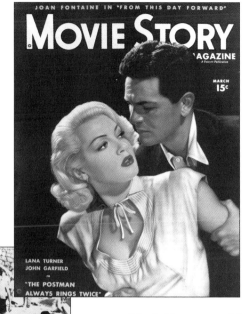

ABOVE: *Movie Story* cover, March 1946

The Postman Always Rings Twice, 1946

LEFT: With Lana Turner

BELOW: With Lana Turner and Cecil Kellaway

ABOVE: In a stage production of *Awake and Sing!* by Clifford Odets, Las Palmas Theater, Hollywood, July 1946

Humoresque, 1946, with Oscar Levant (RIGHT) and Joan Crawford (BELOW)

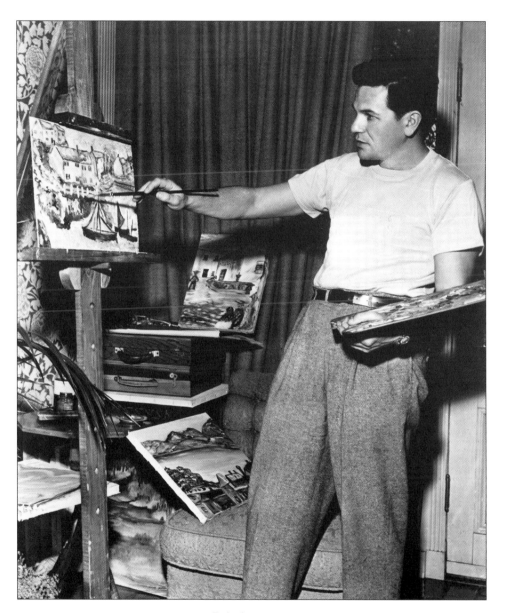

Painting, 1947

Studio publicity shots of Garfield at home, taken shortly after he completed work on *Body and Soul*, 1947

LEFT: With his wife, Robbe

BELOW: "Performing like Nijinsky."

OPPOSITE: *Body and Soul,* 1947

TOP: James Wong Howe filming a scene

CENTER RIGHT: A publicity shot

CENTER LEFT: With Ann Revere

BOTTOM: With Lloyd Gough, seated at left, and Lilli Palmer, at right

OPPOSITE: *Gentlemen's Agreement,*
1947

TOP: With Gregory Peck, Dorothy
McGuire, and Celeste Holm

BOTTOM: With Gregory Peck and
Celeste Holm

RIGHT: Ad for *Force of Evil,* 1948

BELOW: With Thomas Gomez, *Force
of Evil,* 1948

ABOVE: With Orley Lindgren, *Under My Skin,* based on Ernest Hemingway's short story "My Old Man," 1950

LEFT AND BELOW: With Patricia Neal, *The Breaking Point,* based on Hemingway's *To Have and Have Not,* 1950

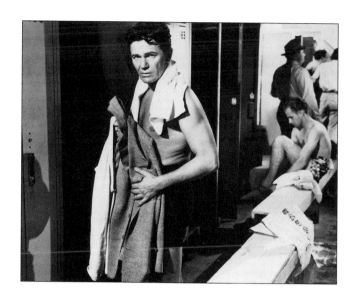

He Ran All the Way,
1951—Garfield's last
screen performance.

RIGHT: With Shelley
Winters

BELOW: With Winters,
Wallace Ford, and
Selena Royle

An anonymous woman, at an unknown place and time,
clearly and happily being tickled by Garfield.

Skipper Next to God, 1948, by Jan de Hartog—
Garfield's return to Broadway after close to a decade in Hollywood.

Garfield's last Broadway perfomances

TOP, LEFT: Odets' *The Big Knife*, 1949

TOP, RIGHT: Ibsen's *Peer Gynt*, 1951

BOTTOM: With Lee J. Cobb in his dressing room, when Garfield at last played the title role in Odets' *Golden Boy* on Broadway, 1952

The
PLAYBILL
for the National Theatre

• THE BIG KNIFE •

1950-51

ANTA

Play Series

Cheryl Crawford and Robert Breen
General Directors

CHERYL CRAWFORD
In association with R. L. STEVENS

presents

JOHN GARFIELD
IN IBSEN'S
"PEER GYNT"

American version by PAUL GREEN

Production directed by LEE STRASBERG

Choreography by VALERIE BETTIS

Setting and Lighting by DONALD OENSLAGER • Costumes by ROSE BOGDANOFF

Music Score and Direction by IAN ADOMIAN

Near East Music by HILLEL and AVIVA

with

KARL MALDEN   MILDRED DUNNOCK   SONO OSATO

PEARL LANG   SHERRY BRITTON

Cast
(In order of appearance)

Aase, A Peasant Widow	MILDRED DUNNOCK
Peer Gynt, Her Son	JOHN GARFIELD
An Elderly Man	RAY GORDON
An Elderly Woman	ANN BOLEY
Aslak, A Smith	JOHN RANDOLPH
Solveig, A Neighboring Girl	PEARL LANG
Her Father, A Minister	JOSEPH ANTHONY
Her Mother	ANNE HEGIRA
A Buttonmolder	KARL MALDEN
Ingrid, The Bride	REBECCA DARKE
Her Father, A Farmer	NEHEMIA PERSOFF
Her Mother	PEGGY MEREDITH
Mads Moen, Her Betrothed	MAHLON NAILL
	EDWARD BINNS
	LISA BAKER
	RAY GORDON
	LUCILLE PATTON
	BARBARA GAYE
	BEVERLEE BOZEMAN
	SHERRY BRITTON
	NEHEMIA PERSOFF
	ED HORNER
	JOHN RANDOLPH

Testifying before the House Committee on Un-American
Activities, in Washington, April 23, 1951

Garfield's body being carried from the Gramercy Park apartment building where he died, May 21, 1952

studied Julie and Baker as if to say "John Garfield and Kenny Baker? Naaahhh... it couldn't be them."

At the induction center the men took and passed their final physical exams and were waiting for orders that would send them to basic training. Julie and Collins were talking when an officer came out of a side room and addressed the sergeant in charge. "He said to the sergeant, 'If any of these men are over thirty, let 'em go. We're not going to induct them. I just got the orders,'" Collins recalled.

According to Collins, the sergeant wasn't pleased. "We already did the paperwork and got them in; why not send them through?" he asked the officer. But the war was winding down and the government was easing up on the recruitment of married men with children. All three, Julie, Collins and Baker, received administrative discharges that day. They took a taxi home. Robbe recalled seeing Julie walk up the front driveway around noon as if returning from a stroll around the block; she broke down in tears when she saw him. For a while, there was peace in the Garfield household.

Julie returned to civilian life and took up Grady's offer to play the male lead in *The Postman Always Rings Twice* on the MGM lot. (Cameron Mitchell had been considered for the role in the interim.) The public remembers the film as one of Julie's best. He's a noir guy in this one; a demobilized soldier returning to an America that has no use for him and who is lured into a web of noir proportions by a wily femme fatale who appears to be worth all the trouble. Julie displayed his newfound maturity as Chambers, a man driven by love and lust to kill, and infused the character with a sense of vulnerability and fear. Chambers is really the antithesis of the type of character Julie had perfected at Warner Bros. in that he is carefree, amusing, and very weak. Watching the film, you may find it hard to blame Chambers, especially since he became a murderer to please Lana Turner, who never looked hotter on film. Turner herself, never considered a great actress, turned in a strong performance in the film, and she and Julie developed an on-screen chemistry that carried over to their off-screen lives. "He was shy, vibrant and intelligent," Turner said of Julie during a 1973 film homage for her at New York City's Town Hall. "And so ahead of his time. He had terrific magnetism. The lines bounced back and forth between us. It kept a girl on her toes." Although extramarital affairs were not uncommon for Julie, sometimes his seductive charm failed to impress his female costars. Turner was an exception to that rule. "The only co-star I know that he had an affair with, actually, was Lana Turner," Vincent Sherman said. "That was a very hot and heavy thing."

The hot and heavy thing started when the duo had too much time on their hands waiting in between camera shots. Unexpected fog delayed location filming at Laguna Beach. Director Tay Garnett relocated to San Clemente Beach. More fog delayed the shoot by another week. Garnett, an alcoholic who was under considerable pressure to turn in an acceptable film under strict production code regulations (MGM had owned the rights to Cain's novel for over a decade but had waited for censorship restrictions to loosen up), couldn't take the strain of the delays. He went on a drunken binge in his trailer, smashing furniture and windows. Julie went in to the trailer to try and calm down the director and was chased by the abusive and incoherent Garnett. The studio reined Garnett in and sent him to a Los Angeles institute for a week of "the cure." Filming was put on halt.

Julie and Turner started hanging out together. They both knew it would be only a matter of time before they got together. "Our eyes would meet and we both knew we were going to have to do it," Julie later told singer Margaret Whiting. "It was like you couldn't let the home team down. Everyone was waiting for it." Instead of playing sly, Julie figured candor was the best policy. One afternoon he said to Turner, "How about it? Let's go down to the beach tonight." Turner was all for it. The moon cooperated fully. So did the sea. But the reality wasn't as exciting as the fantasy, according to Julie. He told Whiting there was no chemistry: "These two super sex symbols and no fireworks." It turned out to be a one-night stand; a disappointment for both parties, but a nice distraction during the delay in filming. The two remained on good terms, and Turner later said Julie was her favorite leading man. Robbe must have suspected something; she showed up on location several times (one behind-the-scenes production still from the film shows Julie and Turner laying comfortably next to each other on the beach while a woman who bears a considerable likeness to Robbe observes them from nearby).

Every Garfield film seemed to have a mishap. A scene in this one called for Julie and actress Audrey Totter (who played a casual pickup) to act in front of a tiger's cage at the Los Angeles Zoo. Midway through the sequence the tiger lifted his leg and sent a steady stream of pee towards Julie and Totter. "Stunt check over here!" Julie jokingly cried out as he and Totter moved out of the feline's urinary range. The tiger was fired and the scene relocated to the train depot.

By the time Garnett returned to direct the film, *The Postman Always Rings Twice* had been in production for nearly four months. Autumn rolled in, and Julie was still at MGM. Jack Warner, knowing Julie's contract would run out in December, was anxious to get his departing star before the cameras at least one more time. Associate producer Steve Trilling felt Julie would be ideal for the role of a street kid turned classical musician in the film remake of Fanny Hurst's *Humoresque* (first filmed in 1926). Barbara Stanwyck was slated to play opposite Julie, but as filming for *Postman* dragged on, it was obvious to Warner Bros. that Julie's contract would expire before he could return to the home lot. *Humoresque's* designated producer, Jerry Wald, decided to move ahead with the film and gave the lead to Dane Clark. In November 1945, Stanwyck left the project and was replaced by Joan Crawford, who was anxious to follow her Academy Award-winning success with that year's *Mildred Pierce*.

For Clark, it was the opportunity of his career. He had been at Warner Bros. for about three years, mostly playing subservient roles to the big boys like Bogart and Garfield. Now he could step out from under Julie's shadow in an A picture opposite Joan Crawford. The young actor began taking violin lessons to prepare for the role. One

day Clark was walking across the Warner lot when he saw a familiar figure heading towards him. It was Julie. The two men embraced
and Clark asked Julie what he was up to.

"They've got me for one more film," Julie said of the studio.

"Great," Clark replied. "What's the picture?"

"*Humoresque,*" Julie said.

Clark nearly fainted. "They took me off that picture and gave it to
him," Clark said years later. "I don't blame him for that. And I never
let on that I was surprised."

Julie had finally finished *The Postman Always Rings Twice* at
MGM in November and he agreed to squeeze in one more film for
Warner Bros., for several reasons: Clifford Odets was writing the
screenplay. Pals Oscar Levant and Ruth Nelson were cast in the
film. Julie wanted to work with Joan Crawford and the story, a combination of Hollywood kitsch and *Awake and Sing!*, appealed to
him. Furthermore, since Bob Roberts hadn't yet made any definite
deals with Enterprise or with any other studio, Julie figured one
more good Warner Bros. film couldn't hurt his career.

It was what was happening outside the Warners lot that did
hurt his career, however. Known as "The Battle of Burbank," it
forged the first link in a chain of events that would ultimately
bring about the noir guy's downfall in real life. Herbert Sorrell, a
former boxer and business agent of the Motion Picture Painters,
had organized the Conference of Studio Unions (CSU), a coalition
of five unions representing 10,000 film employees. CSU had a rival
union, the International Alliance of Theatrical Stage Employees
(IATSE). IATSE sent representative Roy Brewer to Hollywood to see
what CSU was up to. Joining Brewer in Hollywood was IATSE President Richard Walsh. Walsh and Brewer found an important ally
in Senator Jack Tenney (later a major force behind HUAC), who believed that Sorrell was a high-ranking member of the Communist
Party.

CSU had gone on strike on behalf of the set decorators' union in
March 1945. IATSE countered that it had total jurisdiction over set

decorators, and that they couldn't strike. When Walsh told the movie studios that if they chose to negotiate with CSU, all the movie projectionists in the IATSE would strike, the studios found themselves in a potentially untenable situation. But the war was on their side. Few unions would join CSU in its strike due to a union pledge that there would be no striking during the war.

All of that had changed in September. With the war over, CSU garnered support from many motion picture unions. The Screen Writers' Guild, for one, divided its support, with left-leaning liberals backing CSU and right-wing members taking a more neutral stance. But all the guilds, as unions, were required to respect picket lines. In short, if CSU decided to strike outside a particular studio, no union member would cross that line. Screenwriters could stay home and write scripts. Members of the Screen Actors' Guild had a more difficult time choosing sides. Still, the strikers' determination led many actors to remain at home for the duration of the negotiations.

Sorrell figured that if he could focus all of his guns on just one studio, he might succeed in shutting it down. If one studio began to negotiate, the others might fall in line. Sorrell chose Warner Bros. As his main target, and as of October 5, 1945, the studio had been set upon by truckloads of striking union members. Warners all but closed down and Jack Warner called the Los Angeles sheriff's office for support. On October 8 the police arrived in force, watching for a possible riot. They weren't disappointed. By day's end angry strikers had overturned passing automobiles, goon squads had appeared from nowhere, and Warner Bros. security guards were fending off everyone outside with fire hoses and tear gas. Nobody really knew who was on what side of the strike as the violence escalated. Brewer later charged that Sorrell had initiated the violence by hiring thugs from San Francisco to attack the police. Others believed it was Brewer who sent out the pipe-carrying goon squads.

At the time of the strike Julie wasn't even on the Warner lot. He was still in Culver City shooting *The Postman Always Rings Twice.* But he responded to the strike action by joining the Citizens

Committee for the Motion Picture Strikers, another innocuous sounding organization that supposedly had ties to the Communist Party, and drafted a petition protesting the violence. The petition was sent via telegram to the Glendale chief of police, to various civic and political leaders in the Hollywood community, and to the Warner Brothers.

At this time Julie was a member of the Screen Actors Guild executive board and he attempted to convince the Guild to mediate the strike. Ultimately (1947) the Screen Actors Guild recommended settlement through arbitration. However, by that time, most of the Hollywood guilds were against CSU and even Julie voted against them, although as late as February 1947, he was showing sympathy for the CSU strikers. That month he participated in a benefit held at the Philharmonic Auditorium for strikers and their families. It was staged with the help of him, Gene Kelly, Eve Arden, Harpo Marx, Keenan Wynn and others, all of whom performed in comedic and musical skits interspersed with dramatic sequences highlighting the dilemma the striking workers faced. The staged scenes always seemed to portray the police as aggressive brutes while the strikers were repeatedly presented as peaceful, rational and patriotic. The whole thing must have looked like a revival of *Waiting for Lefty*. The long strike focused national attention on Hollywood as a hotbed of political upheaval. HUAC picked up the scent and began making inroads into the film industry.

Julie didn't worry too much at the time, and for that matter, nobody else did either. The actor, having finished *Postman,* returned to the Warner lot to film his commitment to the studio, *Humoresque.* It was a great movie to go out on. It signaled, in many ways, an end to an era. The postwar years would present many changes and challenges for the Hollywood studio system, and the beginning of the end for that system was just around the corner.

In *Humoresque,* Julie plays Paul Boray, a Lower East Side kid who aspires to be a classical violinist. In his quest for artistic and commercial success, Boray forsakes his family, his friends and his values, even falling in love with married socialite Helen Davis. Keep in mind that Clifford Odets wrote the screenplay, because there are obvious references to Garfield's own childhood. His celluloid father (played by J. Carrol Naish) initially has no faith in his son's musical abilities. "He'll never amount to anything," he says, sounding a lot like David Garfinkle. Later still, Boray confides to his pianist friend (Levant) that his father never believed in him: "He doesn't understand me, or my ambitions."

Crawford was probably the biggest female star to play opposite Julie, though this does not mean that she was the best actress. Her role is nearly one-dimensional though she gives it the typical Joan Crawford flourish. At the end of the film, unable to win over the Garfield character, she walks into the ocean to her death. It's a wonderful climax to the quintessential Warner Bros. soap opera of the period. (The ending prompted an angry petition organized by one Gretchin Colnik, a Milwaukee decorator. Colnik and company argued that a mature woman like Crawford's Helen Davis should be able to find a more sensible solution to being jilted.)

Julie and Crawford liked each other. Bob Thomas, in his biography of Crawford, states that when Julie first met Crawford he playfully pinched her nipple. She was not amused, but she decided to use this antagonism to help build a relationship between her character and Julie's. Both of them were sexaholics, but Vincent Sherman, who later had an affair with Crawford, is fairly certain that the two stars did not engage in a physical relationship, perhaps because Robbe was paying more visits than was her norm to the studio during this time, perhaps because Crawford liked to be in control of such affairs, which Julie may not have liked.

Julie did learn how to properly finger a violin bow for the film, but he did not actually play the violin. It was faked, with a violinist's hands tucked through the actor's coat as if he were a ventriloquis's dummy. One violinist's hand came through Julie's coat and fingered the violin. Another violinist's hand took care of the bow. Isaac Stern recorded the musical track. When Oscar Levant saw this ridiculous and confusing spectacle he quipped, "Why don't the five of us make a concert tour?" Julie was always at a loss when fans asked him to play the violin on publicity tours in later years.

Jean Negulesco, who had guided Julie through *Nobody Lives Forever*, was brought in to direct *Humoresque*. Under Negulesco's guidance Julie began painting landscapes. They weren't always particularly good, but they weren't particularly bad either. (Many Garfield friends, upon being asked what they thought of his art, silently shook their heads "no," but Robbe always felt Julie had it in him to be a better artist.) Negulesco's directing style didn't necessarily lead Julie to work harder as an actor; he was a director who favored style over substance, product over process. Robert Blake, who portrayed Paul Boray as a child in the film, categorized Negulesco as a traffic director. "He wasn't terribly sensitive," Blake said. "The good directors—Huston, Stevens, Polonsky—would do whatever was necessary to get what they wanted out of you. Negulesco was more of an interpreter. He knew where to put the camera and he knew where to put the actors and he knew what he wanted, but he never really knew how to get it."

Traffic director Negulesco may have been, when it came to filmmaking, but somebody—perhaps the actors—sure kept the dialogue moving at a fast clip. The film is arch and funny throughout, with Levant getting most of the best lines: "You probably don't recognize me with my clothes on," he says to a stunned woman. "Idealism is a luxury for the very young," he tells Julie in another scene, and Crawford gets a good laugh-line with, "I get the idea that all talented people end up in jail." A funny scene has Julie quoting hearsay on Crawford's alcoholism and promiscuity to a strange man at a party, only to discover that he's talking to her husband.

Negulesco's was unable to get what he wanted out of Blake in an early scene, which prompted Julie to intercede. Blake recalled, "I had to do a scene on a fire escape early in the picture where I was supposed to be unhappy because I didn't have a violin. I was sitting up on a second story set and the cameras were rigged to rise up on me and catch me with a shot of the subway in the background. It was pretty spectacular for a kid my age—I was about ten years old—but it made it difficult for me to do the scene." Blake wouldn't cry on cue. Negulesco was losing patience. Scene after scene was shot and deemed unworthy. "Negulesco was not pleased that I couldn't deliver," Blake said.

Julie showed up on the set. He sized up the situation, took Negulesco aside for a moment and asked for some time alone with Blake. Then he climbed up the fire escape set and sat next to Blake. "He just talked to me for a while, about my childhood, and he got me to go back into my past and talk, and pretty soon I was crying my eyes out," Blake said. "It was his way of teaching me that the Group Theatre's 'method' really worked. Then he climbed through the window behind me, told me not to worry about the crew, and coached me through the entire scene as Negulesco filmed it. It was the beginning of my education as an actor." (Much of this scene ended up on the cutting room floor.)

Blake followed Julie around the set like a stray puppy dog. Julie was receptive to the child's affection. In fact, since Katherine's death he was more sensitive to the needs of children other than his own. Vincent Sherman recalled Julie showing up at his suite at the New York Sheraton bearing a huge teddy bear for Sherman's five-year old daughter. Yet Garfield's daughter Julie, born in January 1946, has less fond recollections of her father's parenting ability: "He blew it as far as being a father. He just blew it. I didn't get the impression that he gave anything to me as a father."

Julie always possessed a charitable spirit towards those in need, including children. During the filming of *Nobody Lives Forever* the company had traveled to the historic Mission San Capistrano to shoot a scene between Julie and Geraldine Fitzgerald. The villagers there made their living by selling locally-grown walnuts to tourists, and when Julie discovered that the children of the mission parish received a huge percentage of those profits, he encouraged the cast and crew to buy all the walnuts in stock. He anted up most of the money himself. When he was overseas he struck up an acquaintance with fighter pilot Ralph Mansberger. After Mansberger was killed in a raid over Austria, Julie helped the pilot's widow find a home in Los Angeles, and he got her daughter Bonnie Lee a small role in *Nobody Lives Forever.* Fulfilling a vow to all the servicemen he met, Julie contacted their families when he got back to the States.

He didn't always take credit for his good deeds. Jack Russell was an ex-serviceman who was running a small bar near MGM when Julie was filming *The Postman Always Rings Twice.* One day after work Julie popped into the bar and anonymously bought everyone in the place a round of drinks. Russell asked Julie where he could buy a good suit; Julie suggested an expensive tailor. "I went down to see the guy," Russell said, "and I picked out two sports coats, some matching pants and a suit. I figured it would come to a couple of grand, and when I asked the saleswoman how much I owed she said, 'It's all paid for.' I said, 'Aw, come on, who paid for it?' And she said, 'I'm not supposed to tell you, but Mr. Garfield took care of the bill.' That was the sort of guy he was."

This generosity tended to attract selfish characters; an array of con men, hangers-on and losers, the sort of riffraff one expected to see in a Warner Bros. crime drama. "He had a coterie of decrepit characters who I found very repulsive," Helen Levitt explained. "There was a pugilist, a writer and a lot of would-be actors. I guess they acted as bodyguards. A movie star needs some kind of protection but I think *he* needed protection from them."

Voices from his past, many of them bogus, clamored for a handout. He always came through whether they were phonies or not. During the 1940 production of *Heavenly Express,* for instance, Julie was approached backstage by a man who reminded him that they had attended P.S. 45 together in the 1920s. The man asked Julie for $200. Julie gave the man the money and wished him well. Conductor Lehman Engel asked Julie if he really remembered being in school with the man. "No," Julie said. "He was a phony." How did he know, Engel asked. "Whenever somebody calls me

John instead of Julie, I know that they're phonies." It didn't prevent him from giving the man the $200.

Midway through the production of *Humoresque*, Julie's Warner Bros. contract ran out. To keep Julie on for the extra month of required filming Jack Warner offered to give his star 16 mm prints of all his Warner films. Julie accepted the offer and carted the films home in the trunk of his car on his last day on the lot. The film ended on a personal happy note when Robbe gave birth to her second daughter, Julie, in January 1946. Of the three children Julie resembled her father the most in terms of personality and talent. To differentiate the two, Robbe took to calling her husband "Big Julie" and her daughter "Little Julie," something right out of Damon Runyon.

Though Julie did not step in front of a movie camera for over a year following his early 1946 departure from Warner Bros., his box-office appeal held fast. Thanks to the commercial successes of *The Postman Always Rings Twice* and *Humoresque* plus the surprising success of *Nobody Lives Forever* (released in October 1946 after sitting on the shelf for over a year), John Garfield made the list of top-ten movie moneymakers for the only time in his career. The public loved all three films; it was the critics who were less impressed.

Time magazine felt that *Nobody Lives Forever* "prompts the suspicion that Warner Brothers' long cycle of expertly documented gangster films—now running into its 16th profitable year—may never die off. The picture's plot has enough holes to drive a black maria through." Critically speaking that may be true, but it remains an awfully entertaining movie all the same. Of *Humoresque*, *The New York Times* wrote that "Joan Crawford wobbles out soused to the ears and having to cast herself tragically into the sea after a telephone conversation with John Garfield, who has told her that he loves his fiddle more." *Postman* fared better; Bosley Crowther said that the film "comes off a tremendously tense and dramatic show, and it gives Lana Turner and John Garfield the best roles of their careers. Mr. Garfield reflects to the life the crude and confused young hobo who stumbled aimlessly into a fatal trap." *Time* magazine was less kind with its reviewer stating, "Garfield is so familiar in the tough-man role that his mere presence threatens the audience's capacity for belief," obviously overlooking the actor's use of economy and focus. The success of all three films reinforced Julie's view that he could work wonders with stronger material. Towards the middle of 1946 the trade papers were suggesting that Julie would sign a long-term contract with MGM or RKO, but there was never any doubt in Julie's mind that he would create his own company, or work as a free-lancer, no matter what the consequences.

"It isn't the money," he told a reporter in 1946. "It's just that I feel I owe it to myself to try new things, things I've never done before. Perhaps a comedy. And I'd really like to do a western." Upon leaving Warner Bros. he was offered impressive single-picture contracts by nearly every major Hollywood studio. RKO wanted him for the lead in *Out of the Past,* 20th Century Fox offered him the murder mystery *Cloak of Innocence,* and Warner Bros. tried to sign him for the psychological western *Pursued.* MGM talked to him about costarring with Judy Garland in a film biography of Sophie Tucker's life. Julie turned them all down. (Robert Mitchum made both *Out of the Past* and *Pursued,* adding to his impressive roster of noir films.)

20th Century Fox came back to Julie with *Nightmare Alley,* a noir nightmare of a film about a high-stakes con artist who is reduced to biting the heads off of chickens in a circus freak sideshow exhibit. For 1947 it was daring stuff, but Julie nixed the film because Bob Roberts was demanding a salary of $275,000, a record sum in those days. Fox put contract player Tyrone Power into the film, and though it did not make money at the time, it is now considered a minor classic containing Power's best work.

Interesting film offers continued to come Julie's way: Republic wanted him to do *Moonrise,* another noir picture based on a Theodore Strauss novel about a man destined to follow his father's footsteps to the gallows. Julie liked the story and wanted to work with director Frank Borzage (a former actor turned director who had made the first version of *Humoresque* in 1926). Bob Roberts urged Julie to hold out for more money and Julie stalled Borzage as long as he could. One day Borzage called Julie at home, urging him to commit or bow out. Julie, fed up, cried out, "Get Dane Clark to do it!" before hanging up on Borzage.

Moonrise was released in 1948 with Dane Clark in the lead.

While Julie understood that Warner Bros. had built him into a star, his tenure there hadn't always aided his career. He was proud of *Four Daughters, Saturday's Children, The Sea Wolf, Humoresque* and *Pride of the Marines,* but few of the other films had provided him with a challenge. He had played the guy on the run, the guy in prison, the guy with a chip on his shoulder, the guy in love with Priscilla Lane, a sad-sack comic Romeo, an oilfield worker, an intern fighting Nazis, a Mexican-American peon, a Hispanic drifter, an Irish-American fighting the fascists, a womanizing sailor and a disgruntled aerial gunner. He had missed the mark with his performance as Porfiro Diaz in *Juarez* and succeeded admirably with his work as Al Schmid in *Pride of the Marines.* But acting in routine melodramas with journeymen directors at the helm led Julie to turn in performances that were, to be kind, no better than adequate. His mannerisms often went unchecked and his performances embraced a flamboyance that seems almost campy today. What is worse, the bad films—pictures like *Flowing Gold* and *Between Two Worlds* and *Dangerously They Live*—have since infringed on the good films, spoiling his reputation as a film icon. Julie understood how important a good script and a good director were to his work. "My problem in movies has been to find the truth," he said in his lecture to the Actor's Lab in 1945. "When I don't, I fail miserably."

He knew he had to break out of the studio system. "A person must do the thing that makes him happy," he also said in 1946. "This freedom I'm attempting may fail. I may take a terrific belly flop. I may meet problems that I'm not able to solve. But no matter what happens, I'll have made the attempt."

He made the attempt. He both succeeded and failed. Over the next three years his career would undergo one of the most meteoric ascents and declines in film history. He would get embroiled in commercial misfires that were politically tinged with Red, find himself involved in a battle with the United States government, and tangle with a beautiful blonde. In the end, he probably felt like one of his screen characters, caught up in a noir scheme that he didn't understand and couldn't escape.

CHAPTER THIRTEEN

Noir Land

*"Film noirs were distress flares launched onto
America's movie screens by artists working
the night shift at the Dream Factory."*
—FILM HISTORIAN EDDIE MULLER

FROM ABOUT 1946 ON, JULIE WAS ONE OF THE ARTISTS working the night shift at the Dream Factory Muller writes about. His characters never wore a trench coat, and it was hard for the femme fatales of noir to really get their nails into them. He no longer fell for the easy line and the soft pickup; he worked hard to achieve success in the noir world, generally coming to his senses and realizing that the price he had to pay to stay in that world was too high. Julie made four noir films between 1947 and 1951; three for his own production company—*Body and Soul* (1947), *Force of Evil* (1948), and *He Ran All The Way* (1951)—and one for Warner Bros., *The Breaking Point* (1950). These films, along with *The Postman Always Rings Twice*, have cemented his position as a major noir actor. Unlike other noir actors like Dick Powell and Robert Mitchum and John Payne, Julie, as a film producer, helped create his own noir world. It was as if he realized he belonged in that strange netherworld of cinema. But he should have remembered the law of the noir world before he entered: Once in, it's nearly impossible to get out.

"I want to make pictures with a point—zing, spit, fire," he told journalist Mary Morris in *PM* magazine not long after leaving Warner Bros. This free-lance stuff was a risky business, but he claimed to have no fears. "Maybe in the next few years I'll make so many mistakes I'll kill my career," he went on. "I can afford that chance." It was Julie hanging off the roof upside down again, and he did it by joining up with fledgling independent film studio, Enterprise. David L. Loew, Charles Einfeld and A. Pam Blumenthal formed Enterprise in 1946. Loew was a producer who had recently engineered the Marx Brothers comeback film, *A Night in Casablanca*. Einfeld, who Julie knew slightly, was an advertising and marketing executive at Warner Bros. Blumenthal was the silent partner with money ties. The trio managed to get ten million dollars in credit from the Bank of America to finance their first six pictures. They leased a small lot on Melrose across from the back gate of Paramount Pictures. Harry "Pop" Sherman was then using the lot to film interiors for a Joel McCrea western, *Ramrod*, which turned out to be the first official Enterprise Production. Enterprise made a deal with United Artists to distribute their first seven films for a 25 per-cent commission. This independent venture attracted some of the biggest stars in Hollywood; Charles Boyer, Dana Andrews, Ingrid Bergman, Ginger Rogers, Joan Crawford and Barbara Stanwyck all negotiated contracts with Enterprise, for the little studio offered something that the majors did not: creative control. It would be the very thing that would bring about Enterprise's demise.

Julie's own deal with Enterprise was coordinated through part-ner/business manager Bob Roberts. *The New York Times* noted on February 2, 1947, that John Garfield had incorporated himself, re-taining 20 percent of what became known as Bob Roberts Produc-tions. Julie's contract with Enterprise gave him script and salary approval, but the deal went no further than that. Enterprise was not formed in any way, shape or form by John Garfield, despite asser-tions to the contrary. His company, Bob Roberts Productions, just set up an office on the Enterprise lot. Though many stars were at-tracted to Enterprise initially, the whole venture was looked upon as a novelty act that wouldn't last long. In the short run, these naysayers were right, but Enterprise did pave the way for the future independents that helped to take over Hollywood by the end of the next decade. "Enterprise was one of the great places to be at that time," Abraham Polonsky said. "Everyone came there to make independent films."

Polonsky had come to Enterprise to do the same thing. He had written a screenplay for Paramount called *Golden Earrings* about a British officer hiding from the Nazis among the gypsies that somehow or other Paramount managed to turn from a fairly dramatic idea into a light comedy, featuring Ray Milland and Marlene Dietrich. Though the film was a major box-office success, Polonsky was disillusioned with the way it had turned out. Enterprise offered the New York-born writer/director a chance to create the sort of film he wanted—sociopolitical drama.

"Enterprise was nirvana," said actor Norman Lloyd, who made two films at the studio. "A guy came around with a cart of juices, sandwiches and coffee around 11 A.M. and again at 4 P.M. And they had a great commissary with a great cook, and the best barber in town. Actors weren't treated that well at any other studio." Marie Windsor, who appeared in the 1948 Enterprise film *Force of Evil,* didn't remember that commissary. She was told to buy her lunch at the hot dog stand around the corner from the lot.

Enterprise embodied an ensemble ideal, a sort of communal filmmaking effort, much like the Group Theatre had done with theater. Director Robert Aldrich remained complimentary about that ideal, as he related to journalist Joel Greenburg: "It was a brand new departure, the first time I can remember that independent film-makers had all the money they needed. The studio, in fact, had everything in the world in its favor except one thing: it didn't have anybody in charge who knew how to make pictures. But for about two and a half or three years before it went down the drain, I would guess that it had a better esprit de corps, and more interest and excitement going for it among the employees, from the laborer to the star, than any place in Hollywood."

Fostering a happy atmosphere, it was at Enterprise that Julie reached the pinnacle of his success as an actor and producer; he turned out two classics of American film noir. The first, *Body and Soul,* was unofficially based on the life story of boxer/war hero Barney Ross, another product of Rivington Street. Ross was an orphaned street kid with ties to organized crime who became Golden Gloves Amateur Lightweight Division champ and later still the welterweight champion. Retiring with only four losses to his record, he enlisted in the Marines during World War II, serving on Guadalcanal. There he earned a Silver Star for single-handedly battling a large Japanese force (shades of Al Schmid). Shortly thereafter he contacted malaria, and in an effort to relieve the pain, became addicted to morphine.

Ross's life story, from his childhood on the streets, his association with gangsters, his boxing and war records, and the drug use, was perfect fodder for a John Garfield film. Julie and Roberts hired writer Arnold Manoff to prepare a treatment based on Ross's life. Manoff went to work while Julie publicized the idea. "If I can do it the way I want, show up the frauds and crooked side of boxing and also relate the story to the times the boy grew up in, I think I'll have something colorful and well meaning too," Julie said. While awaiting Manoff's first draft, Julie and Roberts went about buying other film properties for the actor. Though Bob Roberts Productions company had just one star under contract, both men hoped that the company could produce films for other stars. It never happened. Roberts was not able to draw other film stars into his stable. Perhaps this was due to his fast-talking, hard-sell approach to business. Maybe it was his lack of experience in film production. Several Garfield associates thought Roberts came off as a small-time hustler who managed to hook one big fish: John Garfield.

Still, this hustler was responsible for producing two of Julie's greatest film successes: *Body and Soul* and *Force of Evil.* "He knew how to choose the right scripts, the right people, and the right writers for Garfield's pictures," director John Berry explained of

Roberts. He also understood and respected Julie's desire to grow as an actor, and he sought out appropriate film scripts for possible production. One such film was *Mr. Brooklyn,* a comedy about a Brooklyn streetcar conductor who loses his streetcar. Another comedy, penned by Ring Lardner Jr., was called *The Great Indoors* and had to do with a computer geek (Julie) who falls for a champion swimmer (none other than Esther Williams). Roberts had less acumen when it came to real estate: He urged Julie never to buy property, and Julie listened.

To prepare for the Ross film Julie began training in the ring with professional boxer Johnny Indrisanno. The two spent six weeks working out on a daily basis. Julie got pretty good at it and, caught up in the adrenaline of the ring, he told the press that he had once been a Golden Gloves contender. That was nonsense, as onlookers at a party thrown by producer Leonardo Bercovici discovered. Julius Epstein listened in amazement as Julie bragged to everyone about his boxing prowess. Knowing Julie's talent for exaggerating the truth, Epstein challenged him to a match in Bercovici's living room. Julie agreed; Bercovici produced two sets of gloves, and in about ten seconds Julie was on the floor in a daze. "Not long after that incident I recalled reading that Julie had been a Golden Gloves contender, but there's no truth to that," Epstein said. (There is no evidence that Julie ever boxed, even on the high school level)

All the actor's preparation seemed for naught. In September 1946 the Ross story (called *The Burning Journey*) was put on hold when Ross made headlines by turning himself in to the Manhattan U.S. attorney's office as a dope addict. In 1946, films about drug addicts were taboo, so Enterprise canceled the project. Nonetheless, the seed for Julie's first Enterprise film had been planted. Abe Polonsky got wind of the film's cancellation. "They had already hired the director, Robert Rossen," Polonsky recalled. "They had hired a cast. The sets were built and waiting. I was working at Paramount across the street, and so I walked over to Enterprise. I knew Roberts casually and I told him my idea for a boxing story. I said, 'I have a story

and it's about the Depression, the Jews, the fight game. Interested?"
They said, 'Tell it to us!' And I sold them the story there and then."
The story was *Body and Soul.*

Determined to get *Body and Soul* up and running, Roberts led
Julie, Rossen and Polonsky to Charles Einfeld's office to launch an
assault. The quartet convinced him to agree to the new story
(Rossen reportedly threatened to sue Einfeld for breach of contract
if the picture wasn't made) and filming for Polonsky's boxing picture began in spring 1947.

Actor Joseph Pevney was cast in the film as Shorty, a friend of
Garfield's boxer Charley Davis. "I never had an opportunity like that
in my life," Pevney recalled, "where everybody worked so well together. It was like the best days of the Group Theatre where everyone was working for the best common results." Lloyd Gough was
cast as the villain, appropriately named Roberts (the company was
afraid of being sued by a real life crook if they used any other
name). British actress Lilli Palmer was cast as the boxer's lover, Peg
(the "soul" of the title). Newcomer Hazel Brooks was the body.
Brooks, a model from Cape Town, was the wife of *Body and Soul's*
art director Cedric Gibbons. ("A beautiful girl, but she couldn't act,"
commented the film's dialogue director, Don Weis.) Brooks was a
poor man's Veronica Lake. She wanted to wear a light colored
sweater to show off her ample bosom. Rossen ordered her to wear a
black sweater. "A black sweater doesn't bring out your bosom,"
Brooks told the press. "Why wear one? I told the jerks to make it
light gray." One of the "jerks," Rossen, tried to explain to Brooks
that not all men were interested in looking at her breasts. "I didn't
think we were appealing to that group," she responded.

Bob Roberts had chosen black actor Canada Lee to portray Ben,
the defending champion who Julie's Charley Davis has to fight. The
role was injected with dignity and power. In a pre-production meeting at the studio, an Enterprise executive turned to Julie and
Roberts and said, "Why don't you just avoid any trouble and make
the champion white?"

Julie's eyes narrowed. "Fuck you!" he said to the executive. That ended the debate.

The cast rehearsed the screenplay as if it were a stage play, much to Julie's delight. The actor did most of his own stunts in the boxing sequences, choreographing the movements as if learning a dance routine. He had to prove to everyone that he was the best at everything. While shooting a scene in the ring, Julie turned to former welterweight boxer Art Dorrell and said, "Let's really mix it." Dorrell acquiesced, knocking Julie into the camera boom with a nice right hook that put the movie champion out cold and rewarded him for his cockiness with six stitches.

James Wong Howe, Julie's favorite cameraman, was hired to shoot the film. Howe had an offbeat sense of humor not appreciated by everyone. "He would come on the set carrying a long stick in his hand and look up at the lights and say, 'Gee, it sure is warm," Joe Pevney recalled. "He'd say `I feel a lot of electricity in the air, don't you?' And then he would look up, and then you would look up, and then he'd take that stick and tap your shoe. And you would jump!"

All the people Roberts had chosen shared his liberal sentiments. The entire production was tinged with red as in Communist. Rossen, who had written several films for Julie at Warner Bros., had recently scored a directorial triumph with an RKO crime drama *Johnny O'Clock*. "They hired Rossen because he was a radical, and they wanted a radical," Polonsky mentioned. And Don Weis said, "It amazed me that everyone in that company with the exception of [cameraman] Jimmy Howe was involved politically." Enterprise did have its share of Communist Party members and fellow travelers. Still, as Robert Aldrich pointed out, it didn't produce films of social significance as a matter of course. Two Joel McCrea westerns, *Ramrod* and *Four Faces West*, the Stanley Kramer film *So This Is New York* and the comedy *No Minor Vices* (starring Dana Andrews and Lilli Palmer) could hardly be considered "message" pictures. What is clear is that the Roberts/Polonsky/Garfield unit within Enterprise was made up of individuals who were active in left-wing and progressive causes of the times. "Every day they [Polonsky, Roberts and Garfield] would come down from the office with a petition for us to sign, for good things like housing for the poor, and I signed everything," Weis recalled. "Later, when HUAC started calling up names, I was a little hurt that my name wasn't brought up. Then I realized that I just wasn't important enough."

Politics as a general term doesn't apply either to *Body and Soul* or *Force of Evil,* both of which were written by Polonsky. But corruption—as in the corruption borne of capitalism—does. The first film deals with a fighter who sells himself, piece by piece, body and soul, for money and success. The second film is about a self-made lawyer who sells out his brother in return for financial reward. Polonsky's assertion that capitalism corrupts in itself suggested that an alternate form of social structuring—such as socialism—might be preferable.

It's unlikely movie audiences of 1947 caught any of that symbolism when they first saw *Body and Soul* on the big screen. Coincidence or not, the script smacked of a combination of the Barney Ross story and the Julie Garfinkle story. Right from the opening title and music the film suggests the best of the Warner Bros. crime dramas. It had everything John Garfield fans had come to expect: a rebellious hero scraping his way out of the ghetto, a luscious blonde to lead the hero into trouble, a good girl who tries to save the poor lout before he can get into trouble, gangsters, shadows, sharp dialogue and a thrilling climactic boxing bout, the sort of fight that's rigged from the start in favor of the audience.

The film opens with our scarred and sweaty hero waking up in the darkness from a nightmare. He drives furiously to New York City (the noir capital) to see his mother and his gal. They both reject him, so he turns to a slinky siren, and right away you know this guy's in trouble. The guy is Charley Davis, a Depression-era street kid who turned to the fight game in order to finance his way out of the ghetto. But "money, money, money" becomes Charley's drug of choice, and pretty soon he's overreaching his physical and financial grasp. He sells himself to the ruthless promoter Roberts, beats up a brain-damaged black fighter (Lee) in a championship fight and strays from his loyal gal Peg (Palmer) into the arms of the vixen Alice (Brooks). He loses his fiancée, his friend, his mother and his integrity along the way. At 35, the former champ is graying, flabby, disillusioned. Pressured by the crooked fight promoter Roberts, Charley agrees to throw his last fight, betting everything he has on his opponent in an effort to finance his early retirement. All he has to do is stay in the ring with the young punk Marlowe, "fighting" it out to a 15-round decision.

Charley anguishes over his decision. He's been a heel but he's never thrown a fight. For 12 rounds he and Marlowe dance around each other; earning a lot of boos from the angry crowd. Then in the thirteenth round Roberts double-crosses the champ, unleashing Marlowe (Dorrell) on the out-of-shape Davis. Caught off guard, Davis takes a heavy beating before the animal within him stirs one last time. "I'm gonna kill him," he mutters, stalking the cocky Marlowe around the ring like a tiger. Charley wins (of course), knocking Marlowe out just seconds before the final bell. Peg, watching in the crowd, is ecstatic.

Roberts tells Charley that he can't quit. Charley knows better. "What are you going to do, kill me?" he asks Roberts and his henchman. "Everybody dies." Peg makes her way through the crowd to Charley's side (in an ending later borrowed by Sylvester Stallone for *Rocky*) and the pair walk off together into the night.

Corny—but good—*Body and Soul* is among Julie's most memorable films, though not necessarily the best film. Julie may have seen it as another boxing story, but Polonsky and Rossen knew better. Every scene was injected with the underlying message that fame and fortune corrupt. The word money pops up about a hundred times. "He's not just a kid who can fight," Shorty tells a boxing manager, Quinn (William Conrad). "He's money." After an interesting start shows Charley going into the boxing racket like a kid goes into a new playground, the character pretty much is hooked by the lure of the easy dollar. That he redeems himself in the end has nothing to do with the love of his girl Peg; rather, it has everything to do with Davis's anger that someone turned on him and hurt him.

The dialogue, delivered at a brisk pace, still works. "Everything is addition and subtraction," Roberts tells Julie at one point, "The rest is conversation." Julie gets to inject a little Mickey Borden into the proceedings when he says to Palmer, "You think I like standin' around waiting for the world to decide what to do with me?" When Charley, fed up with his mother's attempts to seek financial assistance to pay the rent, says he'll box to make money, she says, "Better to buy yourself a gun and shoot yourself."

"You need money to buy a gun," Charley shoots back.

That said, Polonsky's transitions are a bit abrupt, and Julie is asked to work extra hard as an actor to make those transitions successfully work. To his credit, he does make them work as he moves from a 20-something kid to a disillusioned middle-aged man in the course of about 30 minutes of screen time. *Body and Soul* is the only film to allow Julie's screen character to mature over the course of ten years (though none of the other actors seem to age a day). He plays a weak, amoral character, a surprisingly unsympathetic man, who is roused out of his slumber not by pride or morals or love but by an unexpected blow to the head.

Julie claimed to understand Davis well. "I didn't have to do much probing into Charley's life and aims," he wrote in *Opportunity: Journal of Negro Life* magazine. "It was all too clear to me because my own boyhood had been so similar." He put Davis on like a suit of clothes and wore him comfortably, but it's still not as much of a successful stretch as his performances in the films *Pride of the Marines* and *Force of Evil* and *The Breaking Point*. He received a Best Actor Academy Award nomination for his work in *Body and Soul*.

The cast and crew knew they had something special in the can when they finished the film, but no one figured it would ever be considered a classic. "We didn't plan on making a film classic," Joe Pevney said. "We just wanted to make a good movie as honestly as we could." Some debate about the film's ending marred the relationship between screenwriter and director. Polonsky had ended the film with a shot of Charley and Peg walking off together, ready to take on the future. Rossen felt the film would have more impact if the gangsters shot Charley dead in the alley. Rossen had attempted to circumvent Polonsky earlier in the shoot by writing new dialogue on pieces of paper and slipping the new bits to the cast. One of the actors tipped off Roberts, who in turn tipped off Polonsky. The duo confronted Rossen. "He denied it at first," Polonsky recalled, "but then we showed him the pieces of paper and his face turned red. He promised to never do it again."

Rossen wanted his hero dead. Polonsky wanted his script respected. Julie sided with Polonsky; Roberts was more ambivalent. Enterprise executive Charles Einfeld solved the problem by suggesting that both endings be shot. Rossen did so. "We went to the rushes the next day and we watched both endings, and everyone was there, and there was no contest," Polonsky recalled. Polonsky's ending remained. Rossen was unhappy about the strained partnership with Polonsky. He told Eileen Creelman of *The New York Sun,* "That's the last picture I've worked on without writing it, and it's going to be the last. Makes me too frustrated." Years later Rossen's widow Sue would maintain that Polonsky was a pain in the neck who took more credit than he deserved for the finished product.

Once the film wrapped, Julie took off for a week of hunting in the Sierra Madre Mountains. He returned to Los Angeles and lent his vocal talents to a children's record for Mercury. *Hermine Ermine in Rabbit Town* was based on a story by Malcolm Child which told of the peaceful coexistence of black and white rabbits in little Rabbit Town until evil Fenimore Fox shows up to stir up trouble. It was a child's fable about racism, and the recording is an absolute hoot to experience. Julie plays all the various voices, joins in the singing of a children's song and does justice to the role of storyteller. About the same time, he provided great copy for Hollywood journalists when he spouted off about his seven-year battle with Warner Bros. "I can't blame them in a way," he said of the studio. "They were afraid to take a chance on me for they had a personality and wanted to exploit it. But I want to take a chance."

For all his talk about taking chances, *Body and Soul,* released in August 1947, was pre-sold to its audience. Slowly, through word of mouth, the film began to make money and critical accolades came pouring in. *The Mirror's* Jack Thompson noted that the film was "probably the most realistic and honest story of prize fighting yet brought to the screen." Julie's work garnered a lot of attention. "It's a striking commentary on Hollywood and its waste of talents that Garfield, an actor who was perfectly capable of doing this job nine years ago when he first left the New York stage, should have had to wait so long and impersonate so many variously repetitious types before he could realize his full capabilities," Archer Winston of *The New York Post* wrote. You would have thought Julie was finally making a comeback after a ten-year hiatus in B movies.

This isn't exactly how it was, to be sure, but it's true that he was riding the comeback trail. But it was a gradual comeback, unlike more dramatic show business stories like Frank Sinatra's turn-around with *From Here to Eternity. Body and Soul* grossed nearly five million dollars for Enterprise, making it the first (and, as it turns out, the only) financial hit for that company. Julie's take was reportedly half a million dollars; the most he would ever earn from one film. The Enterprise executives immediately began negotiating with Bob Roberts Productions for another John Garfield film.

Julie, meanwhile, accepted an offer from 20th Century Fox to play a supporting role in the studio's screen version of *Gentleman's Agreement,* author Laura Z. Hobson's novel about anti-Semitism. Gregory Peck was cast as journalist Skylar "Phil" Green, who agrees to pose as a Jew in order to experience firsthand what it's like to be the victim of prejudice. Fox studio chieftain Daryl Zanuck worked with director Elia Kazan to assemble a strong en-semble cast; Anne Revere as Peck's mother, Dorothy McGuire as his not-so-understanding fiancé, Dean Stockwell as his son, Albert Dekker as Peck's publisher, Celeste Holm as a flirtatious co-worker, and June Havoc as a prejudiced Jewish secretary. Zanuck wanted studio contract player Richard Conte to play Dave Goldman, Green's Jewish friend and the catalyst for much of what happens in the film. Kazan wanted Julie.

Goldman's screen time amounted to about seven scenes totaling 25 minutes. Before the actor read the script, Julie, through Wasserman and Roberts, asked a ridiculously high salary somewhere in the range of $200,000. Upon realizing what the film had to say about anti-Semitism, Julie said, according to Laura Z. Hobson, "I want to be part of the picture. I'll do it for nothing." For years it was reported that Julie was paid $150,000 for his work in it, but there are no documents in the 20th Century Fox archives at UCLA to confirm this claim. Hobson claims he did it for union scale. "This is a part that said something," Julie told the press that year. "One of the things I learned in the Group Theatre: there are no small parts, there are only small actors." He accepted third billing behind Peck and McGuire and costar Celeste Holm was billed further down the cast list although she has more screen time than Julie. She also has a showier role, which helps explain why she earned an Academy Award nomination for Best Supporting Actress.

It wasn't an easy film to get made, according to Peck. An editor tries to talk Dekker's publisher out of doing the article in one of the film's sequences. "Why go stirring up trouble?" the editor asks. Peck says a similar scenario took place in Hollywood when Zanuck announced he was planning to make the film. "Louie B. Mayer, Harry Cohn, all the Jewish studio heads tried to talk Zanuck out of it," he recalled. "They said, 'Why stir up trouble?' You would have thought they had the most to gain by seeing the film get made, but they were concerned that Zanuck's plan would backfire."

Gentleman's Agreement is still seen as a daring, interesting film; for all that, it is fraught with flaws. Peck's character is surprised and outraged to discover that his co-workers, his doctor, and even his

Gentile fiancé are prejudiced in one way or another. In one odd scene Peck views his reflection in the mirror and wonders whether he can pass for Jewish. "No accent, no mannerisms—neither has Dave," he says, as if his view of Jews had been formed by Yiddish vaudeville. Yet, like other Jewish actors, Garfield was asked to downplay his race—including the Americanization of his name—so as not to offend potential film producers, distributors or audience members. Julie had played various ethnic types, including a Hispanic or two and an Irishman, but other than *Gentleman's Agreement,* no other film except *Body and Soul* had referred to his character as a Jew. "John Garfield was not Jewish per se," his cousin Sylvia Maislish Nonkin said of his religious beliefs. "But he certainly had a Jewish identity. He didn't play it down; Hollywood did."

John Garfield fans may get impatient waiting for their hero's entrance for his first scene takes place at the halfway mark (*Gentleman's Agreement* is two hours long). But his presence gives the second half of the film a much-needed energy and focus. "He helped that film more than anybody else in it," Kazan said years later. "God knows we were all tired of Peck and McGuire by the time he came on." Julie's Dave Goldman is an easygoing, fun-loving Army captain, a man who suppresses his angry underside until pushed. Again, he is at his best when utilizing economy, letting his inner anguish remain just that. He plays with quiet authority and humor, offering just a trace of the old tough guy persona when he roughs up a drunk who calls him a "yid" in one brief scene. Kazan felt Julie had matured considerably as an actor: "He was much more confident. He had more of what we call 'stage weight.'" Peck, too, was impressed with Julie's desire to bare everything: "He was vulnerable; his feelings were close to the surface, and he expressed them, which is very important for an actor. He had a strength, a poise, an inner calm."

Julie's best scene in the film involves a dinner table conversation that he has with Cathy (Dorothy McGuire) that lasts all of two minutes. She is trying to prove that she is not anti-Semitic and she tells

Dave of her outrage over an ethnic joke she heard at a dinner party. "This man told a vicious little story," she says, but hesitates to tell him more. "I despised him." Dave, smiling, quietly interrogates Cathy, "What did you do when he told the joke?" Cathy hems and haws and talks about how upset she and all the other dinner guests were. "And what did you do?" Dave asks, still calmly smiling. Cathy, of course, had done nothing. Dave caps off the conversation saying "This is just a different sort of war." Moss Hart had written the entire screenplay based on Hobson's novel, but he asked Hobson to write in that scene specifically for the screen, and it remains one of the film's most powerful.

Even so, courtesy of Hart, the film suffers from an overly loquacious screenplay that includes too many scenes of Peck and McGuire fighting, breaking up, and getting together again. It's easy now to dismiss the film as a well-meaning sermon on the ills of hate and prejudice. "It seems to have dated a bit," Peck admits. "It seems a bit earnest and self-righteous." Peck and McGuire performed admirably, and both Julie and Celeste Holm (who got her Oscar) are superb.

Peck had founded the La Jolla Playhouse in 1946, and during filming Peck told Julie of his plan to create a theater in Los Angeles based on it. Peck's idea was to financially anchor the theater with productions featuring well-known motion picture stars such as Gene Kelly, Rosalind Russell, Henry Fonda, Jack Benny, Mel Ferrer and Julie. He hoped that each performer would commit to ten weeks a year to do a play until the theater got up and running. This became a catch: "We all had to sign a contract guaranteeing ten weeks out of the year," Peck recalled. "And that blew it right there. Gene Kelly couldn't guarantee ten weeks. Roz Russell couldn't guarantee ten weeks. Jack Benny said, 'Gee, I'd love to do it, but I'm not sure about ten weeks.' And so we all sort of parted ways, and that was that. If we had pulled it off we would have been way ahead of our time."

Body and Soul was enjoying a healthy box-office run, and remaining in cinemas through early 1948. Academy voters were putting together their initial ballots as word of the film's success continued to spread. Early that same year Enterprise ran a full-page ad in *The Hollywood Reporter* announcing special screenings of *Body and Soul* for Academy voters because it was hoping for a Best Picture nomination. What they received was a Best Actor nomination for Julie, a nomination for James Wong Howe for his cinematography and a nomination for Robert Parish and Francis Lyon for Best Film Editing. (Parish and Lyon would win.)

Julie was the dark horse that year, and he knew it. The other nominees were Ronald Colman for *A Double Life* (he won), William Powell for *Life With Father,* Michael Redgrave for *Mourning Becomes Electra* and Gregory Peck for *Gentleman's Agreement.* The latter also garnered nominations in the Best Picture, Best Director, and Best Supporting Actress categories and won in all three.

As Julie turned thirty-five in March 1948, he had an Academy Award nomination and two big screen hits running concurrently. In addition, his next film project, *Tucker's People,* was shaping up to be an exciting film. On the professional front, the actor had every reason to quote his final line from *Body and Soul:* "I never felt better in my life." He probably had every reason to believe that his life was just beginning.

CHAPTER FOURTEEN

Force of Evil

"You can't tell about your life until you're all through living it."

—JOE MORSE (JOHN GARFIELD)
IN *FORCE OF EVIL* (1948)

EDMUND HARTMANN, A SCREENWRITER AT PARAMOUNT, was having lunch in the studio commissary one day in 1951 when he was greeted by an amazing spectacle. One by one the diners seated at the tables at the front of the commissary began standing up and cheering and applauding. Hartmann could not see who was meriting all the applause, so he too stood up. He caught sight of studio head Y. Frank Freeman entering with Senator Joseph McCarthy. "He got the damnedest cheers you ever heard," Hartmann said of McCarthy. "They cheered him all the way into the private dining room."

The Red Scare had arrived in Hollywood.

After the war it had reignited. The Nazis had been defeated but there was a strong feeling that a new enemy was waiting to take over America. "When Roosevelt died and Truman took over after the war, that was the end of the illusion," screenwriter Paul Jarrico said. "And it was the illusion that peaceful cooperation between the Soviet Union and the western forces could continue." President Truman had signed Executive Order 9835 in March 1947, establishing a loyalty oath and security program for all government employees, and reviving the attorney general's list of subversive organizations. Truman wasn't the only one preparing for a second wave of investigations. Hollywood personalities helped fuel the fire. During a May 1945 chamber of commerce meeting to enlist aid for Washington to combat subversive groups, Captain Clark Gable of the U.S. Army Air Corps spoke of the need to be wary of the Communists. "I recently left a place where there are no Communists and no anti-Semites," Gable said, "And I hate to see anything like Communism enter the home front."

About the same time Representative Martin Dies reminded everyone that Hollywood was still the greatest source of revenue for the communists. He was joined in his crusade by Mississippi Congressman John E. Rankin, who had stated, "One of the most dangerous plots ever instigated for the overthrow of this Government has its headquarters in Hollywood." Rankin said the House Committee on Un-American Activities was on "the trail of the tarantula." The tarantula was red and he lived in Hollywood. Rankin, Dies and HUAC followed the trial. The real impetus for HUAC's excursion to Hollywood was a radio interview with one Louis Budenz, an ex-Communist who had resigned as editor of the Communist newspaper *The Daily Worker.* In that interview in October 1946 Budenz said that the head of the American Communist Party was a secret agent of the Kremlin. Journalists Howard Rushmore and Frederick Woltman (both fervently anti-communist) surmised that Budenz was referring to Gerhart Eisler, whose brother Hanns was a Hollywood composer. HUAC subpoenaed Gerhart Eisler in February 1947. Eisler refused to testify unless he could first read a short statement. HUAC turned him down, and a young congressman named Richard Nixon charged Eisler with contempt of court. Eisler was jailed, but he posted bail and quite literally jumped ship, stowing away on a Polish freighter bound for East Germany. His flight made him all the more suspect, so HUAC went after his brother Hanns and sister Ruth (Fischer).

Ruth Fischer testified that her brother Gerhart was a communist, a terrorist and a murderer, which is just the sort of thing HUAC wanted to hear (whether any of that is true or not is unclear). Fischer went on to estimate that there were several thousand communists in the United States. HUAC Chairman Robert E. Stripling used Fischer's testimony as a springboard to Hollywood, and went to the West Coast in the spring of 1947 with Senator J. Parnell Thomas and investigator Louis Russell to find Hanns Eisler.

And so the witch hunts resumed.

When HUAC started a round of closed-hearing sessions in Los Angeles, Julie was working on *Body and Soul,* but pulled into the web when Senator Jack Tenney told HUAC that Julie was a communist sympathizer. Julie shrugged the charge off, telling the press, "I voted for Roosevelt and I've always been for Roosevelt. And I guess Senator Tenney doesn't like that. All I can say is that I'm a registered Democrat and vote the Democratic ticket all the time." Tenney went back on the offensive, telling HUAC that both Julie and Charlie Chaplin had given aid and comfort to the communists. Tenney was referring to a May 1946 party aboard a Soviet ship in Long Beach Harbor. The Garfields and the Chaplins had attended. The party was hosted by Soviet journalist Konstantine Simonov (a man who had covered the siege of Stalingrad during the early days of the war). The party was innocuous, Julie said. The group had simply had dinner, toasted to friendship and watched a short film entitled *The Bear,* based on a one-act play by Anton Chekhov. Some right-wing members of the press reported that the film was about the 1917 Soviet Revolution. Unfortunately, Chaplin didn't help matters when he referred to the customs personnel who were monitoring the party as "the American Gestapo."

The party story had merited some front-page headlines in early 1946; a year later Julie had practically forgotten all about the incident. But Tenney now threatened a state investigation into the shipboard party. Julie responded with another press statement: "We felt it was an honor to be invited aboard as a guest of Mr. Simonov because he was here on invitation of the State Department." Julie, like so many others, was more or less unconcerned with the government's investigation. "We didn't think that they had that much power," Paul Jarrico said. "We just didn't think that they could win."

But from the start HUAC was aided by many of the Hollywood power brokers; men who probably didn't realize that they had more to lose than gain by cooperating so fully. In the spring of 1947 fourteen "friendly" witnesses testified in front of HUAC at the Biltmore Hotel in Hollywood. These witnesses comprised a rather eclectic group of personalities including Jack L. Warner, Robert Taylor, the mother of Ginger Rogers, and actor Adolphe Menjou. Taylor griped about being forced to appear in the 1943 MGM pro-Soviet film *Song of Russia*. Menjou said that Hollywood was one of the main staging centers of communist activity in all of the country. Rogers' mother, Lela, suggested that Dalton Trumbo and Clifford Odets were communists.

"I think the Un-American Activities Committee is doing an excellent job here," Jack Warner testified, "And I am happy to have had the opportunity to cooperate with its members." Warner offered up the names of some studio writers who he felt had tried to insert "un-American" ideas into Warner Bros. films. Among the writers were Alvah Bessie, Gordon Kahn, Howard Koch, Albert Maltz, Irwin Shaw, Robert Rossen, Dalton Trumbo and Clifford Odets; all friends of John Garfield's. Also in that list were the Epstein Brothers, who had written several John Garfield films.*

Warner's list gave HUAC hope, and Senator Thomas became intrigued with the notion that communists had infiltrated the Screen Writers' Guild. Emmet Lavery, then president of that guild, seemed unconcerned about Thomas' claim that communist writers were influencing film content. "I personally doubt very much that subversive circles in the city are likely to be trapped by punches tele-

---

* When Julius Epstein looked over Jack Warner's list of subversive writers, he discovered that almost all of them were Warner Bros. employees who were trying to get out of their studio contract at the time. "Not wanting to work at Warners was considered Un-American by Warner," Epstein said.

graphed in advance by eight-column scare headlines," he said. HUAC, wrapping up its West Coast hearings on May 16, 1947, issued a statement that claimed that "90% of Communist infiltration" in Hollywood was due to red-tinged film scripts. HUAC had found its cause. At the same time, a huge Hollywood rally, sponsored by the Progressive Citizens of America, was taking place in support of third-party Presidential candidate Henry Wallace. Some 25,000 audience members attended the event, including the Garfields. Julie pledged $100 to Wallace's campaign, a rather paltry sum that suggests he was ambiguous about his support. Actress Katharine Hepburn was the keynote speaker, and she earned applause when she said, "The artist, since the beginning of recorded time, has always expressed the aspirations and dreams of his people. Silence the artist and you silence the most articulate voice the people have."

In the Wallace crowd were members of Friends of Russia, an acknowledged communist group who began to loudly chant "Wallace in '48." Julie later said he felt the communists had captured Wallace, and that's why he shifted his support to Truman. But he really paid no never-mind to the whole affair, continuing to lend his name to this and/or that liberal cause. Some of the things he petitioned for were worthy; he joined Gene Kelly and Gregory Peck in signing a petition for the American Crusade to Stop Lynching and he registered a protest against discrimination at New York's Ambassador Hotel when well-known black activist and film producer Carter Moss was denied service there.

The spring hearings were not taken too seriously. The autumn hearings would be. In September 1947 Thomas announced that 45 Hollywood artists would be subpoenaed to appear in Washington, D.C., for a round of public testimony on the subject of communism in Hollywood. Of the 45, 19 were considered "unfriendly" by HUAC: screenwriters Herbert Biberman, Lester Cole, Alvah Bessie, Ring Lardner Jr., John Howard Lawson, Albert Maltz, Samuel Ornitz, Dalton Trumbo, Howard Koch, Richard Collins, Bertolt Brecht (he had written exactly one screenplay), Gordon Kahn and Waldo Salt;

directors Lewis Milestone, Robert Rossen, Edward Dmytryk and Irving Pichel; actor Larry Parks and RKO producer Adrian Scott. Among the "friendly" witnesses were Robert Taylor, Adolphe Menjou, Ronald Reagan, Gary Cooper, George Murphy, Lela Rogers and novelist Ayn Rand. HUAC had finally tracked down Hanns Eisler; he would testify first. In October, Eisler appeared before HUAC, telling the committee that he had applied for Communist Party membership and had been accepted, though he chose not to join. HUAC maintained that meant that Eisler was a communist. Eisler spoke about the sociopolitical aspects of his music, and representatives of HUAC drastically reinterpreted his comments to suggest that he was using music to sponsor the overthrow of the United States government. Eisler, waging a losing battle, predicted correctly that HUAC would ruin many careers with "distortions and inventions."

Having gained momentum with Eisler, HUAC moved forward with the so-called "friendly" witnesses. Ayn Rand, self-proclaimed advocate of free thought and author of *The Fountainhead,* which was about to become a major motion picture at Warner Bros., spent a lot of her testimony criticizing *Song of Russia.* Without any hint of irony Rand told HUAC that she was testifying before them because she did not believe that the American people deserved to be lied to. Menjou followed Rand and suggested that Hollywood start making anti-communist films (they would soon enough). Menjou said he was convinced that a communist actor could add subversive elements to a film through a "look, an inflection, or a change in voice." He claimed that communist activity in the United States had increased since the attack on Pearl Harbor, though he could not cite one specific example. He concluded by reading a list of some thirty books that he recommended all Americans read in order to learn the truth about communism, and by saying, "I believe America should arm to the teeth." (Today's Second Amendment supporters would love him.) HUAC ate all of this up.

There was more to eat. Robert Taylor, the movie star Julie had met en route to Hollywood, was all for a blacklist. He told the investigators that he thought the studios should fire "every last one" of the known communists employed. Gary Cooper was more ambivalent, even mentioning that he didn't think Communism was "on the up and up." (In films of these hearings Cooper appears to be the least comfortable of the friendly witnesses.) Lela Rogers and Ronald Reagan testified, repeating earlier claims and egging HUAC on. It's possible that at the time they meant well, but in retrospect, on film anyway, they look like evil incarnate.

By the time HUAC called the unfriendly witnesses, their number had been whittled to ten: Bessie, Biberman, Cole, Dmytryk, Lardner, Lawson, Maltz, Ornitz, Scott and Trumbo. (Bertolt Brecht was also called, but proved to be neither a friendly nor an unfriendly witness. When asked if he had ever attempted to join the Communist Party, Brecht responded, "No, no, no, no, no, never"; he then left the country for good.) The Hollywood Ten, as the remaining unfriendly witnesses became known, decided that their best recourse was to challenge HUAC's right to question their political beliefs. "Trumbo and I and the others decided the only thing we could do was not answer the questions," Ring Lardner Jr. explained. HUAC always maintained control over the dais. Witnesses could plead the Fifth Amendment (protection against self-incrimination) and would end up looking guilty. If they chose to partially cooperate, answering some questions but not others, they ended up waiving their right to plead the First Amendment (free speech). In the end, they decided to answer in their own way, perhaps a very defensive and arrogant way, by refusing to acknowledge HUAC's right to question them about their politics or, for that matter, religion. Their approach turned out to be a mistake.

The Hollywood Ten gained moral support from a band of liberal Hollywood celebrities who joined together to protest the hearings under the banner of The Committee for the First Amendment. Among the members of this committee were John Huston, screenwriter Phillip Dunne, Humphrey Bogart, Lauren Bacall, Danny Kaye, Gene Kelly, Sterling Hayden, Marsha Hunt and John Garfield.

"We formed The Committee for the First Amendment because we thought the people in Washington had gone too far," Gene Kelly said. "Everyone was being branded. If they couldn't brand you a Communist then you were called 'pink.' We formed the Committee not to protect Communism, but to support the right to free speech."

The first meeting of The Committee for the First Amendment took place in early October in composer Ira Gershwin's Beverly Hill home. Julie, in New York City at the time, did not attend. He felt insecure about his role in national politics; guilty about the fact that he wasn't doing more. "I'm a fighting liberal, a progressive," he said in a magazine interview that year. "Only Hollywood has made me a little lazy, a little complacent." He did take part in a national radio broadcast called "Hollywood Fights Back," designed to protest the HUAC hearings. About 40 celebrities, including Helen Hayes, Frank Sinatra, Judy Garland, war hero Audie Murphy, and Bogart, joined Julie and four senators in this program against HUAC. "This is John Garfield," Julie said by remote from New York City. "There is no guarantee that the committee will stop with the movies... If you make a pitch on a nationwide network for the underdog, will they call you subversive? Are they gonna scare us into silence? If this committee gets a green light from the American people now, will it be possible to make a broadcast like this a year from today?"

The members of The Committee for the First Amendment (informally lead by Huston and Dunne) agreed to fly to Washington, D.C. to monitor the hearings and publicly register their disapproval. There was only one communist in the group, actor Sterling Hayden, and he didn't tell the others. Huston and Dunne told everyone they were going to protect the right to free speech and political persuasion and not to defend Communism. There were 30 in the confident group who took a chartered flight (courtesy of eccentric billionaire Howard Hughes) to Washington on October 26, 1947. Julie flew to Washington from New York. "They should either outlaw Communism and have done with it or stop crucifying people on unsupported charges," he told the press that week, and when one reporter asked if he was a communist, Julie reminded them that any performer going overseas during the war had to pass a rigorous FBI clearance test to prove his loyalty.

Morale was bolstered when Eric Johnston, President of the Motion Picture Association, issued a press release that stated, "I will never be a party to anything as un-American as a blacklist, and any statement purporting to quote me as agreeing to a blacklist is a libel upon me as a good American. Tell the boys not to worry. There'll never be a blacklist. We're not going to go totalitarian to please the committee." Despite Johnston's claim and the presence of the Hollywood celebrities, the HUAC hearings took on a more somber tone. Each of the Hollywood Ten had prepared a statement denouncing HUAC. None of them were allowed to read theirs. John Howard Lawson appeared first and proved to be belligerently combative. He refused to answer HUAC's questions and was led away. Dalton Trumbo offered HUAC 20 screenplays to examine to see if they could pinpoint any references to Communist propaganda. HUAC wasn't interested, and Trumbo, in turn, refused to answer their questions. As Trumbo was led out of the hearing room, he decried, "This is the beginning of an American concentration camp."

Ring Lardner Jr. maintained a sense of humor, stating that he wanted to answer the questions, but that he first wanted to question HUAC's right to ask the questions. "Well, we have got the right," Chairman J. Parnell Thomas said, "and until you prove that we haven't got the right, then you have to answer that question." That question was whether Lardner was a member of the Communist Party. "I could answer it, but if I did, I'd hate myself in the morning," Lardner said. He too was led out. This routine was played out by the other seven unfriendly witnesses.

The Committee for the First Amendment sat in the hearing rooms in quiet gloom. Julie, appalled at the hearings, took a step to publicly denounce them on the stairs outside the Caucus Room. Standing next to the Epstein Brothers, he waved a statement that he co-signed with Henry Fonda, Paulette Goddard, Myrna Loy, Gregory Peck, Katharine Hepburn, Van Heflin, Eddie Cantor and others. "These actors are disgusted and outraged by the continuing attempts of the House Un-American Committee to smear the motion picture industry," he said. A large crowd surged forward to hear the actor speak, but HUAC officials asked him to adjourn to the nearby (and then vacant) Caucus Room. Julie and the Epsteins protested but were more or less forced to the room, where the actor finished reading his statement to a mostly indifferent press and no public. Reporters weren't interested in the petition; rather they kept asking Julie if he was a communist. "There's a lot of stupid name-calling going on now on all sides," he said. "I can't be scared by it."

Fear had not set in among the Hollywood Ten or their supporters. Instead they displayed defiance. There were no winners among them that autumn, however. The Ten were charged with contempt of court—a rather nebulous charge, to be sure—and the political and entertainment columnists around the country began running articles that mostly criticized them and The Committee for the First Amendment. Right-wing journalist Westbrook Pegler asked why the Hollywood Ten had sent their legal bills to Enterprise Studios (they hadn't) and suggested that Julie had formed The Committee for the First Amendment. Huston told the press that the Committee stood by itself, that it had no close connection to the Hollywood Ten and that it was not formed by John Garfield.

It wasn't a funny scenario, but journalist Earl Wilson found humor in it. In an article he wrote for the newspaper *PM,* he suggested a two-step solution to the "commie question": 1) Take off your clothes, and 2) Go to bed, get some sleep, and forget about it.

The members of The Committee for the First Amendment began to distance themselves from the whole thing. Julie, to his credit, did not. If newspaper clippings of the period are to be believed, he appeared in a political stage satire, *Sticks and Stones,* which ran for two weeks in Los Angeles. He then agreed to take part in the Liberty Caravan, a group of entertainers who presented a series of skits and songs representing the basic principles of The Bill of Rights, especially the right to free speech. Harmonica-player Larry Adler and dancer Paul Draper (both of whom would soon be blacklisted) also took part in the show, which toured the country in the autumn of 1947. Julie had no fear about speaking out against HUAC and made public appearances in both New York and Los Angeles where he extolled the virtues of free speech and rallied his audiences to speak out against HUAC. "I'm sore, damn sore," he told a cheering crowd of some 8,000 at the St. Nicholas Arena in New York. "We say 'no' and that no has become the fighting slogan of thousands of people who love this country and want to see it free!"

Actor Jack Larson (perhaps best known as Jimmy Olson) was under contract to Warner Bros. in 1948, when he chose to attend a political rally against HUAC at the now-defunct Embassy Auditorium in Los Angeles. Julie was one of the rally's keynote speakers. "The town was so weird then," Larson said of the experience. "It was horrible. Warren Weaver, a studio executive, heard about this rally and he warned me not to go. I went all the same. Garfield was speaking, working really hard to raise money for the defense of the Hollywood Ten, and I admired him. He was electrifying. I thought it was a very brave thing for him to do because it could have meant the end of his career."

As 1948 came in it was apparent that HUAC was gaining ground while support for the Hollywood Ten was beginning to erode. To this day no one can quite say why everyone frightened so easily, though many liberal supporters were disappointed that the unfriendly witnesses had not cooperated more with HUAC. In retrospect, it would have been more effective, perhaps, had the witnesses acknowledged membership in the party (which was legal) instead of engaging the HUAC members in a courtroom conflict of principles. Bogart was among the first to distance himself from The Committee for the First Amendment. He wrote an article for the March 1948 issue of *Photoplay* called "I'm No Communist" that attempted to set his record straight. "I'm about as much in favor of

Communism as J. Edgar Hoover," Bogart wrote. "I despise Communism and I believe in our own American brand of democracy." Bogart went on to write that he had been overzealous in his efforts to support the Hollywood Ten. "We may not have been very smart in the way we did things," he wrote, "we may have been dopes in some people's eyes, but we were American dopes!"

A few weeks later, Eric Johnston said in a national radio broadcast, "We do not defend them [the Ten]. We did not defend them then, we do not defend them now. On the contrary, we believe they have done a tremendous disservice to the industry which has given them much in material rewards and an opportunity to develop their talents." And soon after, at New York's Waldorf-Astoria Hotel, Johnston said, "We will not knowingly employ a Communist or a member of any party or group which advocates the overthrow of the government of the United States by force." He said that the Hollywood Ten would be fired (only four of them were actually under contract at the time) and that they would not be reemployed in Hollywood unless they cleared themselves first.

By the end of the year, Hollywood had given up the fight. Maybe some members of its community were afraid of the government; maybe others were afraid of the communists. But mostly they were afraid of not working. In any event, it got very quiet. "There was a cloud of uncertainty hanging over this town which tarred a lot of us," Gene Kelly said. "People were afraid. They were losing their jobs. They had wives and kids to support. They just caved in. Even the movie moguls, who knew the blacklist was wrong, gave in."

The movie moguls had a lot to worry about in 1947 and 1948. They were fighting new battles on several fronts. Television was coming on strong, and while the studios could proclaim that "Movies Are Better Than Ever," more and more people were preferring to stay home and watch Uncle Miltie (Milton Berle) in drag. Most of the studios would eventually come around and embrace television, but in the beginning they chose to ignore it. What they couldn't ignore was the loss of box-office profits. The second issue arose because in 1947 the government succeeded in divesting the major studios of their theater chains. Until that time the majors had controlled all three phases of the film business: production, distribution and exhibition. Warner Bros., for example, knew a year in advance that one of their films—be it good, bad or indifferent—would be booked into a Warner's theater somewhere. But exhibitors running those theaters understood that if they could break the practice of block booking, then they could show whatever film they wanted in their cinema. The antitrust ruling allowed the studios five years to relinquish control of their theater chains. This relinquishment would mean a further loss of profits to the major studios, and the sudden proliferation of independent film studios like Enterprise.

In those uncertain times, one would imagine that a studio like Enterprise would flourish. Julie was back on the Enterprise lot planning his next independent venture, *The Numbers Racket* (based on Ira Wolfert's recent novel, *Tucker's People*). Though no Enterprise release other than *Body and Soul* had turned a profit so far, business at the tiny studio continued, with much hope placed on the potential success of the Charles Boyer/Ingrid Bergman film *Arch of Triumph*, due to be released early in 1948. *Body and Soul* was still enjoying a healthy run, so Enterprise executives gave Garfield and Bob Roberts the green light to do what they wanted.

What they wanted was to make a crime thriller with an edge to it. Polonsky was adapting the Wolfert book for the screen with some help from the author; he wanted to direct as well. Polonsky approached Bob Roberts and asked, "I'd like to direct Garfield's next one for you even though I don't have any directing experience." Roberts, who liked Polonsky, replied, "Okay, go ahead. But make it a melo." (Melo was short for melodrama.) The deal was done.

One day during filming, Polonsky came across Julie reading a play on the Enterprise lot. The actor was excited. "It's marvelous," Julie said of the piece, waving it in front of Polonsky's nose. "Gadge [Kazan] is going to direct it, and Irene Selznick is producing, and

they want me to act in it." Polonsky had known that Julie wanted to
return to the theater. "So, are you going to do it?" he asked. The
actor calmed down considerably. "No," he said quietly, as if beaten
into submission. The play was Tennessee Williams' searing drama
A Streetcar Named Desire. The role in question was Stanley Kowalski. Kazan cast newcomer Marlon Brando in the part.

How could Julie have turned down one of the meatiest roles in
contemporary drama? Polonsky always felt that Bob Roberts was
behind the actor's decision: "Roberts said to Julie, 'Don't do it. You
can make a picture instead. You'll get more money and it's better for
your career.' And you have to understand the movie business.
Garfield always wanted to go back to Broadway, but when you're in
the movie business, nothing in this world seems more important
than all the intimacies, all the courtesies, all the PR they feed you.
I really think that Roberts thought it was better for Julie's screen career at the time, because he had just had a hit [*Body and Soul*], was
about to make another picture, and was talking to John Huston
about doing a film with him."

That's Polonsky's take, which doesn't add up in the end since
Julie did return to Broadway that season. Ring Lardner Jr. remembered he was in Bob Roberts' office discussing a film project for
Julie when Irene Selznick called to pin Roberts down about Julie's
participation in the play. Roberts refused to commit Julie for more
than a few months. According to Lardner, "Selznick kept saying,
'That's not enough time; we need him for the run of the play,' and
that was the conversation that led her to seek someone else for the
part." (Elia Kazan corroborated this version.)

Actor Joseph Bernard, who befriended Julie around this time, offers another opinion: "Julie felt the part of Stanley was not a star
part. He met with Williams and Kazan, and he asked Williams to
flesh out Kowalski and make him more important. He felt Blanche
overshadowed Stanley, and he felt that his reputation was at stake.
He was a movie star." Robbe agrees with Bernard, suggesting that
Julie wasn't happy with his part in the script.

As for Julie, he publicly stated that he wanted more money. "The reason I didn't do it was just the money," he told *The New York Times*. "I think it's a great play. I wanted what I thought I was entitled to get [15 percent of the weekly gross]." He hemmed and hawed some more about his reasoning, adding, "Stanley is more or less a repetition of the various leads I've played in movies." It was a lame explanation. Up to then he had rarely squawked about the size of a role or the money. To suggest that Stanley was a repetition or variation of the sort of character he had played in Warner Bros. crime dramas is absurd. And Polonsky's belief that Roberts talked Julie out of it seems hardly credible; Julie would return to Broadway twice in the next 18 months for lesser theatrical projects. Robbe shrugged it off years later, saying Julie just didn't want to do it and had no regrets. It is true he tended to look forward, not back. But almost immediately, as if to make up for his poor decision, he accepted the lead in the play *Skipper Next to God*. His salary: $300 a week.

Skipper Next to God is now an obscurity. The play, written by former sea captain and Dutch resistance fighter Jan de Hartog, concerns the plight of postwar Jewish refugees. Julie played Captain Kulper, the Christian skipper of a Dutch merchant ship, who agrees to take on board 460 Jewish refugees from Europe with the hope of landing them at a South American port. Kulper can't find one port that will accept the refugees, and in desperation he sails up the Atlantic to Long Island, hoping America will take in his human cargo. America refuses; Kulper's crew threatens to mutiny and, turning to the Bible, the devoutly religious man seeks guidance and comfort in the passage: "He who taketh not his cross and followeth after me is not worthy of me." So Kulper takes up his cross, puts the refugees in lifeboats and scuttles his beloved ship, counting on the American authorities to take care of the rest.

Scheduled for a one-week experimental run, *Skipper Next to God* opened in January 1948 at the Maxine Elliot Theatre. It was produced by the American National Theatre Academy's Experimental Theatre Wing and directed by Lee Strasberg. Thanks to Julie's box-office clout, the production sold out long in advance, prompting producer Belvin Davis to ask Julie to commit to the play for another three months. Julie agreed, called Robbe and asked her to pack up the kids and come East. They were prepared for a three-month stay in New York, after which they would return to Hollywood so that Julie could begin his next film for Enterprise.

It's unlikely that he guessed it at the time, but when he came back to New York late in 1947, John Garfield was returning home pretty much for good.

CHAPTER FIFTEEN

The Good Life

> *"I began to feel corrupt out there [Hollywood].*
> *It's an easy, pleasant life. Too easy. New York*
> *is alive for me."*
>
> —JOHN GARFIELD

JULIE LOVED NEW YORK CITY. SO DID ROBBE. SHE WAS hoping they'd never go back to Hollywood. "Hollywood was never home to me," she said. "And when people asked Julie what he was doing back in New York he'd make a joke, 'Oh, Robbe wanted to move back to New York, and I just came along for laughs.' That was his excuse. But he wasn't telling people what he really felt about New York."

Temporarily the Garfields rented writer David Ogden Stewart's apartment on Fifth Avenue. Soon afterward they would rent an apartment at 88 Central Park West, where they would remain for the rest of their time together. Julie would stride down the streets of the city, crying out, "New York is a hell of a town, a hell of a town!" Waiters, cabbies and fans would see the movie star and yell out, "Hey Julie, how are ya'?" He was back on his home turf in a city where everyone knew who he was.

Well, almost everyone. One night in January a blizzard forced him to take the subway home from a performance of *Skipper Next to God*. Waiting on the subway platform, he realized that most of the passengers recognized him. A middle-aged woman of some stock, carrying a couple of shopping bags in her arms, circled the movie star tentatively as if sizing him up for dinner. Julie smiled, and she approached him.

"Aren't you Julius Garfinkle who used to live on 189th Street in the Bronx?" she asked.

"Yeah," Julie said, amused.

"Do you remember me? I'm Mrs. Grubstein. We lived upstairs from you. You used to play with my son Mickey."

"Yeah," Julie said. "That's right. How are ya', Mrs. Grubstein?"

"I'm fine," she said, recounting her family's history up to that point. Julie listened politely and then said, "That's great."

The woman paused a moment and then, almost as an afterthought, turned to Julie and said, "So, what are you doing with your life, Julie?" She was oblivious to his fame. Julie loved to tell the story over and over, though as he was not a great joke-teller he often revealed the punch line way in advance.

New York City hadn't changed that much in ten years. The Lower East Side was still predominantly Jewish, with its ranks being swelled by recent immigrants from war-torn Europe. The double-decker buses, known as "Queen Marys," were still around, and you could ride one for a nickel. A trip on the subway cost the same. Brooklyn still had its Dodgers, and Julie loved them.

He could hang out at the Cafe Royal on 12th Street, a haven for artists and intellectuals, at Sardi's on West 44th and at El Morocco on East 54th. He was particularly fond of Toots Shor's on West 52nd. (Toots was famous for his adage, "A bum who ain't drunk by midnight ain't tryin'.") The granddaddy of all the nightclubs was the still popular Stork Club, which columnist Walter Winchell dubbed "the New Yorkiest place in town." It was a happy period for the Garfield family. Robbe was back near her family; Julie played with David and Little Julie in Central Park, and *Skipper Next to God* was winning acclaim. The play ran some 100 performances, earning over $20,000 for The American National Theatre and Academy (ANTA) and becoming the one unqualified Broadway success Julie enjoyed in his post-Hollywood years.

"An actor's got to act and he's better off in a play that suits him and one that he likes," Julie said of *Skipper*. "I wanted to do *Skipper* because it is the story of a man who has to make decisions." Acting before a live audience energized Julie. Even better were the adoring fans, including the women who tore at his clothes. One woman managed to remove the actor's raincoat, escaping into the crowd with it.

It was during this play's run that actor Joseph Bernard, who appeared with Julie in *Skipper Next to God,* became fast friends with the star. "I did a good imitation of Paul Muni, and Garfield heard it one day and it impressed him," Bernard recalled. "We hit it off right away. He liked me and took me under his wing." Bernard was amused at Julie's attempts to disguise himself to avoid detection, as when he took to wearing a huge pair of ridiculous looking sunglasses. "The sunglasses made him look even more conspicuous," Bernard said, "And so he was stopped all the time by people asking for autographs. He would say, 'All right, turn around,' and he'd sign them on their backs."

Backstage his penchant for practical jokes resurfaced, much to the delight and dismay of his fellow performers. He would throw the actors a look suggesting that he might try something new, though he would never actually digress from the written text. He liked to keep his on-stage peers on their toes, and would even give them a cross-eyed glance to throw them off-balance when it was evident that the audience could not see him.

"He was like a little kid," actor Robert Brown said. "During rehearsals for the show his film *Body and Soul* was still playing, and he would take the cast down to the cinema and sneak us in for free. He seemed impressed with his work in that film, but he always seemed to have a great sense of humor about himself as well."

Julie never tired of watching *Body and Soul.* Following a matinee performance of *Skipper,* he said to Bernard, "Let's go over to the Globe and see how my picture is doing." The two men arrived to see a long line winding its way around the corner from the cinema, while a separate crowd waited inside the lobby (the film was still doing good business in the early spring of 1948). The theater manager recognized Julie and let him and Bernard into the lobby. Julie made his way to the auditorium door and opened it, peeking in long enough to see the film's climactic boxing bout. The crowd in the lobby began cooing, "There's John Garfield, there's John Garfield." The hum distracted Julie. Annoyed, he turned abruptly to the crowd and snapped, "Be quiet, will ya'? There's a movie going on in here!"

He was well aware of his stature as a film star. "He loved the adulation of the crowds," Bernard said. "But he loved being a movie star more. I don't think he enjoyed film acting as much as stage work, but he liked being a star."

Actor Robert Brown said, "He was pleased with his fame. I remember he used to wear blue suits, with light blue shirts and a dark blue tie. And a Cavanaugh hat. He seemed to want to pull himself away from the Bronx background through his clothes. But he wasn't a dandy. And he walked in such a funny way because he wore elevator shoes, and he was embarrassed about that part of his image. They were expensive shoes and he had to get them resoled often, and I guess that cost him because he used to joke about how expensive it was to be tall. He was funny that way."

Julie never lost touch with his background. He popped into Pete's Tavern in Gramercy Park for a beer and into Stein and Rappaport's Deli on Second Avenue for a pastrami sandwich. Another favorite of his was McSorley's Saloon. He seemed to be everywhere in 1948. Milton Berle roasted him at the Friars Convention at Trader Tom's Steakhouse in February. He made a guest appearance on the WOR radio show *Quick As A Flash* in March, and the same month spoke on NBC Radio in observation of National Negro Newspaper Week. He was active in the local March of Dimes Campaign, as well as working to raise money for Sydenham Hospital, then the only interracial volunteer hospital in the country. Among other radio work he did in New York was *Something for Thanksgiving* for ABC and *Let Me Do the Talking* (with Mercedes McCambridge) on CBS. A one-night benefit for ANTA had him doing a cameo—cleaning up the stage after comedian Bert Lahr's "Woodman" bit.

At the Hoyle Club he played poker—and lost most of the time. He picked up the LaGuardia Award for stage and screen service in the cause of better understanding between Americans of different religious and racial groups. Meeting novelist Norman Mailer, Julie expressed interest in optioning the rights to the author's novel *The Naked and the Dead.* He put in a day's work playing a cameo role in pal Franchot Tone's low-budget film *Jigsaw* (released in 1949). At the Actors Studio he greeted visitors when it opened its doors. He couldn't get enough of the Big Apple. When he visited a doctor for his annual checkup that spring, he was advised to slow down.

One thing Julie *didn't* do was return to Los Angeles to attend the Academy Award ceremonies at the Shrine Auditorium in March. He knew his nomination was a long shot; the odds favored Ronald Colman or William Powell. When Colman won, Julie didn't take his loss badly. He was barely thirty-five and he had already been nominated twice. He was sure there would be more opportunities. In New York he did accept a Tony on behalf of ANTA's Experimental Theater Wing for *Skipper Next to God* (the Tony was not for *his* work, however).

The 1948 edition of the annual *Current Biography* series listed John Garfield, signaling his importance in the motion picture industry. *Look* magazine published an interview with him that stated, "The gossip columnists have never suggested that the gleam in his eye was meant for anyone but the neighborhood sweetheart he married 15 years ago" (13 years, actually). In the same interview, Julie told journalist Dan Fowler that he held no grudges against Warner Bros.: "I wasn't carrying a chip on my shoulder at Warners. I appreciated the fact that they made me a star, but they didn't pick me up from a filling station."

Inevitably the issue of Julie's patriotism came up. "I am not a Communist," he told Fowler. "I made the Dies list because I helped raise money for the Chinese when it was more popular to ship scrap iron to Japan. Two years later, the Japs were shooting the scrap iron back at us.

"I am a Rooseveltian New Dealer. If Wilkie were alive today, I'd be for him. The trouble is liberalism is unpopular today and anybody who is for the underdog gets labeled a red."

It is ironic now that Julie's 1948 film project has since been cited as one of the most anti-capitalistic films of all time. On the surface, *Force of Evil* looks like just another gangster flick. The story deals with lawyer Joe Morse (Julie), who works with criminal numbers king Ben Tucker (Roy Roberts) to fix a statewide lottery on July 4— the one day that nearly every gambler plays 776. Morse and Tucker figure the small numbers banks will be wiped out when 776 does hit, allowing Tucker to move in and take control of all the banks. One hitch in the scheme is that Morse's brother Leo (Thomas Gomez) runs one of the small numbers banks. The film focuses almost entirely on the Cain and Abel conflict between the two brothers, each of whom has a fundamentally different attitude toward the morality of crime.

Publicity shots featured Julie, cigarette dangling from his mouth, scowling over a caption that read "Numbers King whose number was up!" *Force of Evil* would be sold to its audience on the strength of Julie's tough guy image, but beneath the surface, director Abe Polonsky had a very different idea in mind for the film.

"I figured I had one shot to prove myself," Polonsky recalled. "The numbers racket was a big thing in New York. Always. And New York was good because to me it was a wonderful metaphor for the whole capitalistic system. That's what the picture is about—the monopoly of power that people want. I call it my exposé of capitalism."

Polonsky wanted the best people for his exposé. He approached actor Lee J. Cobb to play Julie's older brother Leo. "I'll do it, but I want to wear a hair piece in the picture," Cobb told Polonsky. Polonsky was bemused. "You're not losing that much hair," he said to Cobb, "Why do you want to wear a hair piece?"

"I'm thinking of becoming a leading man," Cobb said, quite serious. Polonsky asked him to forgo the hair piece, and Cobb refused. But Thomas Gomez, who took the role, seems to be wearing a hair piece.

On Broadway Julie and Bob Roberts saw actress Beatrice Pearson in the comedy hit *The Voice of the Turtle* and Roberts put her under contract. She was more or less forced upon Polonsky as the love interest in *Force of Evil*. On screen Pearson comes off as a sweet waif in the Wanda Hendrix mold; off screen, according to Marie Windsor, she was a pain in the neck. Pearson made unreasonable demands on the cast and crew on a regular basis, to the point where some of the crew members began discussing dropping a sandbag on her head. Windsor didn't think they were joking. Pearson and Gomez couldn't stand each other, which was unfortunate, since they play best friends in the film. Things got so tense on the set that Polonsky began shooting them separately in the same room, giving the impression that they were together the whole time. Pearson is one actress who does not seem to sexually connect with John Garfield on screen. If he was hoping to make a pass at her off screen, he was to be disappointed: According to both Polonsky and Windsor, Pearson was a lesbian.

The production crew included cameraman George Barnes, assistant director Robert Aldrich and dialogue director Don Weis. David Raskin provided the hauntingly memorable music score, which, for some inexplicable reason, Polonsky claimed to forever hate.

For Julie, the role of Joe Morse was a stretch. Morse is an educated man, a college grad who relies on words instead of fists to make his way in the world; the sort of successful lawyer who would have defended the likes of Mickey Borden and Joe Burns (for a price, of course). And unlike the characters Julie had played before, Morse was a conformist, an establishment success story—though he's willing to bend, or even break, the law.

One day Julie approached Polonsky and said, "Abe, I just don't understand this guy. I mean, what is he?"

Polonsky replied, "Just think of him as being the same person you were in *Body and Soul*, only with a college degree."

The following day Julie showed up on the set with an addition to his wardrobe, a Phi Beta Kappa key on a watch chain. From then on he understood Joe Morse.

Interiors were filmed on the Enterprise lot in Los Angeles during the summer of 1948. But Polonsky, Barnes and Julie were eager to take advantage of location shooting in Manhattan, so they incorporated in the film such familiar New York sites as Trinity Church, the Treasury Building, Wall Street and the George Washington Bridge.

Force of Evil is an unusual film by 1948 standards, and it has since been canonized as a classic of film noir. One risks repetition in recounting either the plot or critical analysis. The story is set in the days when the New York lotto was illegal. *Force of Evil* presents capitalism as a crime and money-making as a tragic scheme designed to bring about misery. Unlike other noir films of the period, *Force of Evil* has a lot less to do with double-crossing and pay-offs and more to do with the breakdown of a relationship between two brothers—one convinced that money will buy him the power he needs to take care of everything; the other who just wants to conduct his business "nice and honest," even though that business is illegal. In short, big business in America is trying to run out (or buy out) the mom-and-pop operations. Whether anyone at that time could really decipher the deeper message underneath the basic plot line and high-energy performances is unlikely.

Like *Body and Soul*, *Force of Evil* is concerned with corruption. In *Body and Soul* this corrupt world doesn't collapse, only Charley Davis does. In *Force of Evil*, just about everybody goes down with the ship. Joe Morse seems to enjoy lording over that dark world so prevalent in noir films, but when his brother gets swept into that world, he starts to panic. "A person has to know what's right for them and do it, no matter what," Pearson's Doris tells a guilt-ridden Joe late in the film, and the street kid turned smart lawyer, like Charley Davis in *Body and Soul*, turns on his own kind, engaging in a three-sided gun battle against his partners before agreeing to turn state's witness. Despite this, Joe's brother Leo ends up dead, lying on the rocks below the George Washington Bridge "like an old rag nobody wanted." In the final shot, Joe Morse walks off with his gal by his side to turn himself in, on a long shot for moral redemption.

Julie's work in the film is brisk, clean and sharp. He plays Joe Morse with a confident power, economizing his body movements so that his character almost—but not quite—comes off as a robot. Morse seems almost asexual in the film; more concerned with making money than making love. Some of this is due to the lack of chemistry between he and Pearson, but even when Julie gets a shot to play opposite sultry Marie Windsor (forever known as "Queen of the Bs") he projects a frosty cool that suggests he'd prefer to play canasta on her bed rather than get her into it. Nonetheless it is a strong performance, demonstrating Morse's motivation first by a passion for money and later by a desire to do what's right .

And all this in 82 minutes! Martin Scorsese, who loves the film and says it influenced his own work, notes that *Force of Evil* could be mistaken for a typical B film of the period. It was originally closer to 90 minutes long. Scenes involving Windsor's son (played by eight-year old Beau Bridges) were cut, as were those with Sheldon Leonard as a rival numbers operator, and a framing sequence with Julie in the witness stand. Why and how this footage was cut is a confusing tale; the Breen Office (long arm of the Production Code) may have insisted that the scenes go, or Polonsky may have cut them of his own accord, or the releasing studio, MGM, edited them out. MGM was the most conservative movie studio in town, and they released *Force of Evil* in December 1948 as Enterprise was falling apart. Enterprise had lost nearly two million dollars on its first five pictures, and its original revolving credit of ten million dollars had expired in June 1948. United Artists, Enterprise's usual releasing arm, was also having financial troubles. With all the uncertainties, Roberts wanted to ensure that *Force of Evil* would be released, so he began negotiating with MGM. The Bank of America agreed to extend their loan to Enterprise to permit three films—*Force of Evil, Caught* and *No Minor Vices*—to be completed. Enterprise hoped that at least one of these films would be a hit and save the studio. They had had the same hope with *Arch of Triumph*, which had cost over four million dollars and didn't even break even. Aside from *Body and Soul,* not one Enterprise release ever did make a profit, and only one other broke even: the Joel McCrea western *Ramrod*.

The total creative freedom that had made Enterprise so appealing brought about the studio's downfall. "Everything Enterprise did was wrong," Norman Lloyd said. "The only successful picture they made was *Body and Soul*. And *Arch of Triumph* ruined the studio." Abe Polonsky agrees. "There was nobody upstairs to tell them 'no'," he said. "Nobody to stop over-spending or keep an eye on the budget."

Enterprise suspended operations in September 1948, leaving *Force of Evil* and *Caught* (the last official Enterprise films) to fend for themselves. MGM picked up *Force* and released it at Christmas-time—not an opportune time for a crime drama of morality. The public pretty much stayed away from it. Abe Polonsky said the film never made a dime, though it may have earned back its costs. It baffled audiences in 1948. Maybe *Force of Evil* was too offbeat to comprehend. Since then *Force of Evil* has become the only John Garfield film to attain a cult following, due more to Polonsky's reputation than Garfield's. The vertical camerawork, the lighting and the dialogue, suggesting a Greek choral ode or something out of Shakespeare, made the film stand out in a way that was not decipherable in 1948.

Polonsky's followers consider it his finest work; enough to ensure his place as a major American filmmaker even though he only directed two other films (1969's *Tell Them Willie Boy Is Here* and 1971's *Romance of a Horse Thief,* neither of which was a success in any sense of the word). "*Force of Evil* never died; it never died," Polonsky said in the early 1990s. "And it's a better picture than *Body and Soul*." But the film's commercial failure, coupled with the downfall of Enterprise, signaled an end to Julie's short, happy independent filmmaking career. Bosley Crowther liked the film and Julie's work in it. "The main thing about this picture is that it shows, in plausible terms, the disintegration of a character under the too-heavy pressure of a sense of wrong," Crowther wrote in *The New York Times*. "Mr. Polonsky establishes himself as a man of imagination and unquestioned craftsmanship. True, he was very fortunate in having John Garfield play the young lawyer in the story, for Mr. Garfield is the tough guy to the life. Sentient underneath a steel shell, taut, articulate—he is all good men gone wrong."

Before *Force of Evil* was released, the actor committed himself to another film, the John Huston melodrama *We Were Strangers*. Huston had scored a double bull's-eye at Warner Bros. with his 1948 hits, *Key Largo* and *Treasure of the Sierra Madre*. (Huston had wanted Julie to play the role of Curtain in the latter; the part went to Tim Holt.) Now Huston joined producer Sam Spiegel to form a new independent film company, Horizon Pictures. Horizon's first film project was based on Robert Sylvester's book *Rough Sketch*, which deals with a group of Cuban terrorists who plan to blow Cuban dictator Gerard Machado y Morales to pieces. Julie, eager to work with Huston, agreed to play the lead role of Cuban-American Tony Fenner, leader of the plot to kill Machado, even though Huston and screenwriter Peter Viertel only had 40 pages of script ready. Actress Jennifer Jones, equally keen to work with Huston, signed on as the leading lady, named China Valdez (!). Bob Roberts told Julie he thought the film would be a misfire, and he was right.

"Huston was going through a lot of personal problems at the time, and he was unable to concentrate on the film," Peter Viertel recalled. "It was a very difficult story with an ending that wasn't exactly considered happy by Hollywood standards." (The finale sees all the plotters dead.) Like *Casablanca,* much of *We Were Strangers* was written on the spot, a day ahead of shooting. Julie didn't care, or he pretended not to care. One day he said to Viertel, "Huston's doing this on purpose since the plotters don't know what would happen either." Viertel knew better: "That wasn't true. We just didn't know how to end the film." That ending would be rewritten several times by various writers.

Much of the film has long sequences of the plotters digging a tunnel under the cemetery and filling sacks with dirt. To attain a sense of realism, Huston ordered his prop men to fill the sacks with real dirt so the actors really sweated and strained during shooting. It was a genuine scream when Jennifer Jones came across a hand reaching out of the dirt; Huston had fashioned the hand out of latex to scare her.

Spiegel brought agent Johnny Hyde and a young blonde starlet on the set. Spiegel asked Huston to film a silent test of the blonde, using as little film, time and money as possible. Huston said he would, but as soon as the producer left the set Huston asked Viertel to write a scene for the girl to play on camera with Julie. The next day Huston, cameraman Russell Metty and Julie spent a good part of the day filming this brief screen test with the young blonde, one Marilyn Monroe. Spiegel was furious at Huston's insubordination and blamed the director for letting the film fall behind schedule another day. Indifferent to Spiegel's ranting but appreciative of Monroe's potential, Huston cast her in a small role in his next film, *The Asphalt Jungle*. (No one seems to know what happened to that test film of Monroe and Garfield; one wonders if the actor made a pass at her.)

When filming on *We Were Strangers* ended, Huston hosted a cast party at his home, which Julie and Robbe attended. They watched in amusement as Jennifer Jones presented Huston with a gift—a large female chimpanzee named Trudy. Huston gleefully let Trudy loose, and the chimp took to climbing over furniture, swinging on the chandelier and defecating freely on the guests below. Robbe was hit three times. She excused herself to go wash her hair in Huston's bathroom, only to return for another bombardment. Everyone else thought it was quite funny; spirits were high that night. Julie got so high he passed out under Huston's grand piano.

We Were Strangers was released by Columbia in May 1949 after Spiegel hired Ben Hecht to rewrite the ending so that the bombing is foiled, the plotters arrested and Fenner is killed in a gun battle as the people take to the streets of Cuba in revolt. (That isn't how it happened in 1933, when the events took place.) Julie's performance is devoid of depth or nuance. He may have given over-the-top performances before, but rarely had he given an uninteresting performance. But as Tony Fenner, he is colorless until he springs to life long enough to shoot it out with corrupt politicos in the action-packed climax. Few of the other actors, except for Pedro Armendariz, connect to their roles. The direction is typical of Huston's lesser works: broad, indifferent, and unfinished. That final gun battle is highly watchable, with Huston shading Julie in black, gray and white as he fires a machine gun at his attackers. But the film fades out on a ridiculous note with Gilbert Roland's eulogy to Julie sounding remarkably similar to Henry Fonda's closing speech in John Ford's 1940 film *The Grapes of Wrath* ("Every time a cop's beating up on a little guy, I'll be there," or something like that.). *We Were Strangers* is a mess, though occasionally it is an interesting mess.

The film received mostly poor reviews when it was released, and it gave the right wing reason to target Huston and Garfield as communist sympathizers. *The Hollywood Reporter* considered the film a piece of communist propaganda, stating that it was "the heaviest dish of Red theory ever served to an audience outside the Soviet Union." *The Los Angeles Daily Mirror* mentioned that the Los Angeles District of the California Federation of Women's Clubs, who considered the film a "piece of cleverly designed propaganda to advance the Communist Party line," had sent a letter of protest to Columbia Pictures' head Harry Cohn. It is a politically-charged film, to be sure, but that charge is filled with confusion. Huston shrugged off the criticism (he makes little mention of the film in his autobiography) as did Julie and screenwriter Viertel. "I think in some ways the film was ahead of its time," Viertel said. "In other ways, it just wasn't completely filmed. But none of us thought, at that time, that there would be serious repercussions later on."

Julie didn't seem too concerned that June when the California Un-American Activities named him among hundreds of Hollywood "Communist appeasers or followers." In September Julie subscribed to a brief filed before the U.S. Supreme Court in support of the appeals filed on behalf of writers John Howard Lawson and Dalton Trumbo, both of whom had been convicted of contempt of Congress. Each of the Hollywood Ten had been found guilty of one sort of contempt charge or another and all sentenced to jail terms ranging from six to twelve months. Ring Lardner Jr., displaying his wit to the last, placed an ad in the newspaper classifieds that read "House for Sale; Owner Going to Jail."

If Americans had appeared indifferent to the notion of communists in their closets in 1947, by 1949 they were willing to reconsider their feelings. Senator Joseph McCarthy appeared on radio's *Meet the Press* show and said, "We are at war. We've been at war with Russia for some time now, and Russia has been winning." In 1948 Senator Karl Mundt and Congressman Richard Nixon proposed a bill to require federal registration of the Communist Party and any "front" organizations; the bill passed in the House by a vote of 319 to 58. *Look* magazine published a special issue devoted to the idea that the communists could take over America if the country weren't vigilant. The search for communists in all venues of American society intensified in 1949 and 1950. When a voice of reason did surface, such as that of poet/dramatist Archibald MacLeish, who wrote a splendid article for *The Atlantic Monthly* in August 1949 entitled "The Conquest of America," it was dismissed.

Hollywood's response was to produce anti-communist films. Minor-league studio Republic lead off with *The Red Menace,* a sensationalistic drama about a disillusioned war veteran who becomes a patsy for the commies. RKO countered with *I Married A Communist* and Warner Bros. made *I Was a Communist for the FBI.* Other films such as *Conspirator, The Red Danube* and *Invasion U.S.A.* followed. None of them were successful.

Julie began to draw back from politics by 1950. He made a point of telling journalist Sheilah Graham that "the Marshall Plan is killing Communism in Europe, and that's good." When former secretary Helen Levitt organized a dinner party benefit for the Hollywood Ten, the Garfields made a reservation, but canceled on the day of the affair. "I guess they realized then that it was just too radical for them because by 1950 the Cold War was in full effect," Levitt said.

Writer Paul Jarrico recalled a similar incident regarding the Garfields. "I wrote a pamphlet called *The Truth About Korea,* which was published by the Arts, Sciences and Professions Council," he explained. "No name was on it, though it was fairly well known who had written it. It basically inveighed against America's role in Korea and went into the history of the position of both North and South Korea. I gave Robbe and Julie a copy of the pamphlet, and asked them for their reaction. Julie said, 'I don't know, I don't buy it,' and Robbe said, 'You can't afford to buy it.' "

Robbe's comment had a double meaning. She hated what HUAC was doing but she was concerned for Julie's career. "It was a terrible time in history," she said years later. "And then he and I were having lots of problems. I'm not sure that I was good for him at that time." Bit by bit her influence over Julie had diminished. Katherine's death had relegated Robbe to the position of dutiful wife. She had lost interest in politics, but at the same time the fighter within her would not stand for the moral capitulation that seemed to prevail in the country in the face of McCarthyism. She was beset by a feeling that Julie's fighting spirit was beginning to fade. His health was a concern too. He began taking afternoon naps and complained of tightness in his chest. And as much as he loved New York—where the Garfields were still living—he missed the high life style of Hollywood: the parties, the movies, and the adulation of women. Some of the problems that had plagued the Garfield marriage began to resurface late in 1948 when Julie went into rehearsal for another Clifford Odets' play, *The Big Knife.*

Fittingly, the play—like the films Julie was choosing to make at this period in his life—paralleled the actor's real life problems, both at home and at the movie studio.

The Big Knife was Odets' first play in eight years. Julie helped him in terms of plotting and dialogue; the two men would sit up all night in the Lobster Restaurant in Times Square and work out the scenes. When the restaurant closed, Julie and Odets would help the wait-staff clean up and stack the chairs on top of the tables. Then they'd make another pot of coffee and remain behind, working well into the early morning..

Odets' new play was the most autobiographical piece of work that Julie ever performed. It is the story of movie star Charlie Castle, who has to choose between signing a 14-year contract with his studio or never working again. The studio head knows that years before Castle was involved in a hit-and-run accident which killed a child. The character is a man who once had high ideals and equally high hopes, but has since sold out for fame and fortune. *The Big Knife* was a melding of a little bit of *Golden Boy* and a little bit of *Body and Soul,* and if anyone was going to tackle the lead, it would have to be John Garfield.

Castle was John Garfield as much as Garfield was Mickey Borden. Castle has a wife, Marion, who is a lot like Robbe Garfield. "You used to grab your theater parts and eat 'em like a tiger," Marion chides Charlie at one point. "Now you act with droopy eyes—they have to call you away from a card game." Castle's roles in his last ten films had him going to the electric chair four times. (Julie had only done that once in film to date, although in his next three films his screen characters would die violent deaths.) Castle carries on extramarital affairs, his wife is involved in politics and the untimely death of their young child haunts the actor. The role even has Castle utter the occasional malapropism, as did Julie. The similarities were striking. *"The Big Knife* is no joke," actress Phoebe Brand said. "That's no joke—that's Julie!"

Julie had remained fairly faithful to Robbe since Katherine's death. Now, his two consecutive film failures in a row and his health problems seemed to lead to a resumption of his womanizing. Actor Anthony Quinn, who became acquainted with Julie around this time, was struck by the similarities between John Garfield and Charlie Castle: "I think that motion pictures spoiled him. He became quite irresponsible in relation to women. They seemed to be more important to him than his work. I liked him very much, but he seemed to have changed quite a bit. Once you're a star, you realize that you can have any woman you want—and that changes you." And yet Quinn, himself a ladies' man, didn't categorize Julie as a womanizer. "He did it, I think, out of desperation," he said "It's almost as if he knew he was going to die soon and he wanted to have all the women in the world before he went."

A fan who had caught Julie's performance in *The Big Knife* was one of these women. Julie brought the young woman to a party for Ruth Cosgrove, then the wife of Milton Berle, that press agent Eddie Jaffe was hosting in his Manhattan apartment. Julie cornered Jaffe and asked him if there was a spare bedroom around. Jaffe suggested Julie take the woman to the next-door apartment of writer Jack Pirman and his wife Fawn, who were out of town. Jaffe, house-sitting for Pirman, gave Julie the key. The actor disappeared with his willing guest.

Fawn Pirman decided to return home earlier than anticipated. She entered her apartment, caught Julie and his date copulating and ran into Jaffe's apartment, screaming, "Oh my God. John Garfield's fucking in my bed!" Her comment brought down the house.

Robbe, who presumably had not been invited to this party, had become less tolerant of Julie's affairs. She took out her anger on him at home; and friends noticed a change in the texture and tone of the Garfield relationship.

"Robbe was a marvelous woman, strong and independent," Joe Bernard said. "I know Julie loved her. But they were both volatile people; they let out their anger easily. But they were very much in love. And Julie told me that despite all the other women, he and Robbe had a very good sex life."

Actor Robert Brown offers a more telling description of the Garfield marriage. "She seemed to dote on him, and she really ran the show. Robbe kept the wolf from the door. She took care of the bills, she took care of the household problems, and she took care of him. He was a guy who needed a lot of attention. She was like his mother during that period. And during that time I don't think he wanted to be mothered."

"Women either want to mother me or fuck me, "Julie told singer Margaret Whiting around this time. He seemed disappointed whichever it was. Robert Brown ran into Julie one day at McSorley's Saloon and asked him what he was doing there.

"I'm drying out," Julie replied. Brown was perplexed. One didn't go to a bar to dry out.

"What are you drying out from?" Brown asked.

"Women!" Julie responded. McSorley's was then an all-male club.

Robbe's husband loved and respected her. He also feared her. She could throw a mean temper tantrum, and with good reason. She was tired of hearing about his trysts with this woman or that. To appease Robbe, or maybe because he realized he needed a vacation, Julie agreed to join her for a lengthy tour of Europe in 1949. It also gave him a good reason to get out of *The Big Knife*.

The show had made some money, running for over 100 performances after it opened at the National Theater on February 24, 1949, although the critics panned it. *Time* magazine's reviewer sized up the play's major problem: "He [Castle] is surely one of the very few heroes in history who have been forced to choose between a prison sentence and $3,744,000." Nobody really cared about the financial or artistic plight of a movie star. After its interesting first scene, *The Big Knife* has nowhere to go. Castle immediately gives into his vices: he signs the contract and goes to bed with his best friend's wife (which Julie supposedly did in real life with Odets' new wife,

Betty Grayson). After that first scene, the play tries to maintain sus-
pense with a secondary plot development wherein the studio
threatens to murder a starlet to keep her from spilling the beans on
Charlie's hit-and-run accident. Audiences found it hard to sympathize with the protagonist.

The play was not an out-and-out box-office failure because the
crowds came to see John Garfield in the flesh, though by April that
audience was dwindling. "The play wasn't well received, although
it was a truthful play," Robbe said. "But Julie wanted to get out of it
because it really wasn't a success." So he went to Europe with
Robbe, where they remained for over a month—a very happy month,
by Robbe's account. Away from Hollywood, New York, hangers-on
and agents, the two fell in love with Paris, Florence, Rome, London
and each other. In Europe, Julie's films were popular, and he was
once again revered as he had been during the war years. His problems were quite literally thousands of miles away.

When they returned to New York City, the Big Apple was good to
them. They rented a cottage on Fire Island and spent the weekends
with the kids. In Robbe's view, Julie spent too much time at Ebbets
Field rooting for the Dodgers. Once he attended a game with publicist Sid Garfield (no relation). As they were leaving the ball park at
game's end, people began to point and shout to one another,
"There's Garfield, there's Garfield!" Before Julie could say anything,
Sid turned to him and dead-panned, "You know Julie, I live around
here. Everyone knows me." The line broke Julie up.

He wasn't laughing when he left a Yankees game with Allen
Funt, whose television program *Candid Camera* had just debuted.
Their cab driver instantly recognized Funt and struck up a conversation, virtually ignoring Julie. Garfield wasn't pleased and blurted
out, "Don't you know who you have in your cab?" The driver
couldn't have cared less.

The Garfields were entertaining guests at their Manhattan apartment one evening when Julie abruptly announced that he heading
down to the Lower East Side to one of his favorite delis for a

midnight snack. He convinced Robbe, Joe Bernard and his wife and movie executive Al Crown and his wife to join him. They hailed a cab and rode downtown. After they had eaten, Julie and Bernard went outside to find a cab. A dozen gang members hovered about, casting dark looks towards Julie and Bernard. Bernard sized up the group as street toughs looking for trouble and suggested that they go inside to call a cab.

"No, no, I'll handle these guys," Julie said confidently, still looking for a passing cab.

A gang member yelled out, "Hey you, come here!" Julie, nonplused, walked over.

"Whatdya' want?" Julie said.

"I just bet this guy five bucks that you ain't John Garfield, the movie actor," the kid said.

Julie pulled out his wallet, flipped open his driver's license, and shoved it in the tough's face.

"What's it say there?" he snapped.

"John Garfield!" the astonished street kid replied.

"You lost! Pay the guy the five bucks!"

He was John Garfield in Hollywood, but in New York City he was still Julius Jacob Garfinkle. And New York City was his to have.

CHAPTER SIXTEEN

The Breaking Point

> *"No matter how a man alone ain't got no*
> *bloody fucking chance."*
> —HARRY MORGAN IN ERNEST
> HEMINGWAY'S NOVEL
> *TO HAVE AND HAVE NOT*

ONE AFTERNOON ROBBE GARFIELD RETURNED HOME FROM a day of shopping to find Julie sitting in an easy chair watching television. The spectacle threw her because they hadn't owned a television set when she had left. A local merchant had given it to Julie that day in hope of receiving a commercial endorsement. The 1950s had arrived.

Once the studios began divesting themselves of their theaters, the next step was the divesting of talent. The major studios let their contract players go. By 1952 Jack L. Warner had released Humphrey Bogart, Errol Flynn, Ronald Reagan, Dennis Morgan and Joan Crawford from their studio contracts (Bette Davis had left in 1949). Even Clark Gable, the King of Hollywood, was not immune. In 1954, after some 25 years on the MGM lot, Gable drove off for the last time. The heyday of the Hollywood studio system was over.

In the wake of the big studios came the independents, often spearheaded by major box-office stars. Burt Lancaster, Kirk Douglas and Humphrey Bogart, to name a few, formed their own film companies. Julie still had Bob Roberts Productions, but it was a company without a releasing venue or a strong financial base. The actor's last two films had been financially disappointing, and despite the gains brought by his growth as a screen actor, he had to face the fact that the times were changing.

Julie was at the top of the heap in 1946 and 1947. By 1950 there were new screen rebels ready to succeed him. One was Marlon Brando, who made the transition to film in 1950 with *The Men* and followed it up with the screen adaptation of *A Streetcar Named Desire* (1951). A second was Montgomery Clift, who created a sensation when he appeared in two back-to-back films, *Red River* and *The Search* (both 1948). Clift would inject new life into the on-screen anti-hero, offering the public a different type of loner. The Garfield rebel of the late 1930s and early 1940s had been intense, loud, and fast-talking, but he wanted in, though he was reluctant to admit it. With Brando and Clift the anti-hero changed. He wasn't sure he wanted in, and he wasn't sure he had a cause at all. The difference in their approach is perhaps best described by examining the reaction of the fans. With Clift and Brando, young people discovered that it was cool to be anti-establishment. The fates weren't against them; they just decided to be against the fates—and everything else.

Julie knew both Brando and Clift, and he admired their talent. He could also be envious of their position in Hollywood. Because neither actor had to sign a long-term contract with a studio, both worked out lucrative one-picture deals for themselves along the way. Julie and Clift met for the first time in nearly a decade (since the *Juarez* shoot) at a 1948 party thrown by MCI agent Edith Van Cleve. The two actors sat in a corner discussing their craft and Hollywood. Julie told Clift that if he had not become an actor, he would have been a runner in the numbers racket (perhaps he was living out the film realities of *Force of Evil*). Clift called Julie "John" and said he'd never sign a long-term film contract.

"MGM wanted Monty to play Greer Garson's son in *Mrs. Miniver* in 1942 but he could only get it if he signed on for seven years," Jack Larson remembered. "And he did not want to do that. And

John [Garfield] told Monty that he admired him for not signing a long-term studio contract, because he told Monty he felt he had signed over his life to Warner Brothers."

Out on his own, Julie kept looking for good film properties while listening to several one-picture deal offers from the major studios. "I'm looking for a script with laughs," Julie said around this time, "When I find the right one I mean to play it." Instead, he bought the rights to two very serious novels, David Lord's *Joey* and Nelson Algren's *The Man with the Golden Arm.* The Algren book, about a drug-addicted musician's attempts to get clean, was more controversial. Roberts put down $15,000 of Julie's money for the rights to make the film, and he promised Algren 5 pecent of the profits. He also agreed to pay Algren 50 percent of any profits if he and Julie could not get the film made and sold rights to another producer. Negotiations between Algren and Roberts soured quickly.

In the book *Conversations with Nelson Algren,* the novelist recalled his surreal experiences dealing with Roberts and Garfield. (For some reason Algren repeatedly refers to Roberts as "Moxon"; one wonders if Roberts was using a pseudonym or whether Algren was simply confused.) Algren didn't trust Roberts. "I felt that Moxon [Roberts] was a con guy," he said. "His action was phony." Algren had kinder words for Julie—sort of. "He was a very friendly little guy," Algren recalled. "He always had his shirt out and he always had that sweat shirt tied around his middle and the arms of the sweat shirt tied around him. He played tennis like mad." Algren was less impressed with Julie's sense of himself as movie star. "He worked very hard at being who he was supposed to be. He knew he wasn't who he was. I mean the screen image. He was trying to be like the screen image." Perhaps he was more like the screen image than Algren understood. Don Weis said Julie was the only actor he ever met who was the same off screen as on: "He knew he was John Garfield, and he didn't have anything else. He was exactly what he was on the screen."

Algren did like the idea of John Garfield playing his novel's protagonist, Frankie Machine. Roberts told Algren that no other producer in Hollywood would try to buck the Johnston Office to make the film. (In 1930 the Motion Picture Association of America had adopted a production code that stated among other points that "illegal drug traffic must never be presented." This code had helped kill the Barney Ross story back in 1946.) According to Algren, Julie paid scant attention to the business angle of it all. All he wanted to talk about was the character of Frankie Machine. "He liked the humor of the book and wanted to do it," Algren said.

Algren found Roberts to be condescending, and when the author began to waffle over his decision, Roberts threatened to serve him with a summons. Algren refused to be intimidated and sought refuge at a Chicago hotel. Roberts took the unethical step of hiring an actor to appear as a summons server in the hopes of forcing Algren to sign over the rights. In a scene that played out like a slapstick two-reel comedy, Algren began chasing Roberts and the actor around his hotel room. "None of them made any sense," Algren said. Nonetheless, admitting he was making a lousy business deal, Algren sold Roberts the rights to his novel. Roberts then hired Paul Trivers (a blacklisted writer) to work with Algren on the script over the summer of 1950. In the interim, Julie had another film commitment to fulfill, for right after *We Were Strangers* Roberts had lined up a financially healthy one-picture deal with 20th Century Fox for Julie. The pay of $135,000 was good, but the material was lousy.

"If there's a real good heel around, I sooner or later end up with him," says Paule, a French nightclub singer in the film, *Under My Skin*. The heel is Julie, who plays Dan Butler, a crooked jockey. Casey Robinson wrote the script, based on Ernest Hemingway's short story "My Old Man." The film comes off about as well as one of Julie's old assembly line quickies from a decade earlier. Jean Negulesco, the traffic director of *Nobody Lives Forever* and *Humoresque*, handled the directing chores (he had moved from Warners to 20th Century Fox in 1949). Luther Adler reunited with Julie for the film, playing a crooked promoter.

One day in September 1949, Julie was filming a scene where he had to skip rope while talking to his film son, Orley Lindgren. Lindgren kept blowing his lines, and Julie kept skipping rope take after take. Finally Negulesco got the scene in the can, and Julie asked to take the rest of the day off as he was short of breath. Negulesco consented, but then Julie went off to the Beverly Hills Hotel to play tennis—ten matches worth. It amazed his friends. "I remember he was playing tennis in the intense heat, and I thought, 'Jesus, that's not good for him,' " Peter Viertel recalled. "But he didn't seem to mind the heat or the intense strain."

He finished his ten matches and then lay down by the pool. He had a pain in his left side and he could barely speak. He began to call out Robbe's name; bystanders called for a doctor. Julie was taken to Cedars of Lebanon Hospital, where he was told that he had suffered a heart attack. This heart attack was probably the first serious one, although Robbe later reflected that he had probably suffered earlier, less obvious attacks. Bob Roberts informed 20th Century Fox that his client would need at least four weeks of bed rest before he could return to the set. Production of *Under My Skin* came to a halt.

In order to bolster Julie's spirits Roberts called Abe Polonsky and asked him to invent a film project to discuss with Julie at the hospital. The two men visited Julie and Polonsky pitched his fictional film project to the actor. "He looked terrible," Polonsky recalled. "His spirits seemed very low."

A few days later Gregory Peck ran into Julie in downtown Hollywood.

"How are you doing?" Peck asked Julie. "I heard you had a heart attack."

"Ah, the hell with that," Julie said, defiantly. "There's nothing wrong with me. I couldn't have a coronary. I'm only thirty-six. I'm not going to be a heart patient and I'm not going to take heart pills. If I'm going to die, I'll die with my boots on."

It was bravado, but it was pure Julie. He had simply left the hospital after three nights there. "He tried to brush away the pain,"

Peck said, "even though they told him he had suffered a coronary. He didn't want to accept it."

Was he still trying to test his own mortality, or did he truly believe he was immune to pain and death? Robbe believes that he didn't know better; that he was still the 12-year-old kid hanging upside down from the building and loving every minute of it. A hospital meant bed rest—and if Julie was going to do anything in bed, it wouldn't entail rest. Rest would mean bad publicity, a slowdown, medication, the works. He couldn't buy into it.

Bob Roberts was smarter. He knew Julie needed a rest, so he talked him into a vacation in Palm Springs. It was a vacation of sorts, but Julie got very little rest. What he did get was romance and sex. He met actress/singer Margaret Whiting there and the two embarked on a fast affair. She later described him as restless and worried about both his health and the whisperings of communist ties that surrounded him. According to her memoirs, he would cling to her at night and say, "I care for you because you're so alive. And I'm so afraid of dying." The heart attack had frightened him more than he wanted to admit. He told Whiting that he was smitten with Micheline Presle, his costar in *Under My Skin*. Presle had rejected his advances in favor of producer Bill Marshall's (whom she married). Julie's ego was damaged, and he was looking for a good time on the rebound. Whiting offered him a no-strings-attached arrangement, something he liked. He certainly didn't need another woman who was going to chase Robbe around the house with a kitchen knife.

He returned to Fox right at the end of the year to finish filming *Under My Skin*. The film, released on Saint Patrick's Day 1950 (the fifth anniversary of Katherine's death), was received with indifference by both the critics and the public. "In a portrayal that is all mannerism and no meat, actor Garfield summons up neither the appeal of a hero nor the fascination of a heel," *Time* magazine stated. For Julie it was sort of a no-win situation. After taking two risks with *Force of Evil* and *We Were Strangers,* he had returned to his cinematic roots to once again play a man destined to fall at the hands of the fates, "Now look at me," Julie's Dan Butler says of his life, "The places I run away from. The places I can't show my face. A guy ends up playing tag with himself." *Under My Skin* never rises above a flat film, except for good performances by both Luther Adler and Noel Drayton. Julie looks drawn and tired throughout, and it's obvious that a stunt man is performing the more strenuous action scenes. The film was a big step backward for Julie, and its failure, coupled with the realization that he had to start slowing down, sent the actor into a depression.

What he felt he needed at this point was one good script to put him back on top. And when that script was thrown to him, like a life preserver, nobody was more surprised by who tossed it than Julie.

In recent years Jack L. Warner had been inviting the old guard of Warner stalwarts back to the studio, almost for old times' sake. In 1948 Edward G. Robinson returned to menace Bogart in *Key Largo.* In 1949 Cagney made his comeback film, *White Heat,* at the studio. In 1950, it was Julie's turn. And Warner Bros. had a made-to-order film for him.

Screenwriter Ranald MacDougall felt that a good film could still be made out of Ernest Hemingway's novel *To Have and Have Not.* (The 1944 version, starring Bogart and Bacall, is pretty good, but it owes very little to Hemingway.) MacDougall convinced Jack Warner and Steve Trilling that a faithful version, featuring the right actor as protagonist Harry Morgan, could make for a classic film. Morgan is the sort of guy who has nothing left to peddle except his guts. It was a John Garfield type of role if ever there was one. (A few other names were kicked around in a preproduction meeting, including Kirk Douglas, James Cagney and Errol Flynn. Douglas would have been too young; Cagney too old. And while Flynn seems unlikely casting, it would have been fun to see him give it a try.)

Morgan is the owner of a small fishing boat; a guy who is willing to play along, but who doesn't know what game he's playing. He's 40 or so, and has a wife (Phyllis Thaxter) and two kids. He even has a little house by the bay, the sort of place Mickey Borden sneered at. But he's faced with a pile of debts that forces his wife to work nights, at the same time hot blonde, Leona (Patricia Neal), is threatening the stability of his marriage. Morgan is suffering from low self-esteem; he can't be a good father, he doesn't seem to be a good husband, and the finance company is planning to take his boat—his livelihood—away from him. Harry Morgan was John Garfield in 1950.

Producer Jerry Wald sent the script to Julie. Julie said he'd do it if either Fred Zinnemann or Michael Curtiz directed. Curtiz got the job. In January 1950, after reading the novel, Julie sent an interesting memo (he rarely wrote letters) to Curtiz outlining his ideas for the film.

Dear Mike:

I am most happy to have heard from you. The only reason I didn't answer sooner was because I wanted to reread the Hemingway book, which I did. I quite agree with you about doing it realistically without phony glamour, so that there is a real quality of honesty and truthfulness, which, by the way, I feel Randy MacDougall has captured from the book.

He has followed the book quite honestly, I think, and some of the questions I would like to kind of throw out for consideration or discussion are:

The deepening of the relationship with his wife, so that you get a sense of a man who, although he is married for many years, has a real yen for her, which is usually very rarely shown in films. As Randy indicates, very warm love scenes are played with the man and the wife. I feel, however, that these scenes can still be deeper without making it too slick.

The other girl, I feel, has to be carefully gone over in the sense that Harry should be tempted, as most men are, and almost goes through with it, but in the end kind of gets cold feet. I feel this relationship can be a little clearer.

Since Eddie is to be a Negro, I am of the opinion that the relationship between Eddie and Harry can also be gone into in a little more detail to show that Eddie has similar problems to Harry's, which Randy also indicated in the script, but not with enough detail. Their regard for each other, without being too sentimental, can be kicked up a bit more.

One of the interesting features of the book is that Harry loses his arm. That might be a little too morbid, but it has a wonderful quality, particularly later in the book where he makes love to his wife. This kind of relationship, if you want to include the loss of his arm, has never been shown. It might seem a little grotesque talking about it, but I certainly think it's worth considering, as it will kick up the whole latter part of the script, purely from a characterization point of view. Of course, Mr. Warner might think it's a little too morbid. However, I feel as long as Randy has stuck so close to the original story in many respects, there is no reason why this couldn't be included.

It is indicated in the book, when Harry is in Mexico, that he buys some things for his wife and children. This kind of touch, which makes him not just a tough guy, but human, creates a fuller person.

Hemingway has a marvelous description in the book (to be specific, page 179) with which we can open and close the picture, where Harry is bleeding and unconscious, the blood kind of dripping off into the water and the fish following the blood stream.

I don't mean to go off into effect shots, but this is an example of what exists in the book which you might find very useful, or not, as the case may be. The main theme which seems to me to be quite simple and direct is: the struggle of a man who tries to make a living for his family and to discharge his responsibilities and finds it tough.

These suggestions are all, of course things I have thought
about for quite a long time and I am just telling them to you.
Maybe it will kick off a spark in your thinking.

I, too, am anxiously looking forward to working with you
again, and I think with Randy and Jerry, we might come up
with something which will be a little off the beaten path but
also excellent entertainment and a real joy to us.

With much love and regards,

Johnny G.

To a large degree many of the ideas Julie expressed in the letter
were incorporated into the film, making an excellent script, punctuated with racy dialogue and a nice dose of realism. MacDougall's
screenplay focused on the third part of Hemingway's novel,
wherein Morgan agrees to take some revolutionaries to Cuba for a
price. Since Warner Bros. didn't want to comment on the then-
current state of affairs in Cuba, the revolutionaries were changed to
racetrack bandits and the locale was changed from Key West to San
Diego, where the filming took place. This remake was titled *The
Breaking Point.*

"What's the use of taking a part you don't like?" Julie told Archer
Winston of the *New York Post.* "You're only going to make one or
two pictures a year, and they have got to be good if you want to have
a future. So you read and read. I can't tell you how many terrible
scripts I've read in the past year. And you wait for something you
really want to do, something with meaning."

Later Julie said of the film, "I think it's the best I've done since
Body and Soul. Better than that." (He was right.) Warner Bros. paid
him $175,000 for the film and signed him to a two-picture contract.
They began filming in February 1950 in Newport Beach, Ensenada
and Balboa, California. Jerry Wald sent the cast a memo wishing
them the best and warning them to watch out for low-flying sea-
gulls. With Robbe staying in New York with the children, Julie was
satisfied with renting apartments in the area.

Blond supporting actress Patricia Neal was then involved in a torrid romance with Gary Cooper and met Julie for the first time at a pre-production party in Hollywood. She recalled she didn't know how to take him. "He was a funny man, but I didn't quite understand him," she said. "He came up to me while I was sitting on a couch and he introduced himself, and then he began hitting me on the arm with the back of his hand, saying 'You're all whore, you know that? You're all whore.' I had no idea if he was referring to me personally or the character of Leona." She got a big kick out of his attempts to navigate around the set in his platform shoes. "I was so tall and he was so short, so he would walk around the set in these high heel shoes like the Frankenstein monster," she commented. "I thought that was very funny to watch."

Julie hit it off better with Phyllis Thaxter, who played his wife. "I had just left MGM and was offered a reading for a film with Michael Curtiz," Thaxter said. "I did a brief screen testing costume, and that's when I met Garfield. He was a wonderful man, and I'm positive that he and Curtiz had a big hand in my getting the part. He [Garfield] was very kind to me, and we had a most pleasant and enjoyable relationship. We worked hard on developing the characters and rehearsing those scenes over and over again. I found him to be a very serious person with an inner turmoil that I couldn't quite understand."

The star also spent time with screen newcomer William Campbell, who played one of the hoods who shoots it out with Harry Morgan in the film's climax. "Garfield knew it was my first film and that I was frightened, and he wanted to settle me down," Campbell recalled. "He said, 'Don't worry, it's gonna be a walk in the park with Curtiz.' We'd go over to the drug store and have an ice cream, and he'd tell me how to handle the business, gave me advice like 'Watch your back; it's a tough town,' that sort of thing. He was great to work with. I just loved the guy."

Campbell was just one of many young actors who were enamored of John Garfield at the time. "I thought he was the greatest; we all did," said actor John Ericson, who first came to Hollywood in 1951. Actor Steven Hill recalled sitting in Schwab's Drugstore one day around this time when Julie walked in. Hill was awestruck—John Garfield was his idol. To Hill's delight, Julie sat next to him at the counter to enjoy an ice cream soda.

"What are you doing out here?" Julie asked Hill.

"I want to be an actor," Hill replied.

"What kind of actor?" Julie asked.

"An actor like John Garfield," Hill said.

Julie smiled. "Why don't you try to be an actor like Steven Hill?" Hill took the advice to heart.

Shooting this film, Julie was still trying to find his own way as an actor. Back in New York he had reimmersed himself in acting class in an effort to remain fresh. Taking courses at the Actors Studio, he could begin to revisit the Method, a style that had sometimes eluded him during much of his tenure with the Group. "He talked a lot about acting," journalist/photographer Sam Shaw said of this time in Julie's life. "He was learning how to move, how to walk, and he was working at the Studio. His only concern was about acting and his artistry—and growing up again, as an actor."

Shooting one scene of *The Breaking Point,* Julie took an extra moment to respond to one of the other actors. Curtiz stopped the cameras and chided Julie for forgetting his line. "I didn't forget my lines," Julie said, "I was acting." Curtiz didn't get it.

Despite some differences director and actor got along well. "You know, I'm not the kind of actor that becomes a star in Hollywood," Julie told Archer Winston. "I would normally have been a character actor, but Mike Curtiz made me a star in *Four Daughters,* my first picture. He gave me that screen personality that carried me to stardom. I've always been grateful for that." Ten years after they last worked together on *The Sea Wolf,* it was obvious that Curtiz and Garfield still had a special professional bond. One element of Julie's acting style from the days of *Four Daughters* made a welcome return—subtlety. Curtiz had always been able to get Julie to downplay a scene. But the director was still capable of stringing Julie along for cinematic love scenes. "It's got to be tender and it's got to be violent," was the extent of his direction for a seduction scene between Patricia Neal and Julie. The actors were utterly confused.

Robbe and the kids came West to join Julie towards the latter part of filming, and rented a beach house in Malibu. Their neighbors were director Don Siegel and his wife, actress Viveca Lindfors. "My memory of John is that he was a very nice guy, very warm, but there was also a very shy side to him," Lindfors said. "I think they were having trouble with their marriage then."

Part of the trouble was Julie's recent string of extramarital affairs and his publicized infatuation with Micheline Presle. His inability to take responsibility for his children added to this strain. Once again Julie was tackling a role that seemed to mirror his real-life situation. He never seemed to grasp the responsibility inherent in being a parent. On one occasion he took David with him to the beach. Julie encouraged his son to swim in the ocean, but as his son drifted further and further out into the Pacific, Julie flirted with a pretty blonde on the beach. An alert lifeguard rescued David from a near-drowning. This was just one of several instances where Julie's inattention to his children almost led to serious accidents.

There were perks during the filming. James Cagney, then shooting *Kiss Tomorrow Goodbye* for Warner Bros., dropped by to discuss the good old days. Humphrey Bogart sailed his *Sirocco* down to Newport Beach and offered to lend it to Julie for a fishing excursion. And Julie's old friend Oscar Levant came by one day and watched the scene where the bandits rob the racetrack. Levant sized up the scene, turned to Jerry Wald and quipped, "The hell with the movie—let's do the robbery." (This quote has also been attributed to Jack Warner after he read the script to the 1960 Rat Pack film *Ocean's 11*.)

Curtiz wrapped the film in May after shooting an exciting shipboard shootout between Morgan and the four gunmen. Before filming was completed, Robbe and the children returned to New

York while Julie stuck around Los Angeles for a few days. He called Phyllis Thaxter up one evening and asked her to have dinner with him. She declined. With Thaxter he had been gentle, funny and flirtatious both on and off the set. With Neal he was brusque, rough and sarcastic. "He was kind of macho," Neal said years later with a laugh. "Like he had to play the part off screen as well. It kind of turned me off." It certainly worked on-camera; the pair have a sexy, funny give-and-take relationship.

While Warner Bros. prepared *The Breaking Point* for a summer release, Julie considered an offer from the manager of the Laguna Beach Summer Theater. The manager asked Julie to play Joe Bonaparte in an upcoming stage production of Odets' *Golden Boy*. Though Julie turned the man down, he couldn't get the idea of playing Bonaparte out of his head. He began to make plans for a summer stock tour of the play, with himself as star and director.

Upon returning to New York in late May, he did a ten-minute scene from *Golden Boy* on television, opposite actress Kim Stanley, on the variety program *Cavalcade of Stars*. The surviving kineoscope hints at what Garfield must have been like on stage. There are touches of the young John Garfield in the scene, but the truth is, he had seemed to age overnight. Gray hair at his temples and lines under the eyes suggested a man much older than 37. (This aged appearance imbued his portrayal of Harry Morgan with an honest weariness, however.) On television Joe Bonaparte was presented as being not much unlike John Garfield: tired, underconfident, and still trying to convince himself that he believed in the words he was saying. And he was mad as hell at the world. Between Julie and Kim Stanley, there is an obvious sexual chemistry

The scene did not visibly impress the live audience. Perhaps it was difficult to take a dose of Odets after sitting through such specialty acts as comic Jerry Lester, singer Jane Pickens, ventriloquist Paul Winchell and the dance team of Horatio and Lana. After their scene, Julie and Stanley gamely joined Lester and company in a party celebrating the *Cavalcade of Stars'* first birthday. Julie even donned a silly birthday hat and joined in the singing of "Happy Birthday." His take for the job was $500.

"Live television is just like the theater," he told columnist Darr Smith. "You've got an audience. It's also motion picture technique. You're acting in front of the camera, but you've got an audience that reacts to what you do. This is an actor's dream. Greatest thing that ever happened to me. This is a real medium. It combines everything. In television you play the scene, in movies you move the scene."

Perhaps he foresaw a future as a television star. It was not to be, for overnight he would find it impossible to land any sort of work. The Alger Hiss espionage case, involving supposed state secrets stashed away in a pumpkin patch, had made headlines just before filming began on *The Breaking Point.* John Garfield was connected to it, in an indirect way, when Judith Coplon, a Justice Department employee accused of passing secrets to the Soviets in a related case, testified that the Communist Party used several Hollywood personalities as drawing cards. One of those Hollywood personalities was John Garfield.

The witch hunters were about to come knocking on his door.

CHAPTER SEVENTEEN

Red Scare on Sunset

> *"Don't present me with the choice of either*
> *being in contempt of this Committee and*
> *going to jail, or forcing me to crawl through*
> *the mud to be an informer."*
> —ACTOR LARRY PARKS, TESTIFYING
> BEFORE HUAC, 1951

THE BREAKING POINT WAS FINALLY RELEASED ON SEP-
tember 30, 1950, to uniformly positive reviews. Bosley
Crowther lauded the film and Julie's performance: "Warner
Bros., which has already taken one feeble swing and a cut at
Ernest Hemingway's memorable story of a tough guy, *To
Have and Have Not*, finally has got hold of that fable and
socked it for a four-base hit. All the character, color and
cynicism of Mr. Hemingway's lean and hungry tale are
wrapped up in the realistic picture, and John Garfield is
tops in the principal role—all through his playing of Harry
Morgan is the shrewdest, hardest acting in the show. What
we have here is a good, taut adventure story."

Of three film adaptations of the Hemingway novel *The
Breaking Point* is probably the best. (A 1958 Audie Murphy
B, *The Gun Runners*, is the third.) Yet it is one of the most
obscure films of Julie's career, rarely showing up on television and still not available on video. It features one of his
best performances, as a man who is just trying to get by in
life and finds himself reaching his own breaking point due
to circumstances outside of his control. In that sense, it truly

mirrored what Julie was experiencing at the time, given his uncertain standing in Hollywood, though John Garfield's name still meant something at the box office. Joe Bernard and Robbe attended a preview screening of the film at a cinema in Huntington, Long Island. "The audience didn't know what film they'd be seeing," Bernard recalled, "and when the title came up and John Garfield's name appeared, the audience applauded. He was still a name."

Organizations other than movie studios realized there was value in Garfield's name, too. On June 22, 1950, *Red Channels,* a publication bent on exposing communism in the entertainment field, hit the newsstands. It listed John Garfield in connection with 17 different communist groups; ultimately the actor was tied to 33 so-called communist "fronts," though several of them were merely artistically progressive organizations like the Actors' Lab and the Group Theatre. *Red Channels* was published by American Business Consultants, an organization that was responsible for an earlier anti-communist pamphlet, "Counter Attack." American Business Consultants' goal was to obtain, file and report "factual" information on communist activity in the United States. The three publishers of *Red Channels* were John G. Keenan, Theodore C. Kirkpatrick and Kenneth M. Bierly, all former FBI agents who were looking for a new crusade to launch. In the spring of 1950 they decided to publish the names of anyone in the entertainment field who had even remote ties to communist groups.

In a further irony, while *Red Channels* denounced *The Daily Worker* as the "chief journalistic mouthpiece of the Communist party," a newspaper loaded with "subversive, seditious and treasonable utterances," the three acknowledged that they used *The Daily Worker* as their main source of information for compiling their list of subversive individuals.

The power and importance of *Red Channels* in 1950 cannot be minimized. If a performer was listed in its pages, his or her career was over. Author Merle Miller delved into the effect *Red Channels* had for his book *The Judges and the Judged,* noting that anyone listed in that publication was immediately considered unemployable. "You see this list?" one agent said to Miller. "There are seventeen names on this list, some of the biggest names in the business. I don't even bother suggesting them anymore. I know better. I've had too many turndowns. They're in *Red Channels.*"

Being listed, Julie was in trouble. Among the associations and organizations that *Red Channels* tied him to were sponsor of the Civil Rights Congress in Detroit, 1946; chairman of the American Friends of the Chinese People, 1938; speaker for the Progressive Citizens of America, 1947; sponsor for the Committee to Abolish the House Committee on Un-American Activities, 1947; and sponsor of a boycott of Japanese goods for the American League for Peace, 1938. Julie couldn't remember half of these names or events. He was also one of only two performers listed in *Red Channels* who had an anticommunist quote attributed to him (his comment to Sheilah Graham about the Marshall Plan killing communism in Europe); the other performer was Broadway star Alfred Drake.

The Korean War broke out three days after *Red Channels* was published and as HUAC began preparing for a new round of public hearings, once again focusing on Hollywood.

Where *The Breaking Point* should have been one of the biggest hits of the year, the impact of *Red Channels'* listing of John Garfield may have contributed to its commercial failure. (Studio memos indicate that Warner Bros. felt they had another *Casablanca* on their hands.) For most of the studios 1950 was a lackluster year, but Warner Bros. in particular had few films of merit to promote. Odd that Jack L. Warner dropped *The Breaking Point* on the market with little publicity that September and then, despite good reviews, withdrew it from release soon afterward. Phyllis Thaxter has her own theory on why Warner Bros. downplayed the film. "I don't think there were any political problems when we were making the film," she said, "but by the time the film was released I think Warners were worried that Garfield was hot, and so they did not publicize the film at all. It died a very quiet death." (The film actually made a very slight profit for Warner Bros.)

Montgomery Pittman was a screenwriter at Warner Bros. around this time, and according to his wife, Maurita (whose daughter Sherry Jackson played one of Julie's screen daughters in *The Breaking Point*), her husband once saw a list of suspected communists on Jack Warner's desk. Among the names was John Garfield's. Maurita Pittman always felt that Jack L. Warner experienced an internal struggle regarding the film: "I don't know why the film was unsuccessful. Warner was really too greedy a man not to get whatever money he could out of a picture. But he was fervently anticommunist and maybe he realized that Garfield was trouble, and he didn't put that much publicity into the film." Shortly thereafter, Warner canceled the second film on Julie's two-picture deal.

With Julie being named by *Red Channels,* his career was virtually over and it seemed to happen overnight. He was unofficially blacklisted. When he volunteered to go overseas to entertain the troops in Korea, he discovered that he could not get a clearance from the Department of Defense.

It is amazing that he managed to make even one more film. But smooth-talking Bob Roberts had persuaded Arthur Krim, a top executive at United Artists, to co-produce and release a low-budget crime drama that Roberts was packaging for Julie. The result, *He Ran All the Way*, is a noir thriller steeped in the tradition of the best gangster dramas of the era.

Nick (Garfield) is an overage delinquent, a desperately dumb loser who's hemmed in by the walls of noir. "I got no luck today," he tells his criminal cohort, Al (Norman Lloyd). Still, going along with Al's plan to rob a factory payroll, Nick inadvertently kills a payroll guard during the heist. He's forced to take it on the lam and hides out in the apartment of the Dobbs family. Nick keeps the quartet (Mom, Pop, daughter and kid brother) in line by making sure one member of the family is with him at all times. Of course he falls for the daughter, Peg (Shelley Winters). Both of them are emotionally needy misfits looking for love. Nick hopes to make a break for it with her on his arm and talks her into finding him a getaway car. When the car arrives it's too late for Nick; he ends up in the gutter with a bullet in his belly, courtesy of Peg. The film is a sad but fitting end to Julie's screen career. He portrays Nick as a guy perpetually looking for an angle just to get through the next few minutes of his life. He's a noir guy who can't afford to have any illusions about long-term plans because tomorrow is as far as he's going.

Roberts had bought the rights to Sam Bass's novel for $40,000 (Julie's money) in May 1950. Shooting was done fast and cheap in July and August. The film is considered a Bob Roberts Production, though Julie supplied the money to co-produce. The production crew list reads like a Who's Who in the Communist Party: the director was John Berry; the screenwriters, both credited and uncredited, were Hugo Butler, Guy Endore and Dalton Trumbo; and the associate producer was Paul Trivers. Apolitical James Wong Howe was hired as director of photography.

Roberts lined up a good supporting cast including Wallace Ford (memorable as a sleazy lawyer in *The Breaking Point*) as the father and Gladys George as Nick's unsympathetic mother. (When the police tell George that if she doesn't help them track Nick down they'll shoot him, she replies, "Go ahead. Kill him. Kill him.") Shelley Winters proved to be a challenge for both Julie and Berry. "She would drive Julie nuts," Berry said. "She always took so long to get ready. When the other actors were at their pitch, ready to go, she'd fuck up the scene. I don't know if she did it deliberately or not, but she'd do it until her screen partner would wear out." The novel has Winters' character stabbing Nick with a knife, killing him on the couch when he sexually advances on her. Berry wanted to move the final confrontation outside to give it a stronger sense of drama. Winters told Berry she wanted to kill Julie on the couch.

"I said to her, 'This is Julie's picture. If you stab him on the couch it shifts the emphasis of the movie—he just becomes a rapist.' " Berry recalls. "So we all got together—her agents, Roberts, Julie and me—and argued about it. Roberts tried to convince her the scene would be shot as in the book. Finally, Julie went to Roberts and said, 'You gotta let John do it as he wants; he's the director.' But Winters refused to do the final scene on the street until I threatened to use an extra and put a wig on her. I would have done it, too."

In her autobiography *Shelley II* Winters intimates that Julie directed the film, and says she can't recall whether she had an affair with him or not. Berry thought it unlikely: "I remember he went up to her dressing room once and they had a loud argument about one of the scenes; you could hear them both yelling. She was often not prepared. I remember once she wasn't ready for a scene, and I'd had enough, so I pushed her into it and said, 'Do it!' But she just drove Julie crazy."

He had other problems on the set, as well. Still recovering from his heart attack, Julie found he couldn't work as hard or as long as he used to. He would do his own stunts for the actual takes, but a double filled in for him during the stunt rehearsals. In the swimming pool sequence, in which he teaches Winters' character how to swim, he tired out easily while rehearsing.

With the actor's past four films all having failed to find an audience, both Roberts and Julie were relying on *He Ran all the Way* to revive Julie's flagging film career. It did, after all, offer all the necessary elements that John Garfield fans had come to expect: life's loser battles the fates in a valiant attempt to break free once and for all. And the shadow of HUAC played a role, according to Berry, who said, "It's about doom. That's not coincidental." In many ways the film is the perfect coda to John Garfield's film career. It was well made, belying the short shooting schedule and its low budget. Julie's performance is mostly balanced: some scenes suggest a new-found maturity and a realization of a life ill-spent. Nick, like Julie, is a guy who wants to be loved and tries his best to adopt a family that doesn't want him. Even Julie's former Group Theatre associates were recognizing his potential. "He showed all the possibilities of growth as an actor, but he didn't have a chance after that blow [*Red Channels*] fell," Morris Carnovsky said.

Waiting to see what would happen with regard to Julie's looming political problems, United Artists put *He Ran All the Way* on the shelf. Julie and Roberts talked about doing another film, a whodunit set in Africa called *Port Afrique*. But it was just talk. When Julie left Hollywood for New York in October 1950, it would be for the last time.

He picked up a little radio work, narrating "A Duty of Conscience" on *The Eternal Light* program in October, and making three guest spots on various radio shows, including a Jane Pickens' program in February 1951. And that was that.

Stage work was an option. Julie joined Cheryl Crawford, Lee Strasberg and playwright Paul Green at a lunch meeting at New York's Warwick Hotel to discuss an upcoming production for the American National Theatre and Academy (ANTA). Crawford proposed Ibsen's *Peer Gynt*. "That's a crazy play," Green said. "I've seen it done twice and it bored me stiff."

Crawford agreed, but said she felt Green's style in doing a new adaptation would make the play acceptable to modern audiences. Julie spoke up, suggesting that Green build the play via a series of montage scenes (just like the movies) that would convey all of Peer's trials in dealing with the world. Green decided to make Peer a symbol of Western man: a selfish wastrel, an egocentric lover of women, and a man who runs away from himself in search of material pleasures. Rewriting the English translation into basic colloquial speech, Green managed to reinvent Peer Gynt so that he was one part Ibsen and three parts John Garfield. Julie agreed to play Peer; Strasberg agreed to direct, and Crawford got rehearsal underway in January 1951.

Julie waxed enthusiastic about the play. "This is the most exciting thing I've ever been in, in heart, in tremendous theatrical aliveness," he told reporter Vernon Rice in his own inimitable style of speech. Excited about the physical demands expected of him, including some dance sequences that were worked into the production, he began studying dance at the Actors Studio with instructor Anna Sokolow in an effort to help bring a physical life to his character.

Robbe had not seen Julie so exuberant since *Skipper Next to God* three years earlier. Unfortunately, his enthusiasm was to be short-lived. *Peer Gynt* opened on January 28, 1951, and ran for all of 32 performances. On opening night the curtain was held for over an hour because Strasberg's set wasn't ready. Joe Bernard went backstage to chat with Julie, who said, "Aren't you going to wish me luck?" Bernard laughed and said, "If you want to do *Peer Gynt*, do *Peer Gynt.*" Julie laughed at the comment.

Next morning he wasn't laughing. "The current *Peer Gynt* is lifeless," Brooks Atkinson wrote in his *New York Times* review. "Mr. Garfield is an admirable and likable realistic character. But he never gets Peer Gynt off the ground. His performance is literal and casual, completely lacking in poetic animation." Audience response was mild; applause was tepid. "We had a flop to end all flops," Paul Green said years later.

Karl Malden, featured in *Peer Gynt,* felt that Strasberg, Green and Garfield were all out of their element in the play. "It wasn't the real *Peer Gynt,*" Malden recalled. "Too much time was spent on the troll scenes and the technical aspects of the play. Lee Strasberg just fell in love with that stuff. So he neglected the personal relationships between the characters. Julie was really excellent as the young Peer, but Lee just didn't give him the help he needed in the latter scenes when Peer grew older, and I think Julie had a hard time with the transition."

To promote the play, Julie and actress Mildred Dunnock did a scene from *Peer Gynt* on ABC's short-lived television program *ANTA'S Playhouse* in February 1951. It was Julie's last television appearance, and like everything else he did at the time it was doomed to fail. "Unfortunately the full impact of the scene was lost as the final lines had to be cut due to overtime," *Variety's* reviewer noted. No surviving record of the kineoscope has been found.

Julie wasn't entirely well during this period. Bernard recalled that at least twice during the rehearsal process the physical demands of the role caught up with him. He complained of chest constrictions and had to lie down on a cot in his dressing room until the pain passed. He didn't tell Robbe, Strasberg or his doctor. The play's failure was distressing enough to him. He was about to get more bad news.

Members of the House of Representatives, Donald L. Jackson and Charles E. Potter, vowed to subpoena a number of actors, writers and directors for a new round of Hollywood hearings. Propaganda in Hollywood films that had been the main focus of the 1947 hearings was no longer the issue. This time HUAC was hunting for individual communists. They wanted names. The Committee issued a press release stating that it would start their next round of investigations with actor Edward G. Robinson and include at least ten other movie figures, including Larry Parks. In late February 1951 HUAC sent two representatives to the West Coast armed with subpoenas.

On March 6, the Julius and Ethel Rosenberg trial commenced in New York City. The Rosenbergs were accused of passing atomic bomb secrets to the Soviets. That same day, HUAC announced that subpoenas were being served on Anne Revere, Abe Burrows, José Ferrer and John Garfield. Reached at home by a reporter, Julie feigned surprise. "I did not know until now that I was being subpoenaed," he said. "Until I know what they want I don't know what I can say. I have nothing to hide. Perhaps they want some information from me since I served on the board of the Screen Actors Guild along with Miss Revere."

He knew better. Robbe's membership in the Communist Party was well known, and Julie's participation in various left-wing causes over the past fifteen years was documented. When the subpoena arrived at the Garfield apartment on Central Park West, the Garfields were at home. Robbe answered the door, to two men in suits. "You could see who they were," she recalled. "They had a label that you could smell from miles away." The men asked if Julie was home. He happened to be coming down the stairs from the apartment's upper landing at that moment. Before the men could say anything else, Robbe turned to Julie to brace him. She didn't have to. His face turned ghostly white. One of the men handed him the subpoena, then they tipped their hats and departed.

Julie was scheduled to testify before HUAC on Monday, April 23. The day after receiving the subpoena, he did two things. First, he hired lawyer Louis Nizer, who had represented members of the Group Theatre on various charges back in the 1930s and whose partner, Arthur Krim, was the United Artists executive who had helped spearhead the production of *He Ran All the Way*. (The law firm also represented Paramount.) Second, with Nizer's help, Julie drafted a brief statement of denial for general release: "I have always hated Communism. It is a tyranny which threatens our country and the peace of the world. Of course then, I have never been a member of the Communist Party or a sympathizer with any of its doctrines. I will be pleased to cooperate with the Committee." In retrospect, it wasn't a smart thing to say.

For Hollywood, it was a frightening time. *The New York Times* noted in a March 18 editorial by Thomas F. Brady that the movie studios would be watching the HUAC hearings in an effort to determine who would or would not be employable in the future. According to Brady, management agreed that the studios must disassociate themselves from any individuals under investigation. Likewise, if any witness invoked the First Amendment, it would lead to the reinstatement of the 1947 Waldorf dictum, which meant blacklisting. Victor Riesel wrote in his March 27 column that "Garfield came out for the Soviet invasion of Finland just like his comrades are now condoning the death of American boys." (A mistruth, to put it mildly.) Riesel also said it was too late for any late confessions from the likes of Garfield and Parks.

Nizer urged Julie to not respond to these charges, but rather to wait until he could have his say before HUAC. But for Julie, the waiting was hell. "He took the accusations much too seriously," Nizer recalled. "I mean, of course we were in the fever then so you can't blame him, but he believed at one point that he could go to jail. He would come to my office and cry, 'What can they do to me? Can they put me in jail? Will it end my career?' He wanted to be cleared and to go back to being a star."

Julie had a lot to worry about. For one thing, he knew that HUAC knew that Robbe was a communist, and for another, he wasn't about to give up his movie stardom easily. (It was slipping away from him bit by bit, anyway, thanks to his recent string of commercial misfires.) And listening to Larry Parks' testimony on March 21 made him and everyone nervous.

One can praise Parks for what he tried to do, as he offered strong resistance to HUAC's methods. But ultimately his testimony damaged his own career and the careers of others. He freely admitted his membership in the Communist Party but said he never saw any evidence of attempts to subvert film scripts. Asked about John Garfield, Parks said he had never seen him at a meeting, nor did he believe him to be a member of the Communist Party. HUAC pushed Parks for names. "Don't present me with the choice of either being in contempt of this Committee and going to jail, or forcing me to crawl through the mud to be an informer," he pleaded. His request fell on deaf ears. HUAC demanded obedience, and obedience meant naming names. Behind closed doors, Parks agreed to give up a few, naming Lee J. Cobb, Morris Carnovsky, Gale Sondergaard, Joseph Bromberg and Anne Revere. All of them suffered, as would Parks. (Cobb did name names and saved his career; the others did not.) Although he did name names, Parks was already finished in Hollywood. When he made *The Jolson Story* in 1946, he was considered one of the top "stars of tomorrow," but he would make only one more film in the 1950s and one last one in the 1960s.

With Parks' headline-making testimony, the media focused its attention on the HUAC hearings again. Sterling Hayden testified on April 10. The members of HUAC, including Jackson and Potter, led off with some easy questions, asking Hayden about his youth, his early experiences in Hollywood, and his service record during the war years. They got around to asking for names, and Hayden, admitting the whole thing was "a load to carry around," obliged. He mentioned that although the Committee for the First Amendment may have been a communist front, no one in that organization real-

ized it at the time. To top things off, the actor said he believed that
the Communist Party was encouraging the overthrow of the United
States government. A lot of people believed him.

Julie was next to testify. He flew to Washington, D.C., over the
weekend of April 21, 1951, accompanied by Nizer and his legal associate Sidney Davis. All three men agreed that it would be best if
Robbe stayed home, which was probably just as well, for she was
not particularly happy about Julie's decision to cooperate at all. "I
wouldn't go and say things I didn't want to say about people I knew
and loved," she said. But she wasn't the one that HUAC wanted. She
wasn't a movie star. April 24 would be Robbe's thirty-seventh birthday. There would be no reason to celebrate.

A story that turned out to be apocryphal concerns a message
that HUAC sent Julie regarding Robbe's politics. In it, according to
Robbe, Julie let HUAC know that he would not testify if they asked
him about his wife. It seems farfetched to think that HUAC would
refrain from questioning Julie about Robbe (who they knew was a
member of the Communist Party). Yet, in fact, that is just what did
happen. The Committee members didn't even ask Julie if he was
married.

HUAC had reason to be accommodating. They had never had a
star as big as John Garfield appear before them. "He was the most famous star they [HUAC] had," said writer Richard Collins (who was
then writing a script about an aging rodeo star for Julie). "No one
had the clout that he had among the witnesses. He was a star and
they didn't have any other actors of his stature." This is somewhat
true. Hayden, Parks, Sondergaard and Cobb were hardly Academy
Award-nominated stars. They were on the second or third tier of the
Hollywood star system.

Though Nizer and Davis sat beside Julie throughout his testimony, they were virtually powerless to do anything for him.
Lawyers were not permitted to counsel their clients during the
HUAC hearings. No allowance was made for rebuttal or cross-
examination, and HUAC members acted pretty much like judge and

jury. Julie's testimony began at 10:30 A.M. on Monday, April 23. Present on the HUAC side were Representatives John S. Wood, Francis E. Walter, Morgan M. Moulder, James B. Frazier Jr., Harold H. Velde, Bernard W. Kearney, Donald L. Jackson and Charles E. Potter. Staff member Frank S. Tavenner acted as HUAC counsel (as if they needed one) and Thomas W. Beale Sr. was assistant counsel.

In just one sense Julie's testimony is unusual: it stands out because he pretended to cooperate without really cooperating. His replies to HUAC's queries are absurdly ambiguous. Typical of his answers are comments like, "That is a familiar name," "I don't want to say yes or no," and "I hardly knew him." He figured HUAC would have a hard time discerning whether he was telling the truth or not, and here is where he made his one big mistake: he perjured himself. He was an unlikely candidate for martyrdom, but one thing he would not do is rat on his friends.

Both Abraham Polonsky and Morris Carnovsky were present for Julie's testimony, for they were scheduled to testify the next day. Polonsky was impressed with Julie's approach; Carnovsky sensed that it was misguided but admired the fact that Julie didn't name names.

The testimony began with the usual introductory comments and questions, such as Julie giving his name, address and a brief personal history. The only surprise in this part of the testimony is that he told HUAC he considered himself a legal resident of California, and not New York (the Garfields had been living in New York City again for just over three years at this point). HUAC counsel Tavenner asked Julie to give a brief history of his experience in Hollywood. Julie replied by playing up the importance of the patriotic war films he made at Warner Bros., and then recounted his work as an independent film producer. Tavenner then read Julie's press statement of the previous month, in which the actor said he hated communism.

> TAVENNER: Is it a fact that you have always hated communism, as stated in that news release?

GARFIELD: Absolutely, yes.

TAVENNER: Are you of the opinion and belief that communism is a tyranny which threatens our country and the peace of the world?

GARFIELD: I believe so. I think it is a subversive movement and is a tyranny which is a dictatorship and is against democracy.

TAVENNER: Have you ever been a member of the Communist Party?

GARFIELD: I have never been a member of the Communist Party.

Tavenner asked Julie whether he took part in a Youth Communist League program supporting an anti-war play in New York in 1936.

GARFIELD: I have no knowledge of lending my name to this organization, particularly an organization called the Young Communist League, because believe me, if I had heard of such a name I would have run like hell. I have absolutely no knowledge of this; none whatsoever.

Tavenner asked Julie whether the Communist Party members within the Group Theatre attempted to influence the productions in any way. Julie replied that it was "purely run on an artistic basis. It was not a political organization." Tavenner then moved to Hollywood, asking Julie what led him to sign with Warner Bros. Julie recounted the *Golden Boy* story and it was obvious that some 15 years after the fact, he still felt slighted over not getting the lead. Tavenner didn't care about that; he wanted to know if there was some communist-backed scheme to get Julie to Hollywood. He then attempted to get Julie to acknowledge that he knew such communist-front representatives as Elizabeth Leech, Margaret Potts, Eleanor Abowitz and Sidney Benson. To each name Julie vaguely replied that he could not remember those particular names.

Tavenner was getting frustrated. Julie remained ambivalent. Tavenner asked about Hugo Butler, about Xanadu Films, and someone named Hyman Kraft. Tavenner got nowhere; Julie was noncommittal. Tavenner finally asked his star witness whether any of the people he was mentioning were communists. "We never discussed politics in that sense," Julie replied. "And second, they didn't trust me. I was a liberal, and I don't think the Communists like liberals, and I was quite outspoken about my liberalism." The idea that communists distrust liberals was an odd one; the committee members would return to the issue later on. Tavenner went on reeling off names—Frank Tuttle, George Wilner (an agent Julie knew), Alexander Trachtenberg, and the Actors' Lab. Julie gave Tavenner no satisfaction. Then Tavenner asked Julie about his position during the 1945 Hollywood labor union strike:

TAVENNER: In 1945, during the period of the strike in the moving-picture industry, the Communist Party is alleged to have been interested in influencing the various groups in connection with that strike. Do you have any knowledge on your own part regarding that effort?

GARFIELD: Well, I had no knowledge of what the Communist Party was doing, because I had no association with anybody like that, but I was on the executive board of the Screen Actors Guild for 6 years, and during the period of the strike, and I know pretty well what went on in terms of the strike, in terms of the guild's position, and in terms of the general atmosphere of that time.

TAVENNER: What effort was made by the Communist Party to influence the action of the guild with regard to the strike?

GARFIELD: Well, the strike started in 1945. We of the Screen Actors Guild tried in every possible way to stop it. We played a very impartial role at the beginning. As a matter of fact, some of us were accused of being sympathetic to the CSU, which was the other side, at the beginning. We

then proceeded to get all the information we could, and
we did. This took us until about 1946, and we discovered
that the culprits in the thing were the CSU. They didn't
want to settle the strike.

TAVENNER: The culprits were who?

GARFIELD: The CSU, Conference of Studio Unions. Mr.
Tavenner, I have here the minutes of the board of directors of the Screen Actors Guild from 1945—March 15,
1945, to be specific—to 1947, when the most important
decisions were made, with motions and secondings, motions which I personally made, which clearly bear out the
statement that I make that I was against the strike and felt
that this was a strike which was uncalled for and unwar-
ranted. I would like to give this to the committee, because
these minutes show quite conclusively my position, anyway, personally, on how I voted.

Representative Wood accepted the minutes but made it clear that
they were for use by the Committee only and not for the record.
There was more talk about the CSU strike, and Julie invoked right-
wing "friendly" witness Ronald Reagan's name in an effort to show
that even loyal Americans like Reagan could show up at political
meetings at private homes. (It was revealed later that Reagan was
working undercover for the FBI; he told about seeing Howard
Da Silva, a communist character actor of the period, silence Julie at
a politically charged meeting in Hollywood around 1949.) Tavenner
asked Julie if he could identify any persons who were members of
the Communist Party. Julie dodged the question, but Representative
Velde followed up on it.

VELDE: I don't think you have answered the question that
counsel asked you. He asked if you knew any of the Communist Party members.

GARFIELD: Officially, do you mean?

VELDE: Either from statements they made to you or from
    what you learned about them?
GARFIELD: No, sir.

It was a risky approach, but for the moment it paid off. At this
point Representative Walter stepped in to ask some questions on
why Julie changed his mind on the CSU strike. Tavenner asked how
Anne Revere voted on the strike; Julie didn't know. The interroga-
tion moved back to the issue of Julie's participation in various
communist-front groups, such as his sponsorship of the Joint Anti-
Fascist Refugee Committee. Julie feigned memory loss, saying he had
no recollection of such an event but admitted that it "might" have
happened. Velde then returned to the subject of Julie's liberalism.

VELDE: You mentioned a while ago that the Communist
    Party didn't trust you.
GARFIELD: They don't trust liberals.
VELDE: Many times they use liberals
GARFIELD: They try, yes sir.

Committee members kept firing questions at him, asking him
about his membership in the National Council of American-
Soviet Friendship, the Congress on Civil Rights, the Council on
African Affairs and the National Council of the Arts, Sciences and
Professions. Julie denied any association with all four groups,
though it is possible he had signed petitions for any and all of
them at one time. Tavenner asked him about his relationship to
the American Committee for Yugoslav Relief in 1945. Julie acknowledged that he had visited a Yugoslavian partisan camp during his USO tour and admitted that he had donated to the relief
fund via Colonel Dedijer.

Then Tavenner and the other members turned up the heat by asking him about his participation in the Committee for the First
Amendment.

GARFIELD: I received a telephone call—I am not quite sure whether it was from John Huston—asking me to come down to Washington for two reasons. One was that the industry as an industry was being called unpatriotic and un-American, and we felt that we had done an outstanding job in the war, and we felt it was our duty as people who worked in the industry to come to its defense. That was point No. 1. Point No. 2 was the issue of free speech. Mr. Eric Johnston said at that particular time, "I may be against everything you believe in, but I will fight for the right for you to say so."

JACKSON: I think the record should show that Eric Johnston was anticipated a number of years in that remark.

GARFIELD: I don't know about that, but I remember the instance.

TAVENNER: I think it was Victor Hugo who first said that, or Voltaire.

POTTER: You stated you wanted to make sure there were no Communists identified with this movement, Committee for the First Amendment. You must have known of a certain movement and of certain communist activity in Hollywood or you would not have been suspicious of it?

GARFIELD: That was because of the hearing, you know.

POTTER: But if you were so cautious as to make sure no communist was identified with your group, certainly you knew of communist activity in Hollywood or you would not have been so cautious?

GARFIELD: No, not necessarily; not necessarily.

Representative Wood then asked Julie about his view of the Committee for the First Amendment. The actor found himself defending his purchase of *The Daily Worker* and fending off personal insults from Representatives Velde and Jackson.

GARFIELD: As I have said, I wasn't in on the organization of it. I wasn't in California. Some 2 or 3 months later I did a play, "Skipper Next to God," and *The Daily Worker* panned me and said I was a little punch-drunk for playing in a religious play like "Skipper Next to God."

VELDE: How did you know about *The Daily Worker* saying that?

GARFIELD: I look in all the papers and try to find out all information about myself.

VELDE: I was interested in how you happened to see it.

GARFIELD: Would you like to see the copy?

VELDE: No. I have seen many copies of *The Daily Worker*. I asked how you happened to look at *The Daily Worker*.

GARFIELD: They review all plays.

VELDE: There is nothing sinister in my question.

GARFIELD: Most actors, if they are actors at all, like to see all the reviews, regardless of what paper publishes them. That was a review of a play I was in.

VELDE: You still haven't answered the question, Mr. Garfield. How did you happen to get hold of a copy of *The Daily Worker?*

GARFIELD: It was a review in *The Daily Worker.*

VELDE: I realize that. Do you remember where you obtained the copy?

GARFIELD: Yes. I got a copy by buying a copy. They have a dramatic critic and they review plays just like *The New York Times* or *The Herald Tribune.*

MOULDER: We subscribe to *The Daily Worker* here.

JACKSON: And the witness should know that this committee also shared the criticism of *The Daily Worker.*

Jackson's remark was a cheap shot at Julie's acting. Moulder seemed to be in Julie's corner, but Tavenner, Potter and Velde began to drive harder. Tavenner returned to the Committee for the First

Amendment and Julie's participation in it, trying to get the actor to admit some knowledge of Communist activity in Hollywood.

> TAVENNER: As you look back upon your activity in connection with the Committee for the First Amendment, do you now take the same view you took then, or do you feel that this committee should properly investigate communism in the motion picture industry?
>
> GARFIELD: Pretty much, except for one thing. There is a big difference between fighting for a legitimate political party and fighting for a subversive group, which I consider the Communists to be, and that is where I would differ today.
>
> TAVENNER: You now consider it a subversive group rather than a political party?
>
> GARFIELD: Exactly. For instance, I am a Democrat, and if you were a Republican I would fight like the devil for your right to speak up. But I feel that these people are not a legitimate political group.
>
> TAVENNER: In 1947, Mr. Garfield, it was no secret that the Communist Party was a conspiratorial group that intended to overthrow the Government, even by use of force and violence if necessary.
>
> GARFIELD: It is much clearer now than it was then; much clearer.

Bogart said it best: they had all been American dopes. Julie's answers moved from being vague to vacuous. He still refused to name names, even if he had to lie or play dumb. Testifying wasn't his best performance. Wood pressed for names.

> WOOD: Let me ask you categorically, have you any knowledge of the identity of a single individual who was a member of the Communist Party during the time you were in Hollywood?

GARFIELD: No, sir.

Tavenner asked whether Julie had sponsored a call to abolish
HUAC in 1947; again Julie feigned ignorance. A similar chain of
events followed as Tavenner asked Julie about his ties to the American League for Peace and Democracy and the China Aid Council.
Tavenner asked whether Julie had made a speech extolling the
virtues of Communist China—in 1940. Julie's knowledge of history
was better than Tavenner's. "There was no such thing as a communist government in China at that time," he told Tavenner. It continued like that; Tavenner (or one of the other representatives) asking
Julie about a specific organization, event or person; Julie back-
pedaling, dodging the question, or playing dumb.

Tavenner asked Julie about his 1940 visit to Washington, D.C.

> TAVENNER: Back in 1940—in fact, on April 1, 1940—while
> the non-aggression pact between Russia and Germany
> was in effect, I believe you were an honored guest at a
> meeting here in Washington at which you delivered an
> address attacking the intensive war drives then in
> progress and urging your listeners to read Dalton
> Trumbo's *Johnny Got His Gun.*
>
> GARFIELD: That is absolutely untrue. I was never in Wash-
> ington in 1940 and I never made such a speech. As I ex-
> plained to you, I went overseas at that time, when the
> communists considered the war an imperialistic war. It
> doesn't make much sense.

Nor did his answer make sense. He had been in Washington in
1940 while *Heavenly Express* played there; newspaper articles corroborated his presence. It would be one sticking point for HUAC
when they tried to prove he was lying.

Tavenner asked about Julie's stand on Finnish War Relief (which
led to some unintentional comic byplay when both men kept mix-

ing 1940 up with 1950), the 1945 Russian ship visit with Charlie
Chaplin, and Julie's support of the Hollywood Ten in a Supreme
Court case. The actor's responses continued to be vague, though he
seasoned his answers with a few out-and-out lies. Tavenner gave
up, more or less, saying he had no more questions for the witness;
it appeared that Julie was free. Representative Moulder took this
moment to compliment Julie. "I feel morally inclined to express my
opinion that nothing has been presented by the Committee which
associates you with the Communist Party."

From his vantage point watching the proceedings, Morris
Carnovsky thought Julie acquitted himself well so far. He recalled
that Julie and his lawyers, thinking the hearing was over, began to
gather up their belongings. But Representative Velde was not finished, and he asked Juile again about the petition Julie had signed in
1947 to abolish the House Committee on Un-American Activities.

VELDE: You are very positive you did not sign such a peti-
    tion?

GARFIELD: Quite positive, yes sir.

VELDE: Did you attend any meetings or do anything other
    than sign a petition?

GARFIELD: Yes; I did.

VELDE: Will you go ahead and explain that?

GARFIELD: There was a meeting that had to do with the
    Committee for the First Amendment.

VELDE: And in that meeting that was held, did you recog-
    nize any other Communists - or any communists; rather,
    I beg your pardon—did you recognize any Communists
    as being present?

GARFIELD: No, sir.

VELDE: Did you know of any communists during your ex-
    perience in Hollywood or elsewhere?

GARFIELD: I said before that I did not, and I say again, very
    honestly and very truthfully.

After some discussion of Julie's military service—or lack of—Velde got back to asking when, if ever, Julie realized that there was a Communist Party movement in Hollywood. Julie replied that he didn't know that there were any communists in Hollywood until he considered supporting the 1948 Presidential campaign of Henry Wallace. It was naïve of him to believe that HUAC would accept that sort of logic.

> VELDE: Do you want to go on the record as saying you had no knowledge whatsoever of any Communist Party movement in Hollywood until the time you broke with the Wallace Party?
>
> GARFIELD: Absolutely and positively.

Representatives Kearney and Jackson then began working together to trip Julie up. It wasn't hard to do.

> KEARNEY: I would like to ask Mr. Garfield whether he ever made any statement regarding the Marshall Plan?
>
> GARFIELD: Yes. I came back from Europe and I was questioned by reporters, and I made a statement which ran as follows: quote, "The Marshall Plan is killing communism in Europe, and that is good," quote, unquote.
>
> KEARNEY: You say "quotes," is that from memory?
>
> GARFIELD: That is the fact.
>
> KEARNEY: Is that the memory that you just gave?
>
> GARFIELD: Yes.
>
> KEARNEY: That is from the record as I have it, also. That is all, Mr. Chairman.
>
> WOOD: Mr. Jackson?
>
> JACKSON: Mr. Garfield, I am afraid I am not entirely convinced of the entire accuracy and entire cooperation you are giving this committee. It is your contention that you did not know, during the time you were in New York affiliated with the Group Theatre, which for all its artistry

was pretty well shot through with the philosophy of communism—

GARFIELD: That is not true.

JACKSON: That is a matter of opinion. You contend during all that time in New York you did not know a communist?

GARFIELD: That is right.

JACKSON: And you contend during the seven and a half years or more that you were in Hollywood and in close contact with a situation in which a number of Communist cells were operating on a week-to-week basis, with electricians, actors, and every class represented, that during the entire period of this time you were in Hollywood you did not know of your own personal knowledge a member of the Communist Party?

GARFIELD: That is absolutely correct, because I was not a party member or associated in any shape, way or form.

JACKSON: During that period, it might interest you to know attempts were made to recruit me into the Communist Party, and I was making $32.50 a week.

GARFIELD: They certainly stayed away from me, sir.

JACKSON: Perhaps I looked like better material.

Jackson asked him about all the communists who had worked on *He Ran All the Way*—Guy Endore, Hugo Butler, John Berry, and so on, and then asked, "You have never been approached at any time to join the Communist Party?"

GARFIELD: That is right, Mr. Jackson. I might say, if at any time that had happened, I would have run like hell.

JACKSON: I must say, Mr. Chairman, in conclusion, that I am still not satisfied.

Jackson then read a letter from the National Council of the Arts, Sciences and Professions calling for the abolition of the House

Committee on Un-American Activities. He rattled off a list of sponsors who had signed the letter; Julie was one. Potter again asked Julie if he had ever been approached to join the Communist Party. Once again, Julie said no. Then he squirmed through the next part of the testimony:

> POTTER: Looking back, do you believe that any of the so-called liberal movements that you were affiliated with were used by the Communist Party, in looking back at it now?
>
> GARFIELD: Yes, sir. They were captured like the Wallace Party thing; sure, they were used. But how do you protect people like me? That is what I want to know. That is why I feel we should outlaw the party. We are in a tough spot. Don't you think so, Mr. Potter?
>
> POTTER: I agree that the party should be outlawed. I would go along with that. It is difficult for me to understand how you could have been affiliated with organizations that, looking back now, you believe were being used by the Communist Party, and have so little knowledge as to the fact that they were being used.
>
> GARFIELD: I was not affiliated with these organizations. Some of them used my name without my permission. I was not affiliated with any political party except the Democratic Party and the Liberal Party. I never attended any meetings of these groups. I attended board meetings of the Screen Actors Guild for 6 years, and the minutes speak for themselves. I was also vice president and organizer with Bette Davis of the Hollywood Canteen in 1941. I sold over $5,000,000 of bonds. I was a busy fellow with a lot more things to do than getting involved with a lot of crackpots.
>
> POTTER: Apparently the committee has received not only testimony but certain evidence from publications of alleged membership that you had that you now deny. Did you have any knowledge of articles, for example, which

appeared in *The Daily Worker,* which lauded you for such and such activities?

GARFIELD: I also have proof they panned me. I know the organizations I am a member of: YMCA, Hoyle Club, Democratic Club, B'nai B'rith.

POTTER: You don't appear to be a naïve man.

GARFIELD: I am not, I don't think.

POTTER: It is difficult to understand. If I got lauded in *The Daily Worker,* I would begin to suspect—

GARFIELD: You mean anyone mentioned in *The Daily Worker* is suspect?

POTTER: I would try to find out what they were up to.

GARFIELD: Senator Taft was praised by *The Daily Worker* for his refusal to send troops to Europe. Does that mean he is on their team, so to speak?

Jackson wasn't satisfied.

JACKSON: I do say that, for one who is intelligent and as well established as this witness has proven himself to be, it shows a naïve or unintelligent approach to his problem for him to have lived with this activity 10, 11 or 15 years and not know more about it than this witness knows.

GARFIELD: Mr. Jackson, may I answer that? I went overseas twice. I was too busy with war work. I am now conscious of what you are saying, more conscious than I ever was, but in that time I was more conscious of my bigger duty, which was to my country, and where I as an artist can contribute.

JACKSON: Unfortunately, the work in which you were engaged became more suspect than the work of those overseas.

GARFIELD : I went overseas. I wasn't here joining parties while they were shooting over there and dropping bombs.

JACKSON: A great many witnesses have been produced who
were members of the Communist Party and working for
the overthrow of the Government. That is why you are
here—not because you are John Garfield. You are here because you were associated with an industry that has become suspect in the eyes of many people.

The questioning returned to Tavenner, who asked Julie whether
he knew where John Berry and Hugo Butler were. Both men were
subpoenaed to appear before HUAC but had disappeared. (Butler had
gone to Mexico; Berry to Europe.) Julie said he had no knowledge of
their whereabouts and asked if he could read a brief statement:

GARFIELD: When I was originally requested to appear before
the committee, I said that I would answer all questions,
fully and without any reservations, and that is what I
have done. I have nothing to be ashamed of and nothing
to hide. My life is an open book. I was glad to appear before you and talk with you. I am no Red. I am no "pink."
I am no fellow-traveler. I am a Democrat by politics, a liberal by inclination, and a loyal citizen of this country by
every act of my life.

And so, at 1:15 P.M., after nearly three hours of testimony, Julie
was excused. He later told Robbe that many of the committee members approached him for an autograph or to shake hands. They even
quarreled with each other over who might take him out to dinner
that night.

CHAPTER EIGHTEEN

Sucker for a Left Hook

"Some people prefer to work on their knees."
—ARNOLD FORSTER

JULIE WAS RELIEVED THAT HIS TESTIMONY WAS OVER. Nizer and Davis felt he had acquitted himself well. "His testimony before HUAC was a success," Nizer later said. "He was sincere, and he told the facts." Abe Polonsky also admired Julie's stance. He felt Julie had more to lose careerwise than a lot of hard-line communists who had named names. "Garfield took an interesting path," Polonsky said. "I think it was brave. He didn't want to take the Fifth Amendment and he wasn't a member of the Communist Party. So when they asked, 'Do you know any communists?'" he said, 'No.' He didn't know any communists. His wife did!" John Berry was also complimentary towards Julie: "I thought he was terrific. He was being loyal to his street traditions—you don't give names. It's a tradition that should exist in all human morality."

Nice accolades, but they wouldn't help Julie. The country's mood was changing; there was a very real fear of a Communist attack, particularly with the Korean War continuing. The U.S. government sentenced Julius and Ethel Rosenberg to death for espionage. Passing the sentence, federal Judge Irving R. Kaufman told the Rosenbergs, "Your crime is worse than murder."

Robbe was less impressed with Julie's testimony, especially when he repeatedly denounced communism as a tyranny that should be outlawed. "She was anti anything that had to do with cooperating with the committee," Polonsky explained. "He disagreed with her. He wanted to cooperate but not give names, but to her it wasn't a question of politics. It was a question of morality." Young Julie Garfield agrees about her mother's view, but sympathizes with her father. "Robbe didn't understand what it was like to love something—like acting—and then lose it," she said. "She acted as if she knew what was best for everyone. She used to say 'Don't sell out!' to both Daddy and me regarding acting work. We ended up like fish swimming upstream. That was her power over Daddy. She had no other power. He turned her into a mother, and she was a matriarchal figure to him to the end."

What the aftermath of Julie's testimony would be was not immediately clear to any of the players. The initial signs looked good; *The New York Times* suggested that he might have cleared himself. "The reaction of the Committee members towards Mr. Garfield was largely complimentary," *Time* magazine wrote, citing Senator Moulder's comment that Julie was a "a thoroughly and intensely loyal American citizen."

A turn for the worse came soon after. Tough-guy actor Marc Lawrence testified a few days after Julie, and when asked to respond to Julie's claim that he didn't know a single communist in Hollywood, Lawrence said, "Why, that's silly." The latest issue of the anti-communist journal *Counter Attack,* published on April 27, blasted Julie's testimony and criticized HUAC for not grilling him more. Meanwhile HUAC leaked to the press that they had sent Julie's testimony to the FBI for an accuracy check. By June 6 New York's *Daily Mirror* stated that Congress was considering a special session to see if Julie was withholding information. Representative Bernard Kearney issued a statement regarding Julie's testimony: "The committee definitely disbelieves the greater portion of the testimony of Garfield, especially those portions where he denied ever knowing anyone who was a Communist." Columnist Victor Riesel suggested that the Justice Department look into who held Communist party card no. 25,192 in 1943: "It will get itself one of the great human interest stories of the year, for it may show why a great star perjured himself." The reference was to Robbe. Even if HUAC had struck a deal with Julie regarding his wife's activities, she was fair game to the media and the FBI. Robbe didn't care. She felt Julie could set aside his film career and return to the theater.

Somehow United Artists felt confident enough to give *He Ran All the Way* a limited release in June 1951. The reviews were mixed. Otis L. Guernsey of *The New York Herald Tribune* fell in line with many reviewers when he wrote that the film was "a middling thriller" that looked as though "it had been designed with a typical Garfield tough-guy performance in mind." Julie looks tired in the film, and heavier too, but his appearance (the bags under his eyes, for example) helped convey the impression that this was the end of the line for his screen character, Nick Robey. The film joined the ranks of Julie's previous four films as a commercial disappointment. Its failure depressed Julie even more.

Professionally speaking, there was little else for him to do. He made an interesting one-shot attempt at writing, penning a strange little story called "Door of Mystery" for *Coronet* magazine that summer. The story told of an odd experience Julie had while filming *Juarez* in Mexico that involved a door that mysteriously appeared and then disappeared. The story didn't do much for his career.

Things were not going well between the Garfields either. Julie needed to get back to work to bolster his self-esteem; Robbe couldn't understand why he didn't take a year or more off and just wait it out. She felt he had been so weak in terms of sexual temptation that perhaps here he could display some strength; she didn't understand his need to work, or how much he defined himself by his profession. Robbe knew that her sway over Julie had diminished considerably over the past decade. He had proved that he did not need her to become a star. She felt that she didn't need him, and she wasn't so sure whether the children did either.

These feelings, coupled with Julie's decision to return to some sort of acting work, led the couple to agree to a trial separation. He felt it was the perfect opportunity to follow through with his idea of touring with *Golden Boy*. Clifford Odets gave Julie special permission to stage the play, and Julie, as director, set about auditioning and casting an ensemble of six actors to travel with him on a two-month tour of the New England area. In each town Julie would rehearse with the cast for two days before opening for a week's run. The cast included Harold J. Stone, Joe Bernard, Constance Ford and Anna Berger.

Berger, who had just finished working with Mae West in a revival of *Diamond Lil'*, recalled Julie as being a gentle man with a good heart, boundless energy and a boyish curiosity about everything. Her audition for him was memorable: "I had heard all sorts of stories about him being a ladies' man and everything, but I didn't know what to expect. I was reading onstage for my audition and he was in the audience watching me. I could feel his eyes piercing me. As soon as I finished reading he leapt onto the stage, took me by the hand and led me back to his dressing room."

Berger wasn't sure what Julie had in mind, although she had her suspicions. She wanted the job, but she wanted to put off his advances in a polite manner. So while she sat there in the dressing room thinking of what to do or say, Julie closed the door, turned to her, knelt down in front of her and said, "Okay, so tell me the truth: what's Mae West really like?" That's all he wanted from her. She got the part.

The tour played to sold-out houses and critical accolades. It also exhausted the actors. Constance Ford recalled that after a few weeks on the road she no longer knew what town she was in, what town she was going to, or what costume she was to wear onstage as the tour played from the Lake Whalom Playhouse in Fitchburg, Massachusetts, to Princeton, New Jersey's McCarter Theatre. When

Golden Boy played at the Matunuck Theatre in Providence, Rhode Island, midway through the tour, Robbe and the Garfield children popped in for a visit, supplying the local paper with some cozy front-page Garfield family photos. *The Providence Journal's* critic reviewed the play and praised Julie's work: "One of the nicest things that can be said about an actor is that he does not act. This was amply illustrated last night by John Garfield. He didn't act the part of Joe Bonaparte. He was Joe Bonaparte." That was music to Julie's ears. After 15 years he was finally playing the role that had been written for him.

Only at the last stop was there any sign of trouble. The managing director of the McCarter Theatre was Herbert Kenwith, a 21-year-old theater professional who made it a habit to announce each show a week in advance. "After I went out and announced to the audience that next week John Garfield would be appearing here in *Golden Boy,* I immediately began receiving letters asking me why I was letting this 'commie pinko' in my theater in New Jersey," Kenwith recalled. Kenwith was against the blacklist and for John Garfield: "I wrote a letter to the editor of the Princeton paper explaining why I thought it was important for us to let Garfield appear; that we shouldn't cave into the witch hunt." There were no further protests, and sometime later Robbe wrote Kenwith a letter thanking him for his public stand.

Despite the protesting letters, the last stop was as successful as all the rest. The 1,200 seat McCarter Theatre played to full houses all week. "The theater came alive when Garfield was onstage, you could just feel the energy in the air," Kenwith said. "It was just dynamic." Kenwith, who had worked with film stars Joan Crawford, Dane Clark, Zachary Scott and others, found Julie easy to deal with, and recalled with admiration that he was the only major star to ever offer to pick up the tab at dinner.

Offstage, Julie was aloof and preoccupied. He spent a lot of time in his hotel room listening to the radio and reading the newspapers. To cheer him up, the rest of the cast got together to concoct a practical joke. In the play, Joe Bonaparte opens his violin case in front of his father (played by Harold J. Stone). Stone placed some plastic dog dung in the case because the cast figured the surprise would throw Julie. They had underestimated him. When the time came for him to open the violin case onstage, Julie didn't register surprise. He maintained his concentration, said his lines as if everything was in place, and moved the scene forward. He could take it and dish it out with the best of them. A few moments later Joe is offstage and Stone speaks some lines commenting on Joe's violin playing, as offstage music is heard. A professional violinist was to play a classical piece; but Julie had instructed the man to play "Hey Diddle Diddle, the Cat and the Fiddle," dismaying Stone and throwing the onstage cast off-balance.

Julie wasn't in the habit of discussing his personal feelings with anyone in the cast, but he was attuned to other people's problems. He sensed that something was bothering Berger, and one day he asked her what was wrong. "My younger brother had a serious ear infection and it was possible that he was going to lose his hearing," the actress recalled. "I told Julie about it, and he said 'Well, let me know if there's anything I can do for you.' At the end of the run he gave me his costume, his robe, his trunks and his boxing gloves, and he said, 'Give these to your kid brother.' I did, and he loved them. He kept them until his death."

When the *Golden Boy* tour ended, Julie announced his plans to take the show to Broadway. Drama critic Elliot Norton suggested that Julie take the project to ANTA. Robert Whitehead was then the driving force behind that organization. "This sounds terrible, but the early 1950s was a boon period for me because I could hire a lot of blacklisted actors and use them in ANTA productions," Whitehead said. "The blacklist brought a lot of them back to Broadway." Julie asked Clifford Odets to direct the Broadway production, which went into rehearsal late in 1951.

While trying to work his way back to Broadway, Julie was pushing his new agent, George Chasen, to line up some film work for

him. (Sometime in the late 1940s or early 1950s Julie and Lew
Wasserman split ways; when or why is unclear, but Roberts' personality may have put off the equally strong-willed Wasserman.)
The right-wing press was still pushing the FBI to take a second look
at Julie's testimony. Walter Winchell's radio broadcast of Sunday,
September 9, referred indirectly to Julie: "A male moving picture
star who testified that he never knew a communist in Hollywood or
any other place may be indicted soon for perjury." *American Legion
Monthly* printed an article by J.B. Matthews in their December issue
entitled "Did The Movies Really Clean House?" in which Matthews
claimed HUAC had not done enough to ferret out communists in
Hollywood. "If it were not so serious in its implications, Garfield's
entire testimony before the committee would be one of the funniest
scenarios of 1951," he wrote.

To get a reprieve from the attention, Julie traveled to Europe with
Bob Roberts. He reportedly met with British film producer J. Arthur
Rank to discuss doing a film in England. John Berry ran into Julie in
London and tried to convince the actor to move to Europe until the
fever broke. Julie wouldn't do it. "He was a deep American guy, a
kid from New York," Berry said. "As John Garfield he was a big
symbol of the American dream, and to deny that and act in Europe
was to turn his back on America."

1951 had shaped up as the worst year of Julie's professional life.
He maintained some hope that the Broadway revival of *Golden Boy*
would renew Hollywood's interest in him, but he had to take stock
of the fact that there were no prospective film projects on the horizon. On Christmas Eve 1951, he made out a new will, designating
Robbe the main benefactor.

Julie and Robbe had been apart for most of that summer, but he
returned to the Central Park apartment in the autumn. Julie's con-
tinual desire to land another film was at odds with Robbe's belief
that he could ride out the storm. She was willing to move to Mexico or Europe if Julie was. He couldn't cast aside his image as a
movie star. After more than a decade of Hollywood success, it was

nearly impossible for him to consider downshifting gears. The couple separated again in January 1952 (after Julie's death the press would make the period of separation out to be a matter of days, not months).

Julie spent what would be his last five months on earth either in hotel rooms or in his dressing room at the theater. He stayed to himself more and more, not wanting to unload his problems on others. He made excuses for his current standing in Hollywood. Viveca Lindfors invited Julie to dinner one night, and she asked him why he wasn't making a film. "He wouldn't say that he was blacklisted," Lindfors said. "He would always say, 'I'm discussing a part now but you know, I'm getting too old for that sort of part,' or, 'I'm too short.' He was mysteriously quiet; it was difficult to really know why he did not get the part." Anthony Quinn felt Julie was going out of his way to avoid people: "I don't think he wanted to face many people. I think he got so used to being a movie star that he may have been slightly embarrassed at not being able to work, not being able to be the star."

Let it be said, he kept trying. He and Roberts still wanted to get *Port Afrique* made and Chasen was trying to land Julie the lead in a 20th Century Fox movie, *Taxi*. When Chasen's efforts led nowhere, Julie felt persecuted. "He reminded me of Fagin in *Oliver Twist*," lawyer Sidney Davis said, "crying out, 'Why are they doing this to me?' " as the mob approached to kill him."

Julie could accept the fact that film work was out of his reach. The smaller things hurt more. Grossinger's, the famous summer retreat resort in the Catskills, had agreed to hire Julie as emcee for a benefit for the Damon Runyon Cancer Fund. Columnist Walter Winchell was one of the members of the board for that fund; he vetoed Julie's participation. Julie couldn't get a TV gig either. Milton Berle attempted to get him on his show as a guest star and was rebuffed by his network, NBC. ABC was planning to produce a version of Elmer Rice's *Counsellor-At-Law*. Rice was given control over the script, the production values and casting. His first choice for the lead was Paul Muni. Muni was away making an independent film in Italy, so Rice next picked Julie. ABC said no. Julie's listing in *Red Channels* and his subsequent testimony left too many unanswered questions for the network. Rice realized he actually had little say in casting and canceled the deal; he issued a public statement denouncing ABC and HUAC for "judging artists by political standards."

All of these out-of-reach projects accentuated the problem Julie was facing. In light of his testimony before HUAC, he found himself in a strange no-man's-land. Officially he was not blacklisted, but he wasn't "cleared" to work. He was in a holding pattern, waiting to see what the FBI and the media would do next.

The FBI was cross-checking his sworn testimony. They also began following him, and it's possible that they tapped his phones (a chilling parallel to a scene in *Force of Evil*). But they couldn't disprove much of what he had said before HUAC. The one thing they could make stick was his contention that he had not been in Washington, D.C., in 1940. *The Washington Daily Post* had photographs of the event. Much of the rest of the time, energy and money the FBI spent in compiling a case against Julie was for naught.

Their FBI file on him would add up to about 1,000 pages, most of it of little or no importance. But here and there a fascinating memo appears, including one dated June 18, 1951, which states "Available informants of the Los Angeles Office and past investigation locally . . . have not definitely shown actual Communist Party membership on the part of John Garfield—at least in the Hollywood area." A February 8, 1952, FBI memo, in which it was recommended that a special security index file be compiled of individuals who should be arrested and held for the Detention of Communists Program, strikes a more chilling tone. Thirty-five candidates, including John Garfield, were listed in that file. At the time it was suggested that Julie not be detained should the program be initiated, but the memo itself paints a frightening picture of the political atmosphere of the country during the McCarthy era.

Fortunately, Broadway remained a work option, and rehearsals for *Golden Boy* began in January 1952. Odets worked with Julie and Robert Whitehead to line up a first-rate cast: Art Smith as Tom Moody, Lee J. Cobb as Papa Bonaparte, Joseph Wiseman as the gangster Fuselli, and newcomers Jack Warden, Jack Klugman and Arthur O'Connell in supporting roles. Some concern was expressed over casting Odets' wife, Bette Grayson, as Lorna Moon; she was seen as a possible detriment. Julie's old friends Joe Bernard was on board too, and he recalled director Odets' opening comment to the cast: "Lee J. Cobb is afraid he won't do well as Papa Bonaparte, so keep on your toes." And that was it.

They proved to be a happy ensemble, and the cast and crew sub-titled the play *Garfield's Revenge.* Julie worked out, trying to lose weight so he could still pull off the part of a 21-year-old boxer. He seemed happy to be returning to Broadway, but he still wanted back to Hollywood. He just didn't know how to make that happen.

Then a film project fell in his lap. It looked like a real winner. It was called *On The Waterfront.*

Sam Shaw, who at that time was writing about the movie busi-ness for magazines like *Look* and *Life,* contacted Julie to discuss a possible film version of Malcolm Johnson's 1949 Pulitzer Prize-winning series, "Crime on the Waterfront," which dealt with cor-ruption on the waterfront docks of New York City. Shaw and writer Ed McSauler had already prepared a first draft of a screenplay based on the series. Shaw was connected to Harry Cohn via Joe Curtis, son of Jack Cohn, president of Columbia Pictures and Harry's brother. Jack Cohn and Charles Feldman (one of the founders of Enterprise) said they would produce the film if Shaw could interest some financiers. With Jack Cohn's help, Shaw man-aged to secure financing from a group of Jewish businessmen who wanted to fight the blacklist.

Joe Curtis asked Shaw to speak to Julie about playing the film's protagonist, ex-boxer turned loser Terry Malloy. "My talent was get-ting along with actors," Shaw explained, adding that he had never met Julie before. "The money was raised to do the film as an independent. And this was before Kazan, and even before Schulberg came in, because we had a script that was very strong. And we had some interesting industrial people in New York who were very much disturbed by what was going on with the blacklist, and they were really anxious to fight it. I realize now that it wasn't a matter of money to them. I mean, if they lost money they could write it off as a tax loss. It was a matter of conscience.

"I began meeting with Julie, and I gave him the script. And the backers also wanted Robert Rossen, who was also on the list, to direct. So Julie and I would walk along West End Avenue to discuss the project. He was anxious; you could feel it. He was interested in the idea that independent money was coming forth to fight the blacklist. But that was the only thing that he was concerned with. He wasn't talking about the blacklist and the difficulty of getting work."

What happened next, according to Shaw, was Marilyn Monroe. Shaw had her in mind to play Malloy's girlfriend (a role eventually played by Eva Marie Saint). Shaw gave Monroe the script while she was in New York to take in the Broadway production of *Gentlemen Prefer Blondes*. Monroe read the script and passed it on to her lover, director Elia Kazan. Shaw, who called himself a "half-assed observer at the Actors' Studio," had met Kazan on the set of the 1950 film *Panic in the Streets*. "Kazan had heard about my script (before Monroe gave it to him) and wanted to see it," Shaw said. "I wouldn't give it to him, because he was involved with Arthur Miller on a similar project, *The Hook*." But after Monroe gave Kazan the script, the director called Shaw. "You've got an interesting script, but it needs a lot of work," he told Shaw. "Let Budd Schulberg work on it." Shaw, seeing the merit in Kazan's suggestion, raised $40,000 to pay Schulberg to work on the script. According to Shaw, at this point Jack Cohn turned the script over to Sam Spiegel, who had just produced John Huston's 1951 hit *The African Queen*. Within a year Kazan, Spiegel and Schulberg were preparing the film for Columbia Pictures with Marlon Brando in the role of Malloy. By that point, neither Shaw nor Garfield were involved in any way.

A fascinating story, but is it true? Kazan, Schulberg and others connected with the film tell a different story about the picture's origins and casting, but Shaw does have some corroborating evidence on his side. Al Ryelander, then a press agent for Columbia, insists the story is accurate. "I worked for Joe Curtis at Columbia in New York," Ryelander recalled, "And the plan was for Shaw and Curtis to produce *On the Waterfront* independently—and cheaply—and get Robert Rossen to adapt it for the screen. They were looking for a star, and thought Garfield would be good, and realized he would probably do it for a smaller salary because he was blacklisted."

Kazan's reaction to Shaw's story is typically terse: "I don't think either of those gentlemen were in a position to know what was going on with the film." But Robbe Garfield confirmed that Julie mentioned to her that he might do the film if things worked out, and Budd Schulberg, in his preface to the published script of the film, says he met with Julie to discuss Terry Malloy. "But Julie's life and career were being destroyed by political pressures from right and left and he died of a heart attack before our project was under way," Schulberg wrote. "He would have been good, maybe great."

Lack of work gnawed at Julie. "The pain [of not working] was too much for him," Joseph Bernard said. "He finally got what he wanted—stardom—and now it was taken away from him." Bernard recalled that Julie landed a television commercial for the Red Cross. At the last possible moment it was canceled. "Well, they're just after me, aren't they?" Julie said to Bernard upon hearing the news.

There were people who wanted to help. In March 1952, on the eve of the opening of *Golden Boy* on Broadway, Sam Shaw suggested that Julie see lawyer Arnold Forster, who was then working for the Anti-Defamation League of B'nai B'rith, serving as interme-

diary between HUAC and suspected communists. Forster's concern
was for people who had been unfairly accused, for he realized his
chances of helping a bona fide member of the Communist Party
were slim. Julie called Forster and set up an appointment. Though
the two had been childhood pals, when they met Julie never mentioned their childhood days, which Forster found odd. Forster also
was shocked to see an angry, bitter man of 38, looking more like 48,
in front of him. "He was absolutely defeated," Forster said. "He was
angry, and he was frustrated. He felt that there was no way he was
going to get out of the problem he was in. When he came to me I
guess it was a last desperate effort."

Forster laid out a multi-step plan for Julie to follow. First, they
had to win support from Forster's newspaper contacts. They would
use the press to portray Julie as a dupe of the communists. Julie
would have to go public on a strong anti-communist campaign as
well. The actor agreed to co-write (with Forster) an in-depth article
explaining how he had been "suckered" into contributing his time,
money and talent to the Communist Party. As if trying to tie the
piece in with Julie's screen image, the article was titled "I Was A
Sucker for a Left Hook." Both men, however, agreed that Julie
would not name names.

When Julie told Robbe about his plans, she wouldn't abide by it.
"What we were trying to do may well have led to his being able to
work at a price that Robbe couldn't accept," Forster said. "Robbe
would have preferred that Julie starve rather than bend at the knees
to those bastards. She may well have been right, and in the final
analysis if nobody had bent to these bastards they may have lost
their strength and their power, but if you're a great star, and you
can't work, principle be damned. Some people prefer to work on
their knees."

"I Was A Sucker for a Left Hook" is a fairly innocuous article that
basically reprises Julie's testimony before HUAC the previous year.
In it, he claimed to have been ensnared in a trap and coerced

against his better judgment into lending his name and support to several communist-front groups. "I was gulled into association with high-sounding committees that later turned out to be fronts for communist enterprises, like the China Aid Council," Julie wrote in the article. "Worse still, many fine groups to which I gladly lent my name were successfully infiltrated and exploited by Communists, and I did nothing about it." Robbe couldn't tolerate this half-measure of contrition on Julie's part.

John Berry sympathized with Julie's plight at the time. "The committee was going to charge him with perjury, you know," he said. "If he were to name people he could strike a bargain and go back to work. Once that was planted in Julie's mind, even if he had all the resistance one can imagine, there must have been a flaw. He must have given it some thought. The temptation to play ball must have crossed his mind."

Julie wanted to play ball his way. He would appear to be cooperative while refusing to name names. He even managed to deceive Forster and spread rumors. On March 24, 1952, Victor Reisel's syndicated newspaper column reported, "John Garfield will soon blast the Commies, says he's sorry he got roped in, reveals how it was done and says he'll take any anti-Communist platform to tell his story." Forster wondered how Reisel had received this information and asked Julie about it over drinks at the bar in the Warwick Hotel. Julie feigned ignorance, but after his death, Reisel told Forster that Julie had planted the bit.

Julie continued to work on the article whenever he wasn't directly involved with *Golden Boy*. After out-of-town previews in Hartford, Connecticut, the play opened at the ANTA Playhouse on 52nd Street in New York on March 12 to enthusiastic audiences and good reviews. *The New Yorker* said that Julie's work as Joe Bonaparte was excellent, and *Variety* called his portrayal "well balanced." Critic Brooks Atkinson wrote that "Mr. Garfield is giving one of his most eloquent performances, purged of the overeager mannerisms that used to mar his acting." Julie was often fed or starved by the talent that surrounded him, and this revival was, fortunately, chock-full of first-rate talent.

Odets told the press that he was nearly finished with a new play, *By the Sea,* and that he planned to direct it in the autumn with Julie playing the lead role. In the meantime Julie kept making anti-communist appearances in tandem with Forster's plan. On April 30 he showed up at Ebbets Field for the Fourth Birthday Party for Israel sponsored by the Israel Anniversary Committee, and there he denounced communism. The following week he attended a student rally at Hunter College, again attacking communism as a scourge. On Jinx Falkenburg's radio show, Julie mentioned his rather bizarre plan to take *Golden Boy* to Berlin. "I wanted to do it honestly," he told Falkenburg, "and show the people the communists were trying to use it for propaganda."

These actions of his were enough to make Robbe sever ties between them completely. She felt his giving in, even halfway, was the final straw. "Robbe was already so hurt from all his other actions, like screwing around, that she had had it," daughter Julie explained. "I wouldn't say the marriage was necessarily over, but if you were a woman whose husband had neglected you and was unfaithful, maybe you'd want a separation just to think things over for a while. Robbe wanted Julie to take responsibility for his life." During rehearsals for *Golden Boy,* he moved into the Warwick Hotel in midtown Manhattan.

Problems surfaced about this time with partner and business manager Bob Roberts. Money was the issue. "Roberts didn't pay the salary due me and thereby breached our contract," Julie said in a brief press release in April, adding that he had fired Roberts. (Not surprising considering how many previous talent agents had come and gone throughout Julie's 13-year Hollywood career.) Roberts moved to Europe shortly thereafter to avoid a possible subpoena from HUAC, taking Julie's film property rights with him.

On the political front, a lot of people around Julie were giving in. Robert Rossen named names. So did Edward Dmytryk and Lee J. Cobb. Odets and Kazan were considering it. The stress of his failing marriage, the workouts for *Golden Boy* and the slump in his career continued to take their toll on Julie. Actress Marie Windsor ran into Julie on a street in New York around this time; he didn't look well to her.

Solace came in the form of a woman. While previewing *Golden Boy* in Hartford, Julie met actress/interior designer Iris Whitney. A native of Pasadena, California, Whitney had been a child dancer and actress who had played small roles in several hit plays of the 1930s, including *The Petrified Forest* and *Abe Lincoln in Illinois*. She was blonde, vibrant and well built, a good time girl who, some believe, would have made a great courtesan. In 1952 she claimed to be 36; she was actually 42, qualifying her for "mothering" status in Julie's eyes. Robert Whitehead had introduced the two. "He was uncomfortable in his marriage at the time, and I introduced him to Iris Whitney, who had come up to Hartford to see another actor in the show," Whitehead recalled. "They hit it off right away."

They hit it off *too* well. Julie had experienced so many casual affairs over the years that no one felt that he would fall for anyone. With Whitney it may have been something else altogether. "I was surprised when he told me he was going for her," Robert Whitehead said. "I didn't think it was that serious." Garfield's daughter Julie views Whitney and her relationship with her father in a different light. "My father was a drowning man clinging to a life raft," she said. "He needed someone to hold on to, and she was there for him." When Julie returned to New York for the opening of *Golden Boy*, Whitney was there waiting. She rented an apartment in Gramercy Park, and the two saw a lot of each other in March and April. Acquaintances of Whitney maintain that she was just a well-meaning woman who truly cared for Julie, but it's fruitless to speculate how deep their relationship went.

Julie was now working a sixteen-hour day. Daytime hours he worked with Forster on the article, some were good days, and some bad. At times he would regale Forster with anecdotes about his days at Warner Bros. Sometimes he would act out a dueling scene from an imaginary swashbuckler that he hoped to make. "He was not a guy weighted down with burdens in those few minutes," Forster said. "He was never all glum, glum, glum. No one is, even when you lose your loved one." In a sense Julie had lost his loved one: Hollywood.

He continued to look at the theater as an option. Producer Nick Condos hired Julie to act in the summer stock production of *The Cameo* at the Miami Beach Theatre for the summer of 1952. Julie was trying to acquire the stage rights to one of his biggest film hits, *The Postman Always Rings Twice.* He optioned the rights to Norman Brooks' anti-war play *The Fragile Fox,* and in a rather optimistic press release announced his intent to produce, to direct and to act a psychotic, cowardly Army officer in the play. He said he hoped to eventually produce the play as a movie.

"I think Julie accepted the fact that he was blacklisted," Robert Whithead said. "He hoped to return to Broadway full time. We discussed doing other plays in the future. He wanted to work, I think, at being a major theater actor. He had a great respect for the art of stage acting, and he really wanted to be a distinguished actor, like Helen Hayes or Laurence Olivier."

Julie understood his ranking as a theater artist in comparison to the likes of Hayes. When *Golden Boy* previewed in Hartford, he approached Whitehead and asked him what the advance sales were. "About $16,000," Whitehead replied. Hayes had previously opened in Hartford with the play *Mrs. McThing,* so Julie asked Whitehead what the advance for her show had been.

"Do you really want to know?" Whitehead asked.

"Yeah," Julie said.

"$48,000," Whitehead replied.

Julie considered this. "Yeah, that's right," he said. "That's how it should be."

Golden Boy closed in New York after only 55 performances on April 27, 1952. The play was a fitting climax to John Garfield's stage career. He couldn't have known it at the time, but there would be no more curtain calls for him.

CHAPTER NINETEEN

Last Days

> *"This may sound romantic, but I think what
> happened was, faced with the option of nam-
> ing names, Julius Garfinkle of the Bronx said
> to John Garfield of Hollywood, 'You can't do
> this to me.' And John Garfield packed his
> bags and died"'*
>
> —JACK BERRY

JULIE COMPLETED FIFTEEN PAGES OF "I WAS A SUCKER
For a Left Hook" and Forster submitted it to editor Bill Lowe
at *Look* magazine. Lowe sent it back to Forster, rejecting it as
"slick, unspecific and a special plea." It was all that. The article gave a brief recap of Julie's childhood days, his relationship with Angelo Patri, his work in Hollywood and his
affiliation with various communist "front" groups along the
way. There was no naming of names, no admission of guilt.
Forster asked Lowe if he could resubmit the piece if Julie re-
worked it, and the editor agreed. Julie gamely returned to his
desk with Forster in an effort to give the article more punch.

Robbe called Julie to tell him about problems she was having with David, who was almost nine years old. Julie asked if
he could take David with him to Florida while he was doing
The Cameo in Miami. Robbe thought it might give the two a
chance to bond. "Julie didn't know what it was like to have
parents, so he didn't know what it was like to be a parent,"
she explained. "But he was going to take David with him to
Florida. That was his plan, and it was a good plan."

It was another plan that wouldn't develop. Too many monkey wrenches were being thrown into the works. Among Julie's comrades who were called before HUAC, Dmytryk and Rossen had named names, and now Kazan was in closed-door testimony in April. He said he did not know John Garfield to be a member of the Communist Party, but he knew others, and he named them. He then ran a paid ad in *The New York Times* explaining that he no longer believed in the communist cause, and that he intended to go on directing movies and plays. And that's just what he did.

That same month, Julie's former costar Canada Lee, age 45, died, alone and broke, of a heart attack. Lee had been blacklisted since 1950 for his continued and outspoken support of African-American causes and rights, and being a black actor in a pre-politically correct Hollywood had made it doubly hard for him to find work of any note. (After *Body and Soul,* the actor had appeared in only two films.) According to Robbe and (Little) Julie Garfield, one day shortly before Lee's death Big Julie decided to visit Lee at his Harlem apartment. An FBI agent Julie recognized tailed him all the way. Before entering Lee's apartment house, Julie turned on a whim and said to the agent, "Hey, I'm going up to see Canada Lee. Wanna go with me and say hello?" The agent begged off.

On April 30, Edward G. Robinson testified before HUAC, portraying himself as a victim of ignorance. "I was duped and used," Robinson said. "I was lied to. But, I repeat, I acted from good motives, and I have never knowingly aided communists or any communist cause." Robinson was cleared and went back to work, although his career never again reached the heights he had attained in the 1930s and 1940s. Julie couldn't figure out why he wasn't being allowed to take the same route. Every film producer and agent in Hollywood was waiting for Julie to gain some sort of official clearance before they would use him. Julie realized he would have to deal directly with the FBI if he ever wanted to return to Hollywood.

On May 8 Julie called the New York office of the Bureau and asked for an appointment. Accompanied by lawyer Sidney Davis,

Julie showed up on Saturday morning, May 10, for an interview. The FBI files make it appear as if the agency was surprised by Julie's initiative, but Garfield's daughter Julie claims that Arnold Forster once told her that the FBI had corralled Julie on a street corner and coerced him into the appointment. Whatever the case, the FBI met with Julie on the 10th and as of that date, it is clear that Julie still had no intention of naming names. In the interview, according to the files, Julie was asked to supply a list of addresses where he had resided from his birth to the present; he did so. He then gave a brief summation of his life and his career. They asked him about canceled checks dating back to 1945; he replied that he kept them for about five years, meaning he had some dating back to 1947. He reiterated many of the statements he made before HUAC, from his denial of support for various communist causes to the question of his presence in Washington D.C., in 1940. He still refused to admit that he had been there, even when the FBI showed him a photograph of the event. One wonders if he honestly couldn't recall it.

More questions followed regarding certain names affiliated with communist organizations. Most of the names are blacked out in the FBI files, although one that is still visible is Martin Sloane, a puppeteer friend of Julie's from the 1930s. Julie denied knowledge of Communist Party meetings in his home, though Robbe had hosted some in the early 1940s.

The Bureau asked him about a statement he made in 1934 at the Ellenville Hotel where the Group Theatre was staying, in which he supposedly said, "This is a communist group and everything here belongs to everybody." Julie denied making the statement and said he had no knowledge of the Group's political leanings. Robert Whitehead stated that one of the ironies of Julie's situation was that, while he may have tried to join the Communist Party, they wouldn't have him. "He once told me that the Communist Party considered him politically unreliable," Whitehead said.

During the FBI interview Julie said he did not specifically know of any communists in New York or California. He added that he did not want to speculate as to a person's political membership without having seen a Communist Party membership card. The FBI then asked him about a certain woman (name blacked out) he had slept with and who had Communist Party affiliations. Julie replied that he could recall the name of every woman he had ever had an affair with, and that woman's name was unfamiliar to him.

Julie told the interviewing agents that he was no longer employable in Hollywood, either in film or television, and that he wanted to clear his name. He asked if he was free to travel abroad for work, and the FBI said yes. They then raised questions about a certain person who obviously had a lot of influence in Julie's life and who was reported to be a member of the Communist Party. That name is inked out in the FBI files, but it stands to reason the person in question is Robbe. Julie denied knowledge of the person's political activities, but said he would ask this person to come down to the office to testify on her own behalf. According to Arnold Forster, the FBI actually laid out in front of Julie an entire portfolio on Robbe, showing him canceled checks to Communist Party functions and an expired membership card. One agent reportedly turned to Julie and said, "Sign a statement saying your wife is a communist, and we'll call this all off and clear you." Julie, according to Forster, looked at the evidence, then at the agent and replied, "Fuck you." One thing he wasn't going to do was turn in his wife.

He left the FBI office and, according to agent George Chasen, acted as if he had just been awarded a Get Out of Jail Free pass. "Julie called me Monday and said, 'Now it's official. Tell the studios to check with anyone they want. They'll find out I'm in the clear,'" Chasen told *The New York Post* later that year. This scenario seems inconceivable, given his recent experience with the FBI. When he visited Forster the following week, Julie came off as pensive and troubled and he was drinking and smoking regularly.

He accepted a weekend invitation to Lee Strasberg's Fire Island home on Saturday, May 17. Actor Dane Clark, who had just returned from England where he had made a low-budget thriller, was

also at the party. Julie told Clark that he had received some similar
offers from European and English film producers for low-budget
film work, but that he didn't want to do them. (Director John Berry
claimed Julie thought such projects were beneath him.) According
to Clark, Julie then said, "CBS offered me a part in a television production of *Golden Boy*. Should I do it?" Clark, who understood how
many of his peers refused to consider television work, replied,
"Hell, you're an actor. Get out there and kick ass. What do you care
if it's television?" Julie said, "Yeah, I want to work."

The only phone on the island at that time was at the main boathouse. A message came from the boathouse that there was a call for
Julie. "He goes out, and when he comes back he was as white as a
ghost," Clark recalled. "I said, 'What's the matter, Julie?' He said,
'CBS just called. They told me they got someone else for the part.'
He was crushed. That was the final slap in the face—he couldn't
even get a TV role." It's difficult to corroborate this anecdote. And
it's unlikely Julie would have considered television to be beneath
him, given that he had hoped to do Elmer Rice's *Counsellor-At-Law*.
Some sources say the story is true but the facts about the program
are wrong (there is no record of an early 1950s CBS television version of *Golden Boy*, for example). Whatever the case, it appears that
Julie had been turned down for another job, and he left the island
deeply depressed.

On Sunday the 18th he visited Robbe and the kids at the Central
Park West apartment. He chose a book from the library, took the kids
to Central Park for an hour of play and then returned by himself to
the Warwick Hotel. What he did that night remains a mystery.

About twelve hours behind schedule, on the evening of Monday
the 19th, he showed up at Forster's office. He probably heard on the
radio that day at least part of Clifford Odets' HUAC testimony, in
which the playwright named names. Garfield and Forster worked on
"I Was a Sucker For a Left Hook" from about 9 P.M. until past midnight. He should have returned to the Warwick for some rest. Instead
he found his way to playwright Howard Lindsay's apartment, where

he took part in an all-night poker game. He played badly, lost heavily, and left before dawn. Martin Ritt, who was there, couldn't understand why Julie was pushing himself so hard.

He may have caught a few hours sleep at the Warwick, but he was back in Forster's office by 11 A.M. The two men worked until sundown. In her memoirs, actress Hildegard Knef (also known as Neff) claims that she ran into Julie at the Plaza Hotel that afternoon; Forster believes Knef saw Julie on Monday, not Tuesday. After working with Forster, Julie went down to Gramercy Park to see Iris Whitney. The two had dinner at Luchow's on 14th Street. Afterwards, the actor complained to Whitney, "I feel awful." Though she suggested that he call a doctor, he suggested instead that they return to her apartment.

According to Whitney, once they reached her place Julie took off his shirt and pants and laid down on her bed. He went to bed around 11 P.M., she later said, and she checked in on him from time to time after that. She thought she heard him breathing quietly as late as 2 A.M., but when she brought him a glass of orange juice at 8 A.M., she found him dead. But inconsistencies showed up in Whitney's version of events. Robert Whitehead said he received a call from Whitney earlier, perhaps at 5 A.M., in which she said Julie had stopped breathing. Whitehead called his doctor, Charles Nammack, and asked him to meet him at Whitney's apartment. Nammack was also working for the city morgue, and Whitehead thinks the doctor may have called Julie's death into the morgue desk. A morgue attendant could have tipped off the press. At any rate, before Whitehead got to Whitney's apartment, a handful of reporters were already waiting outside. It was just dawn.

An hour or so later, Whitehead hailed a taxi to Robbe's apartment. He wanted to break the news to her before she got wind of it from the press. He was too late. When he arrived, Julie and David were playing on the floor of the apartment. Robbe was sitting in a chair with a blank look on her face. She had already heard the news. She had been taking a bath when the phone rang. Dripping wet, she picked up the receiver. A strange male voice identified himself as a reporter and then blurted out, "Do you have any comment regarding the death of your husband?" Robbe dropped the phone and broke down crying.

Robbe feared that news hounds would accost her children, and she hustled them off to a friend's house for the day. The action recalled what had been played out back in 1920 with the death of Julie's mother; the Garfield children too were not immediately told of their father's demise. Instead, Little Julie recalls waiting patiently all day for her father to pick her up for a date to spend the afternoon together. It was a date he couldn't possibly keep.

It was Wednesday, May 21, and among the headlines of the day were: Concerned mothers in the Bronx were complaining about the growing number of bums hanging around the St. Peter and Paul Parochial School at 159th and Brook Avenue; Mrs. Anna Openshaw was about to go on trial for shielding her fugitive son, who was wanted for the murder of his father, from the police; and the Bronx Chamber of Commerce demanded full restoration of the Third Avenue El. (They wouldn't get their wish.)

And John Garfield was dead. The official cause was cardiac arrest. He probably never knew what hit him.

CHAPTER TWENTY

Nobody Lives Forever

"I think he was a very destructive person. Not
to other people, but to himself. I think he
was always on the tip of the roof, hanging
upside down, you know what I mean?"
— ROBBE GARFIELD COHN

JULIE WAS BURIED IN WESTCHESTER HILLS CEMETERY IN
Hastings-on-Hudson, New York. In an unfortunate case of
bad timing, the day of the funeral Robbe received a bill in
the mail from attorney Louis Nizer for $50,000. She refused
to pay it. "I didn't think Nizer and Davis gave Julie good
counsel at all," Robbe said. "They kind of mucked up the
whole thing."

Nizer and Davis shouldn't bear all the blame for Julie's
testimony. The lawyers, shrewd as they may have been,
were fighting a battle that no one knew how to fight. "Nizer
and Davis were both highly skilled, highly intelligent
lawyers," Arnold Forster said. "They were caught, as most
of us were, in the whirlwind of McCarthyism. No one really
knew how to fight this successfully, because you were dealing with character assassination, you were dealing with an
elusive enemy who you couldn't quite grasp and hold on
to. They did all the necessary things to establish to the satisfaction of the government agencies that their client was, if
anything, a sucker."

Maybe so, but for the rest of her life Robbe would have
nothing but scorn and anger for her husband's legal team.

312

She felt that Nizer paid little attention to Julie, instead referring the bulk of the case to the younger partner, Davis. Daughter Julie Garfield acknowledges that her father probably had his own line of defense in mind anyway, and that Nizer and Davis couldn't have done much to alter his testimony. But she too always felt as if all the lawyers did was show up and sit idly by while her father made his own way in front of HUAC. "Daddy was out there in front of HUAC working instinctively, playing dumb," she said. "Nizer was sitting there doing nothing. My father needed to be taken by the hand and guided through this testimony. I mean, considering that my father was Mr. Malaprop, it's no wonder he didn't know what he was doing. He was testifying as a street boy, adhering to the code of the streets."

Robbe hired Sidney Cohn, a lawyer who had recently represented writer Carl Foreman before HUAC, to take Nizer and Davis to court. The court case lasted for years, but Cohn won, and Robbe never did pay Nizer and Davis. Robbe became friends with Cohn, and they eventually fell in love. They married in the autumn of 1954.

Immediately following Julie's death "the vultures," as Robbe liked to call them, descended. Victor Reisel published a series of newspaper columns in which he asserted that Julie met with him several times before his death. Julie, according to Reisel, told him that he had just completed a full statement describing how Hollywood communists had ensnared him in their nefarious net. Columnist Howard Rushmore claimed Julie told him he had admitted to the FBI that his testimony before HUAC was all a lie, and that he had decided to name names. Both claims are unsubstantiated. Reisel's charges hurt Robbe. His column, three days after Julie's death under the heading "Garfield Leaves Red Exposé," said Julie had a secret meeting with Reisel hours before his death, in which he made it clear that he was going to name names. "Anonymous midnight voices called him a rat and threatened him," Reisel wrote. "Men he had known but little stepped up to him and told him to lay off."

"He had much to tell," Reisel's column continued. "The communists, coming to him in every guise—as businessmen, as secretaries, as publicists, as tennis club friends and as 'do-gooders'—had gotten him into thirty-two Stalinist fronts and pasted his name on forty-two documents." Reisel's series painted the actor as a frightened pigeon who was terrified of death threats from shadowy communists.

[Years later, in the course of a telephone conversation, Reisel said he barely knew Julie, and that he never wrote a column about him: "My image of Garfield was that he was a very decent fellow, not terribly sophisticated in the international intrigue of the weird communist jungle. I don't believe he was ever associated with any communist group. And I don't know that John Garfield was ever blacklisted. I don't think there really was a blacklist." Forty years may have dimmed Reisel's memory, but then again a lot of fervent anti-communists would disavow their past and claim that there was no such thing as a blacklist. Ronald Reagan was one of them.]

Julie had his defenders. Fred Mayfield, writing in New York's *Daily Compass,* said Julie could not find work because he refused to name names. "But it was not a mere issue of names," Mayfield wrote. "Names are not the only thing that is being tortured out of the witnesses in Washington. It is the spirit of men that is being ripped out of them. Getting a man to put his finger on his former friends and acquaintances is the final degradation. This is as low as a man can sink, and once the rodents of the Inquisition have gotten a witness to do this, they have broken him." So there was, here and there, a voice of reason.

Other newspaper articles of the time focused on Julie's acting talent. One of the most memorable was Richard Watts Jr.'s piece for *The New York Post.* "When he had the proper sort of role, there was no more satisfying actor in the American theatre than John Garfield," Watts wrote. "John Garfield, with his intensity, eagerness, his sensitivity and his idealism, grew to artistic maturity in a theater where those particular qualities, which fitted in so perfectly with those it represented, made him symbolic of it."

Speculation on what caused Julie's death overshadowed the articles. He was a married celebrity who died of a heart attack in the bed of a woman who was not his wife, and that sort of thing can still fuel salacious rumors. Probably no one will ever know what happened in those final hours of Julie's life. Iris Whitney issued a general statement for the press: "He [Julie] was deeply troubled and came to me for help. He needed someone who would sympathize with him. I wasn't in love with him. To me he was just a dear, sweet boy."

Unfortunately, Whitney's lack of logical judgment on the morning of Julie's death helped feed the media frenzy. When the unexpected throng of reporters who arrived at her apartment confronted her, Whitney barricaded herself in the apartment, refusing entry to anyone. She didn't even allow the police to come in until nearly noon, according to newspaper reports. "Garfield Dies in Blonde's Room—Police Smash in Apartment Door," read one headline of the day. New Yorkers made their own judgments regarding Garfield's death, and "He came and he went" became a popular catch phrase on the city streets.

Shortly after Julie's death, the FBI came to the Garfield apartment on Central Park West again. Robbe gathered up her children and held them in front of her. "He's dead," Robbe told the agents, "What more do you want of me?" The two men left, and never returned.

In his final days, Julie had been alternately edgy and relaxed, energetic yet exhausted. There's reason to believe he was being shadowed by the FBI. He probably didn't know who to trust most of the time. The obvious cause of his death was the stress brought on by his inability to find work. And the only way to regain his professional self-esteem, it seemed, would be to sell out his personal self-esteem and name names. Director John Berry always felt this is what killed Julie. "The tension was enormous. The temptation to play ball must have crossed his mind. This may sound romantic, but I think what happened was, faced with this option, Julius Garfinkle of the Bronx said to John Garfield of Hollywood, 'You can't do this to me.' And John Garfield packed his bags and died. The only way to clear himself was to rat, and he couldn't do that."

It turned out that Julie was also facing money worries. Thanks to Bob Roberts' counsel, the Garfields had never owned property, nor did they invest in stocks and bonds. When Julie died he had about $130,000 in the bank. For 1952, that was a substantial sum, but not for a major movie star. Julie had earned several million dollars during the 1940s. Where did it go?

Some of it had been spent on film properties. Roberts had bought them, using Julie's money. At the time of his death Julie owned the rights to about half a dozen film properties, including *The Man with the Golden Arm, Port Afrique, The World and Little Willie* and *Mr. Brooklyn.* Julie and Roberts had also hired several writers to develop film properties for the actor. Richard Collins and Sylvia Richards, for example, were writing that script for Julie about an aging rodeo star (the basis of which was used for the 1952 RKO film *The Lusty Men*). Money always went into rent, and Julie had been a soft touch for a loan or a gift of money. He lent or gave money to many of the blacklisted directors and writers, including Hugo Butler and Dalton Trumbo, during the blacklist years. He gambled a lot, and generally lost. He also lost money—perhaps as much as $100,000—on *He Ran All the Way*. Still, that doesn't account for it all.

Robbe, for one, always suspected Roberts. Others are less direct in their accusations. "I don't know what the financial arrangements between him and Roberts were," Norman Lloyd said, "But Julie moved back to New York without much money. As I understood it, he wasn't that wealthy. I mean, he was doing okay, but he wasn't like any of those guys who had millions. I would have thought that he would have had more."

After moving to Europe, Roberts sold off Julie's film properties. *The World and Little Willie* was produced by Universal under the title *Everything but the Truth,* starring Maureen O'Hara and John Forsythe, in 1956; that same year *Port Afrique* was made into a low-budget British film with actor Phil Carey in the lead. Director Otto Preminger bought *The Man with the Golden Arm,* much to author Nelson Algren's dismay. "I thought it was comical," Algren said of the 1955 film that Preminger made with Frank Sinatra. "It had nothing to do with drug addiction. I thought it was cheap. There was no particular honesty about it." Algren took Preminger and Roberts to court and the case dragged out for years; nobody really won. In 1981 Canon Films produced a remake of *Body and Soul* with Leon Isaac Kennedy. Julie's brother Michael had a small role in the film, though his scenes ended up on the cutting room floor. Roberts sued Canon, claiming he still owned the story rights to the film. The film flopped; the outcome of the case was never made public. Roberts lived quietly in England and died there in the early 1990s.

Robbe Garfield Cohn worked as an interior decorator throughout much of the 1950s and 1960s. After Sidney Cohn's death in 1993, she moved back to Los Angeles to be near her family, where today she suffers from Alzheimer's disease.

Both of Julie's children became actors. David Garfield (sometimes listed as John Garfield Jr.) found sporadic film work in big-budget 1960s films like *The Swimmer* and *McKenna's Gold.* But by the early 1970s he felt his career was going nowhere and he turned to film editing, becoming quite successful at it. His editing credits include *The Front* (1976), *Casey's Shadow* (1978), *All the Right Moves* (1983), and *Desert Bloom* (1985). Nonetheless, David lived a very troubled life, and he died of a drug overdose on Thanksgiving Day, 1994, at age 50.

Julie Garfield has lived out her dream of working in the theater. In 1971 she won the Theatre World Award for her performance in the Roundabout Theater Company's production of *Uncle Vanya.* She became an active member of both the Actors Studio and the Ensemble Studio Theatre, winning more critical acclaim for her work in the first American production of playwright Edwardo Machado's *Broken Eggs.* In the 1980s Julie turned to teaching drama, while working steadily as a supporting actress in Hollywood. Her film credits include *Stanley and Iris* (1990), *Goodfellas* (1991) and *Men of Respect* (1992). She now lives in New York City, where she continues to perform, write and teach.

Julie's brother Michael passed away in the autumn of 1996. Julie's stepmother, Dinah Cohen Garfinkle, died on Valentine's Day 1980. Angelo Patri died in 1965; Jack L. Warner in 1973. Iris Whitney gave up acting (her last stage role of note was as Ma Pennybacker in the 1958 revival of *The Remarkable Mr. Pennybacker* opposite Burgess Meredith) and turned to interior decorating as a career. She remained at her Gramercy Park apartment until the mid-1990s, when she moved into a Long Island nursing home, where she later died.

Clifford Odets' life was never the same after he named names in front of HUAC. "I remember he came to the house from Washington, D.C., for the funeral," Robbe said. "And he didn't think he had done anything wrong because he didn't tell them [HUAC] a lot of things that he could have. He didn't seem to find himself after that, though." Odets died in 1962. One of his last writing projects was penning teleplays for *The Richard Boone Show*. Robert Blake, who was Julie as a child in *Humoresque,* played a boxer hooked on drugs in an episode Odets wrote called "Leather Dollar." "He called me his Golden Boy and compared me to Garfield all the time," Blake said. "He loved Garfield, and talked about him up until the day he died. They fought the good fight together."

If it was a good fight, it was one-sided. Until the blacklist disappeared which, depending on which source you choose to believe, didn't occur until at least 1965 and perhaps not until 1975—no one really won against HUAC. And for years rumors of a government conspiracy to "get" John Garfield plagued the actor's legacy. Young Julie Garfield recalls a story being told to her by a source in the know, a chilling portrait of a time gone by when the government could intimidate at will.

"Before HUAC reopened shop in the second round of hearings in 1951, they sent a representative to Hollywood," Julie explained. "This representative met with all the heads of the film studios, and he said, "We're going after Danny Kaye, Edward G. Robinson and John Garfield. Give us just one of them and we'll leave you alone.'

And the studio heads said, 'Take Garfield. He's expendable.' And that's what happened. They had it out for my father."

Young Julie was raised with this story ringing in her ears but, in fact, there is no trace of documentation to corroborate her statement. Whether the studio heads actually needed to acquiesce in order for the government to build a case against Garfield is debatable. Still, HUAC never netted as big a prize as Julie, in terms of witnesses. He was without doubt the only major movie star of the period to be blacklisted. And the blacklist may have played a part in his current lack of standing as a Hollywood icon. The times in which Julie lived and died surely contributed to the relative obscurity of his work—and his name.

It's not as if John Garfield has been totally forgotten. He has a cult following, but it is nowhere near as strong or as large or as vocal as similar cults for James Dean, Marilyn Monroe and Elvis Presley. For one thing, Garfield's body of film work may not be substantial enough to cement his position in film history. Though he made about thirty films, only a few—*The Postman Always Rings Twice, Body and Soul, Gentlemen's Agreement, Force of Evil*—are recalled by most film buffs today. "Daddy never had a *Casablanca,*" young Julie Garfield said with a laugh, and she's right: the actor didn't make enough film classics to buy him immortality. It is difficult to generate enthusiasm for his work in movies like *Flowing Gold,* but when you catch him at his best, in *Pride of the Marines*, for example, you're left with a feeling of exhilaration by the energy, by the desire to live life to its fullest (even when he was playing losers who claimed they didn't give a damn) and by what Abe Polonsky called the humanity. Garfield's charm is seductive, but not always readily apparent, as it is with Robert Mitchum or Steve McQueen.

Of course, our sense of history is narrowing and shortening, and people forget. But with Julie having passed away at the height of the McCarthy era, and as his death was to some degree accelerated by the events of that era, it was unlikely that anyone would try to revive him as a pop icon. "He's been removed," John Berry said.

"He stopped being a public figure in 1952. And nobody has ever tried to change that."

What does remain is the image. Both on and off the screen, Julie was a rebel with a cause, even if he did not always know what that cause was. His greatest success occurred when he played himself on the screen—an eager, intense and cynical man who is determined to make it despite the odds. He embodied a fatalistic sense of cool long before Mitchum, Dean or McQueen did.

Is his story a tragedy? He *is* marked as a tragic hero by his premature death at the hands of forces beyond his control, this guy who could cheat on his wife but couldn't rat on his friends. Whatever his flaws, he had it within himself to sacrifice. On the surface he struck friends as weak, and yet he developed and maintained an inner strength when it came to a sense of integrity and loyalty. His epitaph is best left to newspaper critic Archer Winston, who in 1952 wrote that Julie "was being loyal to people, not to a place, a country, a Constitution. How many films had he acted in in which the worst sin of the gangster was squealing? As a boy he had lived the city and street morality of the gang.

"What he learned first in the neighborhoods, loyalty to his friends, stayed with him as his most memorable act."

And that's not a bad act to be remembered for.

Postscript

"It all seems too simple. Live your life, do
your work. Simple as all that. You find out
it's not that easy. Nothing comes free. One
way or another you pay for what you are."
— PAUL BORAY (JOHN GARFIELD)
IN *HUMORESQUE* (1946)

I VENTURED IN TO THE WARWICK HOTEL ONE DAY IN 1991, shortly after beginning research on this project, to see if there were any employees who had been there since the early 1950s. To my surprise I found one, a doorman named Francisco.

While he was working, I approached him and introduced myself. I told him about the John Garfield project and asked how long he'd been working at the Warwick.

"I started in June 1952," he said.

Garfield had died in May. Nonetheless for some idiotic reason I felt compelled to confirm what he had just told me.

"Then you don't remember John Garfield staying here?" I asked. "He was here in May."

"No," Francisco politely replied, "I started here in June."

Of course he did. He had just told me that. I was grasping for straws.

"I served George Raft," he continued, quietly. "And Errol Flynn too. But not John Garfield."

I nodded, thanked him and began to walk away. He said something that stopped me.

"John Garfield. He was a good actor."

321

Yes, I agreed, he was a good actor.

"I remember one of his films," he said to me. "A good film. It was called *A Man Alone.*"

I know my movies. *A Man Alone* is a 1955 Republic western that actor Ray Milland (of *The Lost Weekend*) directed and starred in. My suspicions were borne out. Nobody could remember the films that John Garfield had appeared in. Nobody could really remember who John Garfield was.

"No, he never made a film by that name," I said, smiling.

"Yes, he did," Francisco insisted. "A man alone. I remember it. He was a boat captain. 'A man alone ain't got no chance.' A good film."

He was thinking of *The Breaking Point.*

"Yes," I said, "it was a good film." I left smiling. He did remember.

Acknowledgments

IN RESEARCHING JOHN GARFIELD'S LIFE, I WAS FORTUNATE
to have the cooperation of his widow, Robbe Garfield Cohn,
his daughter Julie Garfield, his son David Garfield and his
brother, Michael Garfield. In addition, the following people
were interviewed expressly for the purpose of this book:
Ted Allan, Ann Bellamy, Anna Berger, Joseph Bernard, John
Berry, Robert Blake, Phoebe Brand, Robert Brown, Vera But-
nick, William Campbell, Morris Carnovsky, Anthony
Caruso, Dane Clark, Sidney Cohn, Nancy Coleman, Richard
Collins, Michael J. Coppola, Jean Darling, John Ericson,
Frank Fasolino, Geraldine Fitzgerald, Arnold Forster, Ruth
Garfield, Frances Goodrich, Edmund Hartmann, Steven
Hill, Celeste Holm, Eddie Jaffe, Paul Jarrico, Elia Kazan,
Gene Kelly, Herbert Kenwith, Ring Lardner Jr., Jack Larson,
Helen Golden Levine, Helen Levitt, Viveca Lindfors, Nor-
man Lloyd, Katherine Locke, Ann Loring, Salem Ludwig,
Jeffrey Lynn, Karl Malden, Patricia Neal, Louis Nizer, Sylvia
Maishlash Nonkin, Gregory Peck, Joseph Pevney, Maurita
Pittman, Abraham Polonsky, Anthony Quinn, Victor Riesel,
Martin Ritt, Jack Russell, Al Ryelander, Gerry Schlein, Sam
Shaw, Vincent Sherman, Anna Sokolow, Joseph Solanto,
Kim Stanley, Ezra Stone, Phyllis Thaxter, Audrey Totter,
Peter Viertel, Lew Wasserman, Bob William, Tyba Wilner
and Elaine Zambianco. Constance Ford and Micheline
Presle provided additional insight by letter.

Comments by Rosemary DeCamp, Michael Gordon and
Irving Rapper were culled from interviews conducted by
Professor Ron Davis, former curator of the Film Oral History
Project at Southern Methodist University in Dallas, Texas.

There are no "John Garfield" papers, per se—he was not a man of letters. There is, however a wealth of clipping files on Garfield and his film work. General clippings files on John Garfield are housed at the Academy of Motion Picture Arts and Sciences (AMPAS) Library in Los Angeles. The University of Southern California's Film Library, Los Angeles, Lincoln Center's Library of the Performing Arts, New York City, The Museum of Modern Art's Film Library, New York City, and the Wisconsin Center for Film and Theater Research at the University of Wisconsin, Madison, Wisconsin.

The Warner Bros. production files, which include minute details about the making of Garfield's Warner films, are also housed at The University of Southern California's Film Library—special thanks to Ned Comstock and Leith Adams. The MGM film files were unavailable, but the RKO file for *The Fallen Sparrow* is available at the University of California at Los Angeles (UCLA) film library.

Brian Quinn, formerly with the Museum of Television and Radio in New York City, helped me dig up videos of Garfield's few television appearances, and provided me with a fairly complete list of Garfield's radio credits.

James N. Beaver, Billy Colucci, John Cocchi and Julie Garfield provided me with photographs for this book. Dennis Dutton, Jay Fultz, Alex Gildzen, Barth Landor, Devin McKinney and Meg Mc-Sweeney were all gracious enough to read and edit the manuscript for me, offering helpful suggestions along the way.

Special thanks to David Bordelon, Gary and Judy Chase, Denise Kusel, Beverly Marvin, Christopher and Carol Poole, Gregg Rickman, Jill Santoriello and Steve Webster. Thanks to Michael Kaminski for letting me sleep on his couch, to Meg McSweeney for helping me track people down, and to my agent, Jim Donovon, who maintained faith in both me and this project. Special thanks to Mel Zerman of Limelight Editions for taking a chance on both me and John Garfield. And thanks, as always, to my wife Karen, who saw me through the project and did considerable work in her unofficial capacity as research assistant and copy editor.

Bibliography

BOOKS

Barson, Michael, *Better Dead Than Red*, New York: Hyperion, 1992

Beaver, James N., *John Garfield: His Life and Films*, A.S. Barnes and Co., 1978

Bierly, Kenneth M., John G. Keenan and Theodora C. Kirkpatrick, *Red Channels, The Report of Communist Influence in Radio and Television*, June 1950. Published under the auspices of *Counterattack*.

Brenman-Gibson, Margaret, *Clifford Odets, American Playwright, 1906-1940*, New York: Atheneum, 1981

Ceplair, Larry, and Steven Englund, *The Inquisition in Hollywood*, Garden City, New York: Anchor Press, 1980

Clurman, Harold, *The Fervent Years*, NewYork: Harcourt Brace Jovanovich, 1975

Cogley, John, *Report on Blacklisting: Movies*, Fund for the Republic, New York, 1956

Cole, Lester, *Hollywood Red: The Autobiography of Lester Cole*, Palo Alto, California: Ramparts, 1981

Davis, Ronald L., *The Glamour Factory: Inside Hollywood's Big Studio System*, Dallas, Texas: Southern Methodist University Press, 1993

Donahue, H.E.F., *Conversations with Nelson Algren*, New York: Hill and Wang, 1963

Dunne, Philip, *Take Two: A Life in Movies and Politics*, New York: McGraw-Hill, 1980

Engel, Lehman, *This Bright Day*, New York: Macmillan Publishing Co., 1974

Freedland, Michael, *The Warner Brothers*, New York: St. Martin's Press, 1983

Friedrich, Otto, *City of Nets: A Portrait of Hollywood in the 1940s*, New York: Harper & Row, 1986

Funt, Allen, with Philip Reed, *Candidly, Allen Funt: A Million Smiles Later*, New York: Barricade Books, 1994

Gelman, Howard, *The Films of John Garfield*, New Jersey: The Citadel Press, 1975

Golden, Henry, *The Greatest Jewish City in the World*, New York: Doubleday & Co., 1972

Goodman, Walter, *The Committee: The Extraordinary Career of the House Committee on Un-American Activities*, New York: Farrar, Straus and Giroux, 1968

Green, Paul, *Plough and the Furrow,* New York: Samuel French, Inc., 1963

Hamilton, Ian, *Writers in Hollywood, 1915—1951*, New York: Harper & Row, 1990

Higham, Charles, and Joel Greenberg, *The Celluloid Muse: Hollywood Directors Speak*, London: Angus and Robertson, 1969

Hirschhorn, Clive, *The Warner Bros. Story*, New York: Crown, 1979

Howe, Irving, and Kenneth Libo, *How We Lived*, New York: Richard Marek Publishers, 1979

Kanfer, Stefan, *A Journal of the Plague Years*, New York, Atheneum, 1978

Kashner, Sam, and Nancy Schoenberger, *A Talent for Genius: The Life and Times of Oscar Levant*, New York: Villard Books, 1994

Kazan, Elia, *A Life*, New York: Alfred A. Knopf, 1988

Lewis, Robert, *Slings and Arrows*, New York: Stein and Day, 1984

Mast, Gerald, *Howard Hawks, Storyteller*, New York: Oxford, 1982

McGilligan, Patrick, and Paul Buhle, *Tender Comrades—A Backstory of the Hollywood Blacklist*, New York: St. Martin's Press, 1997

Miller, Merle, *The Judges and the Judged*, New York: Doubleday & Company, 1952

Navasky, Victor S., *Naming Names*, New York: The Viking Press, 1980

Reeves, Thomas C., *The Life and Times of Joe McCarthy*, New York: Stein and Day, 1982

Robinson, Edward G., with Leonard Spigelgass, *All My Yesterdays*, New York: Signet, 1975

Sanders, Ronald, *The Lower East Side: A Guide to Its Jewish Past in 99 New Photographs*, New York: Dover Publications Inc., 1979

Schatz, Thomas, *The Genius of the System: Hollywood Filmmaking in the Studio Era*, New York: Pantheon Books, 1988

Schrecker, Ellen, *Many Are the Crimes: McCarthyism in America*, New York: Little, Brown and Company, 1998

Schwartz, Nancy Lynn, *The Hollywood Writers' War*, New York: Alfred A. Knopf, 1982

Shindler, Colin, *Hollywood at War*, London: Routledge & Kegan Paul, Ltd., 1979

Sklar, Robert, *City Boys: Cagney, Bogart, Garfield*, New Jersey: Princeton University Press, 1992

Smith, Wendy, *Real Life Drama: The Group Theatre and America, 1931—1940*, New York: Alfred A. Knopf, 1990

Sperber, A.M., and Eric Lax, *Bogart*, New York: William Morrow and Company, Inc., 1997

Stuart, Jerome, *Those Crazy Wonderful Years When We Ran Warner Brothers*, Secaucus, New Jersey: Lyle Stuart, 1983

Swindell, Larry, *Body and Soul*, New York: William Morrow and Company, Inc., 1974

Thomas, Bob, *Clown Prince of Hollywood*, New York: McGraw-Hill Publishing Company, 1990

Thomas Bob, *Joan Crawford, a Biography*, New York: Simon & Schuster, 1978

Warner, Jack, with Dean Jennings, *My First Hundred Years in Hollywood*, New York: Random House, 1964

Whiting, Margaret, and Will Holt, *It Might As Well Be Spring*, New York: William Morrow and Company, 1987

Wilk, Max, *The Wit and Wisdom of Hollywood*, New York: Antheneum, 1971

Winters, Shelley, *Shelley II: The Middle of My Century*, New York: Simon & Schuster, 1989

MISCELLANEOUS ARTICLES AND ESSAYS

Clurman, Harold, "Critique of the American Theatre," *The Drama*, April 1931

English, Richard, "What Makes A Hollywood Communist," *The Saturday Evening Post*, 19, May 1951

Eyles, Allan, "The Films of Enterprise," *Focus on Film*, No. 35, April. 1980

Gersch, Harry, "The Day The FBI Came To Our House," *Commentary*, January 1952

Lardner, Ring, Jr., "My Life on the Blacklist," *American Legion Magazine*, March 1962

Laurence, Frank M., "The Film Adaptations of Hemingway: Hemingway and the Hollywood Legend," Ph.D. dissertation, University of Pennsylvania, 1970

MacLeish, Archibald, "The Conquest of America," *Atlantic Monthly*, August 1949

Matthews, J.B., "Did the Movies Really Clean House?" *American Legion Magazine*, December 1951

Nugent, Frank S., "Super Duper Epic: Hollywood Canteen," *The New York Times Magazine*, 17, October 1943

Schulberg, Budd, "The Inside Story on Waterfront," *The New York Times Magazine*, 6, January 1980

Sheridan, Ann, "Ann Sheridan," interviewed by Ray Hagen, *Screen Facts*, November 1966

Somon, Rita James, "As We Saw the Thirties: Essays on Social and Political Movements of a Decade," University of Illinois Press, 1967

Spiro, J.D., "At the Hollywood Canteen," *The Milwaukee Journal*, 7, March 1943

Talbot, David and Barbara Zheutlin, "Albert Maltz: Portrait of a Holly-
    wood Dissident," *Cineaste*, Winter 1977/1978, Volume 8, #3

"Warner Brothers," *Fortune*, November 1937

ARTICLES BY JOHN GARFIELD

"Lady Luck," 4 March, 1939. Garfield, filling in for Ed Sullivan's syndi-
    cated column, writes about his preconceptions of Hollywood.

"Show Business as Usual," *Theatre Arts*, March 1943. Garfield (ghosted
    by writer Al Levitt) discusses the 1941 Flying Showboat tour.

"Speaking of Garfield," *Photoplay*, March 1943. Garfield on his life, the
    film *Air Force,* and his family.

"Overseas Report From Garfield," *Silver Screen*, August 1944. A war-
    correspondent-type piece (probably ghosted by Al Levitt), in which
    Garfield talks about the USO Camp Troupers tour.

"What I Believe," *Silver Screen*, April 1946. Typical movie fan magazine
    fare, with Garfield espousing his political beliefs.

"Our Part in "Body and Soul," *Opportunity: Journal of Negro Life*, Janu-
    ary 1948. Garfield discusses the making of *Body and Soul* and talks
    about his friendship with Canada Lee. A more genuine piece than
    most.

"Door of Mystery," *Coronet*, April 1951. A real oddity in which Garfield
    writes of an incident that took place in Mexico during the 1939 film-
    ing of *Juarez.*

In addition, comments from "John Garfield's Lecture on Film Acting,"
given to the Actors' Laboratory on December 10, 1945, were taken from *The
Drama Review*, vol. 28, no. 4, Winter 1984.

MAGAZINE AND NEWSPAPER ARTICLES

Carrol, Harrison, "John Garfield Declares He Is In The Films To Make
    Good Stories," *Boston Daily Record*, 3 March, 1941

Coons, Robin, "Actors and Politics," *Motion Picture*, May 1946

Cooper, Marion, "Once Was Enough," *Silver Screen*, May 1940

Crene, Regina, "John Garfield Too Busy to Return to Stage," *New York Journal American*, 14 December 1938

Crichton, Kyle, "No Part Too Tough," *Colliers*, 15 April 1939

Crowther, Bosley, "A Man Who Means to Make A Dent," *The New York Times*, 18 December 1938

Dana, Robert W., "He Lost His Aim in Drifting to Hollywood To Be a Failure," *New York World-Telegram*, circa 1938

Darnton, Charles, "Garfield, On The Evils of Money: Affluence A Big Danger to Art," *Los Angeles Times*, 4 January 1942

Duffy, William, and Oliver Pilat, "The Life of John Garfield." A well done six-part series covering all aspects of Garfield's life and career, published in *The New York Post* between 23 May and 27 May 1952. The series was supplemented by articles revolving around Garfield's stage career and life.

Fowler, Dan, "Box Office Tough Guy," *Look*, 13 April 1948

Garfield, John, interviewed by Eileen Creelman, *The New York Sun*, 14 January 1939

Garfield, John, interviewed by Gladys Hall, *Screenland*, May 1946

Garfield, John, interviewed by Edwin Miller, *Seventeen*, January 1949. Miller visited the set of *Force of Evil* where Garfield discussed his career and his hopes for the future.

Garfield, John, interviewed by Darr Smith, *The Los Angeles Daily News*, 4 July 1950

Garfield, John, interviewed by A.H Weiller, *The New York Times*, 4 May 1947

Hawkins, William, "John Garfield His Own Skipper Again," *New York World-Telegram*, 2 February 1948

Jonesby, Ed, "Tough Guy," Fan Magazine, circa autumn 1938

Keller, Alan, "Tramp's Life Comes in Handy for the Stage," Fan Magazine, circa 1940

Marder, Murray, "John Garfield Urges Ban on Communism," *The Washington Post*, 24 April 1951

McKay, Margaret Morton, "Turn Troubles Into Triumphs," *Motion Picture*, 1945

Morris, Mary, interview with Garfield, *PM*, 5 May 1946

Ormsbee, Helen, "Unfettered in Real Life, He Plays a Shackled Star," *New York Herald Tribune*, 20 February 1949

Palmer, Constance, "Good for Garfield," *Movieland*, November 1946

Paul, Elliot, "Citizen Garfield," *Photoplay*, December 1945

Rice, Vernon, "Garfield Not Patronizing the Stage in Skipper," *The New York Post*, 9 February 1948

Robinson, Selma, "Skipper Next To God Talks About Desires," *PM Daily*, 25 January 1948

Ross, George, "Garfield Is Frightened as Film Fame Beckons," *New York World-Telegram*, 28 August 1938

Shafler, Rosalind, "Bronx Tough Makes Good," *The Baltimore Sun*, 9 July 1944

Smith, Frederick James, "No Glamour Boy, But...," *This Week* magazine, 26 March 1939

Strauss, Theodore, "Dialogue Ad-Libbed From a Dentist Chair," *The New York Times*, 26 September 1943

Thirer, Irene, "A Year in Films Changes the Viewpoint of John Garfield," *The New York Post*, 19, April 1939

Walsh, Thomas, "Garfield Has 'Em Guessing," *Screen Life*, March 1940

Waterbury, Ruth, "Close Up on John Garfield," *Liberty*, 1 July 1939

Winston, Archer, "John Garfield's Fight to Grow," *The New York Post*, 27 November 1950

Woltman, Frederick, "John Garfield on Being a Gangster," *New York World-Telegram*, 8 September 1939

Zeitlin, Ida, "It Pays to Be Tough," *Photoplay*, January 1939

Zigmond, Helen, "John Garfield Looks at Hollywood," *The Advocate*," 21 July 1939

In addition, quotes were taken from John Garfield's published testimony before the Committee on Un-American Activities, House of Representatives, Eighty-Second Congress, First Session, 23 April 1951.

Arnold Forster graciously provided me with a copy of Garfield's unpublished article "I Was a Sucker for a Left Hook."

Filmography

Four Daughters (1938), Warner Bros. *Director:* Michael Curtiz. *Producer:* Hal B. Wallis. *Screenplay:* Julius J. Epstein and Leonore Coffee, based on a story by Fannie Hurst. *Cast:* Claude Rains, Priscilla Lane, Rosemary Lane, Lola Lane, Gale Page, John Garfield, Jeffrey Lynn, Frank McHugh, May Robson, Dick Foran, Vera Lewis, Tom Dugan.

Blackwell's Island (1939), Warner Bros. *Director:* William McGann. *Producers:* Hal B. Wallis and Jack L. Warner. *Associate Producer:* Bryan Foy. *Screenplay:* Crane Wilbur, based on a story by Crane Wilbur and Lee Katz. *Cast:* John Garfield, Rosemary Lane, Dick Purcell, Victor Jory, Stanley Fields, Morgan Conway, Granville Bates, Peggy Chandler, Charley Foy, Anthony Averill, Milburn Stone, William Gould, Leon Ames.

They Made Me A Criminal (1939), Warner Bros. *Director:* Busby Berkeley. *Producers:* Jack L. Warner and Hal B. Wallis. *Screenplay:* Sig Herzig, based on a novel by Bertram Milhauser and Beulah Marie Dix. *Cast:* John Garfield, Billy Halop, Bobby Jordan, Leo Gorcey, Huntz Hall, Gabriel Dell, Bernard Punsley, Claude Rains, Ann Sheridan, May Robson, Gloria Dickson, John Ridgley, Ward Bond, Louis Jean Heydt.

Juarez (1939), Warner Bros.—First National. *Director:* William Dieterle. *Producer:* Hal B. Wallis. *Screenplay:* John Huston, Aeneas MacKenzie and Wolfgang Reinhardt, based on the play *Juarez and Maximilian* by Franz Werfel and the book *The Phantom Crown* by Bertita Harding. *Cast:* Paul Muni, Bette Davis, Brian Aherne, Claude Rains, John Garfield, Gale Sondergaard, Donald Crisp, Gilbert Roland, Henry O'Neill, Joseph Callelia, Pedro de Cordoba, Harry Davenport, Louis Calhern.

Daughters Courageous (1939), Warner Bros.—First National. *Director:* Michael Curtiz. *Producer:* Hal B. Wallis. *Screenplay:* Julius J. Epstein and Philip G. Epstein. *Cast:* John Garfield, Claude Rains, Priscilla Lane, Rosemary Lane, Lola Lane, Gale Page, Jeffrey Lynn, Fay Bainter, Donald Crisp, May Robson, Frank McHugh, Dick Foran, George Humbert.

Dust Be My Destiny (1939), Warner Bros.—First National. *Director:* Lewis Seiler. *Producer:* Louis F. Edelman. *Screenplay:* Robert Rossen, based on a novel by Jerome Odlum. *Cast:* John Garfield, Priscilla Lane, Alan Hale, Frank McHugh, Billy Halop, Bobby Jordan, Charlie Grapewin, Henry Armetta, Stanley Ridges, John Litel, John Hamilton, Ward Bond, Moroni Olsen, Marc Lawrence, Victor Killan, Frank Jaquet, William Davidson.

Castle on the Hudson (1940), Warner Bros. *Director:* Anatole Litvak. *Producer:* Hal B. Wallis. *Screenplay:* Seton I. Miller, Brown Holmes and Courtney Terrett, based on the book *20,000 Years in Sing Sing* by Warden Lewis E. Lawes. *Cast:* John Garfield, Ann Sheridan, Pat O'Brien, Burgess Meredith, Henry O'Neill, Jerome Cowan, Guinn "Big Boy" Williams, John Litel, Margot Stevenson, Willard Robertson, John Ridgley.

Saturday's Children (1940), Warner Bros. *Director:* Vincent Sherman. *Producers:* Jack L. Warner and Hal B. Wallis. *Screenplay:* Julius J. Epstein and Philip G. Epstein. *Cast:* John Garfield, Anne Shirley, Claude Rains, Lee Patrick, George Tobias, Roscoe Karnes, Dennis Moore, John Qualen.

Flowing Gold (1940), Warner Bros. *Director:* Alfred E. Green. *Producer:* Bryan Foy. *Screenplay:* Kenneth Gamet, based on a novel by Rex Beach. *Cast:* John Garfield, Frances Farmer, Pat O'Brien, Raymond Walburn, Cliff Edwards, Tom Kennedy, Granville Bates, Jody Gilbert, Frank Mayo.

East of the River (1940), Warner Bros. *Director:* Alfred E. Green. *Producer:* Bryan Foy. *Screenplay:* Fred Niblo Jr., based on a story by John Fante and Ross B. Willis. *Cast:* John Garfield, Brenda Marshall, Marjorie Rambeau, George Tobias, William Lundigan, Moroni Olsen, Douglas Fowley, Jack LaRue, Jack Carr, Russell Hicks, Paul Gulfoyle, Roy Barcroft.

The Sea Wolf (1941), Warner Bros.—First National. *Director:* Michael Curtiz. *Producers:* Jack L. Warner and Hal B. Wallis. *Screenplay:* Robert Rossen, based on a novel by Jack London. *Cast:* Edward G. Robinson, John Garfield, Ida Lupino, Alexander Knox, Gene Lockhart, Barry Fitzgerald, Stanley Ridges, Francis McDonald, Howard da Silva, David Bruce, Cliff Clark, Louis Mason, Frank Lackteen, Dutch Hendrian.

Out of the Fog (1941), Warner Bros. *Director:* Anatole Litvak. *Producer:* Hal B. Wallis. *Screenplay:* Robert Rossen, Jerry Wald and Richard Macauley. *Cast:* Ida Lupino, John Garfield, Thomas Mitchell, John Qualen, Eddie Albert, George Tobias, Aline MacMahon, Robert Homans, Bernard Gorcey, Leo Gorcey, Ben Welden, Paul Harvey, Jerome Cowan.

Dangerously They Live (1941), Warner Bros. *Director:* Robert Florey. *Producer:* Bryan Foy. *Screenplay:* Marion Parsonnet, based on her novel *Remember Tomorrow*. *Cast:* John Garfield, Nancy Coleman, Raymond Massey, Moroni Olsen, Lee Patrick, Christian Rub, Roland Drew, Frank Reicher, Ben Welden, John Ridgley, Cliff Clark, Charles Drake

Tortilla Flat (1942), MGM. *Director:* Victor Fleming. *Producer:* Sam Zimbalest. *Screenplay:* John Lee Mahin and Benjamin Glazner, based on a novel by John Steinbeck. *Cast:* Spencer Tracy, Hedy Lamarr, John Garfield, Frank Morgan, Akim Tamiroff, Sheldon Leonard, John Qualen, Donald Meek, Connie Gilchrist, Allen Jenkins, Henry O'Neill, Arthur Space

Air Force (1943), Warner Bros.—First National. *Director:* Howard Hawks. *Producer:* Hal B. Wallis. *Screenplay:* Dudley Nichols. *Cast:* John Garfield, John Ridgley, Harry Carey Sr., Gig Young, Arthur Kennedy, Charles Drake, George Tobias, Ward Wood, Stanley Ridges, Moroni Olsen, Edward Brophy, Richard Lane, Faye Emerson, Ann Doran

The Fallen Sparrow (1943), RKO. *Director:* Richard Wallace. *Producer:* Robert Fellows. *Screenplay:* Warren Durf, based on a novel by Dorothy B. Hughes. *Cast:* John Garfield, Maureen O'Hara, Walter Slezak, Martha O'Driscoll, Patricia Morison, John Banner, Hugh Beaumont

Thank Your Lucky Stars (1943), Warner Bros.—First National. *Director:* David Butler. *Producer:* Mark Hellinger. *Screenplay:* Norman Panama, Melvin Frank and James V. Kern. *Cast:* Eddie Cantor, Joan Leslie, Dennis Morgan, Edward Everett Horton, S.Z. Sakall, Ruth Donnelly, Don Wilson, Henry Armetta, Hank Mann, James Burke, Paul Harvey, Mike Mazurki, Stanley Clements, Hattie McDaniel, Willie Best. Guest stars (as themselves): Humphrey Bogart, Bette Davis, Olivia de Havilland, Errol Flynn, John Garfield, Ida Lupino, Ann Sheridan, Dinah Shore, Alexis Smith, Jack Carson, Alan Hale, George Tobias, David Butler, Mark Hellinger, Spike Jones and his City Slickers

Destination Tokyo (1943), Warner Bros. *Director:* Delmer Daves. *Producer:* Jerry Wald. *Screenplay:* Delmer Daves and Albert Maltz. *Cast:* Cary Grant, John Garfield, Alan Hale, John Ridgley, Dane Clark, Warner Anderson, William Prince, Robert Hutton, Peter Whitney, Tom Tully, Faye Emerson, Warren Douglas, John Forsythe, Whit Bissell, Mark Stevens

Between Two Worlds (1944), Warner Bros. *Director:* Edward A. Blatt. *Producer:* Mark Hellinger. *Screenplay:* Daniel Fuchs, based on the play *Outward Bound* by Sutton Vance. *Cast:* John Garfield, Paul Henreid, Sydney

Greenstreet, Eleanor Parker, Edmund Gwenn, George Tobias, George Coulouris, Faye Emerson, Sara Allgood, Dennis King

Hollywood Canteen (1944), Warner Bros.—First National. *Director:* Delmer Daves. *Producer:* Alex Gottlieb. *Screenplay:* Delmer Daves. *Cast:* Joan Leslie, Robert Hutton, Dane Clark, Janis Paige, Jonathan Hale. Guest stars (as themselves): The Andrews Sisters, Jack Benny, Joe E. Brown, Eddie Cantor, Jack Carson, Joan Crawford, Bette Davis, John Garfield, Sydney Greenstreet, Alan Hale, Paul Henreid, Peter Lorre, Ida Lupino, Dennis Morgan, Eleanor Parker, Roy Rogers and Trigger, Zachary Scott, Alexis Smith, Barbara Stanwyck, Craig Stevens, Jane Wyman, Jimmy Dorsey and his Orchestra, others.

Pride of the Marines (1945), Warner Bros. *Director:* Delmer Daves. *Producer:* Jerry Wald. *Screenplay:* Albert Maltz, adapted by Marvin Borowsky from the book *Al Schmid, Marine* by Roger Butterfield. *Cast:* John Garfield, Eleanor Parker, Dane Clark, John Ridgley, Rosemary DeCamp, Ann Doran, Ann Todd, Warren Douglas, Anthony Caruso, Mark Stevens, Moroni Olsen, Don McGuire, Tom D'Andrea, Rory Malinson

The Postman Always Rings Twice (1946), MGM. *Director:* Tay Garnett. *Producer:* Carey Wilson. *Screenplay:* Harry Ruskin and Niven Busch, based on the novel by James M. Cain. *Cast:* Lana Turner, John Garfield, Cecil Kellaway, Hume Cronyn, Leon Ames, Audrey Totter, Alan Reed, Jeff York, Morris Ankrum, Cameron Grant, Wally Cassell, Edward Earle

Nobody Lives Forever (1946), Warner Bros.—First National. *Director:* Jean Negulesco. *Producer:* Robert Buckner. *Screenplay:* W.R. Burnett, based on his novel *I Wasn't Born Yesterday. Cast:* John Garfield, Geraldine Fitzgerald, Walter Brennan, Faye Emerson, George Coulouris, George Tobias, Robert Shayne, Richard Gaines, James Flavin

Humoresque (1946), Warner Bros. *Director:* Jean Negulesco. *Producer:* Jerry Wald. *Screenplay:* Clifford Odets and Zachary Gold, based on a story by Fannie Hurst. *Cast:* Joan Crawford, John Garfield, Oscar Levant, J. Carroll Naish, Joan Chandler, Tom D'Andrea, Peggy Knudsen, Ruth Nelson, Craig Stevens, John Abbott, Bobby Blake

Body and Soul (1947), Enterprise Studios, released through United Artists. *Director:* Robert Rossen. *Producer:* Bob Roberts. *Screenplay:* Abraham Polonsky. *Cast:* John Garfield, Lilli Palmer, Hazel Brooks, Anne Revere, William Conrad, Joseph Pevney, Canada Lee, Lloyd Goff, Art Smith, James Burke, Virginia Gregg, Johnny Indrisano

Gentleman's Agreement (1947), 20th Century Fox. *Director:* Elia Kazan. *Producer:* Darryl F. Zanuck. *Screenplay:* Moss Hart, based on the novel by Laura Z. Hobson. *Cast:* Gregory Peck, Dorothy McGuire, John Garfield, Celeste Holm, Anne Revere, June Havoc, Albert Dekker, Jane Wyatt, Dean Stockwell, Nicholas Joy, Sam Jaffe, Roy Roberts, Kathleen Lockhart, Gene Nelson, Virginia Gregg, Jesse White

Force of Evil (1948), Enterprise Studios, released through MGM. *Director:* Abraham Polonsky. *Producer:* Bob Roberts. *Screenplay:* Abraham Polonsky and Ira Wolfert, based on Wolfert's novel *Tucker's People*. *Cast:* John Garfield, Beatrice Pearson, Thomas Gomez, Roy Roberts, Marie Windsor, Howland Chamberlain, Jack Overman, Tim Ryan

We Were Strangers (1949), Horizon, released through Columbia Pictures. *Director:* John Huston. *Producer:* Sam Spiegel. *Screenplay:* John Huston and Peter Viertel, based on the "China Valdez" episode in Robert Sylvester's novel *Rough Sketch*. *Cast:* Jennifer Jones, John Garfield, Pedro Armendariz, Gilbert Roland, Ramon Navarro, Wally Cassell, David Bond, Jose Perez, Morris Ankrum, Tito Rinaldo

Under My Skin (1950), 20th Century Fox. *Director:* Jean Negulesco. *Producer:* Casey Robinson. *Screenplay:* Casey Robinson, based on the story *My Old Man* by Ernest Hemingway. *Cast:* John Garfield, Micheline Presle, Luther Adler, Orley Lindgren, Noel Drayton, Steve Geray

The Breaking Point (1950), Warner Bros.—First National. *Director:* Michael Curtiz. *Producer:* Jerry Wald. *Screenplay:* Ranald MacDougall, based on the novel *To Have and Have Not* by Ernest Hemingway. *Cast:* John Garfield, Patricia Neal, Phyllis Thaxter, Juano Hernandez, Wallace Ford, Edmond Ryan, Ralph Dumke, Guy Thompson, William Campbell, Sherry Jackson, Donna Jo Boyce, Victor Sen Young, Peter Brocco, John Coucette, James Griffith, Norman Fields, Juano Hernandez

He Ran All The Way (1951), Bob Roberts, released through United Artists. *Director:* Jack Berry. *Producer:* Bob Roberts. *Screenplay:* Hugo Butler and Guy Endore (uncredited help from Dalton Trumbo). *Cast:* John Garfield, Shelley Winters, Wallace Ford, Selena Royle, Gladys George, Norman Lloyd, Bobby Hyatt, Clancy Cooper

In addition, John Garfield can be seen in a flashback sequence (as Mickey Borden) in the Warner Bros. film **Four Wives** (1939). He has one line of dialogue in a cameo appearance in **Jigsaw** (1949), a Tower Production released through United Artists. He appears unbilled in a silent cameo at the bar in the Stork Club scene in the 20th Century Fox film **Daisy Kenyon** (1947). He appeared in several short subjects: **Swingtime in the Movies** (WB-Vitaphone, 1938, color), **Chinese Garden Festival** (Republic, 1940), **Show Business at War** (Fox, 1943), **Stars on Horseback** (Hollywood Novelties, 1943), **Screen Snapshots No. 4** (Columbia, 1946) and **Out of This World Series** (Columbia, 1948).

Then there's the issue of **Footlight Parade** (Warner Bros., 1933). For years it has been widely believed that John Garfield appears briefly in the "Shanghai Lil" sequence. Larry Swindell, in his book *Body and Soul*, states that Garfield put in a day's work on the Busby Berkeley feature in New York City. But **Footlight Parade** was shot in Hollywood, not Manhattan, and Garfield was in New York during 1933. Robbe Garfield Cohn said it is not Garfield in the film. Film historian Gene Stavis once asked Berkeley if the bit player was Garfield. Berkeley first said yes but, some time later, said no. Film buffs continue to argue the point. This author does not believe that the extra is John Garfield.

Stage Appearances

Counsellor-at-Law by Elmer Rice. Staged and produced by Rice. Opened on November 6, 1931 at the Plymouth Theatre. *Cast:* Paul Muni, Constance McKay, Lester Salkow, Malka Kornstein, Victor Wolfson, Jack Collins, Ned Glass, Gladys Feldman, Angela Jacobs, J. Hammond Daily, Sam Bonnell, William Vaughn, Anna Kostant, Marvin Kline, John Waulen, Martin Wolfson, June Cox, Jules Garfield. **Note**: Garfield played Harry Suskind in the Chicago production of the play in spring 1932. When the play reopened on Broadway in September 1932 Garfield again played Suskind.

Lost Boy by T.C. Upham. Staged by James Light. Produced by Burton Hartford. Opened on January 5, 1932, at the Mansfield Theatre. Ran for 15 performances. *Cast:* Edgar Barrier, Mooney Diamond, Elisha Cook Jr., Ann Thomas, Ruth Chorpenning, William Balfour, Ralph Chambers, George Price, Jules Garfield, Richard Ross.

Peace on Earth by George Sklar and Albert Maltz. Staged by Robert Sinclair and Michael Blankfort. Produced by The Theatre Union. Opened on November 29, 1933, at the Civic Repertory Theatre on 14th Street. Ran for 126 performances. It reopened on March 31, 1934, and ran for 18 more performances) *Cast:* Julie Colin, Robert Keith, Ethel Latropidi, Clyde Franklin, Walter Vonnegut, Alice Carrol, John Boruff, Fred Herrick, Victor Kilan, Elliot Fisher, David Losen, Mara Tartar, Earl Ford, James MacDonald. **Note**: Garfield played a messenger boy but did not receive billing.

Gold Eagle Guy by Melvin Levy. Staged by Lee Strasberg. Produced by the Group Theatre in association with D.A. Doran Jr. Opened on November 28, 1934 at the Morosco Theatre. Ran for 65 performances. *Cast:* Roman Bohnen, Walter Coy, J. Edward Bromberg, Morris Carnovsky, Luther Adler, Stella Adler, Lewis Leverett, Russell Collins, Margaret Barket, Clifford Odets, Alexander Kirkland, Sanford Meisner, Bobby Lewis. Garfield did not receive billing for his bit participation.

Awake and Sing!! by Clifford Odets. Staged by Harold Clurman. Produced by the Group Theatre. Opened on February 19, 1935, at the Belasco Theatre. Ran for 185 performances. Reopened on September 9, 1935, and ran for 24 performances. *Cast:* Art Smith, Stella Adler, Morris Carnovsky, Phoebe Brand, Jules Garfield, Roman Bohnen, Luther Adler, J. Edward Bromberg, Sanford Meisner.

Waiting For Lefty by Clifford Odets. Directed by Sanford Meisner and Clifford Odets. Produced by the Group Theatre. Opened on February 25, 1935, at the Civic Repertory Theatre. *Cast:* Morris Carnovsky, Art Smith, Ruth Nelson, Gerrit Kraber, Walter Coy, Phoebe Brand, Jules Garfield, Russell Collins, Elia Kazan, Alan Baxter, Paula Miller, William Challee, Luther Adler, Bobby Lewis, David Korchmar. Voices in audience: Clifford Odets, Herbert Ratner, Lewis Leverett.

Weep for the Virgins by Nellise Child. Staged by Cheryl Crawford. Produced by the Group Theatre. Opened November 30, 1935, at the 46th Street Theatre and ran for 9 performances. *Cast:* Eunice Stoddard, Art Smith, J. Edward Bromberg, Tony Kraber, Margaret Barker, Ruth Nelson, Phoebe Brand, Paula Miller, Evelyn Varden, Jules Garfield, Virginia Stevens, Dorothy Patton, Marie Hunt.

The Case of Clyde Griffiths, a dramatization by Erwin Piscator and Lina Goldschmidt of Theodore Dreiser's *An American Tragedy*. Directed by Lee Strasberg. Produced by the Group Theatre and Milton Shubert. Opened on March 13, 1936, at the Ethel Barrymore Theatre. *Cast:* Morris Carnovsky, Alexander Kirkland, Phoebe Brand, Art Smith, Margaret Barker, Ruth Nelson, Paula Miller, Roman Bohnen, Virginia Stevens, Walter Coy, Kay Laughlin, Sanford Meisner, Elia Kazan, Jules Garfield.

Johnny Johnson by Paul Green, music by Kurt Weill. Staged by Lee Strasberg. Produced by the Group Theatre. Opened November 19, 1936, at the 44th Street Theatre. Ran for 68 performances. *Cast:* Bobby Lewis, Phoebe Brand, Roman Bohnen, Russell Collins, Grover Burgess, Sanford Meisner, Lee J. Cobb, Art Smith, Tony Kraber, Elia Kazan, Joseph Pevney, Luther Adler, Jules Garfield, Albert Van Dekker, Paula Miller, Morris Carnovsky, Ruth Nelson.

Having Wonderful Time by Arthur Kober. Directed and produced by Marc Connelly. Opened on February 20, 1937, at the Lyceum Theatre. Ran for 112 performances. *Cast:* Jules Garfield, Katherine Locke, B.D. Kranz, Mona Conrad, Ann Thomas, Irene Winston, Irving Israel, Henrietta Kaye, Connie Lent, Tony Kraber, Kay Loring, Philip Van Zandt, Cornel Wilde, Sheldon Leonard, Janet Fox.

Golden Boy by Clifford Odets. Staged by Harold Clurman, Produced by the Group Theatre. Opened on November 4, 1937, at the Belasco Theatre. Ran for 250 performances. *Cast:* Roman Bohnen, Frances Farmer, Luther Adler, Art Smith, Lee J. Cobb, Jules Garfield, Morris Carnovsky, Phoebe Brand, Bobby Lewis, Elia Kazan, Michael Gordon, Martin Ritt, Howard Da Silva, Charles Crisp, Karl Malden.

Heavenly Express by Albert Bein. Directed by Bobby Lewis. Produced by Kermit Bloomgarden. Opened on April 18, 1940, at the National Theatre. Ran for 20 performances. *Cast:* John Garfield, Harry Carey Jr., Art Smith, William Sands, Phil Brown, Curt Conway, Harry Bratsburg, Randolph Wade, Will Lee, Phillip Loeb, Russell Collins, Nicholas Conte, Aline MacMahon, Burl Ives, Jack Lambert, Charles Thompson.

Awake and Sing! by Clifford Odets. Directed by J. Edward Bromberg. Produced by the Actors' Laboratory. Opened in June 1946 at the Las Palmas Theatre in Hollywood, California for a six-week run. *Cast:* John Garfield, Phoebe Brand, Alfred Ryder, Morris Carnovsky, Art Smith, Roman Bohnen.

Skipper Next to God by Jan de Hartog. Staged by Lee Strasberg. Production supervised by Cheryl Crawford. Presented by the Experimental Theatre under the sponsorship of the American National Theatre and Academy. Opened on January 4, 1948, at the Maxine Elliot Theatre. After a six-performance run the play reopened on January 29 at the Playhouse Theatre and ran for 93 performances. *Cast:* John Garfield, Joseph Anthony, Robert White, Si Oakland, Carmen Costl, John Becher, Wallace Acton, Wolfe Barzell, Michael Lewin, Peter Kass, John Shellie, Richard Coogan, Joseph Bernard.

The Big Knife by Clifford Odets. Staged by Lee Strasberg. Produced by Dwight Deere Wiman. Opened February 24, 1949, at the National Theatre. Ran for 108 performances. *Cast:* John Garfield, Nancy Kelly, J. Edward Bromberg, Frank Wilson, William Terry, Leona Powers, Paul McGrath, Mary Patton, Joan McCracken.

Peer Gynt by Henrik Ibsen, American version by Paul Green, with musical score and direction by Lan Adomian. Directed by Lee Strasberg. Revived by Cheryl Crawford in association with R.L. Stevens under the sponsorship of the American National Theatre and Academy. Opened on January 28, 1951, at the ANTA Playhouse and ran for 32 performances. *Cast:* John Garfield, Mildred Dunnock, Ray Gordon, Ann Boley, John Randolph, Pearl Lang, Joseph Anthony, Anne Hegira, Karl Malden, Rebecca Drake, Nehemiah Persoff, Peggy Meredith.

Golden Boy by Clifford Odets. Directed by Clifford Odets. Produced by the American National Theatre and Academy. Opened on March 12, 1952, at the ANTA Playhouse. Ran for 55 performances. *Cast:* John Garfield, Bette Grayson, Art Smith, William Hansen, Martin Green, Michael Lewin, Lee J. Cobb, Peggy Meredith, Jack Klugman, Joseph Wiseman, Arthur O'Connell, Jack Warden, Norman Brooks, Joseph Bernard, Tony Kraber.

Television Appearances

To the best of my knowledge, John Garfield made only four official television appearances:

Toast of the Town, Christmas 1948. Garfield made a surprise appearance on Ed Sullivan's show, coming out of the audience to read a letter to Santa Claus that was written by a small boy. It's a moving moment.

Candid Camera, 29 May 1949. Garfield, sitting in the studio audience, stands up and takes a bow before the antics ensue.

Cavalcade of Stars, 8 June 1950. Garfield and Kim Stanley perform a scene from *Golden Boy.*

ANTA's Playhouse, February 1951. Garfield and Mildred Dunnock perform a scene from *Peer Gynt.* There is no record of a surviving print.

In addition, Garfield can be glimpsed in a brief television moment speaking outside the lobby of New York City's Globe Theatre at the April 1948 premiere of the Enterprise film *Arch of Triumph.*

Radio Appearances

This is a fairly comprehensive (but not definitive) list of John Garfield's radio appearances in chronological order.

April 1, 1937	Rudy Vallee's *Standard Brands* program, NBC. Julie and Katherine Locke did a scene from *Having Wonderful Time*.
June 6, 1937	*RCA Magic Key*, NBC. "Trouble Night" by Arch Oboler. With Katherine Locke.
February 12, 1939	*Silver Theatre*, CBS. "Escape From Tomorrow."
November 19, 1939	*Standard Brands* program, NBC. "My World."
December 18, 1939	*Lux Radio Theatre*, CBS. *Four Daughters* with the Lane Sisters.
December 25, 1939	*Lux Radio Theatre*, CBS. *Pinocchio* with Cliff Edward and Walter Catlett.
March 5, 1940	*DuPont's Cavalcade of Stars*, NBC. "The Stolen General."
July 4, 1940	*Kraft Music Hall*, NBC.
August 29, 1940	*Kraft Music Hall*, NBC.
November 4, 1940	*Suspense*, CBS. "Death Sentence."
April 14, 1941	*Lux Radio Theatre*, CBS. *Dust Be My Destiny* with Claire Trevor.
May 7, 1941	*Bristol Myers' Time to Smile*, with Eddie Cantor, NBC.
June 6, 1941	United China Relief Program, NBC.
July 24, 1941	*Kraft Music Hall*, NBC.
February 5, 1942	*Kraft Music Hall*, NBC.

March 15, 1942	*Listen America*, NBC.
March 28, 1942	*This Is War*, NBC. "It's in the Works."
April 1942	"I Wonder If They Know" by Sydney Ryand and Milton Gieger (network unknown).
May 18, 1942	*Bristol Myers' Time to Smile* with Eddie Cantor, NBC.
June 4, 1942	*Kraft Music Hall*, NBC.
October 22, 1942	*The Abbott and Costello Show*, NBC.
March 30, 1943	*The Bob Hope Show*, NBC.
April 14, 1943	*Bristol Myers' Time to Smile*, NBC.
May 10, 1943	*Lady Esther Screen Guild Players*, CBS. *Johnny Eager* with Carole Landis.
September 26, 1943	The Editors Speak, NBC.
October 4, 1943	*DuPont's Cavalcade of Stars,* NBC.
November 25, 1943	"Soldiers in Greasepaint," NBC.
January 19, 1944	*Bristol Myers' Time to Smile*, NBC.
May 4, 1944	*The Abbott and Costello Show*, NBC.
May 15, 1944	*DuPont's Calvacade of America,* NBC.
May 25, 1944	*Birdseye Open House* with Dinah Shore, CBS.
November 6, 1944	One Thousand Club of America, NBC. A political rally on behalf of President Roosevelt. Five of Warner Bros. "tough guy stars"—James Cagney, Humphrey Bogart, George Raft, Edward G. Robinson and John Garfield—made announcements.
November 28, 1944	Brown and Williamson Tobacco Group, Inc., NBC. *Rally Round With Hildegarde.*
December 25, 1944	*GI Christmas,* NBC.
April 27, 1945	*Duffy's Tavern* NBC.
December 31, 1945	*Lux Radio Theatre*, CBS. *Pride of the Marines* with Eleanor Parker and Dane Clark.

March 17, 1946   FW Fitch, *Fitch Bandwagon,* NBC.

May 8, 1946   *The Eddie Cantor Show,* NBC.

May 19, 1946   *Theatre Guild on the Air,* ABC. *They Knew What
                      They Wanted* with June Havoc and Leo Carillo.

June 15, 1946   *Academy Award Theatre,* CBS. *Pride of the Marines.*

July 19, 1946   *Colgate Palmolive Peet's Bill Stern Sports Newsreel
                      of the Air,* NBC. Garfield filled in for Bill Stern.

October 8, 1946   *Cresta Blanca Hollywood Players, Golden Boy* with
                      Lynn Bari.

October 16, 1946   *Academy Award Theatre,* CBS. *Blood on the Sun.*

December 25, 1946   *Cresta Blanca Hollywood Players, All Through the
                      House* with Janet Leigh, Gene Kelly and Gregory
                      Peck.

May 1, 1947   *Radio Readers' Digest,* CBS. "Dr. Mamika."

June 2, 1947   *Lady Esther Screen Guild Players,* CBS. *Saturday's
                      Children* with Jane Wyman.

August 8, 1947   *Colgate Palmolive Peet's Colgate Sports Newsreel,*
                      NBC. Garfield filled in for Bill Stern.

September 28, 1947   *Theatre Guild on the Air,* ABC. *Saturday's Children.*

October 26, 1947   *Hollywood Fights Back,* ABC. Garfield was one of
                      some 50 celebrities who spoke out against the
                      House Committee on Un-American Activities.

November 6, 1947   *Radio Readers' Digest,* CBS. "Death Across the
                      Table."

November 25, 1947   *Quiz Kids,* NBC.

December 3, 1947   *Something for Thanksgiving,* ABC.

December 5, 1947   *Hi Jinx* with Jinx Falkenberg, NBC.

December 1947   *Studio One, Let Me Do the Talking,* CBS.

January 18, 1948   *Quick As a Flash,* WOR. Garfield as mystery guest.

March 13, 1948   *Public Affairs,* NBC. "Eleven for Democracy."

July 2, 1948	*Colgate Palmolive Peet's Colgate Sports Newsreel,* NBC, Garfield filled in for Bill Stern.
September 26, 1948	*Anacin Hollywood Star Theatre,* NBC.
May 29, 1949	*The Martin and Lewis Show,* NBC.
July 28, 1949	*Right by Request,* NBC. "The Door."
November 15, 1949	*Lux Radio Theatre,* CBS, *Body and Soul* with Jane Wyman and Marie Windsor.
December 25, 1949	*Hotpoint Holiday Hour,* DuPont. *The Man Who Came to Dinner.* Garfield introduced the program, which starred Jack Benny.
October 8, 1950	*The Eternal Light,* NBC.
February 8, 1951	*Pickens Party* with Jane Pickens, NBC.
February 8, 1951	*Welcome Travelers,* NBC.
February 11, 1951	*The Wayne Howell Show,* NBC.

Garfield also appeared on two "Free World Radio" programs during World War II: "Tomorrow" written by Budd Schulberg and Jerome Lawrence, and "The Second Battle of Warsaw" by Irving Ratech. He reportedly took part in the March 9, 1943, radio broadcast of the Ben Hecht, Billy Wilder and Kurt Weill production *We Will Never Die,* with Edward G. Robinson and Paul Muni.

And on April 23, 1951, ABC affiliate WMAL (Washington, D.C.) broadcast 30 minutes of Garfield's HUAC testimony at 12:05 A.M. Eastern Standard Time. The author was unable to track down this recording.

INDEX

(The entry for John Garfield includes an alphabetical listing and page references for all the films and plays in which he appeared.)